08/21/09

THE STRANGEST FRIENDSHIP IN HISTORY

THE
STRANGEST FRIENDSHIP
IN HISTORY

Woodrow Wilson and Colonel House

GEORGE SYLVESTER VIERECK

GREENWOOD PRESS, PUBLISHERS
WESTPORT, CONNECTICUT

Library of Congress Cataloging in Publication Data

Viereck, George Sylvester, 1884-1962.
   The strangest friendship in history.

   Reprint of the 1932 ed. published by Liveright, New
York.
   Includes index.
   1. Wilson, Woodrow, Pres. U.S., 1856-1924. 2. House,
Edward Mandell, 1858-   3. United States--Politics
and government--1913-1921. 4. European War, 1914-1918--
United States. I. Title.
E767.V52 1976   973.91'3'0924   75-26222
ISBN 0-8371-8413-4

Originally published in 1932 by Liveright, Inc., Publishers,
New York

Reprinted with the permission of Liveright Publishing
Corporation

Reprinted in 1976 by Greenwood Press,
a division of Williamhouse-Regency Inc.

Library of Congress Catalog Card Number 75-26222

ISBN 0-8371-8413-4

Printed in the United States of America

CONTENTS

CONTENTS

THE AUTHOR CHARTS HIS COURSE

I PROPOSE to tell the true story of the Wilson Administration, curiously entwined with the story of the friendship between Woodrow Wilson and Edward Mandell House—the strangest friendship in history. In writing this book I have had the unconscious collaboration of Woodrow Wilson. His constant intimate letters to Colonel House have been opened to me, and I have found in them a key to his character. Colonel House, Woodrow Wilson's other self, has answered numberless questions and elucidated for me some unsolved mysteries of the Wilson Administration. Other distinguished contemporaries have also guided my sometimes faltering footsteps. Emperor William and Colonel House read and revised my account of their momentous interview which almost stopped the World War.

Dr. Constantin Dumba, the Ambassador of Francis Joseph in Washington; Count Johann von Bernstorff, the envoy of William II; Bainbridge Colby, Wilson's Secretary of State; General T. W. Gregory, Wilson's Attorney-General; David F. Houston, Wilson's Secretary of Agriculture and McAdoo's successor as Secretary of the Treasury; Newton D. Baker, the pacifist Secretary of War of a pacifist President; Frank L. Polk, legal adviser of the State Department; Joseph P. Tumulty, the most loyal of secretaries; the late Sidney E. Mezes, Chief of the Inquiry, the body established to prepare the American data for the Peace Conference; Justice Charles Evans Hughes, Wilson's opponent in 1916; Louis Seibold, the brilliant Washington correspondent; Professor Charles Seymour, the editor of *The Intimate Papers of Colonel House;* Miss Frances Denton, the Colonel's able secretary who knew and kept more secrets than the State Department; Shaemas O'Sheel, who graciously delved into musty records for me, and innumerable others have been kind enough to aid my researches. Nor should I fail to mention the help which I received from my wife, Margaret Hein Viereck. Last, but not least, I express my gratitude to my old associate, A. Paul Maerker-Branden, who lashed me into writing this book, and to my brilliant and versatile friend, Charles Fulton Oursler, without whom my inspiration would have lagged before I reached the end of my course.

No one except myself is responsible for my conclusions. Many of those to whom I am indebted for information will disagree emphatically with some of my interpretations. I am the cook. If I have spoiled the broth the fault is mine, not theirs.

I draw freely upon my own experiences. My slant is somewhat more intimate than that of the historian, because I have met and known personally many of the personages who stalk through these pages: President Wilson and his daughters, Clemenceau, McAdoo, Bryan, Page, Burleson, Gregory, Colby, Morgenthau, Ludendorff, Foch, Briand, Sir William Wiseman, once head of the British Secret Service in the United States, President Roosevelt, Colonel House, William II, etc., etc.

Books, especially *The Intimate Papers of Colonel House, The True Story of Woodrow Wilson,* by David Lawrence, and *Woodrow Wilson,* by William Allen White, have helped me in my task. I have dipped freely into these works and I have gathered information wherever I could. The *Intimate Papers* especially have yielded so much valuable material that it would be impossible to acknowledge my indebtedness in each instance. Houghton Mifflin Company, authorized publishers of Colonel House's book, have been gracious enough to grant me special permission to borrow freely from this inexhaustible source. Joseph P. Tumulty's *Woodrow Wilson As I Know Him,* Ray Stannard Baker's *Woodrow Wilson: Life and Letters,* Henry L. Stoddard's *As I Knew Them,* D. F. Houston's *Eight Years with Wilson's Cabinet,* Josephus Daniels's *The Life of Wilson,* George Creel's *The War, the World and Wilson,* William G. McAdoo's *Crowded Years,* William E. Dodd's *Woodrow Wilson and His Work,* Arthur D. Howden Smith's *The Real Colonel House,* Colonel House's *Philip Dru—Administrator,* James Kerney's *The Political Education of Woodrow Wilson,* Woodrow Wilson's *History of the*

American People, and other studies, too numerous to recite, have supplied here and there a flash that illuminates the amazing psychology of Woodrow Wilson and Edward Mandell House. I shall pilot the reader through uncharted seas of history without attempting to follow strictly the order of events in time. Where a conflict occurs, I shall be guided more often by psychology than by chronology. Those who follow me will discover that for six and one-half years the United States was governed by a Duumvirate, a Committee of Two. They will note the confusion prevailing in the diplomatic service of the United States because the Duumvirs, scorning official avenues of diplomacy, chose to communicate with foreign governments through channels of their own. We shall witness the spectacle of a President disowning his own ambassadors, and of ambassadors disowning their government. We shall catch intimate glimpses of monarchs and of premiers. We shall hear what Colonel House said to the Kaiser and to King George, and what they said to him. We shall discover the origin of the "strangest and most fruitful alliance in history," and tell, for the first time, the true story of why it was broken. I shall lift the veil that hides the real causes of the rupture between Woodrow Wilson and Colonel House, even from House himself.

There will be no doubt as to who was the real author of the Fourteen Points and who tried to save them in Paris. Woodrow Wilson's secret agreement pledging the United States to intervention before he was reëlected will cast its shadow across our page. It will be made clear why Woodrow Wilson reversed himself on the Panama tolls, and why he plunged us into war. We shall learn why, in spite of his Gentleman's Agreement with England, Wilson called the British "boobs," and why the United States was on the verge of war with Great Britain during the Wilson Administration. We shall see why, twice in his career, President Wilson was on the point of resigning the Presidency, why Wilson refused to support his son-in-law McAdoo's Presidential ambitions, and other carefully guarded secrets. In this connection we shall make the astounding discovery that for six and one-half months Edith Bolling Wilson was virtually President of the United States; for a longer period, ten months and two and one-half weeks, the sprightly widow of the Washington jeweler was Wilson's co-regent. When I began my study I looked upon Woodrow Wilson as the villain of the ensuing drama. As I proceeded to delve into the débris of reminiscences and unwritten history, he gradually assumed some aspects of a martyr and a saint. There was a time when there was no one in the world whom I distrusted more than Edward Mandell House. To-day he seems to me a genuine philos opher and a gifted statesman. Even if his good intentions, like Wilson's, have helped to pave mankind's way to hell, they gave us a glimpse of the Promised Land where peace abides and a new sanction governs the fate of nations.

GEORGE SYLVESTER VIERECK

THE STRANGEST FRIENDSHIP IN HISTORY

I
UNCHARTED SEAS OF HISTORY

David Meets Jonathan – Woodrow Wilson's *Alter Ego* – A Psychic Enigma – Unpublished Letters – Genius or Dummy? – Lifted Veils

MY DEAR friend, we have known one another always." The speaker, a tall, clean-shaven man, with sparse blond hair turning to gray, put his arm around the other man. His light blue eyes revealed unsuspected depths. Under the influence of emotion his features, sternly intellectual, almost forbidding, lost their accustomed rigor. It was as if a lamp had suddenly been lit in a darkened room.

The friend thus apostrophized was slighter in stature. His small gray mustache bravely strove to hide the sensitivity of his mouth. His luminous hazel eyes were searchlights. But to-day they were veiled. The souls of the two men were instruments attuned to each other.

It was only three weeks before, on Friday, May 31, 1912, in the same place, the Hotel Gotham, then a rendezvous of the elegant world in New York, that Thomas Woodrow Wilson for the first time met Edward Mandell House. Thus began what Sir Horace Plunkett has called "the strangest and most fruitful personal alliance in human history."

Twelve years later, February 6, 1924. Muffled drums accompany Woodrow Wilson, the twenty-eighth President of the United States, to his last slumber in the crypt of the Episcopal Cathedral at Mount Saint Alban, Washington. Amid sorrowing crowds in Madison Square Garden, New York, stands a gray figure, shivering slightly as the familiar words of the funeral service are broadcast. Although, like fourteen nails, the Fourteen Points rivet his

3

name immortally to Wilson's, few in the teeming throng recognize Edward Mandell House. A seat at the ceremony in Washington had been reserved for him, but the invitation mysteriously miscarried, like Tumulty's. But whereas Wilson's secretary heard his name called out after the doorkeeper's from Keith's vaudeville, there was no call for Wilson's *alter ego!*

Between the first scene and the last, interlocked with the friendship of two men, lie the most tumultuous years in the history of mankind. We cannot disentangle the events of the World War without analyzing the relationship between Woodrow Wilson and Colonel House. The history of America between 1912-1920 is the history of their friendship.

For seven long years Colonel House was Woodrow Wilson's other self. For six long years he shared with him all but the title of the Chief Magistracy of the Republic. For six years two rooms were at his disposal in the North Wing of the White House. For six years his apartment in New York City was the second White House. In his summer home at Magnolia, not far from Salem, Massachusetts, where once the witches were burned, all wires converged. "All roads," said Lord Northcliffe, "lead ultimately to Magnolia." Super-ambassador, he talked to emperors and kings as an equal. He was the spiritual generalissimo of the Administration. He was the pilot who guided the ship and assisted the skipper in stormy waters at home and abroad.

From the friendship between Colonel Edward Mandell House and Woodrow Wilson blossomed the Fourteen Points and the League of Nations. Out of this friendship sprang the Federal Reserve Act and other reforms upon which Wilson's fame as a Progressive rests. Under the soft persuasion of Colonel House, Woodrow Wilson reversed himself on the Panama tolls and forced his party to eat its own platform pledges. Under his spell Woodrow Wilson typed with his own hand the text of a gentleman's agreement with Sir Edward Grey which gave the British Government a call on American intervention. Edward Mandell House practically averted war between the United States and Great Britain. His hand steered us, for better or for worse, into the war against Germany.

Rome was, at times, ruled by two Cæsars. But never before

in the history of our country were there two men holding in their hands simultaneously the reins of government. Kings have been swayed by mistresses, ministers, mentors and minions. Presidents have been bossed. But never was there a relationship so utterly removed from the ordinary experience of mankind as the friendship between Woodrow Wilson and Colonel House. Wilson's soul was knit to House's as David's was to Jonathan's. It was not the straw fire of boyish enthusiasm, nor the robust comradeship of two "buddies," born in the fiery ordeal of the battlefield. It was not the love of an older for a younger man, springing from the same root as the affection between father and son. It was an intellectual infatuation based on some deep chemical affinity between two human souls. Wilson was fifty-six, House fifty-four, when they met. Both were happily married. House was a grandfather. Wilson a father.

I shall attempt to trace the intimacy of the two men from its mysterious beginning to its equally mysterious end, and to unfold its effect on the destiny of the United States. Colonel House himself never admitted that his friendship with Woodrow Wilson was broken. "There were," he writes, on April 20, 1928, to Professor Charles Seymour, the keeper of his archives and the editor of his *Intimate Papers*, "many doors in the temples that men of old reared to their gods, to the sun, to the moon, to the mythical deities, Isis, Jupiter, Mars. Behind the innermost door dwelt the mysteries." Colonel House professes to have no key to the innermost door. "My separation from Woodrow Wilson was and is to me a tragic mystery, a mystery that now can never be dispelled, for its explanation lies buried with him."

I believe that I have discovered the key to that innermost portal. I found it in long, soul-searching conversations with those who knew the facts and in the confidential letters from Woodrow Wilson to his other self.

These letters have not been published, except for a paraphrase here and there in Seymour's book, that inexhaustible mine of information and dynamite. I, too, am barred from reprinting the letters. However, I have gone over them with a fine-toothed comb. I have read and reread them and the intimations between the lines. The advice of Colonel House enabled me to thread my way through the labyrinth.

The law decrees that letters remain the property of the man who writes them. The letters written by Woodrow Wilson to Colonel House from October 17, 1911, to November 21, 1920, belong to the Wilson estate. Mrs. Edith Bolling Wilson refused the request of Professor Seymour to garnish his chronicle of House with her husband's letters, although Ray Stannard Baker, Wilson's official biographer, freely appropriated letters written by the Colonel to President Wilson.

This one-sidedness gives to the Colonel's recollections, in spite of the adroit editorship of Professor Seymour, the semblance of an egotism that is alien to House. It was unjust to both Wilson and House to withhold Wilson's share in the correspondence. Its publication could in no way impair the stature of President Wilson. "There is, in all the letters of Woodrow Wilson," Colonel House exclaims, "not one ignoble word, not one unworthy thought." It is impossible to envisage the relationship of the two men and to assay the policies enunciated by Woodrow Wilson from his preëlection campaign to his lamentable breakdown, without a minute study of his letters to Colonel House.

Edith Bolling Wilson's refusal places both House and her husband in a peculiar position. It makes House appear in the light of a garrulous busybody, thrusting unwanted advice upon his friend in the White House, if we doubt the trustworthiness of his memoranda. If we judge by his records alone, Wilson seems like a ventriloquist's dummy, squeaking and squawking as his master wills. The absence of the Wilson letters obscures the element of reciprocity, the give and take, upon which the relationship of the two men rests. Always enigmatic, House becomes almost inscrutable. "What," asks Henry L. Stoddard, "did this man without title contribute to Wilson that led him to make him his confidant, his spokesman, his guide? Colonel House's *Intimate Papers*," Stoddard goes on to say, "give a clear impression that he was all three; the only authentic challenge to that picture of their relations lies in the unpublished letters of Wilson to House."

I cannot persuade those who guard the posthumous fame of Woodrow Wilson to lift the ban. But no one can prevent any honest historical student, properly qualified, from investigating the archives where these letters are preserved in the House collection at Yale. Nor is there any seal upon the lips of Colonel House himself, if any one approaches him in good faith for information.

It is curious that most historians prefer to go to libraries rather than to living men for their knowledge of recent events. William II once remarked to me: "These busy professors who constitute themselves the judges of the living and the dead do not take the trouble to consult me about events which I am better acquainted with than any one else." Colonel House harbors the same sentiment. Yet Colonel House is the last living link between posterity and the cryptic personality of Woodrow Wilson. No member of his Cabinet, no member of his family, knew the curious vacillations of Wilson's mind so well as House. He was behind every scene. He knew the skeleton in every cupboard of Wilsonian diplomacy. "Once," he said to me, "only two people knew—Wilson and I. Now," he added softly, "only one knows."

My perusal of Wilson's letters and my conversations with Colonel House reveal a new Wilson, battling in vain against the maze of circumstance which led him against his will into the War. Instead of a hypocrite purchasing his second election with false pacifist promises, I see a tragic and solitary figure, not unlike Abraham Lincoln's, with the tongue of a poet and the dreams of a saviour. House sought, by different channels, ultimately the same goal as Wilson. Both failed. Wilson's failure springs partly from the limitations of his own temperament, partly from the fact that he had essayed too gigantic a task. The burden he strove to carry alone, after parting with House, was too heavy for one man's shoulders. The odds against him were too many. He could well have exclaimed with François Villon: "I was one and the fates were three."

The story that unfolds itself before the reader will astonish those who have never looked behind the stage where history is made. A famous Swedish Chancellor once said: "My son, you do not know with how little wisdom the world is governed." Those who are privileged to meet the actors who strut across the historic scene know that the Swedish statesman was right. They will discover amazing duplicities and amazing folly. But they

will also find astonishing foresight and unflinching idealism.
There are neither heroes nor villains in our drama—only poor
struggling mortals, each striving vainly to play his part without
fumbling his lines.

II

DEAR, DEAR FRIEND

Statesman or Sleuth? – A Lobe of Wilson's Brain? – The Thermometer of
Wilson's Affection – Guardian of the Privy Purse – The Dark Angel – Exit
Ellen Axson Wilson – Enter Edith Bolling Wilson

PARTISANS of Woodrow Wilson are inclined to minimize
the intellectual coöperation between Woodrow Wilson and
the Texas Colonel. Ray Stannard Baker and George Creel ignore
his importance. Josephus Daniels, in his *Life of Woodrow Wilson*, contents himself with two brief references to House. Apologists for Woodrow Wilson falsely portray House as a glorified
courier, or, at best, a diplomatic sleuth, slouching through the
corridors of divers foreign offices on gumshoes, snooping for information. However, men of independence are not inclined to
join the detractors of House.

"House," said Clemenceau, "was the window through which
light came to Wilson." Lord Balfour, in his *Retrospect*, speaks
admiringly of the Colonel's qualities. "History," the British
statesman insists, "will assign him a unique position. I saw him
under the most varying and often the most trying circumstances,
and found him always resourceful, and always with unruffled
temper. Few, indeed, have been the confidants and constant advisers of rulers who have escaped, as he has deservedly done, any
suspicion of self-seeking or desire for personal power in the
course of their efforts to further a particular policy."

David Lawrence adduces the testimony of Wilson himself
on the subject. "What I like most about Colonel House," Woodrow Wilson explained to a group of newspapermen whose curiosity was piqued by the growing friendship between the two
statesmen, "is that he holds things at arm's length—objectively.

He seems able to penetrate a proposition and get to its very essence quickly. He wants nothing for himself. He will not hold office and is a truly disinterested friend—the most valuable possession a man could have."

Lawrence vouches for the authenticity of this statement. "Mr. Wilson," he adds, "used to refer to Colonel House as his eyes and ears." This, too, is an understatement. House, as one observer shrewdly remarks, was the left lobe of Wilson's brain. He was his most intimate, in some matters his sole, confidant. "I have an intimate personal matter to discuss with you," Woodrow Wilson confided to Colonel House in the summer of 1915. "You are the only person in the world with whom I can discuss everything.... There are some I can tell one thing and others another, but you are the only one to whom I can make an entire clearance of mind." This was after the death of Ellen Axson Wilson and before his remarriage. "I would not," wrote House, "exchange the confidence and friendship that Governor Wilson seems to have for me for any office in the land."

It may be that Clemenceau and Balfour were blinded by the cordiality of their own relations with House. It may be that David Lawrence and others who write in a similar vein deliberately misrepresent Woodrow Wilson. It may be that Colonel House, who reports some of these statements in his notes, unconsciously distorts his reminiscences in a manner flattering to himself. However, Woodrow Wilson's letters to Colonel House in the archives at Yale fail to substantiate such suspicions. They confirm every statement made by Balfour, Clemenceau, Lawrence and many others. The emotional intensity of Wilson's friendship fluctuates with his moods. But from the first letter to the last there is not one word of serious disagreement nor of criticism. The friendship reaches its highest peak after the death of the first Mrs. Wilson.

The degree of Wilson's devotion is reflected in the salutations and subscriptions of Wilson's letters. In the first letter, dated October 18, 1911, Wilson, then Governor of New Jersey, addresses the Texan as "My dear Colonel House," and subscribes himself "with warmest regards, Sincerely yours." Then the thermometer rises. The address remains, "My dear Mr. House," until June 24, 1912. But a warmer tone creeps into the subscription—"Cordially," "Faithfully," "Gratefully," "Cordially and sincerely," "Always affectionately," etc., etc. Wilson assures his political mentor that he will be very careful not to act independently in any matter on which he is not perfectly confident.

Though absent from the Baltimore convention, House had been largely instrumental in pulling the wires which insured the nomination of his candidate. On July 17, 1912, the temperature climbs once more. Wilson for the first time calls House his "dear friend." He thanks the Colonel for the plan of campaign which, though outlined orally, made such an impression upon him that he has carried it in his head ever since with great distinctness. He looks forward with eagerness to the time when House can rejoin him, "with"—the phrase is Wilson's—"your hand beside ours on the steering gear."

Other letters follow. Wilson acknowledges the Colonel's "mighty good counsel" and hopes his advice will be taken not only in Vermont and Maine but everywhere. "Your advice is as necessary as it is acceptable." After the election, the President-elect, attributing to Colonel House "no small part" of the result, once more declares his dependence upon the counsel of the sagacious Texan. Dexterously he impresses upon the Colonel how "full a freight of affectionate regard" his lines carry. The scene next shifts to Bermuda. Wilson acknowledges the Colonel's suggestions for the construction of the Cabinet.

Wilson's last letter from the Governor's Mansion in New Jersey bears the date of February 5th. The first letter from the White House is written on April 25, 1913. "The hot weather," Wilson insists, "will be detrimental to the government if it takes you away." In most of these letters there is also some word conveying regards from Ellen Axson Wilson. "We think constantly of our dear and faithful friends," etc., etc. Wilson looked to House for advice on the investment of his little personal fortune, which amounted to thirty-five thousand to thirty-eight thousand dollars when he entered the White House, and divested himself of every security likely to embarrass him in the future. From a letter in the House-Wilson archives at Yale, it appears that Ellen Axson Wilson likewise consulted Colonel House on investments.

Wilson's letters are interspersed with references to Cabinet selections, political happenings, frank discussions of men and measures. William Jennings Bryan, Colonel Goethals, Walter Page, W. F. McCombs, Paul Warburg, W. P. G. Harding, A. Mitchell Palmer and other important political figures bob up in the correspondence. In one letter he requests the Colonel to make a speech in his stead before the American Committee celebrating the 100th Anniversary of Peace among English Speaking Peoples. Now and then personal problems intrude. Woodrow Wilson asks House to secure a job for a young nephew, J. Wilson Howe, "who has been slaving, slaving, slaving for the Pennsylvania Railroad for years." When McCombs, his campaign manager, suggests Wilson's brother-in-law, Elliott, for the presidency of the College of the City of New York, Wilson urges House not to let this interfere with the candidacy of Dr. Mezes for the same post. It was Mezes, the Colonel's brother-in-law, who received the appointment.

No personal friend was closer to Wilson than House. When Woodrow Wilson remarried in 1915, James Gerard, American Ambassador to Berlin, entrusted to House one thousand dollars to buy a wedding gift. From the interchange of letters between Wilson and House it appears that the latter, realizing that a bride prefers to select her own presents, promptly forwarded a check for the amount to the White House. I cite this instance merely as evidence of the complete trust and the intimacy existing between the President and his adviser.

Whenever Colonel House embarks upon one of his trips to Europe, Woodrow Wilson writes him with deep affection. Letter follows letter. Telegram crowds telegram. After his return, he "fairly longs to see him" and is impatient for cool weather, chiefly because it will re-unite him with House. The Colonel's contemplated trip to Texas makes Wilson's heart "sink." He thanks God every day that he has so generous and disinterested a friend. "You seem tremendously far away ... this part of the country seems empty without you."

Now and then the illness of Ellen Axson Wilson darkens his page. On April 2, 1914, Mrs. Wilson's condition prevents the President from joining his friend in New York. In spite of the ailment that grips her, Mrs. Wilson's mind takes an unflagging interest in public affairs. There was, a heritage of his Irish forebears, something of the rebel in Woodrow Wilson. Something of this rebel found a responsive echo in his first wife. John Kenneth Turner's muck-raking articles on *Barbarous Mexico* make Ellen Axson blush on her sick-bed "for our share in it all."

Events move rapidly. Colonel House starts upon his "great adventure." That was Wilson's conception of the Colonel's historic trip to stop the World War. Then a shot, heard in all the chancelleries, blasts Wilson's hopes. An Archduke is slain by a Serbian assassin. The dykes that held back the racial hatred of Europe break. A crimson flood inundates the world.

Woodrow Wilson shares the Colonel's deep sorrow for the dreadful conflict, consoled only by the thought that "Providence has laid deeper plans than we could possibly have laid ourselves." He does not yet realize the full measure of the calamity that threatens civilization itself. His wife's illness preoccupies his mind. The Dark Angel casts the shadow of his wings over the White House. Wilson cannot find it in his heart to go away for a night, although there are a "thousand very pressing things" which demand discussion.

Three days later Ellen Axson dies.

Her death stirs depths in Colonel House.

"I never dreamed that Mrs. Wilson was so mortally ill, and her death leaves me unnerved and stunned. It only proves again how near to us the Angel of Death hovers. I know as few do how deeply you are stricken, but I thank God you have the fortitude to withstand the blow. My affection for you is such that your troubles must ever be my troubles and your sorrows must be mine, as well. It has fallen to your lot to bring a great nation safely through an epoch-making time and the noble, gentle spirit that has gone would be the first to bid you bring to bear now that splendid courage which is yours and yours alone."

"Your troubles must ever be my troubles" and Wilson's equally lyric answer sound like a colloquy between David and Jonathan. Conventions break down. The friendship between the two men reaches its highest emotional pitch. "My dear, dear Friend," bursts from the restrained pen of Woodrow Wilson. It would be wearisome to catalogue the letters that follow. Each throbs with affection, each gravely discusses affairs of state, each looks to the Colonel for guidance. The praise of House is "very sweet" to the lonely man in the White House. "I would rather have your judgment than that of anybody I know." "With the help of counsellors like yourself I hope that it will be possible to guide the old ship in a way that will bring her credit and make her serviceable to the world."

Occasionally there is a gap in the intimate correspondence between the Duumvirs, when House is in Europe on some important mission, or when Wilson is over-burdened with details of government. "I never worry when I do not hear from you," writes House. "No human agency can make me doubt your friendship and affection. I always understand your motives." Wilson is annoyed by the chronically recurring rumors of a disagreement between himself and House. "The only things that distress me in the malicious work of the day against us are those things which touch not me but those who are dear to me." In his solitude and grief, the widowed Wilson clings to House. "Your letters," he writes, "come like the visit of a friend." This takes us to July, 1915, several months after the first meeting between Woodrow Wilson and Mrs. Edith Galt, and several months before his engagement to her.

On December 18, 1915, a new mistress entered the White House. Neither Wilson nor House had a premonition of the change in their relationship which the second marriage portended. For more than one year House remains in Wilson's thoughts and in his letters "my dearest Friend." In January, 1917, the sentimental salutation is dropped. There is no quarrel, no explanation, no flourish of trumpets. But the thermometer falls. Except for an occasional relapse into the more affectionate form of salutation, the Colonel becomes "My dear House." The President, basking in the sunshine of his nuptials, no longer needs the comradeship of the man from Texas. His new marriage monopolizes Wilson's emotional life. The tone of the letters is cordial. Wilson seeks the advice of House whenever clouds arise on the horizon. His trust is unshaken. He still leaves in his hands the thread of destiny. Perhaps the President is scarcely aware of the precipitate decline in the temperature of his affection. House, whose soul was a psychic barometer, must have sensed that the change in address betrayed a change in heart. But he never refers to the subject.

Under the surface, the fire of Wilson's affection still smolders. His feeling for House is intertwined too deeply with the unconscious forces in his own soul to be uprooted even by marriage. Warm-hearted messages still fly between the two men like carrier pigeons, until after the débâcle of Wilson's hopes in Paris. The few letters that passed between them after that are grave polar birds flapping their wings in the snow.

The various passages, cited almost at random, stress primarily the personal and emotional significance of Wilson's letters. Their amazing political import will appear as the story develops. The letters themselves are only a partial record of what passed between Wilson and House. There were countless personal conferences and telephonic conversations. In New York and Magnolia the Colonel had a private wire to Washington at his elbow. Fortunately, House kept a diary.

III

SYMBIOSIS

Astral Bodies – Wilson in Slippers – Exchanging Budgets – The Secret of
Colonel House – First Impressions – The Passion of Politics – Vicarious
Thrills – A Biological Parallel – Psychic Messmates

THE psychology of Wilson and House presents a fascinating
problem. One must constantly remember that one is dealing with extraordinary men and one must constantly bear in
mind that House was not an official but the friend, the personal
friend of a man wielding sovereign powers and responsible for
fateful decisions. House never forgot this. Neither did Wilson.

The two were bound together by a deep mutual affection and
by similar aims and principles. All this made their conferences
pleasant and easy, and enabled House to act for his friend freely
and with an assured touch. Wilson never repudiated House or
any arrangement that House had made on his behalf. House's
part was to get information far and wide for his chief, to work
out policies in fulfillment of their common principles, and to
speak for him whenever distance or Wilson's disinclination to
encourage personal contact barred him from the discussion. The
Hindus believe that they can send their astral bodies over land
and sea, while they remain at home comfortably regarding their
navels. House was the astral body of Woodrow Wilson.

The discussions between the two men were remarkable not
only for what they said but for what they left unsaid. Silence
on Wilson's part meant agreement. Silence on the part of House
indicated dissent. When two men understand and trust each
other, a tone, a look or an omission may be eloquent. Practically
all the time, by letter and in person, the resourceful House was
presenting, sometimes pressing, plans, while Wilson was deciding

or holding back. Often his holding back was amusing and touch-ing; a tired and overburdened man knowing he must take on a hard task, but postponing, evading, all but dodging it, and House often too sympathetic to press further. Occasionally there was a little fencing between them. When Wilson did not wish to come to a decision, he artfully evaded being alone with House. Then House, instinctively sensing what was going on, would discuss some philosophical abstraction or the immortality of the soul.

The surprising and delightful feature of their meetings was the time they gave to enjoying each other's society—reading, mostly poetry, discussing books, history and great men, while urgent problems waited. When, refreshed, these last were taken up, decisions were reached and frequently hammered out on the President's typewriter with appalling rapidity. In the tense, con-tentious, jealous atmosphere of Paris all lightness vanished and the stage was laid for tragedy.

Wilson, like the first Napoleon, liked to surprise his friends. He never found Colonel House napping. There was always a comfortable chair or a couch and a pair of slippers ready for him at the Colonel's hearth. The Colonel disconnected the telephone, barred the door, and then the two men would talk. Sometimes the subject of their confidences was secrets of state so profound that the President of the United States hesitated to entrust them to the United States mails! Between state dispatches Wilson would read aloud some stanza from Gray's "Elegy," of which he was very fond, or a sonorous poem by William Watson. Some-times, toward the end of the evening, Wilson would abandon the problems of the nation and recite limericks of which he knew an enormous number.

Occasionally they wandered through the streets of New York, like Harun-al-Rashid and his Vizier. "I remember," the Colonel remarked, "taking a walk with Wilson during the War from my home at Fifty-third Street. We reached Times Square without being noticed by any one. At Times Square we saw a crowd reading war bulletins. Wilson said: 'Let's see what the news is and how the people react.' We stood there quite a while listening and watching, when suddenly one man recognized Wil-son. The news immediately spread. We walked down to the

Waldorf followed by a crowd of over five thousand. We took the elevator, went up one flight and came down by another elevator, then we continued our walk undisturbed and returned unrecognized on a Fifth Avenue omnibus."

House, like a wise bee, brought to Wilson honey gathered from many fields. Often curt with others, Wilson was almost courtly with House. Once, when House stayed with him in Windsor, Wilson rose half an hour earlier every morning merely to give his friend the uninterrupted use of their common bathroom. When, after his election, House wished to yield precedence to Wilson in entering a room, Wilson remarked somewhat testily: "The fact that I am President of the United States is no reason why I should not be a gentleman."

When the two met, Wilson invariably asked House: "What is your budget?" House, with equal courtesy, urged Wilson to unburden his mind first. Then each would consult his notes and they would discuss the momentous issues which faced the nation. In one such conversation they re-made the map of Europe.

For almost a year before they set eyes on each other, House had been working quietly for Wilson. His original candidate for the Presidency had been Gaynor, then Mayor of New York. But Gaynor's eccentricities induced House to strike his name from the list. Two editors, Edward S. Martin of *Life* and Walter Page of *World's Work*, were the living bridge between Wilson and House. The moment the Governor and the Colonel met, a kindling spark leaped from the one to the other.

"What," I asked House, "cemented your friendship?"

"The identity of our temperaments and our public policies," House replied without hesitation. "Perhaps Wilson liked me because talking to me was like arguing with himself. It was my desire to see him President. He very much wanted to be President. There, from the first, was our common goal."

House selected Wilson because he regarded him as the best available candidate. "He is not," he wrote to Dr. Mezes, "the biggest man that I have met, but one of the pleasantest. And I would rather play with him than with any prospective candidate I have seen. From what I had heard I was afraid that he would have to have his hats made to order. But I saw not the slightest evidence of it. Never before have I found the opportunity and the man."

For many years House had been compelled to curb his ambition to enter national politics. Always moving quietly in the background, he made and unmade several governors of Texas. His disagreement with Bryan's financial heresies frustrated his desire to play a part in national politics until the star of Wilson rose in Trenton.

"Why," I asked the Colonel, "did Wilson accept your judgment so unreservedly?"

"Because," Colonel House replied, with a shrug of his shoulders, "he realized that I had more experience than he in politics. Wilson was not lacking in caution. Before he tied up with me closely, he made thorough inquiries as to my character, my affiliations and my political experiences. The echo of these inquiries drifted back to me long before he called on me at the Gotham. In a sense, he knew more about me than I knew about him. I understood his type, perhaps, better than he understood mine. Our thoughts ran along the same channels; a common purpose united us."

"What was your purpose and his?"

"To translate into legislation certain liberal and progressive ideas. Texas, under Governor Hogg and Governor Culberson, was the pioneer progressive among the States. The Progressive movement in the United States was fathered by Hogg, not by La Follette or Roosevelt. Many of the laws which we wrote on the statute books of Texas were subsequently adopted by the nation at large. The regulation of railroads, for instance, was first attempted in our State. I wanted to carry the Texas idea into national politics.

"Politics was always my passion. In school and college I studied most subjects solely to pass my examinations. They did not interest me deeply. Public affairs held my attention. I knew every Congressman, every Senator by name. As a young man I had much more respect for them than now and overestimated their importance. I understood the machinery of Congress. Even in Grant's day I had access to the White House. I spent hours listening to debates in the two Houses of Congress. My political

activities were confined to Texas so long as Mr. Bryan dominated the national politics of the Democrats. I could not swallow
free silver. I told my associates that the nation would never
accept it. Wilson, as you know, held the same opinion. He voted
for Palmer and Buckner in 1896."

"Did you find it difficult to get along with Wilson?"

"No. We found it very agreeable to work together."

"Wasn't Wilson intolerant of contradiction?"

"Wilson was intolerant only of fools. He did not want any
one to tell him what he already knew. If somebody agreed with
him, he did not want the other fellow to point out to him
laboriously by what steps he had reached his conclusions. If he
agreed with me, as he most often did, he would immediately start
another subject. If he did not agree with me, he would patiently
listen to every argument.

"Bryan irritated Wilson because he insisted on telling him,
in every detail, why he agreed with him. Wilson did not care
for such details. His mind worked so quickly that he had already
digested the other man's argument before it was started. He saw
no necessity for re-stating the obvious. He regarded that as an
intellectual insult. I remember his once saying to me: 'That
amiable ass, Mr. Blank, called on me this morning and insulted
me without knowing it.'

"Once in a while I made a suggestion more or less for the
sake of argument. Occasionally he pounced upon it, much to my
surprise, and accepted my point of view, sometimes before it was
completely settled in my own mind. Even his snap judgments
were more often right than wrong."

"There are," I remarked, "curious gaps in your conversation
and in your correspondence with Wilson. If he acted contrary to
your advice or if he suddenly changed his mind, did you never
question him to discover his motives? It seems strange that two
men who were as intimate as you were should not have insisted
upon complete candor in every case."

"Wilson had a mind that worked along ways of its own,
that was at times impenetrable even to his closest friends. I, too,
did not care to discuss an issue after the decision was made,
even if I disagreed with the decision. I never wasted tears crying

over spilt milk. Wilson was not politically minded himself, but
the moment a plan was submitted to him, he immediately seized
upon the point and had the courage to act upon it without hesitation. His mind responded instantaneously, intuitively. A whole
process of reasoning and cerebration which would take days and
weeks in others was precipitated in his mind like a flash."

"You are said to have a genius for friendship," I remarked.
"Did that genius ever flower as perfectly before as it did in your
relations with Woodrow Wilson?"

"I had several similar political friendships. Perhaps the most
intimate of these was with Governor Culberson. Innumerable
letters and notes from him bear eloquent testimony to the kin-
ship of our minds. I frequently went to his office and stayed
there all day. After being Attorney-General and Governor of
Texas, Culberson represented his State in the Senate for twenty
years. We never ceased to be friends, although in one case I
thwarted his wishes."

"Did Woodrow Wilson have a genius for friendship like yourself? It is frequently pointed out that his career is strewn with
wrecked friendships. Consider Harvey, McCombs, Tumulty and
yourself."

"Wilson," House remarked thoughtfully, "loved humanity,
but he did not like people. His intimacies were few. But it is not
true that all his friendships were broken. His friendship with the
two Joneses in Chicago and with Cleveland Dodge lasted for many
years. He never had a real break with Tumulty or with me. I am
confident that, had his health not failed, he and I would never
have drifted apart."

"Why did you never accept office?"

House smiled.

"Because I prefer the intellectual pleasure without the responsibility. I never liked the idea of traveling from place to
place, shaking hands with the electorate. There was, perhaps,"
he added seriously, "a time when I would have liked to be Governor of Texas. But before that time came I had already tasted
the fruit of office by proxy. Moreover, I did not wish to compete
with friends for public honors."

"Would the Presidency have appealed to you?"

"If some one had offered me the Presidency on a silver charger, like the head of John the Baptist, probably I would have accepted the gift. But I was too well aware of the realities of politics to indulge in such speculations. I knew that no one could be President who had not gone the route of office. I would have had to be Governor or Senator first. That did not appeal to me. I do not like to make speeches. I abhor routine. I prefer the vicarious thrill which comes to me through others. I gladly gave my best for the satisfaction of seeing my ideas carried out."

"Didn't most constructive ideas in your relations with Wilson emanate from you?" I interjected. "It seems to me that Wilson had the vocabulary and you had the ideas."

"That is hardly fair to either of us," House countered. "We supplemented each other. I could not have done what he did and he could not have essayed some of the things that I did. It betokens genius in a statesman if he is able to get from others something he lacks himself."

"A distinguished British historian (E. P. Gooch) says that Wilson was the pupil and you were the teacher, especially in foreign affairs."

"It is not important," House replied calmly, "to determine who was the master and who was the pupil. The fact is that two minds attempted to collaborate. History alone can declare to what extent the experiment was successful. It may decide that the League of Nations, however imperfect, marks a new milestone in the history of the human race. The Fourteen Points may not have been successfully translated into the Peace Treaties. But mankind can never forget the message of Woodrow Wilson. Ideas, like wine, need time to ferment. The turmoil in which the world is seething denotes the birth pangs of a new epoch."

The relationship between Wilson and House was not that of host and parasite. It was a psychic messmateship for which a parallel exists among plants and animals. Some plants, while living upon others, in turn confer upon their hosts certain benefits. The mistletoe, for instance, retaining its green, helps the tree to breathe when its own leaves are dead. Some crustaceans form a close partnership with other sea animals in which each assumes a certain share in sustaining the common household. One supplies the larder, the other maintains the defenses. This relationship, well known to nature students, is called symbiosis. The relationship between Wilson and House transfers symbiosis from a biological to a spiritual plane. Some men are strongest when they are alone. Some draw unsuspected strength from union with others. Their combined strength is greater than the sum of their separate strength if it remained disunited. Music and literature offer such instances. Collaboration of this type existed between Emperor William I and Prince Bismarck. However, the Iron Chancellor was incomparably the stronger. Wilson and House were evenly matched. The relationship between Bismarck and his sovereign was clearly defined. The relationship between Wilson and House was one for which no name exists. It was based not only upon their strength but also upon their weakness.

House, throughout his maturity, was in delicate health. Until the age of eleven or twelve he was a robust youngster. But one day, while swinging high, a rope broke and he was thrown on his head. Brain fever followed. For a long time the boy hovered between life and death. Upon his recovery malaria fastened upon him. Some years later he suffered from a heat stroke. Again he recovered, but he acquired a new handicap. His sensitivity to heat made him an exile from his own native Texas and from Washington in the summer.

The Colonel's frail constitution was such that he could not have lived through the tussle of a political campaign. He was the brain of every campaign, but he never, with one unimportant exception, assumed officially the reins of party leadership. Capable of terrific exertion at times, he could not chain his body and mind to the wheel of office routine. His powerful mind, keenly aware of his lack of physical equipment, utilized others. It pleased him to play with human beings, to direct their moves as if they were kings or pawns in a game of chess. A master psychologist, he turned their emotions on and off like faucets. As a little boy he sometimes provoked quarrels among his playmates solely for the pleasure of patching them up!

If life had compelled House to contend with other men for a living he would have overcome the handicap of his health or perished. But his father left him a sufficiency—not a great fortune, but enough to enable him to indulge in his intellectual pastime. Necessity became a virtue. It gave him an impish pleasure to remain in the background while pulling his wires. Seymour suggests that his sardonic sense of humor was tickled by the thought that he, unseen and often unsuspected, without great wealth or office, merely through the power of personality and good sense, was actually deflecting the currents of history. House would have rendered himself invisible if he could. To this day he does not like to be photographed or painted. "I want to be a myth," he said to me once. There was a smile on his lips. But the confession, like many a jest, affords a glimpse into the mystery of the unconscious. Possibly, in the terminology of Adler, almost hackneyed by repetition, the Colonel's intellectual conceit hides an inferiority complex springing from the defects of his physical constitution.

Woodrow Wilson represents a parallel case. Some strange feeling of inferiority made it difficult for him to deal with other men as equals. Many considered Wilson good looking. Wilson did not share this opinion. Though Wilson joked about his appearance, a sense of his homeliness made him exceedingly shy. His humility disguised itself as haughtiness. Conversation, except under conditions pre-determined by him, was an ordeal. In congenial company he could be delightfully genial and human. But these occasions were rare. Ordinarily he carried a psychic chip on his shoulder. He quarreled with a fate that had not made him an Apollo, and did not give him a face reflecting the fineness of his mentality. William Allen White describes "the wrong side of his face" as "reptilian" and his hand as "cold, stiff, moist, extended like a fish which a clerk, desiring a larger sale, casually pokes across a counter." I was equally repelled the first and only time I met Woodrow Wilson, a year or two after his election, although White's portrait seems somewhat exaggerated to me. Age softened, and suffering spiritualized Wilson's features.

In his recital of a subsequent meeting the distinguished Kansas editor admits Wilson's painful effort to manifest some show of grace, some weary attempt at charm. Wilson longed to be understood but something within him thwarted the impulse. Unwilling to expose his soul, he withdrew sullenly into his shell.

He surrounded himself with a wall. From behind that wall he spoke as a teacher to his pupils. But he entered no arena where he would be compelled to compete with others on equal terms. He needed a shield against the world. His academic rank gave him the protection he craved. Later he hid himself behind the Presidency. His temperament compelled him to depend always upon others for certain contacts. Ellen Axson, who understood his psychology, smoothed his path socially. In politics he depended upon House.

Wilson was never an athlete. In his Princeton days he was handicapped by hernia. The strain of overstudy affected his sight. It is not generally known that, like President Roosevelt, he was blind in one eye, the result of a retinal hemorrhage. His digestive system was lamentably impaired. A lifelong sufferer from migraine, he entered the White House armed with a large supply of coal-tar tablets and a stomach pump. Dr. Grayson, his physician, threw the tablets out of the window and forced a regular course of exercises upon his patient. Grayson's régime, coupled with the stimulation of power, improved Wilson's health. Although deriving new strength from the air of the White House, he still suffered from frequent headaches, and from a painful neuritis of the left arm and leg.

House, limited in his physical activities, turned to politics, Wilson to rhetoric. Wilson's frustrated energies made him an artist in words. He could express the longings of the race, the soul of the world in a speech, and seize in a phrase the inarticulate and inchoate hopes of mankind. He could move men not by personal contact but by his oratory. House was the negotiator, Wilson the prophet. House gathered the ideas, Wilson gave voice to them. House manipulated individuals, Wilson the masses.

House, as Dr. Constantin Dumba remarks in *The Memoirs of a Diplomat,* had all the qualities which Wilson lacked. To the outside world, Wilson was the senior member of the partnership— House the silent partner. But for all of his silence, the initiative for most moves came from him. All this expresses only crudely the intricate inter-relations between two complex personalities. Not all ideas originated with House, not all felicitous phrases with Wilson. The "Freedom of the Seas," for instance, was invented by House. "House," Wilson exclaimed, "is my second personality; he is my independent self. His thoughts and mine are one." This was true. But it was not the whole truth. In Wilson several personalities struggled for mastery. He had more selves than one. House was not his other self. He was only one of his other selves. This Wilson never knew; House only dimly suspected.

IV

HOUSE—SVENGALI OR STATESMAN?

The Daydream of Colonel House – A Book That Made History – *Philip Dru* Unlocks the Secret of Wilson Policies – House and Bryan – House Performs a Miracle – The Omen of Colonel Harvey – Bryan Swallows a Cocked Hat – Two Colonels Make a President

WAS Colonel House the Svengali of the Wilson Administration, misusing the mysterious power which he wielded over Woodrow Wilson, or was he a constructive statesman who attempted, jointly with Wilson, to transform his progressive visions into realities?

There seems to be no doubt of the unselfishness of Colonel House; there are some, however, who maintain that he followed the whim of the moment without definite plan or policy. Some believe that he was unduly under the influence of his British friends. Still others hold that he told Wilson merely what Wilson wished to be told. Ray Stannard Baker insinuates somewhere that House never disagreed with Woodrow Wilson if he could help it. This is a baseless accusation. House did not hesitate to irritate Wilson, to contradict him, and to clash with him on important matters.

There were times when Wilson seemed to perform at his bidding, like Trilby for Svengali. There were other times when only the Colonel's matchless tact prevented serious friction. He never wrestled with Wilson without wearing his velvet gloves. But there is no doubt that he was iron underneath. Nor is there any doubt that he had definite policies of his own before he met Woodrow Wilson.

In his political fantasy, *Philip Dru, Administrator*, published in 1912, House gives us an insight into his conception of gov-

27

ernment. The significant part which the author was destined to play in fashioning the policies of the Wilson Administration endows this book with extraordinary importance. Out of this book have come the directives which revolutionized our lives and plunged us into the World War. *Philip Dru* was written hastily. House deprecates it as a literary achievement, but he admits that it formulates his ethical and political faith.

The radical note that runs through the story from the first page to the last is not far removed from State Socialism. The book itself, Colonel House assures me, was never discussed between him and Wilson. But evidently silence implied consent. Although there is no evidence that Wilson ever read it, his ideas ran along parallel lines. Both Franklin K. Lane, Secretary of the Interior, and William Jennings Bryan, note the influence of *Dru* upon the Administration. "All that book has said should be comes about," says Franklin K. Lane, in one of his letters. "The President comes to *Philip Dru* in the end."

The Wilson Administration transferred the Colonel's ideas from the pages of fiction to the pages of history. One of the institutions outlined in the book, though under another name, is the Federal Reserve System. In *Philip Dru* is found the genesis of the Tariff and the Federal Trade commissions, also the roots of the quasi-dictatorship which Wilson assumed to make the world safe for democracy. House dedicates his opus "to the unhappy many who have lived and died lacking opportunity because in the starting the world-wide social structure was wrongly begun."

Woodrow Wilson's ancestry was British. Steeped in English tradition, he never admired the inflexibility of the American Constitution. Wilson would have preferred a government responsible to parliament, without a written constitution, based on the British model. The forebears of Colonel House, like the Roosevelts, came from Holland. But before they crossed the Atlantic they lingered for generations in England. House, like Wilson, regarded the British system as more essentially democratic because it responds more quickly to the demands of the people.

In *Philip Dru,* House chronicles a civil war in the first half of the century. "Wealth had grown so strong that the few were about to strangle the many and among the great masses of the people there was sullen and rebellious discontent. The laborer in the cities, the producer on the farm, the merchant, the professional man, and all save organized capital and its satellites saw a gloomy and hopeless future." The Colonel's hero, Dru, a young West Point cadet, graduating in 1920, predicts the advent of a new era. "Nowhere in the world," he exclaims, "is wealth more defiant, and monopoly more insistent than in this mighty republic, and it is here that the next great battle for human emancipation will be fought and won. And from the blood and travail of an enlightened people, there will be born a spirit of love and brotherhood which will transform the world; and the Star of Bethlehem, seen but darkly for two thousand years, will shine again with a steady and effulgent glow."

Philip Dru discusses these things with his sweetheart. The time is now measurably near, he insists, when it will be just as reprehensible for the mentally strong to hold in subjection the mentally weak and to force them to bear the grievous burdens which a misconceived civilization has imposed upon them, as it is wrong for the physically strong to destroy the physically weak. Government, according to Dru, must be inspired by the spirit of charity rather than the spirit of ruthless efficiency. Philip Dru maintains that the United States Government is unresponsive to popular desires. It is a "negative government," for "it is at more pains to do nothing with safety than to attempt desirable reforms which might disturb vested interests and alienate voters." The theory of checks and balances reënforces the negative character of the government.

Philip Dru proposes to make government positive. His opportunity soon arrives. Disclosures of gigantic corruption lead to an armed revolt. Placing himself at the head of the army, Philip Dru seizes the government. He is not afraid to pay the price of reform in blood. Thousands perish in the battle between his followers and the defenders of organized privilege. But the victory is his.

Dispensing with both houses of Congress, Philip Dru proclaims himself Administrator. As such he promulgates a number of measures to assure the ultimate triumph of democracy. He appoints a board composed of economists and others well versed in matters relating to the tariff and internal revenue, who are instructed to work out a tariff law which contemplates the abolition of the theory of protection as a governmental policy. He directs the tax board to work out a graduated income tax and formulates a new banking law affording a flexible currency based largely upon commercial assets, the real wealth of the nation, instead of upon debt as formerly. The primary object of his financial reform is to destroy the credit trust, the greatest, most far-reaching and in every direction the most pernicious trust of all.

Dru compels corporations to give a voice on their boards of directors and a share in their profits to labor and to the government, and launches old age pensions and a labor insurance law. Labor, he proclaims, is no longer to be classed as an inert commodity to be bought and sold by the law of supply and demand. He borrows certain ideas from Henry George, by taxing the unearned increment of idle land. He emancipates woman, stresses the importance of sex education, rewrites the Constitution of the United States, makes parliamentary government supreme, and robs the Supreme Court of the power to invalidate acts of Congress.

The House of Representatives elects an executive whose functions resemble those of a British Premier. The President is chosen by a majority vote of all electors for a single term of ten years and receives a pension after his retirement. His duties are entirely formal and ceremonial, corresponding to those of the King of England. State constitutions are similarly rewritten and uniform statutes governing such questions as divorce are adopted.

Philip Dru, by purchase and negotiation, acquires ample coaling stations along the Atlantic and Pacific coasts, and in the Bahamas, Bermuda, the British, French and Danish West Indies. He places the entire continent, including Canada and Mexico, under the American flag. In the case of Mexico, this is not accomplished without bloodshed. But again he does not shrink from war to achieve his goal. Philip Dru, though hating war, is not a pacifist. In this respect Dru and his creator differ from Woodrow Wilson. Dru creates a navy "second only to that of England."

The two great English-speaking nations "hold in their keeping the peace and commercial freedom of the Seven Seas." He arranges an international coalition in which England and America join hands with Germany and Japan. Then, like his creator, Dru aspires to become a myth, and exiles himself with Gloria. "Where were they bound? Would they return? These were questions asked by all, but to which none could give answer."

Philip Dru is the daydream of Colonel House. He sees himself in his hero. Philip Dru is what he himself would like to have been. Every act in his career, every letter, every word of advice that passed from him to Woodrow Wilson was consistent with the ideas enunciated by Philip Dru. We may or may not agree with his philosophy and his conclusions, but we cannot deny his fidelity to his ideal. In the light of Philip Dru we can understand many policies of the Wilson Administration in Mexico and in Europe which baffle the historian who ignores the book. It is the secret code which, once understood, illuminates the minds of the Duumvirs.

The inbred radical strain of the author of *Philip Dru* won the heart of William Jennings Bryan. Having faith in the Colonel, Bryan took the Colonel's friend to his bosom. Colonel House performed a miracle of political tact when he reconciled Bryan and Woodrow Wilson. House convinced the Commoner that everybody south of Canal Street was in a frenzy against Governor Wilson. He whispered into his ears strange echoes of a conversation with Colonel George Harvey, editor of *Harper's Weekly*, one of the original Wilson men, darkly hinting that Wall Street's coffers were bulging with money to ensure the defeat of Wilson. Two hundred and fifty thousand dollars would be distributed in New Jersey alone to defeat Wilson delegates. In the background appeared threateningly the figure of J. Pierpont Morgan the elder, virulently opposed to the Governor of New Jersey. Harvey attributed this opposition to some derogatory remark made by Wilson in Morgan's presence on banking methods, which the great banker took as a personal insult. The antipathy between Morgan and Wilson was mutual.

Bryan leaped with joy at the welcome news from House. He expressed the hope that Wilson would use the opportunity furnished by a forthcoming banquet in honor of Washington to speak out against the "trusts" and the "Aldrich currency scheme." In 1911, Wilson and Bryan were opposed to the reforms propounded by Aldrich. Colonel House, biding his time, induced in both men a change of heart.

Bryan's nascent cordiality toward Wilson increased when Wilson, dissembling his love, kicked the editor of *Harper's Weekly* downstairs. House had admonished Wilson that the undampened enthusiasm of Colonel Harvey, who was associated in the public mind with the powers that rule the street called Wall, was likely to injure his prospects. Harvey, attracted to Wilson by some curious quirk in his own normally conservative mind, had proclaimed Wilson's candidacy from innumerable housetops for years.

"Did Wilson know the intimate affiliation between Colonel Harvey and Morgan?" I asked Colonel House.

"He must have known. It was possibly one of the reasons for the eventual break with Harvey. This break with Harvey has been the theme of many comments. I am afraid I was largely responsible for it. My friend E. S. Martin, who was associated with Colonel Harvey on *Harper's Weekly*, had written many of the pro-Wilson editorials. I suggested to him to go slow for political reasons. When Colonel Harvey came back from a vacation, Martin conveyed the suggestion to him. Thereupon Harvey replied: 'Is that so?' and straightway wrote a two-page editorial in favor of Wilson. He then asked Wilson if he thought his advocacy was harming his candidacy. Wilson had dinner with me on that day. I asked him: 'What did you say?' He said: 'I told him my friends think so.' I asked: 'Was he very angry?' Wilson replied: 'I do not think so.' But he was mistaken. Harvey never forgave him.

"I remember that dinner because Houston had come especially from St. Louis to present his tariff views to Wilson. Wilson usually made up his mind very quickly. Sometimes I was frightened by his suddenness. I think that Wilson, once his mind was made up, spoke somewhat gruffly to Colonel Harvey, but from the point of view of political expediency nothing was more favorable to his success than his break with Harvey."

"Was Harvey's friendship with Wilson as intimate as yours?"

"I do not think so," Colonel House replied. "But Wilson owes more to Harvey than to any other man. He owes his nomination largely to two things: first to Harvey's support and then to his opposition. Wilson would never have gotten on the right track except for this incident and the acrimonious discussion by Colonel Watterson that followed. Bryan would never have trusted Wilson if he had not broken with Harvey, whom he regarded as Morgan's agent."

Gratitude for political favors was not one of Wilson's virtues. Never gifted with tact, he forced the pill down Harvey's throat without sweetening. House was not prepared for the brutality with which Wilson showed the door to his first and most enthusiastic sponsor. He saw no forewarning of his own fate in Harvey's!

Then a bomb fell into the lines of the Wilsonites. Some one unearthed a letter, written in 1906 by Wilson to Mr. Adrian Joline, with a phrase that is now political history: "Would that we could do something at once dignified and effective to knock Mr. Bryan once for all into a cocked hat." Colonel House carefully picked up the explosive and immersed it in a pail of water before it could damage the Governor's fences. Hypnotizing Bryan with subtle flattery, he induced the Commoner to swallow the cocked hat. With the active opposition of Bryan and his cohorts, Wilson could not have been nominated in 1912. Bryan was pledged to support Champ Clark. But the shadow of Tammany Hall and Thomas Fortune Ryan, hovering over Clark, impelled Bryan to desert his lifelong friend. In defiance of the instructions of the State convention, he cast his vote for the candidate of the Texas magician.

House had the Texas delegation in his pocket. He carried it with him even when he traveled abroad. With the aid of his friend Gregory he had organized the delegation into a militant phalanx for Wilson. Tammany Hall, alarmed by the growth of the Wilson boom, offered to support Senator Culberson of Texas for President, if the Texas delegation would abandon the Governor of New Jersey. The proffered bribe was rejected with scorn, in spite of its deft appeal to local patriotism. Culberson was the intimate friend of House. The Colonel's strategy had made him Governor and Senator of his native State. Personally, he was closer to House than Wilson. The Colonel's friendship for Wilson did not then burn with the steady incandescence which was to distinguish it later. House knew that he could trust Culberson absolutely, while his mind always harbored a slight uneasiness about Woodrow Wilson. Even when their mutual devotion was in its noon-day, some quivering premonition in the unconscious sounded vague alarms like a distant bell. Perhaps the Colonel sensed the other submerged personalities of Woodrow Wilson to which he was not attuned. But his sense of reality told him that Wilson could be elected. Culberson's chances were nil.

Wilson looked upon himself as a candidate of the people against entrenched privilege. He regarded Clark, Underwood and Harmon, his rivals for the Democratic nomination, as conspirators darkly united against him. The evidence that the combination was financed by Wall Street, Wilson insisted, fell short only of legal proof. Conscious of his own high mission as the champion of democracy, Wilson feared that the things done and the alliances formed would render the Democratic party utterly unserviceable as a free unit to the country.

If Wilson's nomination was maneuvered by Colonel House, he must share the credit for Wilson's election with Colonel Roosevelt. House freely admits this. The two colonels made a President.

"It is only by accident," House remarked to me in a confidential moment, "that a man of genius enters the White House by the front door. Lincoln was a compromise, Roosevelt an accident. Wilson was elected by Theodore Roosevelt."

Without the schism in the Republican party Woodrow Wilson's ambition to reach the White House would have died stillborn. With the aid of Roosevelt, the daydream of Colonel House was fulfilled. President by proxy, he could carry out the policies of Philip Dru.

TWO PRESIDENTS FOR ONE

COLONEL HOUSE picked up the receiver.

"Washington on the wire."

"Who is this?"

"This is the White House."

It was Ajax speaking.

"Ajax" was one of the names chosen by Wilson for secret communications with House. At other times he called himself "Aaron" and "Angus." House was "Beverley," "Bush" and "Roland." Eagerly the two men pilfered mythology and the dictionary to designate their associates. Each had a code name. In work and play their thoughts were one. House was the double of Wilson. It was House who made the slate for the Cabinet, formulated the first policies of the Administration and practically directed the foreign affairs of the United States. We had, indeed, two Presidents for one!

In his letters to Wilson, House always speaks of *"your* policies," *"your* plans," but consciously or unconsciously he identified himself completely with Wilson. House insists that there was nothing unconstitutional in his relations with Wilson. "Other Presidents," he remarked to me, "have had personal advisers and agents." But no other President entrusted to them affairs of state so unreservedly. It is a matter of record that Wilson sent his co-regent on missions involving not only his own reputation, but the destiny of the nation, *without instructions.* It is doubtful

35

whether a President has the right to divest himself to such an extent of his authority. However, questions such as these left the Duumvirate untroubled.

Although he carried the Electoral College by an overwhelming majority, the combined popular vote of Taft and Roosevelt exceeded Wilson's. Wilson, like Abraham Lincoln, was a minority President. His prospects were not propitious. Wall Street was afraid not only of Wilson but of House. Some business leaders looked upon the Colonel as a wild man from Texas. The reputed radicalism of the newly elected President loomed like a gigantic scarecrow over Business. Colonel House moved swiftly and softly to restore confidence. In spite of his radical streak, the Colonel was not without friends in the dwelling of Mammon. His feelers were everywhere, even in that sublime region where the Bakers spoke only to Morgans, and the Morgans spoke only to God!

J. Horace Harding, a private banker who belonged to the inner group of those reigning in Wall Street, arranged a dinner to sound House on the policies of the Administration, for with its facilities for gathering information, Wall Street knew that House was the power behind the throne. House accepted the invitation, but not—the Colonel moved ever warily—without first securing the sanction of the President-elect. The men who put their feet under the banquet table owned or controlled enough cash to vie with the United States Treasury itself. Their potential credit was incalculable. They were the supermen of American business. The dinner was like a masque in which copper, oil, steel, iron and gold personified were the guests.

The House of Morgan was represented by Robert Bacon and H. P. Davison. There were Otto H. Kahn of Kuhn, Loeb and Company, James Speyer of Speyer and Company, A. H. Wiggin of the Chase National Bank, Charles H. Sabin of the Guaranty Trust Company, James Farrell, head of the United States Steel Corporation, C. A. Coffin of the General Electric, Julius Kruttschnitt of the Southern Pacific. There were H. C. Frick, James McLean, D. G. Reid, Percy Rockefeller, Jay Cooke 3rd, W. S. Pierce and others of equal might.

Colonel House did not arrive until after the dinner. He made no formal speech. He never does. But he talked to them as a group, and then quietly, now to this, now to that man, in Banker Harding's drawing-room. No one kept a record of what he said, but before the last sparkle died in the long-stemmed glasses, House had convinced the financial overlords that the Democratic donkey, with Wilson in the saddle, would not kick over the traces.

House did not disguise or conceal from Mr. Harding's guests Wilson's desire to accomplish certain financial reforms along sound principles accepted by the bankers themselves. The Colonel's words smoothed the turbulent waters. The stock market, which had registered a fever, subsided, and the panic which had been predicted after Wilson's inauguration remained where it was, on the knees of the gods. The Schiffs, the Warburgs, the Kahns, the Rockefellers, the Morgans put their faith in House. When the Federal Reserve legislation at last assumed definite shape, House was the intermediary between the White House and the financiers. But he was not their tool.

House realized that in a capitalistic society no government can be carried on successfully without the coöperation of business. He impressed this conviction vividly upon Woodrow Wilson. Wilson rendered unto Mammon that which is Mammon's.

In dealing with business, Wilson, according to House, avoided the sensationalism of his predecessors in office. "When Taft or Roosevelt wanted to assault Big Business, their attorney generals swooped down upon the strongholds of the corporations without previous warning. Wilson preferred to reason it out. He asked his attorney general to confer with the corporations, explained to them what was wrong, and the whole thing was ironed out without expense to the government, and without disturbing the economic peace of the country."

The financial skies being clear, the Duumvirate now undertook the difficult task of constructing a Cabinet. Personal, political and geographical considerations complicated the job. The human material at their disposal was somewhat inadequate. No one felt this more keenly than House. The Democratic party had been inured to defeat. It was not trained for constructive work. The tentative list which House submitted to Wilson was recruited largely from his own calling list. The following letter, written on January 9, 1913, two days before Wilson left for Bermuda, sheds light on how House dominated the selection of Wilson's advisers:

> DEAR GOVERNOR:
> Here is a slate to ponder over:
> Secy. State ....W. J. B. (William Jennings Bryan)—Nebraska
> **Secy. Treas.** ......W. G. McA. (William G. McAdoo)—New York
> Atty. Genl. ....J. C. McReynolds—Tenn.
> Secy. of War
> *or* P. M. Genl. ....Chas. Crane—Ill.
> P. M. Genl.
> *or* Secy. of War ....T. W. Gregory—Texas
> Secy. of Agriculture
> *or* Secy. of Interior ....Walter H. Page—New York
> Secy. of Agriculture
> *or* Secy. of Interior ....David F. Houston—Mo.
> Secy. Navy ....H. C. Wallace—Washington
> Secy. Com. Labor ....Brandeis or Gardner—Mass.-Maine
> In Reserve ....
> Daniels—N. C.
> Thos. Ball—Texas
> Redfield—New York
> Burke—So. Dakota
> This would give you a Cabinet well distributed geographically and about the best material. I hope to see you as soon as you are back from the West. Mrs. House and I had a memorable evening with you. You can never know how deeply I appreciate your wanting me in your Cabinet. As an ex-officio member, however, I can do my share of work and get a little of the reflected glory that I am very sure will come to your Administration.
> Yours affectionately,
> E. M. HOUSE.
> January 9, 1913.
> P. S. If I put in Crane I would leave out Brandeis, and vice versa. It would be too much La Follette.

On February 7 Wilson asked for a final conference about the official family. He begged House to sound Houston, and added that the Treasury had been offered and accepted as they planned. Here is the Cabinet appointed by Wilson:

Secretary of State..................................W. J. Bryan
Secretary of the Treasury ....W. G. McAdoo
Secretary of War ....Lindley M. Garrison
Postmaster General ....Albert S. Burleson

Attorney General ....J. C. McReynolds
Secretary of the Navy ....Josephus Daniels
Secretary of the Interior ....F. K. Lane
Secretary of Agriculture ....D. F. Houston
Secretary of Commerce ....W. C. Redfield
Secretary of Labor ....W. B. Wilson

Even a cursory examination reveals that Wilson picked most of his associates from the Colonel's list. Some modifications were suggested by House himself. The men named by House, William Jennings Bryan, W. G. McAdoo, Josephus Daniels, W. C. Redfield, D. F. Houston, J. C. McReynolds, made up the majority of Wilson's official family. Charles Crane, Walter H. Page, Brandeis, etc., received other posts. It was merely an accident that the editor of *World's Work*, Walter H. Page, did not become Secretary of the Interior. If he had not been week-ending when Colonel House called him upon the telephone, the job would have been his. Unfortunately Mr. Page was away. It was thus that he became Ambassador to the Court of His Britannic Majesty.

David F. Houston, erstwhile Chancellor of Washington University, was the funnel through which House infiltrated into Wilson's mind his ideas on the tariff. Woodrow Wilson's tariff speeches were rhetorical echoes of his dinner conversations with Houston at the home of Colonel House. Houston remained close to Wilson until the end. "I wish," Wilson exclaimed a few years later to House, "there were two Houstons!"

Franklin K. Lane, Secretary of the Interior, who does not appear on the original list, was an intimate friend of a member of the Colonel's family. He, too, was suggested by Colonel House. The influence of Colonel House was also evident in the appointment of his friend Alfred Sidney Burleson, who received the portfolio of Postmaster General. When McReynolds resigned from the Cabinet, another devoted friend of Colonel House, hailing, like himself, from Texas, T. W. Gregory, succeeded as Attorney General.

In the secret communications between House and "Ajax" the various members of the President's official family figured under names borrowed primarily from classical lore. Bryan be-

came Priam—McAdoo became Pythias—Garrison, Mars—Mc-
Reynolds, Coke—Burleson received the appellation of Demos-
thenes—Josephus Daniels was nicknamed Neptune—Houston
became Mansion—and Redfield, Bluefields. Subsequently, as foreign affairs occupied the attention of the Duumvirate, von
Jagow, Germany's Foreign Minister, was christened Othello,
Bernstorff figures as Jones, the Kaiser as David and Dante, Grey
as White, Asquith as York, England as Zenobia—and Germany
as Zadok, in their conversation and correspondence. It requires
no Black Chamber, no code expert, to decipher the mystery of
these names.

House was somewhat disturbed by the nonchalance with
which Wilson appointed his Cabinet. "I can see no end of trouble
for him," he writes in his diary, "unless he proceeds with more
care." Wilson, even more than House, was bored by details. He
never took the trouble to apprise Houston officially of his appointment. Important decisions were made casually, with a jest. House
proposed Henry Morgenthau as Ambassador to Turkey. Wilson,
mindful of the defeat of the Ottoman Empire by the Balkan
League in the war of 1912, jokingly retorted: "There ain't going
to be no Turkey." "Then," House replied in the same vein of
levity, "let him go look for it."

Poor McCombs, Wilson's campaign manager, was left in the
ice box. Avid for a place in the Cabinet, he refused the Ambassadorship offered to him by Wilson. After that he sulked, and
wrote a book. "I have always felt," Colonel House confided to
me, "that it was distressing that W. F. McCombs did not reap
the advantage which should have come to him by reason of his
great service to Woodrow Wilson. When others were working
casually and intermittently he devoted his entire time to the
furtherance of Governor Wilson's nomination for President. If
he had not fallen ill, he might have gone far, for he had real
ability and much charm with a sense of humor. His illness was
of such a nature that it soon put him in direct antagonism not
only with the President but also with those with whom he had
to work politically."

It was impossible to feed all the hungry Democrats. Even
some of those who deserved consideration found the trough empty.

There were many grumblings and heartaches. House smoothed the President's path wherever he could. His frail figure interposed a granite wall between office seekers and Woodrow Wilson. So skillfully did he conduct himself that he made few enemies. "Take my word for it," Senator Gore remarked to Postmaster General Burleson, "House can walk on dead leaves and make no more noise than a tiger."

THE HAND ON THE STEERING WHEEL

WILSON meekly accepted the suggestions emanating from his *alter ego*. Once he balked. He did not want to kick Bryan upstairs into the Cabinet instead of knocking him into a cocked hat. House pleaded that it would be best to make Bryan Secretary of State in order to have him at Washington and in harmony with the Administration, rather than outside and possibly in a critical attitude. House hoped that Mrs. Bryan would temper the tantrums of the Nebraskan. "Mrs. Bryan," House insists, "is the salt of the earth. Her intellectual qualities command my respect. She was always steadier than her husband, less inclined to fly off at a tangent."

The Colonel's diary records his struggle in behalf of Bryan. "I called up Governor Wilson, and he asked if I still held to my advice about Mr. Bryan and I answered yes. This is the third or fourth time he has asked me this. It shows how distrustful he is of having Mr. Bryan in his Cabinet." Even on the day on which he invited Bryan to join his Cabinet, Wilson telephoned House once more, hoping against hope that the Colonel could suggest an escape!

"Why," I asked Colonel House, "did Wilson make Bryan his Secretary of State?" We were facing each other in the library of his little apartment on Park Avenue. From the wall a picture of Woodrow Wilson regarded us sternly.

"Wilson would have ignored him if I had not pressed upon him the political urgency of enlisting the Commoner. A lady once lambasted Wilson most frightfully in my presence for having put Bryan in his Cabinet. I said: 'Dear lady, don't blame Wilson, blame me.' I think she never forgave me."

"Bryan's domination of the Democratic party sealed you up in Texas like a djin in a bottle. Why did you reward him for this by forcing him upon Wilson?"

"No lash of the Administrative whip could have compelled Congress to adopt the Federal Reserve Act and other financial reforms, upon which the domestic fame of Wilson rests, without Bryan. President after President had tried it and failed. When I first recommended Bryan," Colonel House continued musingly, "the world was at peace. Foreign affairs were dull. Bryan's presence in the Cabinet made Wilson's hold on Congress impregnable. Bryan was the best possible Secretary of State in 1912. The War turned the world topsy-turvy. Bryan was not the best Secretary of State after 1914."

The Colonel gazed at the portrait of Woodrow Wilson over his couch.

"Bryan was a man with excellent intentions. His moral courage was like a flame. He was a doctrinaire. But he was also, like Lloyd George, a shrewd politician. Unfortunately for his aspirations he ceased to grow. His environment clung to his coat-tails. His oratory invariably carried the West, but the very qualities that endeared him to his followers were a barrier to his success in the East."

"It would have been better for Woodrow Wilson if you had accepted the responsibility of office."

House smiled.

"If I had been Secretary of State, every day a new gulf might have arisen between Wilson and myself. I could remain his informal adviser even if my advice were rejected. Had I gone into the Cabinet I could not have lasted eight weeks." Outside of the Cabinet, as Seymour points out, House lasted for eight years! This, I may add in parenthesis, is one year longer than the lease of power which House grants to the hero of his fantasy, *Philip Dru.*

Tempted to probe deeper, I asked: "Could Wilson have forced you to assume the responsibility of office?"

House shook his head.

"No. If he had made that the condition of our coöperation I would have stepped out."

"Did Bryan never resent the fact that you were Mr. Wilson's super-Secretary of State?" I queried.

House did not attempt to evade the question.

"Bryan would not have been human if he had been entirely free from resentment. He told one of the members of the Cabinet that he resigned on my account. I am not disposed to criticize Bryan. I admire his great qualities; some of these qualities," the Colonel added, "he has bequeathed to his daughter. Ruth Bryan Owen has inherited winsome and intellectual qualities from both her parents."

"Did you ever discuss your policies with Bryan while you were unofficially exercising his functions?"

A smile suffused the features of Colonel House.

"I discussed these policies only with Woodrow Wilson."

"But surely," I countered, "Bryan must have talked to you about the issues involved."

Colonel House grew a little hazy.

"I suppose he did."

"Did he agree with you?"

"In spite of the fundamental difficulties of our position, in spite of temperamental and political differences, we had some aims in common. We both wished for peace. Our roads traveled side by side for a long time before they converged. We still sought the same goal, but we could not agree on the shortest route."

It was no secret, even while Bryan retained his post, that the Secretary of State had no voice in formulating the foreign policies of the United States. He was not in the confidence of the Duumvirs. But who was? Vice-President Marshall, like the Secretary of State, never figured in their consultations.

"Why is it," I inquired, "that Marshall played a negligible part?"

House scratched his head.

"Marshall was held too lightly. An unfriendly fairy godmother presented him with a keen sense of humor. Nothing is more fatal in politics. Many politicians destroy themselves by their wit. Wit makes enemies. It stirs up the hornets. Marshall made friends, not enemies. But they looked upon him as a jester. Marshall was spontaneous and genuine. Once he presented a book to Woodrow Wilson. "How," Colonel House asked, with the ghost of a chuckle, "do you think he inscribed it?—'To Woodrow Wilson from his only Vice.' "

There was one instance when Vice-President Marshall might have seized the reins of government from the palsied hand of Wilson. That was after the President's return from his Western trip. But Marshall lacked the stamina or the desire to play a decisive part in the destiny of his country. The Vice-Presidency is what the Germans call a "first-class funeral." Marshall resignedly accepted his fate. The men who wrote the Constitution did not have such a rôle in view when they created the office of Vice-President. It would be preferable for the country if our Vice-Presidents officially exercised some of the functions which Colonel House exercised unofficially! That would assure continuity of policy even if fate struck down the President.

Marshall aided his chief by helping to pilot some of his measures through the Senate. The legislative record of the Wilson Administration, in the first four years, justified the fondest hopes of his progressive advisers. Colonel House looks upon the reform of the monetary system as the crowning internal achievement of the Wilson Administration.

"To pass the Federal Reserve Act, with the aid of a party shot to pieces by financial heresies, was nothing short of a miracle!"

The Colonel's own interest in currency reform was kindled by a personal experience. "My brother, a banker, failed in the panic of 1907. His bank had plenty of assets. But the assets were frozen. That brought the whole problem of money and banking very close to me. I studied the reform proposed by Aldrich because I wanted to find something that would prevent failures like my brother's."

"Was Wilson interested in the matter?"

"Very much so, in spite of the fact that at one time he was

opposed to the Aldrich plan. Wilson," House continued, with an enthusiasm that did not seem artificial, "was wonderful. He was ever willing to lend his ear to any sound proposition, nor did he hesitate to sacrifice his personal idiosyncrasies if need be. He conquered his aversion to Bryan to place the money of the United States on a sure basis. By a paradox of fortune the man who almost destroyed our money structure was the instrument chosen by destiny to make it secure."

"Did Bryan blindly accept the plan, or did he labor to change it?"

"He worked over it very hard, and made several important suggestions. At first we did not think well of them. But events have shown that he was right."

"Along what lines were Bryan's suggestions?"

"Bryan insisted upon strengthening the hold of the government on the Federal Reserve System."

"The Federal Reserve Act seems to be the product of many minds. Who really put it over? Both Owen and Glass claim the honor of having delivered the baby."

"Glass had charge of it in the House, Owen in the Senate. McAdoo did much, perhaps more than even Owen or Glass. Wilson backed it with all the power of his office. But all would have failed without the Commoner."

House collaborated in every direction. His first task was to remain at the President's elbow and to prevent him from committing himself to any scheme without thorough investigation. Then he guided the measure so that it was left in the control of experts and preserved from the assaults of political incompetents.

After floating the ship, it was almost equally important to man it. Here, as in the case of the Cabinet, Wilson relied primarily upon House. The name of W. P. G. Harding crops up in their correspondence. Wilson admits his gratitude to House for suggesting it. A few days later Wilson writes that Houston and McAdoo, having met Harding on a recent trip, consider his ability and talents very ordinary. They urge instead A. Martin Baldwin of Alabama. However, as usual, the advice of House prevails. On April 28, 1914, he records in his diary: "After dinner we went to the office for the President to sign his mail. We read the Mexican despatches together and afterward got down to the real finish of the Federal Reserve Board. He took his pen and wrote down their names: Richard Olney first, then Paul Warburg, Harding, Wheeler and Miller. He turned to me and said, 'To whom would you give the ten-year term?' I advised giving it to Miller, which he did. He gave Olney the two-year term, Warburg four years, Harding and Wheeler the six- and eight-year terms." Olney and Warburg were also sponsored by House. Olney did not accept the appointment.

Space does not permit me to detail here the manifold activities of the Colonel. When Wilson's lackadaisical attitude toward his Cabinet created difficulties, House persuaded the President to restore the old custom of meeting his official family at least once a week. However, the members of the Cabinet were not permitted to formulate in public any policies of their own. Their speeches were limited, their utterances censored. There was no god but Wilson, and House was his only prophet.

The Colonel's opinion was constantly sought by members of the Cabinet on departmental matters, and in matters governing their relations with the President. His advice was asked in the appointment of judges. There was no department of the government over which the Colonel did not exercise some influence. To him flocked every politician with an ax to grind. Every reformer with a scheme for saving the country, finding the White House barred, left the infant on the door-mat of Colonel House.

"Good morning, Your Excellency—"

It was the voice of Colonel House at his favorite instrument, the telephone.

"What do you mean?"

"A great deal—"

There was a gasp.

"Are you joking?"

"Not at all. I am authorized by the President to ask you if you will accept the Ambassadorship to the Court of Saint James'."

At the other end of the wire sat Walter Hines Page.

"Do you accept?"

Page, all aquiver with delight, coyly reserved his decision.

"I am immensely pleased, but I doubt my ability to fill the place. It is entirely different from anything I have previously done."

He promised to inform House of his decision. Forty-eight hours later he called up and mysteriously announced: "I have decided to turn my face towards the East." That was his playful way of saying that he accepted the honor. He expected to be called to the White House for a conference, but having made the appointment, Wilson promptly forgot his Ambassador. He was appointed but not received by his own chief!

Having disposed of this matter, the Eternal City was conferred upon another Page—Thomas Nelson. House's doorbell must have been busy in those days. One of his callers was James W. Gerard. After consulting with House, Gerard drew Berlin from the ambassadorial grab bag. Gerard, throughout his Berlin career, remained in constant communication with House. House, in turn, advised Gerard with the punctuality of a clock. Brand Whitlock wrote from Brussels, Willard from Madrid, Penfield from Vienna, Morris from Stockholm, Thomas Nelson Page from Rome and Walter Hines Page from London.

Most of the diplomatic appointees, like most members of the Cabinet, were personal friends or acquaintances of the Colonel. There was in this no sinister motive on the part of Wilson's co-regent. He realized that some man must be appointed and that, other things being equal, it was better to entrust delicate missions to people whom he knew than to strangers. He expected no gratitude and exacted no personal service in return from those upon whom he bestowed his favors.

House enjoyed the distribution of diplomatic plums because they enabled him to gratify his passion for world politics. The Colonel was growing tired of home politics. House had made, even in Texas, a ceaseless study of current diplomacy. Through all his diaries runs the desire to free himself from the details of domestic politics and to participate in the formation of a positive foreign policy for the Wilson Administration.

Although the mind of Colonel House was more and more immersed in world affairs, he found it difficult to interest Woodrow Wilson in Europe. "I wish," he notes somewhat impatiently in his diary, "the President would pay more attention to foreign affairs. He seems to be interested mainly in domestic matters, which bears out his own assertion that he has a 'one track mind'. I do not believe he reads Gerard's or Penfield's messages which come to him through me and are sent in that way for his information as well as mine. If he would keep himself informed he would not destroy his influence abroad as he does from time to time by things he says in his speeches." The letters of the Ambassadors were received but not read!

Unlike the President, Colonel House read the letters of all the Ambassadors with meticulous attention. Their reports to the State Department were rather cursory. They felt that their missives would receive scant attention from Bryan or Wilson. They knew whose hand was on the steering wheel.

VII

THE PRICE OF HUERTA'S HEAD

Panama Tolls Trouble Wilson – Grey Converts House – The Colonel's Advice – England Wins a Trick – Colonel House Upsets a Platform – Woodrow Wilson's Ruse – Huerta's Head on a Silver Platter – A Dream of Pan-America – The Embryo of the League

WHEN the American people built the Panama Canal they little thought that they were building it for Great Britain. They did not clearly understand that Great Britain had sacrificed certain rights to dig a canal of its own, in return for the promise that British ships should pass through the big ditch on the same terms as our own. The clause in the treaty covering this point was somewhat shadowy. It was susceptible of divers interpretations. President Taft and his Secretary of State, Philander Knox, both men learned in law, sided with those who denied Great Britain's claim. The Democratic platform insisted upon the exemption of American ships from paying tolls in the American-built canal. The Democratic party in Congress was pledged to abide by the platform. The country at large looked askance at any concession to England. Wilson was committed to carrying out the policy of his party. However, one of the Duumvirs decided otherwise.

A discussion with Sir Edward Grey had convinced Colonel House that the English contention was incontrovertible. Sir Edward Grey, on that memorable occasion, lightly touched upon both the Panama Canal tolls and certain difficulties which were facing the Administration in Mexico. What was said is not clearly recorded. But ever after that conversation, Mexico and the Panama tolls were curiously interlocked in the minds of all concerned. While these conversations were going on, the President was stubbornly pursuing a policy of his own in Mexico. Hating carnage and bloodshed, Wilson refused to shake the blood-stained, if competent, hands of Huerta, the dictator of Mexico.

Both Wilson and House believed with Philip Dru in the destiny of the United States to dominate the North American Continent. To House, the idea of violence was abhorrent but not unthinkable. Wilson, preferring the ferrule to the sword, was determined to achieve his end without actual warfare. Huerta's resistance to his benevolent purpose enraged the pedagogue in the White House. Europe, led by England, egged on Huerta. The secret of her policy was writ in oil. Great Britain balked Wilson's attempt to enforce his will in Mexico without resorting to armed intervention. Pershing was sent to Mexico on the pretext of pursuing the bandit chief, Villa. Actual warfare, however, was still avoided. It could not indefinitely be postponed unless Huerta backed down.

The situation fascinated Colonel House. He proceeded to straighten it out in his own fashion. An involvement in Mexico at this time was not to his taste. He wanted America to keep its powder dry, in view of various eventualities that were shaping themselves in Europe. The Colonel now employed the arts of reconciliation, which he had so assiduously practiced even in school, upon Sir Edward Grey and Woodrow Wilson. The British Cabinet was urging Sir Edward to take energetic steps to make England's protest effective. Grey was on the point of demanding the arbitration of the moot point by an International Court. House urged him to desist.

"If you press your point," he admonished Sir Edward, "you invite an adverse answer from Wilson. The President has had no leisure to familiarize himself with the question; if you force a decision now, he will stand on the party platform and will be backed by the majority of both houses of Congress."

Grey accepted the Colonel's advice. He challenged the entire Cabinet and took upon himself the responsibility for delaying negotiations. Wilson gratefully appreciated Sir Edward's compliance with the request of the Colonel. Somewhat later Sir William Tyrrell, the right-hand man of Sir Edward Grey, appeared in America. House arranged a meeting between the President and Sir William. The audience was satisfactory—to Great Britain. England won a trick!

Wilson's surrender, Colonel House insists, revealed his moral courage. "No public official ever had more. When he felt an act or policy was right he would sponsor it, no matter what the cost to his personal fortunes. He reversed himself in face of the fact that Senator Underwood, Democratic leader in Congress, Kitchin, Democratic leader in the House, and Champ Clark, Speaker of the House, held views to the contrary. He did it, too, knowing that the sentiment of the country was against him."

"What," I asked Colonel House, "changed Wilson's mind about the Panama tolls?"

House looked at me unperturbed.

"Possibly I did."

His reply solved the riddle that has puzzled most historians of the Wilson Administration. Wilson never deigned to explain his change of mind. He did not even take the Committee on Foreign Affairs of the Senate into his confidence.

"Colonel," I asked excitedly, "what made you do it?"

"I thought we were wrong," House calmly replied.

Nothing exemplifies more vividly the amazing power exercised by the Colonel. The ethical scruples of a private citizen upset the platform of the Democratic party, reversed the policy of two Administrations and the deliberate judgment of the people.

"The arguments of Sir Edward Grey," House continued, "were incontestable. Tyrrell was a wise messenger. Page, our Ambassador in London, sided with him and me. Wilson's decision confirmed the faith of the American Government in the sanctity of treaties at a critical point in the history of the world."

Both Wilson and House knew that the opposition of Congress was a tough nut to crack. House pulled every wire at his disposal. Senator O'Gorman, the staunch friend of Ireland, was one of the leaders of the anti-British faction. House induced the Senator's son-in-law, Dudley Field Malone, to reason with that formidable antagonist. Wilson, unwilling to explain his real reasons even in confidence to the Senate Committee, resorted to stratagem. He overawed and alarmed Congress by hinting at a mysterious catastrophe that was bound to involve our country if we insisted upon sending our ships through the canal toll-free without granting the same privilege to Great Britain. He made the adherence of Congress to his policy a matter of personal confidence. "I ask this of you," he solemnly announced, "in support of the foreign policy of the Administration. I shall now know how to deal with other matters of even greater delicacy and nearer significance, if you do not grant it to me in an ungrudging measure."

The stratagem worked.

Wilson's mind moved on a high ethical plane; nevertheless he exacted a price for his conversion. England paid for Wilson's surrender with the head of Huerta. The moment Wilson had promised to yield on the tolls question, Great Britain instructed her Ambassador, Sir Lionel Carden, not to block Wilson's policy in Mexico. Deprived of his British prop, Huerta abdicated and fled. That was in July, 1914.

Wilson and House now contemplated peaceful intervention in Mexico with the A. B. C. powers, Argentine, Brazil and Chile. Colonel House urged upon Wilson a system of coöperation between the North and South Americas. "I thought the Federal Reserve Act was the greatest constructive work and the thing that would stand out and make his Administration notable. Now," the Colonel records in his diary, "I would like him to place beside that great measure a constructive international policy.... I thought the time had arrived to show the world that friendship, justice and kindliness were more potent than the mailed fist. He listened attentively to what I had to say and asserted that he would do it and would use the speech in San Francisco, when he opened the exposition, to outline his policy."

Colonel House contemplated a League of American States guaranteeing security from aggression and furnishing the mechanism for peaceful settlement of disputes. Eventually, he succeeded in kindling Wilson's enthusiasm. "I thought," House explains in his diary on December 16, 1914, "Wilson might not have the opportunity to play a great and munificent part in the European tragedy. But there was one thing he could do at once and that was to inaugurate a policy that would weld the Western

Hemisphere together. It was my idea to formulate a plan, to be agreed upon by the republics of the two continents, which in itself would serve as a model for the European nations when peace is at last brought about."

The Colonel's plan carried forward the policy of his hero, Philip Dru, who takes Mexico under the wings of the American eagle. "We must," he advises Wilson, "either ourselves or jointly with the A. B. C. people keep a hand on the throttle for many years to come. Restoring order for a moment is only one part of the job. The other part is giving right direction to affairs, so that your policy as a whole may be justified."

Wilson asked him to explain his ideas a little more fully. "I take it," the President confides to Duumvir House, "that we have no authority in law to put this government under such obligations as you suggest without legislative action by both Houses and treaty action by the Senate." The President hesitates to adopt a course not unlike that of Roosevelt when he "took" Panama, but is unwilling to summon an extra session of Congress to authorize the steps involved.

The plan failed. Chile balked. Bryan and Lansing were neglectful. Wilson lost interest when House was away. Colonel House himself was engrossed in Europe, and could give little personal attention to the child of his brain. But it was not a question of love's labor lost. Article X of the League covenant is a replica of the plan proposed by Colonel House for his new Pan-American doctrine. It was the League of Nations in embryo. Conquerors and poets have dreamed of some Parliament of Man. Napoleon brooded over Pan-Europe. Kant, the German philosopher, advocated a League of Nations. For years the minds of American and British statesmen had played with some such plan. It was Colonel House who first attempted to try it out on a small scale in the Western Hemisphere. It is not unfitting, therefore, that his hand was destined to write the first draft of the covenant of the League of Nations.

VIII

THE INTERVIEW THAT ALMOST STOPPED
THE WORLD WAR

Schrippenfest in Potsdam – The Geographical Colonel – Between Two Generals – Half an Hour That Might Have Changed the Fate of the World – Queen Victoria's Favorite Grandson – Great Britain's Choice – Germany, the Cockpit of Europe

IN June, 1914, Colonel House had an audience with the Kaiser. "The visit of Colonel House to Berlin," the Master of Doorn said to me on one occasion, "almost prevented the World War."

Colonel House reported the gist of his exchange of thoughts with the Kaiser to Wilson. The present version, revised and amplified by Colonel House and the Kaiser, has the approval of both actors in that momentous scene. It is authentic history.

Mid-day, June 1, 1914. A crescent-shaped luncheon table in a gaudy hall of the Imperial Palace at Potsdam, where the walls are made of sea shells. The Kaiser in military uniform, surrounded by officers glittering with buttons and decorations. Opposite him, in somber evening dress, looking like two black crows—the phrase is the Kaiser's, not mine—Colonel House and James Gerard. It is the day of the *Schrippenfest,* held annually on Whit-Monday for the *"Lehr-Infanterie-Battaillon,"* founded by Frederick William III. This unit is a school battalion drawn from every regiment of the Prussian Army. In honor of the occasion the common soldiers are regaled with white rolls and beef and rice pudding. The Empress and the imperial princes are present. Colonel House and Ambassador Gerard are the only civilian guests.

House is wedged in between two generals. He is flanked on the one side by General Falkenhayn, Chief of the General Staff.

The other is a Saxon general who must go down to oblivion. Neither Colonel House nor the Kaiser seems to remember his name. The generals insist on discussing with House highly technical problems of military strategy. House vainly protests that he is not a military man. But his efforts are futile. "I had cautioned Gerard before coming to Berlin not to use the title of 'Colonel' referring to me, or in introducing me after I arrived. This did not serve my purpose, for Bernstorff had cabled on my coming, so I became 'Colonel' immediately.

"Most of my time at luncheon was used in explaining to my neighbors the kind of Colonel I was—not a real one in the European sense, but, as we would say in America, a geographical one. My explanation finally reached Falkenhayn's consciousness, but my neighbor from Saxony was hopelessly befuddled and continued till the last to discuss army technique."

Governor Hogg of Texas had bestowed the title of Colonel upon his friend in an unlucky moment. Unwilling to offend the Governor, House had accepted the designation, although he immediately presented the resplendent uniform that came with it to an old Negro butler, who proudly wore it at lodge meetings and funerals! There is a photograph of the butler in the Colonel's military accoutrements. The title of "Colonel" pursued House for the rest of his life. It will go with him to eternity. He could escape from it no more than the Ancient Mariner from his albatross. To friend and foe alike he became the "Colonel."

It was "Colonel" House who, immediately on his arrival in the German capital, was invited to view the aviation field. The military authorities were anxious to demonstrate to their American colleague Germany's mastery of the air. It was here that he met a Dutchman by the name of Fokker, whose name is linked with the history of aviation. Fokker engaged in spectacular flights for the benefit of the "Colonel." It was "Colonel" House to whom Admiral von Tirpitz unfolded his heart. It would have been better if Colonel House on his first visit had met the pacific and scholarly Chancellor von Bethmann-Hollweg, or Rathenau, philosopher and business executive. But Bethmann-Hollweg was on a vacation. The Foreign Office thought that an American "Colonel" would be more impressed by an Admiral than by a business man or a Chancellor.

Dr. Gottlieb von Jagow, then Foreign Minister, confirms my interpretation. "Unfortunately," he writes, "we did not know in Germany the meaning of certain American military designations, such as Kentucky- or Texas-made 'Colonels.' His Majesty, the Emperor, misinterpreting the courtesy title of 'Colonel' prefixing the name of President Wilson's confidential emissary, desired to confer a special distinction upon House by inviting him to an ancient military festival, the so-called *Schrippenfest,* a luncheon given to the school battalion after a solemn religious service." The welcome he thus received, and the insistence with which the military point of view was dinned into his ears by other distinguished Germans, accentuated in the mind of Colonel House the impression that Germany was obsessed by militarism.

The experience of Colonel House in the German capital colored his report to the President. "The situation," he writes from Berlin, "is extraordinary. It is militarism run stark mad. Unless some one acting for you can bring about a different understanding, there is some day to be an awful cataclysm. No one in Europe can do it. There is too much hatred, too many jealousies." This was exactly the task upon which Colonel House and Woodrow Wilson had set their hearts. The thought came from House. Catching the Colonel's enthusiasm, Wilson urged House to impress upon the statesmen of Europe that the United States was a disinterested friend. It seemed inconceivable to German officialdom that a mission of such importance would be left in the hands of an American who was neither a professional diplomat nor a professional soldier.

In spite of the military honors showered upon House, the Kaiser rattled the saber not even once in his conversation with the Duumvir. The luncheon in the Shell Hall, during which any intimate discussion was impossible, lasted fifty minutes. Then the Colonel saw the Kaiser alone. He talked to him for half an hour. That half hour might have changed the fate of the world, if circumstances had been propitious. But before it was possible to work out a more definite plan for world coöperation, the shot of a Serbian assassin loosened the hounds of hell in Europe.

The Emperor and the Duumvir are walking up and down a terrace in Potsdam, overlooking the park of Sans Souci. Ten or fifteen feet away from them, out of hearing, stand Ambassador Gerard and Dr. von Jagow, in earnest conversation.

HOUSE: President Wilson feels that Europe is divided into two armed camps, guarding huge stores of ammunition. He fears the spark that may set the world on fire.

THE KAISER: We Germans keep our powder dry. But we don't play with fire. Germany wants no war; she has nothing to gain from war. I have maintained the peace of Europe for twenty-five years. Germany was poor. She is now growing rich. A few more years of peace and she will lead the Old World in commerce.

HOUSE: But why, Sir, do you constantly increase your military and naval budgets? Having already the largest army in Europe, why do you insist upon rivaling Great Britain on the high seas?

THE KAISER: I challenge the statement that ours is the largest European army. I admit that we must maintain our strength. We are menaced on every side. (*The Emperor brings his face close to Colonel House. The Colonel involuntarily retreats. The Kaiser continues earnestly.*) The bayonets of all Europe are directed at the heart of Germany. We are surrounded by jealous and unfriendly neighbors.

HOUSE: Your neighbor across the channel is not unfriendly. My conversations with Sir Edward Grey and Sir William Tyrrell convince me that England is willing to coöperate with Germany. She recognizes Germany's right to more colonies and "a place in the sun." It seems to me that an understanding between England and Germany would make it possible to reduce the frightful burden of armaments. There are new worlds to be peacefully conquered. Asia, Africa, South America offer vast fields for concerted action. England and Germany, with the aid of the United States, can explore and exploit the waste spaces of the world.

THE KAISER: Nothing would be more pleasing to me. I have always loved England. Every one knows that I was Queen Victoria's favorite grandson. Do you think that I could ever forget her love for me? I have been attacked in my own country because I love England too well. Germany and the English-speaking nations are kinsmen. Many years ago, when I began the culture exchange between the United States and Germany, I paved the way for closer coöperation between England, Germany and the United States. My hopes were frustrated by England. How could English statesmen form an alliance with Latins and Slavs, who have no sympathy with the ideals and purposes of our race, and who are vacillating and unreliable allies? England, Germany and the United States are the light-bearers of the world; they alone can evolve the ultimate ideal of a Christian civilization.

HOUSE: I believe that the culture and the history of France entitle her to participate on equal terms with the Germanic group.

THE KAISER (*dubiously*): Perhaps. I have pocketed my pride more than once to conciliate the French, but my friendly gestures have been misunderstood. Now France is tied to Russia, and England to France. Both will pay dearly for the Russian alliance.

HOUSE: I agree with Your Majesty that Russia is a liability to Great Britain. The Muscovite is the most formidable menace to England's future. He would be even more formidable if Germany did not stand like a living wall between him and Europe.

THE KAISER: The English will learn by bitter experience the impossibility of making permanent or satisfactory alliances with either Russia or France.

HOUSE: But, Your Majesty, it is your ever-growing navy that, together with your enormous army, frightens England into an unnatural alliance with her natural enemies. England cannot permit Germany, almost a next-door neighbor, to possess the largest navy as well as the largest army.

THE KAISER: It is Russia, not I, that threatens Great Britain in India.

HOUSE: Nevertheless, Your Majesty, the day may come when English statesmen will have to decide whether they run more danger from a successful German invasion than from the possibility of losing their Asiatic colonies to Russia.

THE KAISER (*interrupting*): We never even dreamed of such an invasion.

HOUSE: British statesmen include every contingency in their calculations. Great Britain has no desire to see Germany crushed.

THE KAISER (*looks at* HOUSE *questioningly*).

HOUSE (*continuing*): Germany's downfall would leave her to reckon alone with her ancient enemy, Russia. But she would rather envisage that possibility than the spectre of German naval supremacy.

THE KAISER: I am not building my fleet to attack Great Britain. Germany, without coaling stations, without naval bases, must build a navy capable of protecting her commerce everywhere on the seven seas, a navy commensurate with her growing importance and power. We must be strong enough to defend ourselves against the combined attack of Russia and France. We do not seriously consider the possibility of a clash with our British cousins. What grounds for conflict exist anywhere between England and Germany, or between Germany and the United States? Like Germany, America and England have nothing to gain from war. They can only lose.

HOUSE: I recognize the community of interest between England, Germany and America. If they will stand together they can maintain the peace of the world. But there can be no understanding between England and Germany so long as you, Sir, continue to increase your navy. The English statesmen to whom I have spoken wonder when Germany will reach the end of her naval program.

THE KAISER: That is no secret. The matter has been threshed out in the Reichstag. We have formulated a definite policy. We shall make no attempt to expand beyond the point needful to our defense. I am, I repeat, a friend of England. My army and I render an incalculable service to her by holding the balance of power against Russia in Europe.

HOUSE: Your Majesty's point of view and that of the British statesmen is so nearly identical that it should not be difficult to harmonize the policies of the two countries. Both President Wilson and I feel that an American may be better able to compose the difficulties which still remain and to bring about understanding with a view to peace. There is too much distrust and dislike in Europe. We are in a better position to act as go-betweens because we have no selfish interest at stake.

THE KAISER (*nods approvingly*).

HOUSE: This is the work I have undertaken. I have come to Germany before going anywhere else to win, first, the approval of Your Majesty. After leaving Germany it is my purpose to go directly to England, where I shall take up the negotiations with the British Government in the same informal manner in which I have talked to you. If the reaction is favorable, I shall return and report to Your Majesty.

THE KAISER: By all means keep in touch with me. Any communication will reach me through our friend Zimmermann here in the Foreign Office. (*One of the Emperor's sons appears upon the terrace to convey to the Kaiser the fact that the special train from Potsdam is waiting. But he waves him away. Later the Empress herself comes out, but the Emperor continues to talk to House. Finally the Grand Chamberlain approaches and in an embarrassed manner explains the difficulty to the Emperor. The Kaiser dismisses him curtly and continues the conversation.*) Tell the President from me that nothing is nearer to my heart than to preserve world peace.

HOUSE: May I ask Your Majesty why Germany refused to sign the Bryan Treaty for Arbitration providing a "cooling-off period" of a year, before hostilities can be inaugurated?

THE KAISER (*very seriously*): You would not ask this question if you realized Germany's unfortunate geographical position. For centuries Germany has been the cockpit of Europe. No natural borders protect her from her enemies. Our only advantage is that we are ready. We have not signed and never will sign a treaty that would deprive us of this advantage. Our strength lies in being always prepared for war at a second's notice. We will not resign that advantage and give our enemies time to prepare.

(*House bids farewell to his host. The two men clasp hands, never to meet again.*)

THE MOST ABYSMAL BLUNDER IN HISTORY

AFTER his talk with the Kaiser, House went to Paris. When he arrived in the French capital, the shooting of Calmette by Madame Caillaux had provoked a political crisis. The Cabinet had fallen and there was no one in authority with whom he could discuss a matter of so much importance. After remaining in Paris for a week, the Colonel started for London. The English agreed with him "in principle," but dillydallied. Sir Edward always agreed in principle. But if Sir Edward Grey had shown a little more energy it would have been possible to strait-jacket Mars. There would have been no World War in 1914.

On July 7, 1914, House writes an enthusiastic letter to Emperor William thanking him once more for his gracious reception. He sugar-coats the recalcitrance of Paris, and assures the Emperor that Sir Edward Grey was "sympathetic to the last degree." He adds that England "must necessarily move cautiously lest she offend the sensibilities of France and Russia."

> While this communication is, as Your Majesty knows, quite unofficial, yet it is written in sympathy with the well-known views of the President, and, I am given to understand, with the hope from His Britannic Majesty's Government that it may bring a response from Your Majesty which may permit another step forward.
>
> Permit me, Sir, to conclude by quoting a sentence from a letter which has come to me from the President:
>
> "Your letter from Paris, written just after coming from Berlin,

gives me a thrill of deep pleasure. You have, I hope and believe, begun a great thing and I rejoice with all my heart."

I have the honor to be, Sir, with the great respect, Your Majesty's

Very obedient servant,
EDWARD M. HOUSE.

Unfortunately, when this letter arrived William II was already on his Norwegian cruise, from which he was recalled only after the war clouds had gathered. House regrets, in a letter to Woodrow Wilson (on July 31), that Sir Edward Grey let matters drag until after the Kaiser had gone to Norway, before giving him any definite word to send him. "It was my purpose to go back to Germany to see the Emperor, but the conservative delay of Sir Edward and his confrères made that impossible. The night before I sailed, Sir Edward sent me word that he was worried over conditions, but he did not anticipate what has followed." Sir Edward failed to reveal to Colonel House the binding character of his engagement with France.

Dr. von Jagow, Germany's Foreign Minister, commenting upon the situation, exclaims: "American innocents abroad can hardly be blamed if they permitted British diplomacy to pull the wool over both their eyes. But there is no excuse for any serious student of history, now that German, Russian and other archives lie exposed, if he fails to revise his impression, if he permits his judgment to be guided by sentiments rather than facts."

"House," says the Kaiser in a letter to me, "may have been misled. Grey knew the land-grabbing hunger of Russia directed against Germany and Austria-Hungary; he knew the burning desire of France to re-conquer the 'lost provinces'—the old German territory of *Elsass-Lothringen;* he knew the envy in British industrial and capitalistic circles against Germany's successful competition.

"Hence, he 'engineered' the necessary events and complications that presented the Russian hate, the French lust for revenge, and British commercial envy with the wished-for opportunity to satisfy their criminal intentions at the expense of unsuspecting Germany.

"Result: A junction of pirates surprising a tranquil land and a tranquil people profoundly at peace with themselves and the world. Sir Edward Grey played the rôle of interested observer who shrugs his shoulders, when appealed to, exclaiming, 'Not my fault. Can't help it! Those Germans *are* exasperating.'

"Realizing the heinousness of their offense, those responsible for the conspiracy, knowing that in time truth, like murder, will out, created a scapegoat to turn away the wrath of the world from themselves. They chose for their victim the monarch of the nation they feloniously attacked and saddled him with their crime by inventing the *War-Guilt Lie*.

"International capital and the press placed itself at the disposal of the pirates and by propaganda (Northcliffe) they disseminated the *War-Guilt Lie* all over the world, until even their victims, the Germans, began to believe it.

"Ever yours,

"WILLIAM, I. R."

Colonel House had been in London many times before he came to Berlin. He was imbued with the British point of view. England's leading statesmen were his personal friends. In England, Colonel House was at home. Spiritually and literally, Sir Edward Grey and the men he met in London spoke the same language as he. The Colonel's knowledge of German was elementary. In Paris and in London, Colonel House established intimate personal contacts which made it unnecessary for him to rely solely upon diplomatic channels for information. In Germany he had only one friend, a cousin of General von Moltke, who exchanged thoughts with him. But poor von Moltke was not sufficiently conversant with American affairs to make an ideal interpreter.

Colonel House was not unsusceptible to the Kaiser's fascination. He recognized in him "all the versatility of Roosevelt with something more of charm, something less of force." But the false impression of German militarism engendered by his reception in Berlin warped his point of view. It was to exert a disastrous influence on Woodrow Wilson.

"What," I asked Colonel House, "was Wilson's opinion of the Kaiser?"

"Probably," House replied, "whatever impression I had created in his mind. He did not hate the Kaiser. He believed that the Kaiser had built up a military machine, or permitted such a machine to be built up, which finally overshadowed him.[1] He looked upon these men, not upon the Kaiser, as the military masters of Germany."

The influence of the Duumvir's reports upon Wilson was profound. "I was interested," Colonel House writes in his diary, "to hear him (Wilson) express as his opinion what I had written him sometime ago in one of my letters, to the effect that if Germany won it would change the course of our civilization and make the United States a military nation. He also spoke of his deep regret, as I did to him in the same letter, that it would check his policy for a better international code."

In the crash that followed the momentous audience of Colonel House with the Kaiser, three great empires have fallen. The Czar is dead, Austria-Hungary disrupted, the Kaiser an exile at Doorn. Another great empire is battling for its existence. There are those who believe that Great Britain is on the brink of her dissolution as an imperial power. All this wreckage, Colonel House thinks, would have been avoided if the Kaiser and Sir Edward Grey had acted upon his advice. House is inclined to blame Germany most for the disaster.

"I cannot," the Colonel remarked to me, "understand Germany's inability to realize her increasing navy would necessarily lead to a conflict with England. If Germany had not given England an excuse for war, England might have been forced to provoke a war. She could not tolerate a Germany disputing her naval supremacy."

"This disposes of the theory that England entered the war to save 'poor little Belgium'!" I interrupted.

Colonel House waved aside my interpolation.

"Germany's failure to meet the terms of Great Britain was the most abysmal blunder in history."

"The most abysmal blunder in history," I interjected, "was the World War itself."

"The veriest amateur," Colonel House continued, without

---

[1] "Colonel House fails to realize that the military machine to which he refers was two centuries old. It was not created by William II." Marginal note by the Kaiser.

contradicting my statement, "the veriest schoolboy, could have foreseen the result. It was the blind spot in Germany's mental vision. I put the matter as plainly as I could in my talk with the Kaiser. He seemed to understand my point of view. But his advisers lacked his mental elasticity. Bethmann-Holweg, his Chancellor, was well-meaning but mediocre. If Germany had possessed a Chancellor like Bismarck—"

"A Bismarck," I remarked, "is not born in every generation."

"If she had produced a Chancellor of even moderate capacity she would not have stumbled into the trap of the World War. She would not have given the Allies the pretext she did, and she would not have permitted the shadow of her sword to scare all mankind. The Allied powers feared Germany. Paris and London were both afraid—"

"The Germans, too, were afraid," I said.

"Why," Colonel House resumed, ignoring my interruption, "did Germany refuse the proffered hand of England? England made several gestures in the direction of a German alliance. The last of these was the Haldane Mission."

"I discussed this point with the Kaiser," I remarked, "and he assured me that no definite offer of alliance was ever made by Great Britain. The second volume by Nowak on William II reveals that an offer was made, but that the Kaiser was either misinformed, or only partly informed, of its implications and scope. Though the Germans were not convinced of England's good faith, they welcomed Haldane when he came on a diplomatic mission to Berlin, shortly before the War. The Germans permitted him to look behind the scenes of their war machine. They feel that the noble lord abused their hospitality, that he came as a spy, not as a friend."

"That," House quickly retorted, "is an injustice. Haldane had a warm admiration for Germany."

"But," I asked, "Haldane used the military secrets which he obtained in Germany?"

"Haldane undoubtedly used whatever knowledge he acquired for the benefit of his country after England was at war with Germany. I spent many hours with Haldane in the privacy of his library. He discussed with me every detail of his mission to Germany. England was willing to go far toward meeting the wishes of the Kaiser."

"You mean," I said, "that England would have raised no objection to the acquisition by Germany of the Portuguese colonies. England was always liberal in disposing of other men's property."

House raised his hands deprecatingly.

"Portugal was ready to dispose of her colonies under certain terms. England was prepared to concede to Germany a sphere of influence in the Near East. She had withdrawn her last objections to the Bagdad railroad."

"This, too, is questioned."

"The pact was ready for the signature of the two governments when the war broke out. Germany's path was clear. Backed by her army and by the British navy she could have achieved primacy among the powers of the Old World, if she had bided her time. Her star was obviously in the ascendant, while England's had reached the zenith. But Germany refused Haldane's hand and continued to increase the fears of the world by rattling the saber."

I pointed out that, according to official statistics, Germany expended less for her army and navy than her neighbors. "English navalism," I insisted, "was as much of a menace to the world as German militarism. England, in addition to the vast amounts devoted to the maintenance of her supremacy on the seas, spent almost as much on her army as Germany did. France and Russia spent more."

"Nevertheless," House replied, "Germany's army was the most formidable, and Germany managed somehow to put on the worst possible face in every international dispute. She put too much trust in her sword, too little in the good faith of men like Sir Edward Grey and Haldane. During the War Haldane was forced out of office because he was suspected of being pro-German. Haldane was Germany's sincere friend, but," House went on musingly, "he was also the best Secretary of War England ever had. He made the English army, small as it was, the finest in Europe. It was even finer than the German army because it was composed entirely of veterans. The Germans had no veterans because they had not been at war for nearly half a century."

"Germany had kept the peace of the world since 1870, yet," I interposed, "you say that Germany was a menace. Every other great European power not merely rattled the saber, but drew it from its sheath between 1870 and 1914. England, France, Russia, Italy, all were actually engaged in hostilities with one power or another. We were at war with Spain. Japan clashed with Russia."

"Nevertheless," House insisted, "the psychology of the generation that dominated Germany at the time of the outbreak of the War was militaristic and imperialistic. Had Germany been content with her army, without challenging England's supremacy on the seas, the conflagration of 1914 would have been confined to the Balkans."

"Then you do not believe that Germany started the War?"

"Not deliberately." He paused. "But her actions brought it about."

"Your signature is attached to the Peace Treaty of Versailles. How do you justify paragraph 231, which forces Germany to admit her 'war guilt'?"

"I think," House replied without hesitation, "it is shortsighted to put anything into a peace treaty that is likely to rankle in the mind of the vanquished. The very name 'peace treaty' suggests that such a thing should be avoided. The inclusion of the paragraph in question, under the spell of war psychosis and war propaganda, was an egregious blunder. Some men in Germany wanted the War.[2] This is equally true of some men in England and France. Germany lacked finesse. Luck was against her. But to saddle the war guilt upon her exclusively is neither good history nor good sportsmanship."

[2] "No," says Emperor William, in a marginal note.

X

WOODROW WILSON SEES A GHOST

Shades of Madison – Two Princeton Men in the White House – Woodrow Wilson's Deadly Parallel – 1812 and 1914 – "A Tragic Accident" – The Duumvirs Intercept a Letter – House Averts Break with Great Britain – Super-Diplomacy

W ILSON'S enemies called him "the best President England ever had." This sarcasm is undeserved. It is true that Wilson's roots clung to the soil of England. They did not go back to colonial or revolutionary America. His grandparents on both sides of the family were born in England. No President of the United States, with one exception, Ray Stannard Baker admits, had a briefer American background than Woodrow Wilson. Nevertheless America, under his Administration, was repeatedly on the verge of war with Great Britain.

A sitting-room in the White House, September 30, 1914. The two Duumvirs, Wilson and House.

W I L S O N : (*with a sigh of relief*) I am glad we caught that message.

H O U S E : (*quietly*) It certainly would have raised the devil in London.

W I L S O N : (*earnestly*) The language of the note was undiplomatic, but it espoused an unimpeachable principle. The United States (*He speaks with considerable asperity*) never accepted England's theory that the ocean is her backyard. We were confronted by the same difficulty one hundred years ago. Then, as now, England was at war with a Great Empire. England's policy was a war measure against the Corsican, not against us, but it cut America to the quick. Then, as now, a Princeton man was President—

H O U S E : Was Madison a Princetonian?

W I L S O N : (*smiles*) Madison and I are the only Princeton men that have become President. The circumstances of the War of 1812 and now run parallel. I sincerely hope that they will not go farther. Madison, like myself, was a peace-loving man, but he was forced into the war by public opinion. History may repeat itself.

H O U S E : God forbid!

W I L S O N : If I were superstitious—

H O U S E : But you are not superstitious!

W I L S O N : Hardly. Except (*He laughs*) about the number thirteen.

H O U S E : You, Governor, are singularly favored of fortune. A number regarded as unlucky by most people seems to bring good luck to you. There is no reason why you should not extricate yourself from the fate that enmeshed Madison. You are not the ghost of Madison, you are Wilson!

W I L S O N : Still it is interesting to indulge in historical speculation. You know that I have written a history of the United States.[1] I am not very proud of it. I wrote it largely not to teach others but to teach myself. That may have been an expensive process for the fellow who bought the book, but I lived in the United States and my interest in learning our history was not merely to remember what happened, but to find out which way we were going.

H O U S E : I am more familiar with your thoughts than with your books. I shall remedy this fault presently.

W I L S O N : Don't trouble. It is a work in five volumes. Here (*He takes a volume from the desk*) is the one that deals with the War of 1812. It may amuse you to listen to a few passages. (*He reads*) Mr. Madison loved peace as Mr. Jefferson did, and was willing to secure it by any slow process of law and negotiation. But presently he found himself caught in the tangled network of policy which, as Secretary of State, he had woven for Mr. Jefferson. ... Mr. Madison was left to face two unfriendly pow-

---

[1] *History of the American People,* by Woodrow Wilson, published by Harper & Bros.

ers, to the more false and dangerous of whom it was his cue, it seemed, to play the complacent servant.

H O U S E: I hope history, the old plagiarist, will not repeat herself.

W I L S O N (*still reading*): Napoleon promised that his decrees against American shipping should be revoked on the 1st of the following November, provided England would before that date withdraw her Orders in Council. England replied that she would rescind the Orders when informed that the Emperor had revoked his decrees. The Emperor sent word to Mr. Madison that his decrees were in fact revoked, and should cease to have effect after the first of November, if, in the meantime, the United States should "cause their rights to be respected by England." ... (*He walks up and down as he reads*) Napoleon's decrees, like the English Orders in Council, had been nothing less than acts of war against the United States from the first, though not primarily aimed at her, and would at any time have justified a declaration of hostilities. But Mr. Madison did not want war. The United States were not strong enough, particularly now that the party in power had disbanded its army, dismantled its navy, and reduced its revenues to a minimum. The President's principles clearly forbade war, besides. He wished to fight only with the weapons of nominal peace: embargoes and retaliatory restrictions. If Napoleon would yield his decrees, so much the greater pressure could be brought to bear upon England to yield her Orders in Council, and the vexatious game might at last be won....

H O U S E: I don't recollect the exact course of events. I am so much immersed in the present that the past seems dim. We can no doubt learn from the mistakes of your predecessor. Madison underestimated the obstinacy of John Bull. What is a fault in a mule may be genius in a nation!

W I L S O N (*stressing every syllable*): Ill feeling between England and the United States was seriously deepened, as the astute and unscrupulous master of France had meant that it should be; and every negotiation for an amicable settlement grew the more confused and doubtful. Every sinister influence seemed to draw Mr. Madison towards what he most dreaded and condemned—

towards a war of arms, brought on by a programme of peace.... (*A pause. The President rests his eyes. Then continues.*) Negotiations dragged very slowly then, with the coming and going of tardy ships, which had oftentimes to steal like fugitives in or out of port. But all through the long year 1811, though hopes and plans and anxious fears came and went with doubtful ebb and flow, and no one knew what either England or France would do, it grew more and more evident that the Government of the United States must do something, if only to keep itself in countenance. It had pledged itself to believe that France had in good faith yielded to its demands. England made no pretense of having yielded or of intending to yield. (*Wilson speaks with the skill of the trained orator. House listens attentively.*) Evidence multiplied that France was playing a double and lying part. Mr. Madison's mortification was complete and very bitter; but no one deemed it possible that the United States should fight both France and England at once. Men's minds were slowly made up to stomach France's deceptions and fight England! At least it was so with the President, who saw no way of retreat not too humiliating to be borne; and it was so with Congress, which had passed under the control of new leaders.

H O U S E : Disaster approached with the inevitability of a Greek tragedy.

W I L S O N : A tragedy, indeed! Napoleon was the enemy of the civilized world, had been America's own enemy in disguise, and had thrown off the disguise. England was fighting him almost alone, all Europe thrown into his scale and hers almost kicking the beam; and now America had joined the forces of Napoleon, in fact if not in intention, as he had subtly planned. It was a tragical but natural accident that the war should be against England, not against France.

H O U S E : Put William in place of Napoleon, and Germany in place of France, and you have the situation to-day. Fortunately history is not prophecy.

W I L S O N : The historian is often a prophet.

H O U S E : Madison failed because he vacillated. He lacked a positive policy.

w i l s o n : I hope we may be able to hold a course that will keep us out of war.

House transmits the warning conveyed in Wilson's recapitulation of American history to Sir Cecil Spring-Rice. Sir Cecil Spring-Rice is profoundly stirred and immediately dispatches a cable to Sir Edward Grey calling his attention to the ominous parallel. Sir Edward would have been dumbfounded if he had received the message from the State Department which Woodrow Wilson and Colonel House discussed the night before. The whole course of modern history would have changed, if Colonel House had not stopped its dispatch. House himself tells what happened. Let us re-create the scene from the Colonel's recital.

Mrs. Wilson and the family withdraw to enable the President and his Duumvir to examine the contents of a large portfolio marked "urgent" which has just been delivered by a messenger from the Secretary of State. The President and his *alter ego* get down to work. House reaches into the pouch from the State Department, fishes out a long letter from X (Bryan) to Page. The document dwells with considerable emphasis on the Declaration of London and neutral shipping. As the Colonel reads the note his face becomes very serious.

"Governor," he says, "do not permit this to be sent."

He cites a few passages from the letter which alarm Wilson. Wilson's face grows pale.

"Shall I talk it out with Spring-Rice?" asks the Colonel, controlling his agitation.

Wilson consents; quickly the Duumvirs go to bed that night tired and worried. Colonel House meets the Ambassador at the residence of William Phillips, the scene of many clandestine conferences between the two men in the future. When Sir Cecil reads X's (Bryan's) instructions to Page, he almost jumps into the air. "My dear Colonel House," he says, "one paragraph in this document amounts almost to a declaration of war. If this paper should get into the hands of the press it would be featured in such a way as to indicate that war with Great Britain is almost inevitable. I believe one of the greatest panics the country ever saw would ensue. This," he adds, "is as bad as the Venezuela incident. In fact, it is more critical."

The two men discuss various ways of meeting the situation.

"Never," avows the Ambassador, "would this difficulty have arisen if the State Department had talked the matter over with me frankly in the beginning. My Government's attitude was known at the Department for a month. And yet not a word of objection was raised. If I had known what the feeling of this country was I would have taken the matter up with London and they would have modified their attitude. Unfortunately, they have already published their intention of doing the things to which your Government now objects. It will be difficult to handle now in a way to save the face of my Government."

Then follows one of the most grotesque, certainly one of the most extraordinary, situations in the history of diplomacy. Sir Cecil Spring-Rice and Colonel House together outline a dispatch from the United States Government to Page and another from Sir Cecil Spring-Rice to Sir Edward Grey.

"I do not know," Sir Cecil Spring-Rice said, as he bade good-by to Colonel House, "what you have accomplished in your busy life, but I feel sure that you have never done as important a piece of work as in this instance."

Colonel House had prevented a break between England and the United States. A year later, Sir Cecil Spring-Rice, discussing the matter with Colonel House, reiterated his conviction: "If the message had gone the way it was originally written, good relations between the United States and England could not have been re-established. The insult would have rankled forever."

The extra-diplomatic method of Colonel House was fraught with manifold dangers. The price which the Colonel paid for British friendship was high. He paid for it with the Freedom of the Seas which, in spite of all protests that followed, was trampled underfoot by Great Britain throughout the War. The concessions were all on the side of the United States.

Colonel House tried sincerely but ineffectually to reëstablish the doctrine of the Freedom of the Seas in innumerable conferences with both groups of belligerents. Mr. Wilson protested again and again against English infringements of American rights on the high seas. But England scored in every controversy because England was not afraid to face the ultimate consequences of her position—war. Wilson was unwilling to follow in the footsteps of Madison.

When the pro-Germans acclaimed Wilson's neutrality proclamation insisting upon absolute impartiality, they did not know that he was afraid of a quarrel with England, not with Germany. Wilson did not, at that time, envisage a conflict with Berlin. "It would have been easier," Colonel House insists, "to have steered the American people into war against England than against Germany if Germany had shown more moderation. The traditions of the Revolution and of 1812 still rankled. Wilson was exceedingly angry with the English. On several occasions he was on the point of breaking with England. I don't think he contemplated actual hostility. But it is only one step from a severance of diplomatic relations to war!"

XI

COLONEL HOUSE PACKS HIS TRUNKS

The Star of Bethlehem over the White House – The Pessimism of Colonel House – Woodrow Wilson Looks Westward – Two Secretaries of State – Lansing Plays the Game – The President's Proxy in Europe – The Farewell of the Duumvirs

WILSON'S intellectual interests were many. His primary passion was peace. Peace is the one note he sounds insistently even when he makes war. Innumerable Woodrows and Wilsons who were ministers of the Gospel haunt his unconscious. He encouraged the Duumvir's first trip to Europe in the vain hope of preventing a world conflagration. He commissioned six more trips across the submarine-infested seas to extinguish the fire. He twice crossed the Atlantic himself to prevent similar catastrophes in the future.

On August 5, when war declarations came thick and fast, he was so wrought up that he acted without consulting his *alter ego*. He dispatches messages to all belligerent nations offering mediation "It can at least do no harm," he apologetically remarks to House. The drums of war drown out the voice of Woodrow Wilson. He receives no response from any government. But his Scotch-Presbyterian conscience is satisfied. He has done his duty.

Mindful of Madison's dilemma, he proposes, come what may, not to stain his own hands with blood. About the middle of August he urges all citizens to be neutral even in thought. "Every man who really loves America will act and speak in the true spirit of neutrality, which is the spirit of impartiality and fairness and friendliness to all concerned." Roosevelt, Gerard, Page approve. Even British statesmen express the hope that America will be able to resist the temptation of plunging into the fiery furnace of war. The Duumvirs agree.

The situation saddens House. He sees no good outlook. "If the Allies win, it means largely the domination of Russia on the continent of Europe; if Germany wins it means the unspeakable tyranny of militarism for generations to come. Fundamentally," he assures Wilson, "the Germans are playing a rôle that is against their natural instincts and inclinations, and it shows how perverted men may become by habit and environment. Germany's success," House continues—and here is the keystone of his policy in the World War—"will ultimately mean trouble to us. We will have to abandon the path which you are blazing as a standard for future generations with permanent peace as its goal and a new international ethical code as its guiding star, and build up a military machine of vast proportions."

Fearing a German victory, House seeks to impress upon Wilson the necessity for "preparedness." He ably defends his attitude. "If we had strengthened our army and navy, when the forces of hell broke loose in Europe, both England and Germany would have been inclined to think before violating our rights. An America able to turn the scale of naval and military victory could have strangled the dragon of war before its fiery breath reduced civilization to ashes."

But Wilson stands by his guns, or, shall we say, by his doves of peace. Determined to follow in the footsteps of the Prince of Peace, Wilson rejects "preparedness." In the end, House, as usual, prevails. But it took him two years before he convinced Wilson. Colonel House believes that the world paid dearly for the delay.

It was America, not Europe, that most engaged Wilson's attention. "The President," writes House, "appeared almost more interested and absorbed in local situations than in the foreign crisis. I, myself, am so little interested in them that I talk of them with reluctance and it's immaterial to me whom he appoints."

Taking affairs into his own hands, Colonel House negotiated directly with all the foreign Ambassadors in the United States. Bernstorff, Spring-Rice, Jusserand and Bakhmeteff, all found their way to New York or to Magnolia. The Duumvirs hoped that the informal conversations might develop a frankness which would be impossible in the rigid atmosphere of official business.

The Secretary of State looked wise and knew nothing. Both Bryan and his successor, Robert Lansing, accepted the situation. Only the routine of the State Department, and matters which did not interest the President and House, remained in their hands. Even to-day we look in vain in the files of the State Department for the records of important negotiations. Lansing owes his appointment to the complaisance with which he acquiesced in the situation.

"Wilson," House explained to me, "did not want to appoint Lansing after Bryan walked out in a huff. He would have preferred to make one of the Joneses from Chicago, his lifelong friend, Secretary of State. I urged Lansing, for Lansing, after two years' service in the Department, knew my relations with Wilson. If he stepped into Bryan's shoes, he tacitly accepted the existing conditions."

Lansing played the game. Wilson, House thinks, never appreciated Lansing, because Lansing disagreed with him on a number of points. When the United States joined the Allies, Wilson wanted to put Newton D. Baker in Lansing's place. House persuaded him to make no change. Lansing fitted into the scheme of the Duumvirs. Baker's attitude was unknown.

Early in 1915, Europe irresistibly calls the President's double. Once more Colonel House packs his trunks. In his valise he carries letters from Woodrow Wilson, conferring upon him the authority to act as his proxy. Wilson desires to minister to the relief of suffering in Europe. He offers, through his personal plenipotentiary, "to put the reserves of the United States at the service of all belligerents in whatever way the rules and practices of neutrality permit for the purpose of mitigating the distress and frictions and the dislocations in the time of war."

"Tell Sir Edward Grey my entire mind," Wilson urges. "Let him know that while you are abroad I expect to act directly through you and eliminate all intermediaries." The President approves all House has in mind to say to Sir Edward and to the Germans. "There is not much for us to talk over," the President writes, "for the reason that we are both of the same mind and it is not necessary to go into details with you."

Then came time to say good-by. "The President's eyes,"

Colonel House reports, "were moist when he said his last words of farewell. He said, 'Your unselfish and intelligent friendship has meant much to me,' and he expressed his gratitude again and again, calling me his 'most trusted friend.' He declared I was the only one in all the world to whom he could open his entire mind.

"I asked if he remembered the first day we met, some three and a half years ago. He replied, 'Yes, but we had known one another always and merely came in touch then, for our purposes and thoughts were one.' I told him how much he had been to me, how I had tried all my life to find some one with whom I could work out the things I had so deeply at heart, and I had begun to despair, believing my life would be more or less a failure; then he came into it, giving me the opportunity for which I had been longing.

"He insisted upon going to the station with me. He got out of the car and walked through the station and to the ticket office, and then to the train itself, refusing to leave until I entered the car. It is a joy to work for such an appreciative friend."

Colonel George Harvey, from his dugout in *Harper's Weekly*, growled: "Instead of sending Colonel House abroad, Wilson should go to Europe to find out just what the people think of him. He could leave House here to act as President during his absence."

XII

WHEELS WITHIN WHEELS

What Bryan Said to Dumba – A Tip for the Germans – Gerard Blusters –
Zimmermann Calls a Bluff – After Bryan's Resignation – Mischief in England
– Walter Page Has His Little Joke – The "Over-Advertised" British Navy –
France Seizes the *Dacia*

WILLIAM JENNINGS BRYAN rises cheerfully to greet
the gloomy Austro-Hungarian Ambassador, His Excellency
Dr. Constantin Dumba. The Ambassador is dressed with meticulous care, from his dark, striped cravat to his patent-leather shoes.
His eyes are melancholy and his white mustache droops sadly
on one side. Bryan's coat-tails flap about him like the wings of a
raven. The nose of the Secretary of State suggests a bird of prey.
His stern features relax into a smile when he gazes into the glum
face of Dr. Dumba.

[May 17th, 1915.] "Permit me," the Austrian Ambassador remarks to William Jennings Bryan, "to convey to Your Excellency
the thanks of His Apostolic Majesty, my gracious Emperor and
King, for your intercession on behalf of Austrian prisoners of war.
I should like very much to show my appreciation by assisting you
in your negotiations with Germany. Germany has no desire for
war. On the contrary, she is anxious to maintain friendly relations
with the United States. If," the Ambassador suavely suggests,
"Germany were to give assurances for the future, would it not be
possible to arbitrate all past disputes?"

"I do not feel that I am authorized to discuss this subject,"
Bryan replies, "without first getting the views of the President.
But you may say to the German Government that there is no
desire for war in this country and that we expect Germany to
answer our note in the same spirit of friendship that prompted
ours."

A light kindles in the Ambassador's eyes, banishing the gloom for a moment. There was a ring in Bryan's words that gave assurance that America did not desire war—the ring of a sacred pledge. Nothing else mattered. But, being a diplomat, Dumba tries to score a second time.

"Mr. Secretary, it would be easier for Germany to fall in with your wishes if she could in her reply say that she expected you to insist upon the freedom of trade with neutrals. Germany's submarine warfare is a measure of retaliation. If you induce Great Britain to abide by the Declaration of London . . ."

"Such an expression," Bryan interjects, "might embarrass us and also make it more difficult to deal with the Allies along that line. Germany should assume that we will live up to the position taken in our protests against British Orders in Council."

The Ambassador leans over eagerly. This, if true, is welcome news.

"Could you give me any confidential assurances of that kind?"

"It should not be necessary," Bryan replies.

Then, with the delighted smile of a politician who has found a solution to a vexing problem, he confidentially adds: "If Germany so desires, she may make a statement to her own people that she takes it for granted that we will maintain the position enunciated in our notes to Great Britain and will insist upon our right to trade with neutrals. But don't let her say so in her communications to us."

The tragic lines in Dumba's face vanish completely. He listens to Bryan as one augur to another.

"If," Bryan continues, "the statement was made to the German people instead of to us, it would not require an answer from us and would not embarrass us. If Germany's answer did contain any expression of opinion as to how we should deal with Great Britain and would seemingly link the two cases together, it would put us in the attitude of acting at Germany's suggestion instead of acting on our own initiative and for the protection of our own interests. It might also be construed as a sort of trade whereby we will settle an account with Germany by opening an account with the Allies."

Dumba sees the force of Bryan's argument. A load falls from his diplomatic heart. Mr. Bryan suggests that Germany should make a statement for home consumption. Perhaps the American protest is also written largely for home consumption? ... Changing the subject, the Ambassador seeks another concession. Knowing Bryan's own views on the subject, he artfully asks: "Would it not be possible for you to refuse clearance to ships that carry explosives and ammunition? In Germany, passenger trains are not allowed to carry explosives. This regulation is made for the protection of the lives of passengers. You might on the same ground refuse to allow ship owners to carry explosives on passenger boats."

Bryan, secretly pleased, smiles.

"Germany is of course at liberty to make any suggestion which she thinks proper in her reply. We cannot consider these suggestions in advance." But every quiver of his voice betokens sympathy with the proposal.

The Ambassador excuses himself as quickly as politeness permits. He no longer fears war and he feels that the severity of Wilson's note was intended to quiet his critics at home. He drafts a message to the Austro-Hungarian Prime Minister, Count Stephan Burian, which is received in Berlin before it reaches Vienna, because he entrusts it to Count Bernstorff who, by some strange legerdemain, is able to hoodwink the British censor.

"The most impossible Secretary of State," Dumba mutters to himself, as he rushes to the Embassy, "but the most sympathetic of American politicians."

When Wilhelmstrasse decodes the Ambassador's report before transmitting it to the Ballplatz, the German Under-Secretary of State, Dr. Zimmermann, laughs.

"I always knew," he says to himself, "that those Yankees were bluffing."

He immediately places before the Chancellor his interpretation of Dumba's message. The Chancellor, who had been quaking in his boots at the thought of adding one more to the long list of Germany's foes, regains his composure. The entire Wilhelmstrasse breathes a sigh of relief.

In the meantime, Ambassador Gerard was enacting his part.

After a stormy interview with the Chancellor, he dispatched an employee of the Embassy to a famous travel bureau on the main thoroughfare of Berlin to make reservations for himself and his staff. He was going to show that America meant business. Unless Germany yielded, he would ask for his passports. Dumba calls this a played-out trick. But it would have been effective except for the good-natured indiscretion of Mr. Bryan. When Gerard went to the Foreign Office to note the effect of his stratagem, Zimmermann laughed in his face.

"My dear Mr. Ambassador," he said, "we know that your protest was a sop to public opinion. The United States will not go to war over the *Lusitania*."

Gerard blustered and fumed. Zimmermann showed him the dispatch from Dumba. Gerard immediately communicated with Colonel House in London:

> "Zimmermann told me yesterday that Dumba, Austrian Ambassador, had cabled him that Bryan told him that America was not in earnest about *Lusitania*."

Colonel House forwarded the message to Mr. Wilson. "Of course," he added, "Mr. Bryan did not say that, but I think you should know what Zimmermann told Gerard."

When the President, infuriated by Gerard's message, asked Bryan what really had happened, the Secretary of State sent a detailed report of the conversation to Wilson through his confidential messenger, Herbert O. Yardley. But, of course, his summary did not reproduce the impression made upon Dumba by the shading in Bryan's voice. Undoubtedly, Bryan's manner suggested to Dumba that he considered war inconceivable, and that was the crux of the problem from the point of view of Wilhelmstrasse. In his report to the President, Bryan urged the immediate dispatch of a note to London:

> "I think the call of the Ambassador was rather significant, especially as I learned from Villard that he had received some of the same suggestions from von Bernstorff. I believe that it would have a splendid effect if our note to Great Britain can go at once. It will give Germany an excuse, and I think she is looking for something that will serve as an excuse. There is much discussion of the

idea suggested by Dumba—in fact mentioned in the first explanation received from Germany, namely, that passengers and ammunition should not travel together. I have no doubt Germany would be willing to so change the rule in regard to submarines as to exempt from danger all passenger ships that did not carry munitions of war."

Ordinarily Bryan took no hand in the formulation of American policy. In this instance his failure to live up to the austere implications of the President's *Lusitania* note defeated Mr. Wilson's intention. The result was disastrous. The difficulty would have been avoided if Wilson had taken Mr. Bryan into his confidence. But a gulf yawned between Wilson and his Secretary of State. The State Department was ignored by the Duumvirs. Confusion ensued and the President's best-laid plans *gang agley*.

Bryan was for peace at any price. Wilson was inclined to agree with the Secretary of State. But he did not carry his heart on his sleeve. He wanted his note to be taken seriously. Bryan's well-meant advice to Dumba weakened Wilson's hand. Nothing he did afterwards convinced the Germans that he was in earnest. After three months' parleying Germany yielded on the main issue. But Wilson's victory was not complete. Germany made no formal disavowal of the sinking of the *Lusitania* or the *Arabic*. Her promise to refrain from attacking passenger ships without warning was implied rather than explicit. Submarine commanders were instructed to abide by Mr. Wilson's demands. But the Imperial German Government reserved the right to rescind its orders. The issue of peace or war hinged on this reservation.

Bryan lost because he made his reckoning without Colonel House. The Colonel no longer acted as a cushion between Woodrow Wilson and his Secretary of State. Wilson's irritation with Bryan, until then banished into the recesses of his mind, flared up at a Cabinet meeting. When the Commoner accused some members of the Cabinet of being "unneutral," a steely glitter came into Wilson's eyes. "Mr. Bryan," he said, "you are not warranted in making such an assertion. We all doubtless have our opinions in this matter, but none of us can justly be accused of being unfair."

The Nebraskan apologized. But he resigned shortly afterwards.

Bryan desired to go abroad to bring peace to Europe in his own fashion. After his resignation, he requested Gerard to secure for him an interview with the Kaiser. Wilson instructed Gerard to ignore this demand, to show Bryan every courtesy if he came, but to let it be understood that he represented nobody but himself. The Commoner threatened to oppose Wilson actively if he showed any signs of breaking off diplomatic relations with Germany. He also informed Gerard that he expected to be the Peace Commissioner of the Administration, but whether appointed or not, he would go and act as he thought best. All this appears in a letter from Woodrow Wilson to Colonel House in November, 1916. Evidently, Wilson exclaims, a great deal of mischief is brewing Commonerwards!

But there is mischief, too, in Great Britain. The scene shifts to Downing Street. Walter Hines Page, the American Ambassador, and Sir Edward Grey, the Foreign Secretary of Great Britain, are shaking with uncontrollable merriment. Before them lies a memorandum from the American Secretary of State insisting upon the recognition by Great Britain of American rights on the high seas. Outside a hurdy-gurdy plays:

> "Rule, Britannia, rule the waves,
> Britons never will be slaves."

At this particular juncture, Great Britain rules the waves and waives the rules at her pleasure.

Mr. Page apologizes whenever he presents a note from the American Government. To-day the American Ambassador is in a particularly apologetic mood. He reluctantly reads to Sir Edward Grey the memorandum from Washington. It seems that public opinion in the United States is boiling over with indignation at British interference with American mails and American ships. Certain shippers are making a test by sending the *Dacia*, a merchantman, carrying cotton to Germany. The *Dacia* was formerly German-owned. Under a law recently passed by Congress, she was sailing under American registry with an American crew. Would England seize this ship? If she did, hell would break loose. Sir Edward Grey is somewhat perturbed by this possibility. But Page brushes away his fears.

"Have you heard of the British fleet, Sir Edward?" Page asks with infinite drollery.

Sir Edward Grey looks at Page uncomprehendingly. His sense of humor is not highly developed, but he cannot deny the impeachment.

"Yes," the Ambassador chuckles, "we've all heard of the British fleet. Perhaps we've heard too much about it. Don't you think it has had too much advertising?"

Sir Edward Grey still fails to catch the subtlety of the Ambassador's joke.

"But have you heard of the French fleet? France has a fleet too, I believe."

Sir Edward nods.

"Don't you think that the French fleet ought to have a little advertising?"

"What on earth are you talking about?"

"Well," Page remarks, with the pleased smile of a schoolboy who has at last solved a conundrum, "there is the *Dacia*. Why not let the French fleet seize it and get some advertising?"

A beatific smile illuminates the features of Sir Edward Grey. He presses the Ambassador's hand warmly.

France seized the *Dacia*. The French were popular. We had no dispute of long standing with France. The newspapers made no fuss. American protests fell flat. Walter Hines Page had thwarted the policy of his Government. Men have been hanged and quartered for less than this!

If Page had dispensed with such pleasantries and had carried out his instructions, it is possible that the British Government would have respected American rights on the high seas. This would have established a precedent of infinite value to all neutral nations. Germany and the neutrals would have been convinced of the sincerity of the President of the United States. The Freedom of the Seas would have been assured, and the course of history altered. The peculiar relationship of the Duumvirate superimposed upon our diplomatic service another system functioning independently. In some instances the two systems harmonized; in others they diverged. It is difficult to escape the conclusion that the resulting confusion played havoc with American diplomacy.

XIII

HEADACHES THAT CHANGE HISTORY

Multiple Chess – Cross-purposes – Departments Go On Forever – Temperamental Tribulations – An Ambassador Disavowed – Wilson's Jibes: Gerard,
Lippmann, Lawrence – Herron's Mission – Münsterberg's Error – The Light-
ning That Struck Hale – Wilson Versus Hoover – Hidden Causes

TWO heads are better than one—sometimes. At other times
two heads, like two cooks, are one too many. Diplomacy, to
change the metaphor, is a game of chess, or rather, a series of
chess games played simultaneously. Those in charge of foreign
affairs must keep in mind not only one but many intricate games
going on at the same time between themselves and a host of
invisible players. There are great chess players who play more
than one game at the same time and keep a clear picture of every
move in their heads. Wilson and House were like two great masters of chess, playing jointly a series of complicated games with
numerous antagonists. Their antagonists were the great powers
of Europe. In order to lose no move, to miss no point, it was
necessary for the two players to preserve complete identity of
purpose. Such identity existed for a long time between Wilson and
House. But even that was not enough. Sleepless vigilance was
needed. Wilson and House were extraordinary individuals. But
they were human!

When Colonel House was away on his missions to Europe,
he could not, in spite of long messages in code, communicate fully
and confidentially with his fellow-player. Nature, too, exacted her
toll. Wilson had headaches, House breakdowns. Some of these
headaches and breakdowns changed history!

When the Duumvirate was indisposed, the game was left in
the hands of subordinates. The State Department and the em-

bassies worked frequently at cross-purposes with each other and with their principals. Now and then, an especially intricate game preoccupied the masters to such an extent that they neglected important moves on other chessboards. That is the penalty for the concentration of power. In the end, a divergence of purpose between Wilson and House caused them to lose the main game in Paris. It meant checkmate for Wilson. But that was still in the future. For the time being, the harmony between the Duumvirs was undisturbed.

Wilson's trust in House was justified. But it was unfortunate that he could not persuade himself to trust any one else. No two men between them can run a great government. House had power without responsibility; Wilson's Secretaries of State and his Ambassadors, responsibility without power. When Wilson's one-track mind was preoccupied with other affairs or when House was absent, officials slighted by the Duumvir assumed importance and made decisions. Bernstorff, Sir Cecil Spring-Rice and other Ambassadors had confidential sessions with the President's *alter ego,* but, unlike Wilson and House, they could not entirely ignore the Secretary of State. In the famous conversation with Dumba, the Secretary of State "gummed the works." When House emerged in London or in Berlin, the American Ambassadors in these capitals shriveled in stature. But under ordinary circumstances, the wheels of the embassies revolved in the regular manner. A slight wink from Page, a misjudged gesture on the part of Gerard were sufficient to defeat the most elaborate stratagems of the Duumvirs.

The permanent officials of the embassies and the State Department exercise more influence than a President realizes. The men in charge of the routine of government to a large extent control that government. Prime ministers, Presidents, come and go. But the Department goes on forever. The fixed attitude of the permanent officials can completely destroy the intentions of the chief. The idiosyncrasies of the permanent officials can be a powerful force with which a chief must reckon. Departmental red tape strangles his initiative. Passive resistance defeats his aim.

Even if the State Department and the diplomatic service had always functioned in unison with the President, there would have been misunderstandings, deflecting currents, wheels within wheels.

But the whole machinery of government was thrown out of gear by the fact that the Duumvirs did not take the Secretary of State and the Ambassadors into their confidence. Sometimes Ambassadors were entrusted with secrets of state. At other times they were left in the dark. As a result, they blundered and miscarried their orders. Some, like Page, had policies of their own. Wilson realized their insubordination. But for some strange reason the schoolmasterly rod did not fall on the offending knuckles.

Wilson's communications with House frequently reflect impatience with his deputies. "What extraordinary stuff Gerard sends us! I admit I am not helped by it at all." "What you tell me about Gerard's having originated the idea of certain immune liners," he says elsewhere, "is extremely interesting and fully confirms my estimate of 'Jimmie'!" Walter Page "needs a bath in American opinion." It may be useful, the President suggests humorously, to have him transmit the English view straight. Undoubtedly, he avers on another occasion, you are right about what Page ought to accomplish and might accomplish if he were to follow the same course that Penfield is following, and that even Gerard would follow if he recognized the occasion. But all these misgivings remained the secret of the Duumvirs.

In the beginning Wilson puts the charge against Page very mildly. He does not wish to criticize his old friend, although he scents danger in the intense feeling the Ambassador manifests for the English case. He does not foresee any actual disloyalty, but senses the peril that Page may put himself out of touch with American feeling altogether. When Page, in a message to House, sarcastically exclaims: "God deliver us, or can you deliver us, from library lawyers; they often lose chestnuts while they argue about burns," Wilson once more deplores the Ambassador's proneness to forget the temper of the folks at home. But he does not recall him. He contents himself with strong letters. Submitting the draft to Colonel House, he asks: "Pull it about, alter and add to it as you think best."

Wilson is one of the most contradictory characters in history. No one, not even Colonel House, can explain him. Wilson, in one of his letters to House, regretted that he made Page Ambassador to London rather than Secretary of Agriculture. If so, why did he not recall him? And why did he leave Gerard in Berlin if he was so little helped by his letters?

Wilson's psychology was rather peculiar. He was convinced that he could conduct all important affairs himself. Details seemed negligible. He did not realize the possibility of Page deriding Mr. Bryan's notes or advising Sir Edward Grey how to circumvent the intentions of the American Government. Neither did he visualize the possibility of Mr. Bryan telling Dumba not to take the *Lusitania* protest too seriously! Wilson had the contempt of genius for routine. This, and his reluctance or inability to confide in others, bore within it the seed of much trouble.

Wilson liked Page, in spite of his irritating attitude, and made allowances for the subtle hypnotism of his London environment. He underestimated Gerard. Page was the more scholarly of the two. But Gerard obeyed orders. Perhaps it would have been better if he had sent Page to Berlin and Gerard to London!

Bismarck always suspected the efficiency of an Ambassador who was too popular in a foreign capital. Page was altogether too popular in the British metropolis. Gerard went too far in the other direction.

There were times when the Germans insisted upon the recall of Gerard. House reasoned with them and persuaded them to bear with this uncomfortable Ambassador. Gerard was helpful to House in Berlin. He was recalled to Washington in 1916 and advised by House how to make himself more popular in the Wilhelmstrasse. It was House who suggested to Gerard the speech on German-American relations which won many plaudits in Germany. Unfortunately it was his Swan Song, and was followed almost immediately by the rupture of diplomatic relations between the two countries.

"That speech," I said to Colonel House, "has been condemned as evidence of American hypocrisy."

Colonel House shook his head gently.

"It was not hypocrisy. Wilson did not want the break. He did not want war. No one can foretell what might have happened if the Germans had maneuvered with more finesse. It is not impossible that we might have stayed out of the War. With the declaration of unrestricted submarine warfare, Wilson's hopes for peace tumbled over like a house of cards."

Wilson not only mistrusted his official associates; his attitude toward his personal representatives was consistently inconsistent. Walter Lippmann was regarded by many and by himself as the mouthpiece of the Administration among the intelligentsia of the Fourth Estate. Yet, according to one of Wilson's letters in the House archives at Yale, the President confessed himself puzzled why that brilliant journalist had been sent to Europe to investigate propaganda. Wilson speaks of Lippmann's judgment as "most unsound and therefore entirely unserviceable in matters of that sort." He looks upon the opinions of Lippmann and his associates in the *New Republic* regarding the purpose of the war as "highly unorthodox." In spite of this, he appointed Lippmann to high office and permitted him to function as Secretary of the Inquiry, the organization created by Colonel House to prepare the groundwork for the Peace Treaty. What strange mental paradox made Wilson entrust weighty matters to men whose judgment he disdained? After giving them opportunity to work all sorts of mischief, he forgot completely about them unless they crossed him in some dark mood. Then they were dropped with a thud from Olympus.

Such was the fate of the brilliant William Bayard Hale. Hale ghost-wrote *The New Freedom* for Woodrow Wilson. He acted as the President's personal scout in Mexico. Wilson enjoyed Hale's stories and his Scotch whisky. But some unguarded word, some act, slight in itself, made him unpopular. The former favorite was barred from the Presence. The Germans subsequently employed him because they thought that Hale still had the key to the back door of the White House. The only man who kept that key, and held the key to the front door as well, was House. Other men who thought themselves depositories of Wilson's confidence secretly annoyed him. He once or twice fell out with Frank Cobb. He occasionally lambasted Seibold, and called David Lawrence a "nuisance."

There were many loose wires in the power house of Wilsonian diplomacy. Professor George D. Herron, utopist and radical, who endowed the Rand School in New York, a Socialist institution, is commandeered by Wilson to establish mysterious contacts in Switzerland and elsewhere. Paris and Vienna whisper with awe. He plays his little part and disappears.

Distinguished men, Americans as well as foreigners, thought they had access to Wilson's confidence. One of these was the eminent Harvard psychologist, Professor Hugo Münsterberg. Not content with his scientific laurels, Münsterberg, who retained his German citizenship, dabbled in international politics. In a letter to Wilson, intended for the President only, he laid down certain conditions for peace which differ from a similar plan sponsored by President Charles W. Eliot of Harvard. Wilson read Eliot's letter to his Cabinet. The letter from Münsterberg engaged his interest. But he passed it on to Colonel House. It did not fit in with his plans at the time. House ignored it. How many important matters may have fallen between two stools in this fashion?

Another name that occurs in the correspondence between House and Wilson is that of Herbert Clark Hoover. The great engineer did not fill Wilson with enthusiasm. House advised Wilson to exploit Hoover's popularity with the women voters. House knew little of Hoover's engineering ability, but he recognized in him even in those days a master of propaganda. The advice of House, not Wilson's confidence, opened the path to the Presidency for Herbert Hoover. Wilson's real opinion of Hoover was later revealed in a zoölogical speech by a Democratic Congressman.

The Peace Commissioners who accompanied Wilson to Paris did not know what was in his mind. No one knew except Colonel House, and there came a time when even House did not know! The known, the unknown and the unknowable enter into an attempt to evaluate personalities and events. Causes apparently trivial may send a psychic avalanche into motion. The menu of a Prime Minister may be the fate of his country! A cup of coffee or a mistress too many may cause or avert a world war.

The historian of the future will examine with the microscope of the new psychology Wilson's temperamental limitations arising from psychic and physical causes, his contempt for the judgment of others, except one, his sporadic personal initiative, his vacillations and his headaches. Such historians, delving in the unconscious, may discover that these factors were more vital in shaping his policies than great external events like the sinking of the *Lusitania*. We who have no such vision, or at best only a glimpse, must patiently thread our way through mazes of circumstantial and documentary evidence, of gossip and correspondence.

XIV

THE COLONEL AND THE KING

The Most Anti-German of Monarchs – The King and the Kaiser – King George Predicts the Sinking of the *Lusitania* – House Makes a Prophecy – The Popularity of George V

COLONEL HOUSE talked intimately to the Kaiser on only one occasion for thirty minutes. But he enjoyed many contacts with the Kaiser's cousin, King George.

"Of all the public personages in England," Colonel House says, "King George was the most violently anti-German." This was also the impression of General Pershing. The King was influenced, no doubt, by the Danish blood of his mother. Possibly King George remembered that his father, King Edward, spoke English with a strong German accent. His grandfather, Prince Albert, and his grandmother, Queen Victoria, preferred German to English in their intimate personal communications.

I believe Frank Harris once published a German letter written by Queen Victoria to one of her ministers, under the significant caption: "The Queen's English"! The King's German antecedents intensified his British reaction. It requires no analytic skill to determine the cause of his emotional intensity. King George was particularly angry with his cousin, the Kaiser.

In the reports of his first audience with the King, Colonel House describes George V as "the most bellicose Englishman" he has met. Though speaking kindly of the German people, George V denounced his cousin and his cousin's military advisers in what Colonel House calls good sailor-like terms. "This," the King exclaimed, "is no time to talk peace."

"How would you establish a permanent peace, Sir?"

"By knocking all the fight out of the Germans, and by

stamping on them until they want peace and more of it than any other nation."

"Can you count on your Allies to see you through?"

"I am certain," the King retorted, "that Russia and France will stick to the last man." The monarch outlined in glowing terms what would happen to the Germans if the French got in there, and quoted his cousin Nicky as saying: "Russia is aflame from one end to the other. We are determined to win, if we must put twenty million men into the field.

"England," the King continued, "is sending the flower of the nation to the front. The world will be forced to acknowledge before the spring or summer is over that her army is equal to her best tradition."

Impressed by the King's energy, House asked: "I wonder why Your Majesty refrains from speaking to the British public in the same forceful manner in which you have talked to me?"

"I don't," the King replied, "because my distinguished cousin, the Kaiser, has talked so much and has made so much of a fool of himself that I have a distaste for that kind of publicity. Then, too, ours is a different sort of monarchy and I do not desire to intrude myself in such matters."

Colonel House showed the King a cartoon in *Life* which Editor Martin had sent to him in advance of publication. This cartoon depicts Emperor William hanged at the end of a yardarm. "I was not sure," the Colonel writes in his diary, "of the wisdom of showing him this, but he seemed to enjoy it thoroughly."

On another occasion the King surprised House by telling him that he had been reading *Life* for twenty-five years. He was interested when House told him that the Kaiser was annoyed with America. George V was particularly pleased when House showed him a fifty-mark note upon which was stamped: *"Gott strafe England und Amerika."*

The conversations between House and George V drifted almost invariably to the Kaiser. When Lord Northcliffe declared that the Kaiser was dying of tuberculosis of the throat, the King branded this statement as nonsense. "The Kaiser," he insisted, "merely has a carbuncle on the back of his neck."

The King believed that the Kaiser's Zeppelins intended to burn up London. Subsequently the world learned that German äerial cruisers were handicapped by the specific order of the Kaiser to spare Buckingham Palace and other distinguished landmarks of London.

On one occasion, discussing with Colonel House in Buckingham Palace the possibility that Germany might sink a trans-Atlantic liner to break the British blockade, George V asked a question that was curiously prophetic. "Suppose they should sink the *Lusitania*, with American passengers aboard?" House, who had traveled on the *Lusitania* himself, replied to the King, as he had to his Foreign Minister: "A flame of indignation would sweep across America which would in itself probably carry us into the War." That was on the morning of May 7, 1915. At two o'clock in the afternoon of the same day the *Lusitania* was sunk off the southern coast of Ireland.

It is fortunate that Captain Schwieger reported the sinking of the *Lusitania* in his log-book. Otherwise some readers might jump to the fantastic conclusion, voiced at the time of the disaster, that England herself had a hand in the torpedoing of her own ship. The *Lusitania* was listed as an auxiliary cruiser of the British Navy. The Germans stoutly maintained that the *Lusitania* carried picric acid and cartridges. We know to-day that this contention was true. We also know that Schwieger could have rendered no greater service to England if he had been in the pay of the British.

The King, unlike his Ambassador in Washington, Sir Cecil Spring-Rice, did not regard Anglo-American relations with pessimism. When House explained some points which were not clear, the King cordially agreed with the American position. House made his usual argument concerning the submarine issue, the German-Americans, and Wilson's difficulties in Mexico, which were at that time troubling the Administration afresh. The King said he understood quite well why the President did not intend to permit Germany to force the United States into war with Mexico.

House read to the King some cables from President Wilson, principally about British interference with American shipping.

"I wish," he said, "all official England to understand our Government's attitude upon this question, in order that there may be no misunderstanding, should it be necessary to act with vigor later." Wilson's messages on maritime freedom may have impressed the King. But they did not alter the policy of the British Admiralty.

"The more I see of the King," House writes, "the better I like him. He is a good fellow and deserves a better fate than being a king. . . ." Unlike the Kaiser, King George is not a man of extraordinary gifts. "But," Colonel House insists, "he is the type of monarch the British people like best. He holds himself well within his constitutional limitations and does not attempt to venture beyond the prerogatives of the crown. His services were of more value than appeared on the surface and his popularity helped Great Britain in many tight places. The Prince of Wales," Colonel House adds, "did what was expected of him, and more. His charm and his courage were an inspiration to the youth of Great Britain."

XV

A BEE IN GERMANY'S BONNET

The Freedom of the Seas – The Dubious Acquiescence of Sir Edward Grey – A Machiavelli of Peace – The *Lusitania* Sinks – House Demands an Ultimatum – Wilson Braves the Tempest – What the Kaiser Said to Gerard – British Beef and German Beer – Colonel House Foresees Trouble

SHORTLY before the sinking of the *Lusitania*, Colonel House whispered into the ears of Germany's Foreign Minister one phrase. That one phrase was: "The Freedom of the Seas." The bee, dexterously put into Germany's bonnet, was to buzz until the end of the War. It is still buzzing to-day. The idea of the Freedom of the Seas is as ancient as navigation. The phrase itself was disinterred by Colonel House. What Germany attempts to gain by force, House tries to secure by persuasion. Woodrow Wilson embraces the idea with enthusiasm. Military and naval disarmament and a League of Nations to secure each nation against aggression and maintain the absolute Freedom of the Seas are the two keystones upon which he rears his edifice of peace. The President pledges himself to exercise to the limit the moral force of the United States on behalf of any belligerent willing to discuss peace on such terms.

Sir Edward Grey gives House credit for bringing up the Freedom of the Seas. House intimates that the first hint of the doctrine came from the British Foreign Office. He makes no claim to originality. "Grotius, one of the world's great authorities on international law, coined the term *mare liberum* in 1609. I," Colonel House says, "merely translated it into English. The same or similar terms emerged at the time of the French Revolution. Free seas, world peace, equal rights of all nations were bandied about freely in 1798. The Freedom of the Seas is an ancient American doctrine. We went to war to maintain it in 1812. Germany justified her submarine campaign with the contention that England had illegally blocked the highroads of the ocean. It is possible," the Colonel modestly admitted, "that my negotiations gave the words new currency. I widened its application in London and in Berlin. Unfortunately, the Germans immediately telegraphed the idea to Dr. Bernhard Dernburg in the United States. Dernburg annexed the idea for his propaganda. That gave the word a black eye in England. When I came back to London the term wore a German label, and," the Colonel smiled, "the English were ready to throw me into the Thames."

The Freedom of the Seas, as House interpreted it, was the right of any merchantman, no matter under what flag it sailed, whether neutral or belligerent, to pass without hold or hindrance anywhere on the high seas once it had crossed the three-mile limit. The Freedom of the Seas did not necessarily end the right of blockade. An enemy fleet, on the surface of the seas, circling the skies, or diving in the deeps, could still prevent any ship from leaving its territorial waters. But once the barrier was passed, the ship was no longer subject to search or seizure.

"If," Colonel House musingly remarked, "the Freedom of the Seas had been an accepted doctrine, Germany would not have attempted to vie with England in naval construction. Free seas would have given her access to her colonies and to world commerce. Great Britain, depending upon sea-borne trade for food and raw materials, would have benefited even more. She could have laughed at von Tirpitz."

Grey agreed, as usual, "in principle," with the emissary of President Wilson. In practice, unfortunately, he saw innumerable obstacles. England was straining every nerve to deprive Germany of foodstuffs and raw materials pouring over her borders through neutral ports. House maintained that England could not effectively block the ports from which Germany drew her supplies without declaring war against all neutrals. "Your blockade," he said, "is an offensive weapon of doubtful legality. It is a bone of contention between you and the United States. You pay too high a price for the restraint which you put upon commerce. Even from a military point of view, you have more to gain than to lose. If the seas are free, Great Britain can concentrate her naval strength, now largely diverted to the protection of her sea-borne commerce, against the enemy fleet and enemy ports. Declare the freedom of the seas," he pleaded, "and draw the teeth of the submarine."

Sir Edward Grey, Asquith and Tyrrell listened politely. But whenever House pressed for action, they hedged.

"Moreover," they said, "what of Germany—?"

House smiled. His bag was packed. His ticket for Berlin was in his pocket. But again Sir Edward Grey intervened. The moment was not propitious for negotiations, in his opinion, because the fortunes of war were with the Germans for the time being. House cables Grey's objections to Wilson. The President is not impressed. Wilson is in an aggressive mood. "If," he replies, "an impression were to be created in Berlin that you were to come only when the British Government thought it an opportune time to come, you might be regarded when you reach there as their spokesman rather than mine."

House still hesitates. "Sir Edward Grey," he cables, "does not so much desire an advantage before I go to Berlin, but there should not be so great a disadvantage as now. His colleagues, as a majority of his people, do not want negotiations to begin now. We must be patient. The general public in Zenobia (England) does not like us very well and Youth (Gerard) says we are now hated in Zadak (Germany)."

However, on reading the President's message, House changes his mind. A few days later we find him in Berlin. He dines with von Jagow and the Chancellor, but avoids von Tirpitz. In a confidential report to Wilson, partly in code, he records his impressions of Germany:

> "The situation of Zadak (Germany) is this: Peace is generally desired, but not having actual facts given them, the people would overthrow the Government and perhaps the throne if parleys should now be commenced upon a basis having any chance of success. The civil government would listen to proposals based upon the evacuation of Belgium and France and about half the military government would consent to this but the people generally would not now permit it. The problem is to save the face of the authorities and enlighten the people.
>
> "I have proposed a way to do this, and it was cordially received

by Alto (Bethmann-Hollweg) and Wolf (Zimmermann). In substance it is for us to try to induce Zenobia (England) to consent to the freedom of the seas as one of the peace conditions. If they yield, as we have reason to believe they will, then Zadak (Germany) can say to the people that the great cause they have been striving for has been won and there is no need to retain Belgium and her coasts in order to be in a position to wage a more successful maritime war at some future time. That to hold an alien people would be a source of weakness rather than strength and would breed future trouble.

"After seeing Yew (Thomas Nelson Page) and Willard (Joseph E. Willard, Ambassador to Spain), I shall go to Zenobia (England) to take this matter up with White (Grey). If you approve, please cable Page permission to meet me at Nice. The blockade is pinching Zadak (Germany) and while there is no real suffering there is great and growing inconvenience. This tends to increase peace sentiment. The feeling against us is still running high because of export of war ammunitions to Allies. In governmental circles this is allayed because of our proposed aid in securing the freedom of the sea but the people are very bitter and unforgiving. Wolf (Zimmermann) asked if we would permit Zadak (Germany) to buy up all munitions of war and hold it. I told him yes, if we could so arrange. I regard this as impracticable.

"I would advise doing nothing to upset our amicable relations with the Allies consistent with our position of neutrality. Zadak (Germany) will use us but will continue to dislike us.... I judge my visit to Zadak (Germany) has been successful on account of the unusual courtesies extended me upon leaving which was not particularly in evidence upon arriving."

House made no secret of his conviction that the Freedom of the Seas would be a boon to Great Britain in his negotiations with Downing Street. In Berlin, House talked in a different tenor. He painted the advantages to be gained by Germany in glowing colors and was amused by the eagerness with which his bait was swallowed. To House the end justified the means. He could be a Machiavelli. Unlike Machiavelli, he did not seek the advantage of some selfish prince, but the welfare of mankind. The Freedom of the Seas would secure perpetually complete harmony between England and the United States. It was the magic sesame to world peace.

Then, crossing the Channel once more, House consults with his friends in Downing Street. His diplomatic letter to Dr. Zimmermann, Germany's Under-Secretary of State, dated May 1,

1915, outlines his labors to convert Great Britain to the Freedom of the Seas.

"I have seen Sir Edward Grey and have mentioned to him the interest which the United States and Germany had in the Freedom of the Seas, and I am pleased to tell you that he was at least willing to listen to the suggestion.

"He explained to me, however, that if he himself could be brought to the idea, it would only be upon an agreement that would guarantee the making of aggressive warfare on land as impossible as it was intended to make it upon the sea. In other words, if the commerce of the world, even in time of war and even between belligerents, was to go free and to have access to its own ports and to neutral ports without molestation, the land should be as free of menace as the sea.

"He did not undertake to commit himself to the suggestion, and he particularly wanted me to know that he was speaking for himself and not for the Government or for the people.

"He has promised to discuss the matter with his colleagues, and I shall undertake to get some estimate of the general sentiment in regard to such a proposal.

"Of course, you understand that the conversation was predicated upon the evacuation of Belgium and France and upon the consent of all the Allies."

From the last two paragraphs, it is obvious that the British Government had not committed itself to the Colonel's suggestion. Grey spoke solely for himself. His hypothetical support was based upon unfulfillable conditions. Encouraged by the support of high-minded British liberals, House was determined, nevertheless, to exert all his influence to convert Great Britain to his doctrine. It is futile to speculate on the chances of his success. The ink of his letter to Zimmermann was hardly dry when the German missile that struck the *Lusitania* torpedoed for the time being the Freedom of the Seas.

House is convinced of his own sincerity in seeking peace. To some students of his papers, it must seem that he sought it with half a heart. An undefeated Germany meant to him that the world would be plagued for generations to come by the nightmare of militarism. The sinking of the *Lusitania* gave him the opportunity to tear Wilson from his pacifist moorings. Like Page, he saw red. With Page he penciled the following cable to Wilson:

"Since (it is now certain that) a large number of American lives were lost (when the *Lusitania* was sunk), I believe an immediate demand should be made upon Germany for assurances within 2 or 3 days that this shall not occur again. If she fails to give such assurances I should inform her that our Government expected to take whatever measures were necessary to insure the safety of American citizens—if war follows, it will not be a new war but an endeavor to end more speedily an old one. Our intervention will save rather than increase the loss of life—America has come to the parting of the ways when she must determine whether she stands for civilized or uncivilized warfare. We can no longer remain neutral spectators. Our action in this crisis will determine the part we will play when peace is made, and how far we may influence a settlement for the lasting good of humanity. We are being weighed in the balance, and our position amongst nations is being assessed by mankind."

In the copy preserved in the archives of Colonel House there is an addition suggested by Mr. Page, which Colonel House did not include in his message. For the sake of the memory of Mr. Page, it is to be hoped that his scribbled suggestion will never be published.

Woodrow Wilson, like House, loved England, but he loved peace more. Instead of sending an ultimatum to Berlin, he made an impassioned speech. "There is such a thing as a man being too proud to fight. There is such a thing as a nation being so right that it does not need to convince others by force that it is right."

For once the Duumvirs disagreed.

A storm burst about Wilson. Theodore Roosevelt bellowed with anger. The pro-Allies portrayed Wilson as a coward and a poltroon. "Unclean!" "Unclean!" "Pro-German!" shouted London and Paris. But he kept us out of war. He not only kept us out of war, but he continued his efforts to mediate before the belligerents had destroyed themselves and civilization. Armored in righteousness, Wilson defied the storm of indignation his phrase had unleashed. Wilson's passion for peace was so strong that in his partnership with Colonel House he for once assumed the dominant rôle. House goes forth once more in search of Freedom of the Seas. Without the recognition of American rights on the high seas by both groups of belligerents, peace is always imperilled.

It is unfortunate that House did not see the Kaiser on his

second and third trips to Germany, one before and one after the sinking of the *Lusitania*. Popular feeling against the United States ran high on both occasions. The Emperor was in no mood to receive Wilson's emissary. William II was very angry because he looked upon the United States as the arsenal of the Allies. Wilhelmstrasse conveyed the impression to House that every German soldier who died was killed by an American bullet. House could not escape these complaints. In their conversations with German statesmen, both House and Gerard defended our legal right to supply the Allies with war materials. But in his private correspondence with House, Gerard asserts that true neutrality would stop such shipments. House, too, in his *Intimate Papers* makes the point that we could have stopped the shipment of munitions and money to the Entente if we had chosen to interpret our neutrality strictly.

Before the third European trip of Colonel House, in January, 1916, a cryptic message from Gerard evokes shudders in Washington. Emperor William, it seems, had cornered the luckless Ambassador, and threatened that he would "attend to America after this war." This was serious, if true. It confirmed the fears of Colonel House, who considered a conflict between a victorious Germany and the United States inevitable. But Gerard added another sentence—a sentence that chilled Wilson's heart. It baldly stated that Wilson's pro-Ally actions had forfeited his right to mediate. No wonder House scurried to Germany!

Gerard amplifies his conversation with the Emperor for the benefit of Colonel House. He quotes the Kaiser as saying: "I and my cousins, George and Nicholas, will make peace when the time comes." The Kaiser, Gerard avers, looked upon war as a "royal sport." House is duly shocked. It does not occur to the Colonel that Gerard's report is colored, consciously or unconsciously, by his bias. He forgets the high intellectual level of his own conversation with the Kaiser at Potsdam.

"I am wondering," the Colonel confides to his diary, "how long any part of the world will continue to be ruled by such masters. Long ago, in my inexperience, I thought governments were controlled by the great, who were actuated solely by patriotic motives. Now that I am playing the game with them, I find that selfishness plays the major part. It is appalling to me to see how heartless some are who are profiting in one way or another by the War. I say this with knowledge, and I wish the world could realize it."

After he recovers from his consternation, House, negotiating with Zimmermann and with the Chancellor, revives their enthusiasm for the Freedom of the Seas. Zimmermann strikes him as "amiable and well meaning but of limited ability." House is chagrined because Chancellor von Bethmann-Hollweg again and again declares: "I am the only belligerent statesman who openly avows his readiness to talk peace."

"Ah," House replies, "but by peace, Your Excellency, you mean a *victorious* peace."

It does not occur to House that no one in England or France had expressed the slightest interest in any peace founded upon the defeat of his country. The Colonel's observations reveal his partisanship. In England every conference involves luncheon or dinner. The appetite of British diplomats does not irritate House. But he notes with obvious annoyance that the Chancellor drinks beer copiously. House, contenting himself with mineral water, matches the Chancellor, glass for glass. "The beer," Colonel House adds, "did not affect him because his brain was as befuddled at the beginning as at the end."

In spite of these tribulations, the Colonel's visit to Germany eased the tension in the relationship between Germany and the United States. The Freedom of the Seas was the Fata Morgana that beguiled Wilhelmstrasse.

XVI

DID WILSON PLEDGE THE UNITED STATES TO WAR BEFORE THE ELECTION OF 1916?

TEN months before the election which returned Wilson to the White House in 1916 "because he kept us out of war," Colonel House negotiated a secret agreement with England and France on behalf of Wilson which pledged the United States to intervene on behalf of the Allies.

On March 9, 1916, Woodrow Wilson formally sanctioned the undertaking. If an inkling of the conversations between Colonel House and the leaders of England and France had reached the American people before the election, it might have caused incalculable revulsions of public opinion. It might have led to Wilson's reëlection by a larger vote, or it might have led to his impeachment.

"What does the United States wish Great Britain to do?" It was Ambassador Page who addressed this question to the emissary of President Wilson. Among those who anxiously waited for the Colonel's reply were Lloyd George, Lord Reading, Reginald McKenna and Austen Chamberlain. It was characteristic of the mental attitude of Page that he made himself spokesman of the four British statesmen.

"The United States," replied House, "would like Great Britain to do those things which would enable the United States to help Great Britain win the War."

This was in January, 1916. The British statesmen were charmed. Page generously said: "You have answered the question with more cleverness than I had the wit to do."

From this conversation and various conferences with Sir Edward Grey grew the Secret Treaty, made without the knowledge and consent of the United States Senate, by which Woodrow Wilson and House chained the United States to the chariot of the Entente. I beg the reader's pardon. It was not a "treaty" but a "Gentleman's Agreement." A Gentleman's Agreement, in the language of diplomacy, is a compact morally binding upon the participants but drawn loosely enough to be explained away if awkward questions are asked. Only the spirit, not the letter of the Constitution, is violated!

To what extent do nations rule themselves? To what extent are their destinies decided by private understandings among gentlemen which may be safely denied because legally they do not exist? Sir Edward Grey suavely disavowed with uplifted eyebrows any binding engagement between Great Britain and France in Parliament. He evaded the questions of Colonel House in 1914. The agreement or understanding between Sir Edward Grey and his French colleagues was entirely "informal." It did not obligate Great Britain legally. Nevertheless, the entire foreign policy of Great Britain, France and Russia rested upon this scrap of paper. And when the War came, England paid with her blood for the I. O. U. of Sir Edward Grey.

We Americans pride ourselves upon the candor of our diplomacy. We feel secure in the knowledge that no Administration can enter into formal engagements on behalf of the United States with a foreign power without the knowledge and consent of the Senate. Nevertheless, we, too, have been victimized by gentlemen's agreements. Woodrow Wilson and Colonel House were not the first offenders. There is some reason for believing that a secret agreement was made between Lord Salisbury and President McKinley in the Spanish-American War. Tyler Dennett, a distinguished American historian, unearthed a secret engagement between President Roosevelt and the Japanese Government which made the United States virtually a member of the Anglo-Japanese Alliance. And in 1916 Woodrow Wilson and Colonel

House, the Duumvirs ruling the United States, made with Sir Edward Grey the most fateful Gentleman's Agreement in history.

This instrument gave England the right to demand American intervention at her convenience, and bound the United States to support the Allies unless victorious Germany accepted a peace dictated by her foes. Sir Edward Grey, England's Foreign Minister, Balfour, First Lord of the Admiralty, Lloyd George, then Minister of Munitions, and Prime Minister Asquith, concurred in the agreement. It was sanctioned and confirmed by President Wilson. I do not question the loftiness of Wilson's motives, nor the integrity and the patriotism of House. The Gentleman's Agreement was the Colonel's reply to the President's pacifism. It pleased Wilson because it assured to America a voice in the peace conference. It pleased House because it guaranteed the victory of the Allies. Strange to say, it did not please England and France —and thereby hangs a tale—the tale of the Secret Treaties.

Though withheld from the American people, and from the Senate of the United States, the Gentleman's Agreement was known in the foreign offices of the Allies. Even the American Secretary of State, Mr. Lansing, was appraised of its terms. This is surprising, since the Duumvirs left Mr. Lansing usually in complete ignorance of what transpired in the rarefied atmosphere where they had their being. After the War the text of the agreement leaked out. Grey was the first to tattle. Page discussed it at length. Colonel House tells its history. C. Hartley Grattan discusses it at length in his book, *Why We Fought*. But for some incomprehensible reason the enormous significance of the revelation never penetrated the consciousness of the American people.

We are indebted to House for tracing the genesis of the document. The idea had been germinating for some time in the Colonel's mind.

On October 17, 1915, Colonel House wrote a now historical letter to Sir Edward Grey in which he first broached the subject. "In my opinion, it would be a world-wide calamity if the War should continue to a point where the Allies could not, with the aid of the United States, bring about a peace along the lines you and I have so often discussed. What I want you to know is that, whenever you consider the time is propitious for this intervention, I will propose it to the President. He may then desire me to go to Europe in order that a more intimate understanding as to procedure may be had.

"It is in my mind that, after conferring with your Government, I should proceed to Berlin and tell them that it was the President's purpose to intervene and stop this destructive war, provided the weight of the United States, thrown on the side that accepted our proposal, could do it."

This seems fair enough. However, the Colonel knows with what bait to snare his British friends. "I would not," he adds, "let Berlin know, of course, of any understanding had with the Allies, but would rather lead them to think our proposal would be rejected by the Allies. This might induce Berlin to accept the proposal, but, if they did not do so, it would nevertheless be the purpose to intervene. If the Central Powers were still obdurate, it would probably be necessary for us to join the Allies and force the issue."

The carbon copy of this letter, which is preserved in the House archives, bears, opposite this paragraph, the following notation in the handwriting of Colonel House: "I have expressed myself badly, and I do not mean to be unfair to Berlin. E.M.H."

House, in concluding his letter, calls Grey's attention to the danger of postponing action too long. "If the Allies should be unsuccessful and become unable to do their full share, it would be increasingly difficult, if not impossible, for us to intervene. I would have made this proposal to the President last autumn," he adds, "but you will remember that it was not agreeable to the Allies."

The suggestion electrifies Wilson. The very next day, October 18, Wilson replies and sanctions the letter except for one or two "unimportant verbal changes." The changes are, however, by no means unimportant. House himself, in his annotations, mentions one of these. The President is unwilling to make American intervention inevitable. The original reads: "If the Central Powers were still obdurate, it would be necessary for us to join the Allies," etc. Wilson adds the word "probably" and the sentence now reads: "It would *probably* be necessary, etc." Wilson considers the rest of the letter all right and prays to God that it may bring results. House is fully alive to the vital significance of Wilson's commitment.

"This," he notes, "is one of the most important letters I have ever received from the President." The letter begins "Dearest Friend" and ends, "Affectionately Yours" but—*the signature is missing!* "The President did not sign this," House remarks in a marginal note, "because of the danger of sending it through the mails." Wilson knew that it was dynamite. The letter is written on the stationery of the White House on the President's own typewriter.

Three weeks later, Sir Edward Grey inquires by cable if the letter from House is to be taken in conjunction with his (Grey's) proposal, made some weeks earlier, for a League of Nations. House consults with Wilson. On November 1st, Wilson authorizes House by telegraph to reply in the affirmative. Duumvir Wilson is now completely under the spell of Duumvir House.

House discussed the idea of American intervention informally with various British statesmen, but he decided to bring France into line before reducing the agreement to writing. He used all his powers of persuasion to convince Aristide Briand, who was Premier of France, and Jules Cambon, his Foreign Minister, of Wilson's desire to bring the War to an end upon a "reasonable" basis. "Reasonable," in the Colonel's vocabulary, meant favorable to the Entente.

On February 7, 1916, Colonel House had a heart-to-heart talk with Briand and his colleague. "We had a complete understanding as to the immediate future," the Colonel reports. "I again told them that the lower the fortunes of the Allies ebbed, the closer the United States would stand by them." House summarizes the gist of the conversation in a letter to Woodrow Wilson dated February 9, 1916:

> "It was finally understood that in the event the Allies had some notable victories during the spring and summer, you would not intervene; and in the event that the tide of war went against them or remained stationary, you would intervene. This conversation is to go no further than between Briand, Cambon and myself, and I promised that no one in America should know of it excepting yourself and Lansing.
>
> "I told them I had had a similar conversation in England and

that there it would go no further than a group composed of the Prime Minister, Sir Edward Grey, Balfour, and Lloyd George. This seemed agreeable to them. ...

"It is impossible for any unprejudiced person to believe that it would be wise for America to take part in this war unless it comes about by intervention based upon the highest human motives. We are the only nation left on earth with sufficient power to lead them out, and with us once in, the War would have to go to a finish with all its appalling consequences. It is better for the Central Powers and it is better for the Allies, as indeed it is better for us, to act in this way; and I have not hesitated to say this to the British and French Governments, and have intimated it to Germany.

"A great opportunity is yours, my friend—the greatest, perhaps, that has ever come to any man. The way out seems clear to me and, when I can lay the facts before you, I believe it will be clear to you also.

"In each Government I have visited I have found stubbornness, determination, selfishness, and cant. One continually hears self-glorification and the highest motives attributed to themselves because of their part in the War. But I may tell you that my observation is that incompetent statesmanship and selfishness is at the bottom of it all. It is not so much a breaking down of civilization as a lack of wisdom in those that govern; and history, I believe, will bring an awful indictment against those who were short-sighted and selfish enough to let such a tragedy happen."

On February 10th, House has an important conference with Sir Edward Grey. He embodies the sense of that conversation in a cable to Wilson. "After going over the situation with great care and taking up every detail of foreign affairs, we finally agreed that it would be best for you to demand that the belligerents permit you to call a conference for the discussion of peace terms. We concluded this would be better than intervention (on the submarine issue), and it was understood, though not definitely agreed upon, that you might do this within a very short time—perhaps soon after I returned. The Allies will agree to the conference, and, if Germany does not, I have promised for you that we will throw in all our weight in order to bring her to terms."

Other conferences follow. In the meantime, Grey had received a communication from the French Ambassador giving in detail the minutes of the conference between House and Aristide Briand and Jules Cambon. The French have a congenital genius for misunderstanding. They understood House to say that America would intervene, no matter how low French fortunes might fall. House asked Grey to correct that impression. "If," he said, "the Allies put off their call for our assistance to a time when our intervention cannot serve them, then we will not make the attempt."

Sir Edward Grey at first coyly refuses to consent to accept Wilson's outstretched hand, but he finally yields to the persuasion of House, who threatens that the United States will withdraw its support unless France and England act quickly. Asquith, Balfour, Lloyd George and Reading enter the plot. They point out the difficulty of securing the consent of England's Allies.

"The next point," House writes in his diary, "that came up was how the British Government could let us know the time they considered propitious for us to intervene, without first submitting the question to the Allies, and, if they did not submit it to the Allies, how to avoid the charge of double-dealing. The solution I suggested for this was that at regular intervals I would cable Sir Edward Grey, in our private code, offering intervention. He could ignore the messages until the time was propitious, and then he could bring it to the attention of the Allies as coming from us and not as coming from Great Britain."

The British gladly accept the suggestion offered by the nimble wit of the Colonel. The conferences continue. They are conspicuous by the absence of Ambassador Page. In a memorandum dated February 9, Page perpetuates his protest:

"House arrived from Berlin—Havre—Paris (the King of the Belgians) full of the idea of American intervention. First his plan was that he and I and a group of the British Cabinet (Grey, Asquith, Lloyd George, Reading, etc.) should at once work out a minimum programme of peace—the least that the Allies would accept, *which, he assumed, would be unacceptable to the Germans;* and that the President would take this programme and present it to both sides; the side that declined would be responsible for continuing the War. Then, to end the War, the President would help the other side—that is, the Allies. House had talked more or less with some members of the French Government, who, he said, were enthusiastic about it. I wonder if they understood what he said, or whether he understood what they said? Then, too, the King of the Belgians approved it. Of course, the fatal moral weakness of the foregoing scheme is that we should plunge into the War, not on the merits of the cause, but by a carefully sprung trick. When I said that the way to get into the War was for a proper cause—to decline to be hoodwinked about the *Lusitania* or (or and) to send Bernstorff home because he gave money to von Papen which went to bomb-throwers, etc., etc.—of which the Department of State has documentary evidence—this is the way to get into the War—then House objected that we must do it the President's own way. Of course, such an indirect scheme is doomed to failure—is wrong, in fact."

House brushes aside Page's misgivings. On February 14th, he agrees with Sir Edward Grey on a definite formula. February 23rd, Sir Edward Grey finally embodies the Gentleman's Agreement, reached between himself and Duumvir House, in the following memorandum:

(*Confidential*)
Colonel House told me that President Wilson was ready, on hearing from France and England that the moment was opportune to propose that a conference should be summoned to put an end to the War. Should the Allies accept this proposal, and should Germany refuse it, the United States would probably enter the War against Germany.

Colonel House expressed the opinion that, if such a conference met, it would secure peace on terms not unfavorable to the Allies; and, if it failed to secure peace, the United States would leave the Conference as a belligerent on the side of the Allies, if Germany was unreasonable. Colonel House expressed an opinion decidedly favorable to the restoration of Belgium, the transfer of Alsace and Lorraine to France, and the acquisition by Russia of an outlet to the sea, though he thought that the loss of territory incurred by Germany in one place would have to be compensated to her by concessions to her in other places outside Europe. If the Allies delayed accepting the offer of President Wilson, and if, later on, the course of the War was so unfavorable to them that the intervention of the United States would not be effective, the United States would probably disinterest themselves in Europe and look to their own protection in their own way.

I said that I felt the statement, coming from the President of the United States, to be a matter of such importance that I must inform the Prime Minister and my colleagues; but that I could say nothing until it had received their consideration. The British Government could, under no circumstances, accept or make any proposal except in consultation and agreement with the Allies. I thought that the Cabinet would probably feel that the present situation would not justify them in approaching their Allies on this subject at the present moment; but, as Colonel House had had an intimate conversation with M. Briand and M. Jules Cambon in Paris, I should think it right to tell M. Briand privately, through the French Ambassador in London, what Colonel House had said to us; and I should, of course, whenever there was an opportunity, be ready to talk the matter over with M. Briand, if he desired it.

Armed with the Gentleman's Agreement, Colonel House returns to Washington. The President assures him that he has accomplished a difficult task in a way beyond his expectations.

HOUSE : I would be proud if you would be given the opportunity to realize the plan.

THE PRESIDENT : You should be proud of yourself, not of me, since you have done it all.

But on studying the document the President's Calvinist conscience asserts itself. He is horrified by the thought that the agreement commits him to war. There is one sentence that he cannot swallow. Knowing Wilson's unwillingness to obligate himself definitely, House no doubt called Sir Edward Grey's attention to the word "probably," which Wilson inserted in the letter of October 17th. The astute Grey, in his memorandum, used "probably" twice. But he omitted it in one very important sentence. "If it failed to secure peace the United States would leave the conference as a belligerent on the side of the Allies, if Germany was unreasonable." Wilson's professorial mind immediately notes the missing qualification. With visions of brutal invasions, limbs torn from limbs, men mowed down and youthful bodies trampled in the mire, assailing his mind, he takes his pencil and inserts between "would" and "leave" once more one word—*"probably."* Thus his conscience is set at rest. He is not unconditionally committed—legally. Morally, however, he is bound to enter the War at the pleasure of England and France!

On March 7, 1916, eight months before his reëlection, the President formally approves the Gentleman's Agreement which gives Great Britain and France a call on American intervention. He himself takes down in shorthand the sense of his discussion with House. He himself types it off.

"I reported to the President the general conclusions of our conference of the 14th of February, and in the light of those conclusions he authorized me to say that, so far as he can speak for the future action of the United States, he agrees to the memorandum with which you furnished me, with only this correction: that the word 'probably' be added after the word 'would' and before the word 'leave' in line number nine.

"Please acknowledge receipt of this cable."

This telegram, typed by the President, signed by Colonel House and addressed to Sir Edward Grey, makes the United States conditionally a member of the Entente.

CLOVEN HOOFS

W HY were the Allies dissatisfied? Why did they not avail themselves of the Gentleman's Agreement?

In order to understand this situation we must remember that the provisional peace terms agreed to by Woodrow Wilson and Colonel House were infinitely milder than the terms proposed in the secret treaties among the Allies themselves, which were not then known, or fully known, to Woodrow Wilson and his co-regent.

Let us first examine the "reasonable" terms sanctioned by Wilson and House, which did not satisfy the rapacity of the Allies. Though shod with fine phrases, the cloven hoof betrays itself. In the light of the agreement itself and their previous conversations, the terms approved by the Duumvirs include: the restoration of Belgium and Serbia, the abolition of competitive armaments and guarantees against military aggression, the transfer of the Italian-speaking regions of Austria to Italy, the cession of Constantinople to Russia, and the annexation of Alsace and Lorraine by France. There could be no objection to the restoration of the invaded countries. But nothing in the military situation in January, 1916, justified the surrender of Alsace-Lorraine and the sacrifices demanded from Turkey and Austria-Hungary. The phrase, "guarantees against military aggression" was a concealed attempt to insure forever the contemplated loot of the Allies.

When these peace terms were drawn, Germany held Belgium and throttled France. Her submarines were paralyzing Great Britain. Italy was demoralized, Russia beginning to crack. Such a peace could not seem "reasonable" to the Germans. It was, on the basis of existing conditions, preposterous. Compensations outside of Europe held no allurements for Germany.

To understand what such a peace would have meant to Germany, let us put ourselves in Germany's place. Let us assume that we were at war with England, Canada, and Mexico, that we had crippled the British navy, conquered every inch of Canadian soil, and held all of Mexico under our thumb. Would we regard any neutral as "reasonable" who proposed that we should cede the State of New York to Canada and Texas to Mexico, in return for a stretch of territory somewhere in Central Africa or Patagonia?

The fact that even more drastic humiliations were laid upon the Central Powers after their defeat does not make the terms proposed in the Gentleman's Agreement "reasonable." It merely explains why the Peace Treaty of Versailles is unworkable and why the attempt to enforce it has upset completely the economic structure of the civilized world.

How was it possible that terms such as these seemed "reasonable" to the shrewd Colonel House and the scholarly Woodrow Wilson? It cannot be explained except upon the hypothesis that they were completely hypnotized by the blandishments of Sir Edward Grey and their own ingrained sympathy with Great Britain.

"The Administration," wrote Lord Northcliffe to Winston Churchill, "is run entirely by these two men (Wilson and House). Wilson's power is absolute and House is a wise assistant. Both are pro-English." When this message came hurtling across the cables America was already at war. But long before this, when Wilson was exhorting his countrymen to be neutral even in thought, he did not hide from Colonel House the fact that his heart was with the Allies. "He" (Wilson), the Colonel notes in his diary on August 30, 1914, "felt deeply the destruction of Louvain, and I found him as unsympathetic with the German attitude as is the balance of America. He goes even further than I in his condemnation of Germany's part in this war, and almost allows his feeling to include the German people as a whole rather than the leaders alone. He said German philosophy was essentially selfish and lacking in spirituality. When I spoke of the Kaiser building up the German machine as a means of maintaining peace, he said, 'What a foolish thing it was to create a powder magazine and risk some one's dropping a spark into it!' "

Wilson was equally outspoken with members of his Cabinet. When the Cabinet discussed retaliatory measures against the Entente for their infringement of our neutral rights, Wilson exclaimed: "Gentlemen, the Allies are standing with their backs to the wall, fighting wild beasts. I will permit nothing to be done by our country to hinder or embarrass them in the prosecution of the war unless admitted rights are grossly violated." He finally asked for the embargo which he could hold as a club over England. But he refused to avail himself of this weapon.

When Brand Whitlock, Mr. Wilson's Ambassador in Belgium, called on the President in December, 1915, the following colloquy ensued:

W H I T L O C K : Mr. President, I am officially representing the interests of Germany as well as of the United States and I can say honestly that I am officially neutral in all things; but I ought to tell you that in my heart there is no such thing as neutrality. I am heart and soul for the Allies.

W I L S O N : So am I. No decent man, knowing the situation and Germany, could be anything else. But that is only my own personal opinion and there are many others in this country who do not hold that opinion. In the West and Middle West frequently there is no opinion at all. I am not justified in forcing my opinion upon the people of the United States and bringing them into a war which they do not understand.

In spite of his own sentiments, Wilson strove heroically to maintain an impartial attitude officially. He keenly felt that he was President of a nation nourished by the blood of all European races. Perhaps the Irish strain in his ancestry helped him to see now and then with other than British eyes. It must have been his Irish blood that coursed through his brain when he rebuked

Page for proclaiming from the housetops of London that the American people were "English-led and English-ruled." Page wrote a long, lame letter of explanation, but did not mend his ways.

When the *Dacia* controversy loomed large, Wilson delivered to his Ambassador in London a much-needed lesson. "The President," Mr. Bryan cabled to the recalcitrant Page, "directs me to send the following: 'Answering your two telegrams in regard to the irritation and apparent change in public opinion regarding the United States you will please discuss the matter again with Sir Edward Grey in effect as follows: We regret exceedingly to learn that the British public entertains any doubt as to the strict neutrality of this Government or as to the support given by the general public to the Government's position. This is probably due to the fact that a portion of the British public is quite naturally uninformed as to the character of our population.' "

It is Wilson the historian, rather than Wilson the partisan, that speaks:

> "While the English element predominated in the original stock the immigration in latter years has been largely from other countries. Germany and Ireland, for instance, have contributed very materially during the last half century, and among those who are the children of foreign-born parents the German element now predominates. This element is not only numerous but it has a strong representation in financial, mercantile life and agriculture. . . .
>
> "There is, of course, not the slightest alteration in the cordial feeling which has always existed between the United States and Great Britain. Mere debate and newspaper agitation will not alter that feeling; but acts which seem to them arbitrary, unnecessary, and contrary to the recognized rules of neutral commerce may alter it very seriously, because the great majority of our people are trying in good faith to live within those rules, and they are sensitive about nothing more than about their legitimate trade. . . .
>
> "The export of arms, ammunition, and horses to the Allies, is, of course, known, and the protest made by German-Americans and by a portion of the Irish-Americans, while entirely without justification, is not unnatural."

Page, shocked and aggrieved, asked the permission of the State Department to delay the presentation of this dispatch and to present its contents to Sir Edward Grey at a more favorable opportunity. "It may safely be assumed," laconically remarks Page's biographer, Burton J. Hendrick, "that this favorable opportunity never came."

In spite of this lecture, Page, while resenting the President's pacifism, took it for granted that Wilson was pro-English. He knew that Colonel House was England's friend. House made no concealment of his leanings. He could not conceive of any save a British peace. But, like Wilson, he looked upon the victory of Great Britain merely as a phase in the struggle of humanity toward a new international ideal. He saw rising, goddess-like from seas of carnage, a Parliament of Man. Wilson believed that he could re-make the world without unsheathing the sword. House did not share this hope.

Wilson, conscious of the ethnic composition of the American people, included the German-American element in his calculations. House, unlike Wilson, discarded the German-Americans. His experience with practical politics had taught him that the German-Americans were not sufficiently organized to play a decisive part in a Presidential election. When he defended President Wilson in Paris against the charge of being pro-German, or of attempting to beguile the pro-German vote, he exclaimed: "A man with the President's intelligence would hardly cater to 15 per cent of the American vote in order to lose 85 per cent of it."

Again, unlike Wilson, House knew the Germans and liked them. Some of the Forty-Eighters cast upon our shores by the German revolution of that year were friends of his father. One of them especially profoundly impressed House as a boy. The Colonel was familiar with the German-Americans. He knew that they were peaceful and law-abiding citizens. Much as he liked these Germans, who seemed to him *gemütlich* and jolly, he regarded the men around the Kaiser as decidedly *ungemütlich*. He feared a recession of the "democratic ideal" throughout the world in case of a German victory, and was alarmed by the possibility of a clash between American democracy and German militarism.

The Gentleman's Agreement was based upon this theory. We may disagree with the Colonel. But if we accept his premise we cannot impeach his actions. Colonel House wished to end the senseless slaughter as soon as possible and leave Great Britain mistress of the seas. It was his conviction that enlightened self-interest would compel Great Britain to share the trident of naval supremacy with the United States. Together the two countries were to safeguard the peace of the world by controlling the ocean. The partnership thus envisaged was to assure to all mankind the Freedom of the Seas. House was not disinclined to take Germany into the partnership. Germany was to keep peace on the land, while the Anglo-Saxon nations maintained tranquillity on the seas. It is extremely unlikely that the hard-hearted Englishmen who made the Gentleman's Agreement with House shared his dream. House had encountered among English intellectuals a few inspired minds to whom his plan did not seem visionary. But the iron realities of war shattered their hopes and his.

The Gentleman's Agreement brought neither peace nor the millennium. It inspired the Allies to reject every peace offer from Germany because they knew that if their backs were against the wall they could count upon the United States. Having nothing to lose by delay, the Allies were in no mood to precipitate America's intervention. Their unsavory secret treaties, dividing the skin of the German bear long before he was trapped, were far more immoderate than the "reasonable" terms discussed between Sir Edward Grey and Colonel House. England and France wanted America to enter the War too angry to ask questions about their secret engagements. They did not want a peace conference dominated by the United States to thwart their greedy schemes for aggrandizement. They were alarmed by the idealism of Wilson. The insertion of the word "probably" in the Gentleman's Agreement aroused their fear that Wilson might let them down at the last moment unless his hand was forced. Their distrust of Wilson was heightened by Page, who frankly sided with the Allies against his own Government and made no effort to conceal from House his contempt for the President's pacifism. Except for these considerations, England and France would have invoked the Gentleman's Agreement to force American intervention long before April 5, 1917, when Germany, equally distrustful of Wilson, resorted to her last weapon, unrestricted submarine warfare.

Germany would have exercised more patience if she had not

gotten wind of the Gentleman's Agreement between Wilson's emissary and England and France. As early as February 29, 1916, Gerard writes: "Both the Chancellor and von Jagow say they are convinced America has a secret understanding with England and that nothing can be arranged." How did the Germans read the mind of the Duumvirs? Herbert O. Yardley, then a young clerk in the State Department, boasts that he deciphered the confidential messages between Wilson and House for his own amusement with the aid of the simple devices employed by Poe in his *Gold Bug*. This would lead one to suspect that every Cabinet in Europe must have been in possession of these messages, for the tapping of cable wires presents no mechanical difficulties to experts of a modern Intelligence Service.

True, the cables of Colonel House were guarded by an elaborate system. When House sent a communication to Wilson from Europe it was put in the special code which he and Wilson had devised for their own convenience. It was then entrusted to the naval attachés of the American Embassy and translated into what was called the Navy Box, an intricate code changed every day, and transmitted to the Navy Department in Washington. The Navy Department re-translated it into the original House-Wilson code and forwarded the message to the Secretary of State. The State Department in turn delivered it to Mr. Wilson. When it reached Mr. Yardley, it was not in the Navy Box but in the simple House-Wilson cipher, which Mr. Yardley was able to decode without difficulty.

Nevertheless, it is possible, in the light of Mr. Yardley's astounding revelations, that the elaborate organizations maintained in all European countries may have had the key to the Navy Box! The German "Black Chamber" would not have been worth its salt if it had failed to discover some reference to the Gentleman's Agreement in the correspondence of the Duumvirs or in the communications between Allied statesmen. Colonel House himself somewhere expressed his fear of a leak! With this knowledge, no matter how vague, the German Foreign Office could no longer believe in the good faith of the President of the United States.

In vain Bernstorff attempted to convince Berlin of Wilson's

sincerity. Wilhelmstrasse repeatedly tried to employ for its own ends Mr. Wilson's desire to emerge from the War as the peacemaker. Without knowledge of Wilson's complex personality, without understanding his intransigent idealism, German diplomats attributed this desire solely to egotism. They did not realize that it was rooted deeply in Wilson's Scotch-Presbyterian conscience. The sophisticated statesmen in the German Foreign Office knew that Wilson was reluctant to countenance an English defeat, but they did not know, as Bernstorff did, that he valued peace more than the success of the Allies. Wilson's messianic complex outshouted the voice of his English blood. He was more interested in saving the world than in saving Great Britain!

But he loved England enough to make the United States in fact, if not in law, a secret Ally of the Entente before the election of 1916. Agreements of this type nullify the treaty-making powers of the Senate and the war-making powers of Congress.[1] Woodrow Wilson's Gentleman's Agreement with the Allies and similar undertakings by other Presidents, reveal an unsuspected breach in the wall of the Constitution.

[1] Colonel House objects to my interpretation. In a letter, dated February 13, 1932, he says:

You are unfair to President Wilson, Lord Grey, and myself. All three of us knew that whatever agreement of the kind made was subject to the consent of Congress, and President Wilson was not overstepping his prerogatives when he accepted it. You might argue that such action of his compelled Congress to sustain him, but you will recall that the President himself, acting in conjunction with the Prime Ministers of the Allies and their representatives, made a solemn agreement at Versailles which was afterwards rejected by the Senate. An Executive must conduct the affairs of state according to his judgment as to the best interest of the country, but the final decision rests with the Congress.

Please bear in mind that the Germans were approached in 1915 and 1916 for their terms of peace and they would not discuss anything excepting a peace based upon the *status quo*. This was manifestly impossible for the reason that Germany occupied nearly all of Belgium, a large part of France and Russia. If peace had been made upon those terms it would have been a victorious peace for Germany and, in my opinion, would have led us into ultimate conflict with her. It would have made her the dominant power in the world, and would have taxed us to the limit to meet any infringement of the Monroe Doctrine which almost surely would have followed her assumption of world power.

Failing with Germany, we turned to the Allies, and naturally had to discuss terms more favorable to them than we would have insisted upon had Germany met our wishes for a peace based on the *status quo ante*.

Replying to an article by C. Hartley Grattan on the Gentleman's Agreement, House admits that the powers of the Presidency should be restricted. History records that in all international crises since that of 1812 the decision for war or peace rested primarily with the President. The die was cast when Congress convened in spite of the fact that the Constitution reserves the right to declare war to Congress alone. Colonel House suggests a constitutional amendment limiting the President's war-making powers. But since these powers are not rooted in the Constitution, it is difficult to see how they could be curtailed by any amendment. Yet a way should be found to protect the American people from executive commitments violating the Constitution by circumvention. Who can say that history will not repeat itself? What was possible in 1916 is possible again. Who knows what Gentleman's Agreement may be in existence to-day which our children may be called upon to seal with their blood to-morrow?

XVIII

THE GHOST OF MADISON STALKS

The Ruler of the Seas – The Patience of Woodrow Wilson – Vain Peace Efforts – House Warns Grey – Scraps of Paper and Paper Blockades – Pigeon-holing Uncle Sam's Protest – Polite Refusals – Wilson's Troubled Sleep

EARLY in 1914, the ghost of Madison stalked. On May 7, 1915, he vanished, frightened away by the ghosts of the *Lusitania.*

The issues between the United States and Great Britain were clearly defined. For centuries Britannia had arrogated to herself the right to regulate the traffic of the seas. In her desire to cripple Germany, she stretched the meaning of contraband beyond the limit in the World War. She claimed the right to seize and search all vessels, both outgoing and incoming, carrying such articles as copper, rubber and foodstuffs, utterly oblivious of the fact that she had signed the Declaration of London, which limited the contraband list and reduced interference with neutral shipping to a minimum. In this instance, as in others, the British Government accepted the new idea "in principle." But the British Parliament never ratified the agreement!

Immediately on the outbreak of the War, Germany agreed to abide by the Declaration. When the United States asked the English to do likewise, Britannia turned a cold shoulder to Uncle Sam. In vain America pointed out that the British Orders in Council presented "a proposed course of action previously unknown to international law," which "destroyed all known standards by which neutrals could measure their rights and avoid danger to their ships and cargoes." The United States was forced to the reluctant conclusion that "the policy of his Majesty's

Government toward neutral ships and cargoes exceeds the manifest necessity of a belligerent and constitutes restrictions upon the rights of American citizens on the high seas which are not justified by the rules of international law or required under the principle of self-preservation."

Sir Edward Grey would have taken these admonitions to respect the Freedom of the Seas more seriously if he had not been strengthened in his resistance to the just demands of the United States by the American Ambassador. When the State Department protests against the illegal seizure of our ships and the violation of our mails, the wires bristle with lamentations from Walter H. Page.

Wilson's patience in the first years of the great trial exceeded that of the camel. There was a danger, nevertheless, that the camel of his patience might balk. But the patience of Wilson's Ambassador in London was infinite—his patience, that is to say, with Great Britain. He adopted, however, a truculent tone in his missives to House. "It is no time to quarrel or to be bumptious about a cargo of oil or of copper, or to deal with these governments as if things are normal. Thank God you are three thousand miles from it. I wish I were thirty thousand . . ." This was while Bryan was still in nominal charge of the State Department.

House assures Page that, "all of us feeling as we do," there is little danger of war, but he warns him to refrain from expressing "unneutral" sentiments even in his communications with Mr. Bryan. He points out that the American people are sensitive regarding their rights as neutrals. "It would not be wise for the President, with all his powers and popularity, to go counter to their sentiments."

The echo of Wilson's lecture on the War of 1812 still reverberated in the Duumvir's mind. Personally he accepted with alacrity the argument of Cecil Spring-Rice that modern conditions of warfare required changes in the old definition of contraband, but rejected the same argument when it was advanced by Bernstorff on behalf of the submarine. When he realizes the litter of trouble likely to spring from these contradictions, Colonel House renews his effort to inveigle the dove of peace. He negotiates with Spring-Rice and with Bernstorff. But he cannot persuade Sir Cecil to meet the German Ambassador. "Make peace now," he urges, "while Great Britain dominates her Allies, a peace based on disarmament, which will compensate Belgium without dismembering Germany."

But England has other secret engagements. These Spring-Rice locks in his bosom, but he declares: "The time is not ripe for peace proposals. Our Allies would suspect us of treason."

"Shall I discuss the matter with Jusserand or with Bakhmeteff?"

"No, Jusserand has an extraordinarily bad case of nerves. The Russian Ambassador," Sir Cecil adds, "is a reactionary of the worst type and little less than mad."

Bernstorff, the Englishman insists, is "thoroughly unreliable." What would Sir Cecil have said if he knew that Wilson in a letter to House calls him "childish"?

Wilson mistrusted Bernstorff. But he despised Sir Cecil and repeatedly urged his recall. House, for reasons of policy, did not press this point in his conversations with Sir Edward Grey. "Spring-Rice," he said to me, "was a charming gentleman. But he was ill and irritable when the War broke loose. The Ambassador had many friends in the Foreign Office, including the Foreign Secretary. It was conveyed to me that it would be better for us to let England withdraw him in her own time and in her own way than for us to make a request for his removal."

Sir Cecil constantly injects into his official reports mischievous notions of Wilson's "pro-Germanism." The impression created by Spring-Rice was largely responsible for England's refusal to trust Wilson. He evidently convinced Sir Edward Grey. "People cannot believe," Grey writes rather bluntly to House on January 22, 1915, "that the United States desires to paralyze the advantage which we derive from our sea power, while leaving intact to Germany those military and scientific advantages which are special to her. I think it is only fair that he (Wilson) should be warned that should people in England come to believe that the dominant influence in United States politics is German, it would tend to create an untoward state of public opinion which we should strictly regret. The above," the British Foreign Secretary adds, "is purely personal and must be so regarded; but I think it is my duty under the circumstances to give this personal and friendly warning as to the probable trend of public sentiment."

Early in 1915 House labored eagerly to destroy Grey's grotesque misconception of Wilson. He assures his British friends that Wilson's heart beats for them. But he warns them that their lawless interference with American cargoes and American mails may lead to grave consequences.

"How," he asks Sir Edward, "is it possible for the President to protest with vigor against German infractions of the law of nations, so long as Germany has some ground for complaint that he permits the British to alter maritime regulations at will? Washington is faced by a strong wave of popular resentment. It may not be possible to prevent the passage by Congress of an embargo on the shipment of arms."

The word "embargo" sounds like the echo of Madison's admonition to the British Government of his day. House is conscious of the parallel. Grey has forgotten his history.

"It was such an embargo," House warningly adds, "that brought on the War of 1812. The President will try to prevent it. But the danger exists. Mr. Wilson sends this warning through me rather than through Page because he wants it to be unofficial."

Sir Edward Grey sympathizes with the attitude of the Colonel personally, but officially he remains unmoved. The Admiralty is too busy to read Wilson's interpretation of Madison.

England, continuing to seize neutral ships wherever possible, makes no attempt to patrol the coast line of Germany. She is unable to stop sea traffic between Germany and Scandinavia. A blockade that is not effectively enforced is illegal. America protests; American public opinion writhes. Copper and cotton barons ask disagreeable questions. The German-Americans and the Irish mass in protest against the strangulation of American trade and the pilfering of American mails. England quibbles and persists, unrepentant, in her paper blockade. Between Germany's scraps of paper and England's paper blockade, the Administration has a hard course to steer!

The *Lusitania* catastrophe shifted the emphasis of America's indignation from England to Germany. England serenely continued her lawless course until even England's friends in America were disgruntled. "The English," Secretary Lane, a Canadian by birth, writes to House, "are not behaving very well. They are holding up our ships; they have made new international law. We have been very meek and mild under their use of the ocean as a toll road. Of course," Lane hastens to add, "the sympathy of the greater part of the country is with the English, but it would not have been as strongly with them, not nearly so strongly, if it had not been for the persistent short-sightedness of our German friends. I cannot see what England means by her policy of delay and embarrassment and hampering. Her success," Lane goes on to say, "manifestly depends upon the continuance of the strictest neutrality on our part, and yet she is not willing to let us have the rights of a neutral." In the same chatty tone Lane continues:

> "You would be interested, I think, in hearing some of the discussion around the Cabinet table. There isn't a man in the Cabinet who has a drop of German blood in his veins, I guess. Two of us were born under the British flag. I have two cousins in the British army, and Mrs. Lane has three. The most of us are Scotch in our ancestry, and yet each day that we meet we boil over somewhat at the foolish manner in which England acts. Can it be that she is trying to take advantage of the War to hamper our trade?"

House waves this letter in the face of Sir Edward Grey. Sir Edward smiles apologetically and pigeon-holes every American protest. Now, as in the War of Independence, in the War of 1812 and in the Civil War, an intelligent minority in England supports America. Francis W. Hirst, editor of *The Economist,* criticizes Grey and Grey's war. Hirst advocates an embargo by America on exports to all belligerents. Such an action by President Wilson, he thinks, would lay the foundation for a new international sanction. Robert Donald, editor of the *Daily Chronicle,* agreeing with Hirst, denounces the paper blockade and maintains that the United States would be warranted in stopping the flow of munitions of war to England as a measure of retaliation. Lord Morley, who resigned from the Cabinet as a protest against Grey's deception, and Lord Loreburn, former Lord Chancellor, hold similar views. These men desire a speedy peace. Perhaps they alone in all England foresee the frightful price in loss of prestige and trade England must pay some years later for Sir Edward's philanderings with Paris!

These opinions fortify the Duumvir's soul. Calling on the Marquis of Lansdowne, once a powerful member of the ruling oligarchy in Downing Street, he argues convincingly: "The sinking of the *Lusitania* was lucky for you. If Germany were not acting so much worse than you, you would certainly be called to an accounting. The President is bending almost to the breaking point to avoid a disagreeable controversy with you. He is a Scotchman with all the tenacity of purpose of his race."

House waits to let the implication sink in.

"Remember," the Colonel adds softly, but emphatically, "that while the President at heart sympathizes with the Allies in their purposes, he is President of the United States. Our people do not differentiate between violators of international law. We must of necessity maintain an equitable attitude between the two groups of belligerents."

But Lansdowne, even if convinced, cannot move the obstinate men at the helm. The Duumvir wanders from pillar to post. "Germany," he tells Lord Crewe, "at least replies to our notes. You file away our protests until the dust settles over them. I shall advise the President not to ask for your reply until the *Lusitania* controversy is settled. But if it is, an immediate answer should be forthcoming. The President is hard-pressed and you cannot deal with us in the future in the manner in which you have treated us in the past."

Duumvir seeks out Grey once more and shows him a personal letter of the President, protesting against the use of the American flag by the English to protect them from German torpedoes. Wilson considers the practice obnoxious.

"You are playing into Germany's hands," insists House, reiterating the argument of the President.

Sir Edward is polite and regretful. But the practice continues. England continues her course, even after Germany seems to yield in the *Lusitania* dispute.

To take the sting out of the controversy with England, House works out an arrangement with Grey by which Great Britain is to give up her food blockade, if Germany stops her submarine warfare. Grey again personally approves. But somehow he is unable to convince the Admiralty or his colleagues in the Cabinet.

And once more the ghost of Madison troubles the sleep of Woodrow Wilson.

XIX

THE PIOUS WISH OF AMBASSADOR PAGE

Deep Waters – A Deal in Cotton – Rumblings from Washington – Lansing
Writes a Note – Wilson Vacillates – Colonel House Loses His Temper – The
Fury of Sir Cecil – Two Prayers

THE pro-British Page scents serious trouble. A brilliant, if
sinister, thought enlivens the imagination of the American
Ambassador to the Court of Saint James's. *"It is a curious thing to
say,"* he writes to House, *"but the only solution I see is another*
Lusitania *outrage which would force war."* The American Ambassador is eager to sacrifice a hundred American lives to gain a
respite for Great Britain from the anger of Mr. Wilson!

"We are in deep water with this Government," Page groans.
"They made the mistake of putting themselves legally wrong by
the Order in Council of March 11th, and the cotton men and the
meat men are being stirred up (being already angry) to keep our
State Department active. I fear this Government will have to put
cotton on the contraband list. The agitation for it has become
almost irresistible. And the Government has bungled so many
things that it has lost its courage and is generally under fire. Sir
Edward is very despondent about the American situation."

Impressed by Page's jeremiad, House advises the English to
throw some of the onus for their high-handed seizures upon the
French. "You will remember," he writes to Sir Edward, "that
the *Dacia* incident was immediately forgotten when France seized
her." The Colonel would hardly have fathered such an idea if he
had not considered the situation desperate.

Snubbed on every side, however politely, House nevertheless
urges Wilson not to press Great Britain too hard. He feels that
the United States can force England to come to terms. "But in

doing so," he advises his fellow-regent, "we would gain their eternal resentment for having taken advantage of their position, and our action would arise to haunt us—not only at the peace conference, but for a century to follow...."

To-day Colonel House knows that memories of nations are short. The Duumvir was impressed by the plea of such men as Lord Bryce, whom he honored highly, that German warfare had degenerated to the level of "savagery." A victorious Germany was a "challenge to mankind"!

When England, still extending her contraband list, wages war against American cotton, House insists that "a break with the Allies must be avoided. In no event," the Colonel writes, "should we take a course that will seriously endanger our friendly relations with Great Britain, France or Russia for ... our friendship with Germany is a matter of the past." Still mindful of Madison, Wilson agrees. But his patience is "worn to a frazzle."

Protests from the South, accelerated by German propagandists, pour in. Page suggests an understanding between American cotton growers and the British commercial attaché in Washington. England is willing to buy our cotton, but she is unwilling to yield to our arguments. Wilson, in a note to House, recommends the suggestion. This is hardly the attitude one would expect from the Sir Galahad in the White House. But Woodrow Wilson was a curiously contradictory personality. In dealing with him one must always be prepared for the unexpected.

The German controversy serves the purpose of the Duumvirs. "America," Wilson informs Bernstorff through House, "is not engaged in arranging passenger traffic, but in defending human rights." Knowing that they must adopt severe measures against England if Germany yields, the Duumvirs are not altogether displeased by the protracted correspondence with Berlin. Great Britain is amazed by the rumblings from Washington. "I am sorry beyond measure," House writes, "that it seems to be our part to be without friends on either side. We have been exceedingly patient with Great Britain, and have done as much as any neutral nation could to aid her without actually entering the War. On the other hand, the British have gone as far as they possibly could in violating our neutral rights, although they have done it in the most courteous way."

In this crisis any false step may be fatal. House, unable to endure the summers of Washington, cannot come to Wilson. Wilson does not dare to join House, because he fears to create the impression that he is not finding Bryan's successor, Robert Lansing, satisfactory. So Duumvir Wilson sends Lansing to Duumvir House and asks him to talk freely to the Secretary of State. Nothing illuminates more vividly the complete control of our foreign relations by the Duumvirate. The Secretary of State is compelled to go to Colonel House for instructions and information!

After a long talk with House, Lansing writes another note to Page. Page sees Sir Edward. The Foreign Secretary, as usual, comprehends the gravity of the situation, and, as usual, takes no action. To open trade to Germany or to the neutral countries about her would practically, he asserts, remove the economic pressure upon Germany and therefore prolong the War.

Wilson admitted that the argument was true but insisted that it did not satisfy the American Government. "How far," he asked House, "do you think they will yield?" He was determined to press for the utmost without seeming unreasonable.

In one of Wilson's letters to House written about this time, he trusts that the Colonel and the Secretary of State will evolve an "effective policy." He "hopes" that such an action will enable him to escape the "consequences" both he and House would "deplore." The state of public opinion is such that he "cannot long delay action." Even in private correspondence Wilson dare not express the thought in his mind. Incredible as it may seem to-day, in July, 1915, hardly ten weeks after the sinking of the *Lusitania,* Wilson trembles at the thought of "war with Great Britain."

Late in 1915 more trouble brews. England decided to arm her merchantmen. This made impossible the search of a merchantman by a submarine, upon which Mr. Wilson insisted. The Senate and the country were aroused against England. Lansing strongly backed the German argument that a merchantman, armed ostensibly only for defense, could sink a submarine. Lansing held that we could not hold the Germans responsible if, under such circumstances, they refrained from warning the victims. Wilson agreed with Lansing. It is hardly fair, he argued, to ask a submarine commander to give warning to some one if, when they approach as near as they must for that purpose, they are to be fired upon, as Balfour would evidently have them fired upon. The question gives the President some "perplexing moments."

House formally presents the American argument to Lord Reading. Lord Reading listens politely. But England continues to arm her merchantmen. House counsels Wilson that it is "inadvisable" to insist upon the American contention. His advice prevails. Some new trouble with Germany gives Lansing the excuse to withdraw gracefully. The shade of Madison can rest in peace. Once more Duumvir House has prevented a serious clash between England and the United States.

Poor Wilson is torn by conflicting emotions. Two souls dwell in his bosom. War with England or with Germany are the horns of his dilemma. He tries to escape from both by mediating between England and Germany. Every now and then his British ancestry stirs his blood. He surprises House by his vacillations and contradictions. "I have never been sure," he confides to his *alter ego,* one night late in September, 1915, "that we ought not to take part in the conflict. If it seems evident that Germany and her militaristic ideas are likely to win, the obligation upon us will be greater than ever."

Unhappily the British Ambassador was not eavesdropping when the President made this confession. Both Sir Cecil and Jusserand, to the annoyance of House, still reiterate in their reports home that the President is "pro-German."

Colonel House lost his temper only once throughout the World War. It was Sir Cecil Spring-Rice who furnished the provocation. "The Ambassador," House reveals, "started to talk in a very disagreeable way about the United States."

"I presume," declaimed Sir Cecil, "that the record will stand forever: when the laws of God and man are violated there is no protest from the United States, but when your oil and copper shipments are interfered with, you protest most vigorously."

House pointed out the number of protests sent to Germany. Sir Cecil, ignoring the Colonel's argument, lost his head completely. "No matter," he shouted, "how low our fortunes run, we will go to war before we will admit the principle of blockade as your Government wishes to interpret it. If we acquiesced, it would be all to the advantage of Germany, whom you seem to favor. Germany has neutral ports, like Malmö and Copenhagen, which are just as much German as Bremen or Hamburg, but Great Britain has none. And the rule you wish to lay down would isolate us in the event our enemies could blockade our coasts. On the other hand, no amount of blockade which Great Britain could bring to bear would shut off Germany."

"Why not submit the controversy to arbitration?" suggested House.

This infuriated the Ambassador. "At one time," he fumed, "this country was composed of pure rock. But now it is composed of mud, sand and some rock; and no one can predict how it will shift or in what direction."

As Sir Cecil's loquacity increased, House grew more and more taciturn. When the Ambassador calmed down at last, Bernstorff's name escaped from the Colonel's tongue.

"I would be glad," Sir Cecil gasped, "if you would not mention Bernstorff's name in my presence again. I do not want to talk to any one who has just come from talking to him or to Germans. At this moment I do not know how many of my relatives have been killed in England by the raid of the German Zeppelins last night."

This was pretty strong language for an Ambassador to address to the President's "other self." The vein in the Colonel's forehead stood out. His hands shook a little.

"I regard your remark as an insult and I will not permit you to say such things to me. You represent neither your Chief nor your Government. Your views are not their views. I know of no official anywhere who serves his country so badly as you."

"In that case," Spring-Rice replied, "I had better relinquish my post and go home."

"Use your own discretion. As far as I am concerned, I do not intend to have any further discussions with you."

Crestfallen, Spring-Rice humbly asked the Colonel's forgiveness. Sir Cecil stayed. He stayed, and he did not alter the tenor of his reports. Sir Edward Grey, alarmed by the Ambassador, complains: "It looks as if the United States might now strike the weapon of sea power out of our hands and thereby insure a German victory."

House takes Grey's letter to Wilson.

H O U S E : The United States cannot risk a German victory. We cannot continue to quarrel with both belligerents, with the Germans over submarine accidents, plots and propaganda, with the Allies over their restrictions of trade.

W I L S O N : Shall we ever get out of this labyrinth?

H O U S E : Only by adopting a positive policy.

This is the reply the Colonel's Dru would have given. House outlines his "positive" policy. It means American intervention. The Colonel embarks for England with Wilson's blessings, to present his idea, which assumes the shape of the Gentleman's Agreement, to Sir Edward Grey. While he discusses these matters in London, Wilson cannot press the Allies unduly. Once more the threatened break with the Allies is delayed. Fascinated by the intricate moves of European diplomacy, House, the Gentleman's Agreement in his pocket, enjoys the game for its own sake. Wilson prays for peace, Page for a German torpedo that, sinking another passenger boat with American women and children, will line up Uncle Sam against the Kaiser.

XX

WILSON CALLS THE ENGLISH "BOOBS"

When Gentlemen Disagree – The German Pot and the Allied Kettle – Grey Digs the Grave of an Empire – Lansing Dissects His Chief – The Turn of the Road – A Stingless Ultimatum – House Argues and Cajoles – Sir Edward's Note – The Rattle of the Skeletons

POOR Boobs!
This is what Wilson calls the English Government in a letter of July 27, 1916, to Colonel House. Hardly four months after he formally approved of a secret Gentleman's Agreement which practically assured an Allied victory, President Wilson is exceeding wroth with Great Britain. His notes to London are meticulously polite. But in his communications to Colonel House the President does not conceal his indignation. He is now on the point of demanding from Congress retaliatory powers against the British blockade of neutral commerce. The German Government having backed down in the submarine question, the various controversies with Great Britain which had slumbered while the dispute with Germany raged clamor for his attention.

The Gentleman's Agreement intended to bind the United States and England more closely together nearly precipitates a conflict. The obstinate refusal of the British Government to avail itself of Wilson's offer irritates the President intensely. It increases his suspicion of the selfishness of the Allies, and confirms his opinion that there is little to choose between the German pot and the Allied kettle.

"Doubtless," says Lansing, "the failure of Mr. Wilson to indorse without modification the tentative promise made by Colonel House as his representative had something to do with the British state of mind, so that the promise, destroyed of its value from the British point of view, hindered rather than helped in obtaining the object sought."

Sir Edward Grey very cleverly assured House that he could not take up the American offer with the French unless they first raised the topic. The French were careful not to permit the slightest whisper on the subject to escape their lips. The opportunity for bringing America into the War was passed over in silence. "Perhaps," Seymour says, "they hoped the German submarines would drive the United States into the War without conditions."

Sir Edward Grey's dilly-dallying may have been clever diplomacy. In the light of subsequent events, it was elephantine stupidity. It deceived House, it thwarted Wilson, and brought the British Empire to the verge of ruin. Peace would have averted the complete collapse of Central Europe and Russia. Not only the British Empire, but the entire economic fabric of the civilized world, would be sounder to-day if Sir Edward Grey and his colleagues had grasped the proffered hand of Woodrow Wilson. History may look upon Grey as the gravedigger of the British Empire. Great Britain owes her salvation, if she is to be saved, not to her diplomacy, but to the inherent strength of her people.

Lansing, moving in a fog of ignorance, where he heard only faint inklings of Wilson's peace plans, justifies the attitude of Great Britain. The Secretary of State was not in sympathy with his chief. "Though," he writes, "at the outset, the motive inspiring the efforts of Mr. Wilson was essentially impersonal, humanitarian and altruistic, I believe that the thought of his actual presence and participation in a conference to arrange terms of peace had appealed more and more strongly to him, until it had become, possibly unconsciously, an end rather than a means. One reason for this change of objective from mediation or good offices, with the object of bringing the parties together for the purpose of negotiation, to the injection of himself into the proceedings as a personal mediator in the conference was due, it would seem, to the President's determination to include in any negotiated peace provisions creating an international concord, association or league devoted to preventing future wars—a plan which Colonel House or Sir Edward Grey appears to have suggested and which Mr. Wilson strongly espoused."

Success, Lansing admits, would have made Wilson not only the leader of international thought but the preëminent personality in the history of modern times. He feels that Wilson's ambition overshadowed his desire for service. No one, least of all Wilson himself, could gauge all the perplexing forces that motivated his actions. Robert Lansing, like House, advocated America's entrance into the War on the side of Great Britain. He could not stomach Mr. Wilson's impatience with England.

By the middle of 1916, when the forthcoming Presidential election begins to loom large in the public mind, the correspondence with London becomes exceedingly acrid. Page, as usual, defends Great Britain. "Sir Edward and other men in high position," he writes to House, "are a good deal disturbed lest the American Government continue to harp on the blockade. They won't relax it; they can't."

What change had come over Woodrow Wilson?

Woodrow Wilson, according to House, felt that America had come to the turn in the road. The German question was no longer acute. We must now, he wrote to House, get down to "hard pan" with the Allies. "Altogether indefensible," were the words with which he characterized interference with neutral trade. "Intolerable" was his word for the looting of our mails on the high seas. His Irish blood, of which he was keenly conscious, revolted against the treatment meted out by the British Government to the Irish rebels.

Wilson believed that the United States must make a decided move for peace on a permanent basis. Failing in this, she must insist to the limit upon the recognition of her neutral rights. He was determined to defend the Freedom of the Seas with the same blunt speaking, the same indomitable firmness with which he had maintained our rights against von Tirpitz. This is the vein in which he talked and wrote to House. He felt that America's choice must be made at once. "Which," he asked, "does Great Britain prefer? She cannot escape both. Inaction is no longer possible."

The settlement the President proposed in no way involved

the United States in the territorial adjustment between the belligerents. Wilson then, as later, refused any material advantage for ourselves. We were, he deemed, in no sense a party to their quarrels. "In this," House remarks, "I did not agree with the Governor. But I entirely agreed with him when he said that our primary interest was to secure permanent peace, based upon a universal alliance assuring the freedom of the seas and outlawing all wars begun in violation of treaty rights and without preliminary warning. He included in his program the idea promulgated by Bryan of a 'cooling-off period' before the sword would be unsheathed. He proposed a new world resting upon mutual guarantees of political independence and territorial integrity."

"It is imperative," Wilson impressed upon House, "that Sir Edward should understand all this. The crisis cannot be postponed."

House immediately prepared a cable embodying the President's suggestions. Unfortunately, House weakened Wilson's idea by embodying in his note the statement that he [Wilson] did not insist upon an *immediate* peace conference. This robbed the note of its effectiveness. It was no longer an ultimatum.

Mr. Wilson called the message "admirable," and said there was nothing which he could add or wished to take away. The English, he insisted, had been "blindly stupid" in the policy they had pursued on the seas. Now they "must take the consequences." He doubted that they would be "either able or willing to be evenhanded" with us in the trade rivalry which must inevitably ensue after the War.

In his letters to Wilson, House, while deploring the utter selfishness of governments, fans Wilson's hopes of peace. "Gratitude," he writes, "is a thing unknown, and all we have done for the Allies will be forgotten overnight if we antagonize them now. Nevertheless, I am convinced that it is your duty to press for a peace conference with all the power at your command—for whether they like it or whether they do not, I believe you can bring it about."

Wilson meant business. Determined to speak his mind before the League to Enforce Peace, the President sweeps aside the Duumvir's contention that the European nations would not consider the establishment of an international tribunal at this time. How else, he asks, can we secure the deliberate consideration of all situations that may threaten war and lay a foundation for the concerted actions of nations against "unjustifiable breaches of the peace of the world?" Wilson feels that the only "inducement" the United States can hold out to the Entente is one which will actually remove "the menace of militarism."

In this spirit, House drafts a number of suggestions for the President's speech of May 27, 1916. Wilson closely follows the argument of his Duumvir. But he lends to the Colonel's logic the wings of eloquence. His keynote is a plea for a new international morality. "It is clear that nations must in the future be governed by the same high code of honor that we demand of individuals.... The principle of public right must henceforth take precedence over the individual interests of particular nations."

House argues and cajoles to secure the adhesion of the Allies to Wilson's plan. "England and France seem to think that the cooperation America is willing to give them in a just settlement of the vexatious questions that are sure to follow peace does not outweigh the doubtful advantage they would gain if Germany were completely crushed. It seems certain if this happens a new set of problems will arise to vex us all. Your seeming lack of desire to coöperate with us will chill the enthusiasm here—never, I am afraid, to come again, at least in our day. There is a fortunate conjunction of circumstances which makes it possible to bring about the advancement and maintenance of world-wide peace and security, and it is to be hoped that the advantage may not be lost. If it is, the fault will not lie with us."

House did all that was possible. In a note written on the same day on which the President made his speech (before the League), he called Sir Edward's attention to the statement of the German Chancellor that Germany would make peace on the basis of the *status quo*. "This," he suggested, "cannot mean anything except a victorious peace for Germany. If England and France, under our invitation, should go into a peace conference now, it would probably lead either to Germany's abandonment of this position or war with us."

Sir Edward replied that he could not act without the consent of France. "No Englishman," he wrote to House, "would at this moment say to France, after Poincaré's and Briand's speeches: 'Hasn't the time come to make peace?'"

Sir Edward Grey suggested that the United States should negotiate directly with France in order to impress the French Government with its good faith. House sought out Jusserand. But the French Ambassador pooh-poohed any suggestion of peace. The Allies as well as the Germans under-estimated our strength. And in Allied closets and cupboards rattled the skeletons of their secret treaties.

XXI

WAR WITH GREAT BRITAIN!

Campaign Hysteria – The Plaint of Captain Guy Gaunt – "The Last Straw"!
– A Club for the President – The Irritation of Colonel House – Page Chides
the Administration – British Bourbons Will Not Budge – Wilson at the
Breaking Point – The Ghost of Madison Stalks Once More

THE Presidential campaign of 1916 unleashes storms of hysteria. The slogan "He kept us out of war" enrages the Allies. The British Naval Attaché, Captain Guy Gaunt, one of the most romantic figures in modern British diplomacy, tells House that his country, Australia, had always looked upon the United States as her ideal. "Now," he says, "she bitterly resents your not entering the War. I have a letter from a friend stating that in the future Australia will purchase from Germany rather than from the United States. There is the same deep undercurrent of feeling in France. The Allies are resolved that America shall not take part in the peace conference."

It almost seems as if the Allies are bent upon forcing a break. In the very midst of the campaign, England issues a black list of American firms with whom English subjects are forbidden to trade. British steamships and British merchants are compelled to boycott the firms thus proscribed. Neutral lines accepting freight from the suspects are denied bunker coal in British ports. Intimidated, neutral bankers deny loans to the blacklisted firms. The British Government uses the black list to coerce American merchants into submission. Practically no ship could leave an American port without a release from the British consul. Practically no merchandise could be shipped from any American harbor without the sanction of Great Britain.

The country rumbled angrily. But no one was angrier than

Wilson. "The Black List," he exclaimed, "is the last straw. I am at the end of my patience with the Allies!" He said this not in public; he confided it in private to Colonel House. The President and the legal adviser of the State Department, Frank L. Polk, had Spring-Rice and Jusserand on the carpet. "Both," Wilson writes to House, "considered the Black List a stupid blunder."

Wilson, like Madison in the same quandary, seriously considers the advisability of legislative action to restrict exportations. The measure he contemplates includes the proscription of loans. In the intimacy of his confidences with House, Wilson reiterates the suspicion that England's policy is not based solely upon the desire to win the War, but upon the wish to prevent American merchants from securing a foothold in markets hitherto controlled by Great Britain. He is "compounding" a very sharp note with Polk. He may feel obliged to make it as "sharp and final" as the one to Germany on the submarines. "What," he asks, "is your own judgment? Can we any longer endure their intolerable course?"

To House the Allied action seemed a criminal folly. But considering war with England even more foolish and more criminal, he once more thrusts himself into the breach. He advises Wilson to let Jusserand and Spring-Rice inform their governments of the contemplated embargo unless the Allies immediately toe the mark. This was in the last week of July. By August no reply was forthcoming. Polk, under the circumstances, sees no possible reprisal except retaliatory legislation. He considers this legislation a "club" for Great Britain. House reluctantly admits that a club may be needed.

The following month, Congress grants the President drastic retaliatory powers and votes prodigious naval appropriations, the largest, Seymour asserts, ever passed by any legislative body of a state not at war. The contemplated program will wrest the trident from the hands of Great Britain. It makes America the second, maybe the first, naval power. Like Madison before him, Wilson is now in the mood to assert our rights on the high seas by force. His prophecy is on the road to fulfillment. Every day the parallel becomes more deadly.

House sees the whole structure of Anglo-American coöperation tumbling. He pleads with Wilson and enlarges upon the peril of disputing with Great Britain the mastery of the seas. House remembers his interview with the Kaiser. He sees America in the rôle cast for Germany. Spain, Holland, Napoleonic France, Portugal, Germany, one by one, challenged the naval supremacy of Great Britain. One by one they fell.

Is America next?

Wilson, unmoved by the arguments of the Duumvir, is prepared to face the consequences. Overcoming his inertia, he now spurs himself and recalls Page to give his Ambassador a dose of Americanism. Never since 1812 had the United States been closer to war with Great Britain!

Duumvir House does not conceal his fears from Woodrow Wilson. "Our only difference with Great Britain now is that the United States is undertaking to build a great navy. We are rapidly taking the position Germany occupied before the War. No one in England would probably admit it, but the growing irritation against us is underneath."

"Then," Wilson replied, "let us build a navy bigger than hers and do what we please." House notes this reply in his diary. He also notes his conviction that the British would not permit the United States to build a navy equal to theirs, if they could prevent it.

The situation is getting under the Colonel's skin. "It is impossible," he tells a British visitor, "to satisfy the Allies. If we went into the War, the Allies, after welcoming us warmly and praising us beyond our deserts, would later, when they found we were not furnishing as many men, chide us just as the French did the English, and say that we were not spilling our blood, that we were shirkers."

Irritated, House forces the reluctant admission from Page that England would have taken arms against Germany, even if France rather than Germany had "violated" poor little Belgium! Drawing a parallel between the United States and Germany, he writes to Page: "Before the War the friendship between Great Britain and Germany was traditional until Germany began to cut into British trade and plan a navy large enough to become formidable. I wonder if England does not see us as a similar menace both as to their trade and supremacy of the seas." Page dissents.

On one point, however, he agrees with House. "Great Britain will never allow America to have a navy equal or superior to theirs. If we build, they will build more, although," the Ambassador adds, "they would do so in a friendly spirit."

Thoroughly aroused, Page chides the Administration. "The relations between England and the United States," he snarls, "would have been better if America had acted differently."

House, retaining his perennial calm, recapitulates to Page the number of ways in which the United States has shown friendship and partiality for the Allies. "And what," he asks, "is the result? Our relations are worse now than in the beginning of the War. If we sent Ambassador Bernstorff home and entered the War, we would be applauded for a few weeks and then they would demand money. If the money was forthcoming, they would be satisfied for a period, but later would demand an unlimited number of men. If," the Duumvir concludes prophetically, "we did it all they would finally accuse us of trying to force them to give better terms to Germany than were warranted."

British Bourbons, though beset by trouble in Ireland, refuse to budge from their position. England has learned and forgotten nothing since 1812. The ruthless suppression of the Irish Easter Rebellion provokes resentment in the United States. Resolutions expressing sympathy with the Irish are adopted in the United States Senate. The sentiment to meet force by force takes root on Capitol Hill. The Government seriously contemplates a convoy of warships for American merchantmen through long lanes on the ocean, grimly guarded by British dreadnaughts and British cruisers. That means the instant collapse of the blockade upon which the Allies stake their hope of victory, or—war.

While Wilson was almost exploding with indignation, the pro-Germans throughout the country looked upon him as the supine tool of the Allies, smirkingly consenting to every violation of American rights. This was the situation three weeks before the election, while the pro-Germans led by *The Fatherland*, assaulted Wilson as the pawn of Great Britain, and Jeremiah O'Leary, one of the leaders of the irreconcilable Irish, sent jeering telegrams to the White House. Wilson felt that he was indeed "sailing in deep waters." Had he kept us out of war with Germany merely to hurl us precipitately into war with Great Britain?

Some friends of England recognized the peril. Frederick Dixon, editor of the *Christian Science Monitor*, calls on House at the request of the British Ambassador. "Dixon," writes House in his notebook, "believes the tension is greater than we realize. He had long talks when he was in England with both Grey and Cecil, and while Grey was moderate, as usual, Cecil said: 'If we attempted to put such measures into effect, it would probably mean breaking off diplomatic relations and the withdrawing of all trade.'"

Spring-Rice adds fuel to the conflagration by intimating in London that the United States is spoiling for a row. To add diversity to our difficulties, the German submarine *U-53* sinks six vessels with contraband for the Allies off our coast.

All England is in turmoil over the matter. Lord Grey threatens reprisal. "If," he tells Page, "a German submarine be allowed by the American Government to sink neutral ships so near to American waters, the British Prime Minister will push the British Government to search neutral ships for contraband in the same waters."

"There is," Ambassador Page telegraphs to Secretary Lansing on October 18, 1916, "abundant confirmation of fierce public feeling. The subject is the prevailing topic of conversation everywhere."

The *U-53* conformed scrupulously to international law, but Captain Guy Gaunt is beside himself. House reports Guy Gaunt's remarks to the President. The President replies: "If our relations with England should be imperiled, as Captain Guy Gaunt seems to think possible, it would only be another illustration of how difficult it is to be friendly with Great Britain without doing whatever she wants us to do."

Once more the ghost of Madison walks through the White House.

XXII

IF HUGHES HAD BEEN ELECTED—

Secrets of the Campaign of 1916 – Wilson Decides to Resign If Defeated –
Anglicizing the Constitution – The Doubts of Justice Hughes – Polk Confirms
House – Gregory's Story – Wilson's Lost Letter

"I SHALL resign if Hughes is elected!"

Fearing war with either England or Germany, uncertain
if the people will abide by his decision, Woodrow Wilson deter-
mines to give up the Presidency some five months before his term
expires, if the election of 1916 should go against him. It was
House who inspired his bold decision. Wilson never acknowledged
that he owed the Presidency to House. But he was ready to relinquish it at his bidding. Surely no ruler, ancient or modern,
ever placed himself more completely in the hands of a friend!

Ellen Axson Wilson, the wife of his youth, had lain in her
grave these many months. Edith Bolling Wilson reigned in the
heart of President Wilson. His mind was dominated by his
Duumvir. The one shadow that interposed itself between the two
friends was temporarily banished: House no longer pressed for
immediate armed intervention. Yielding to political expediency
and Wilson's wishes, the Duumvir acquiesced in the battlecry of
Woodrow Wilson's campaign—"He kept us out of war!"

No one knew better than House how resolutely the face of
the President was set against entangling the United States in
Europe's quarrel. The war sentiment, in the East at least, was so
noisy that it seemed possible that he would court defeat on this
issue. House, ever ingenious, saw the possibility of snatching victory from defeat. Even a beaten Wilson could seize the spotlight
from Hughes. His resignation would make constitutional history.
No President of the United States had ever resigned. Wilson de-

lighted in creating new precedents. Neither of the Duumvirs acknowledges the vassalage of tradition. It was Wilson's dramatic instinct that impelled him to revive the ancient custom of addressing Congress in person. And what could have been more dramatic than his resignation, if the verdict of the people had been thumbs down against him?

We have already seen that the theory of government in the minds of the Duumvirs was English rather than American. More flexible, more responsive to the electorate, it disavows the system of checks and balances which upholds, and sometimes holds up, the government of the United States. The Colonel's hero, Philip Dru, dwells on the shortcomings of the American Constitution. Wilson never concealed his preference for the British theory. Both Duumvirs labored to make the Presidency a more positive force in government. Wilson considered himself a Premier rather than a President. Kings, unless death terminates their reign, wear their crowns until they are dethroned or decapitated. Presidents, barring impeachment or demise, hold their office until their term expires. A British Premier, if defeated, returns to the people that which is the people's. Wilson preferred the rôle of Premier to the rôle of President.

Some fifteen years later the New York *Times* scoffed at the story of Wilson's proposed resignation. It intimated that Wilson had no notion of resigning and that Hughes would not have accepted the offer, because he could not form a government in the short time at his disposal between the election and his inauguration.

Skeptics to the contrary, Wilson's mind was made up. The President had committed himself to the plan in writing. The first reference to the amazing action contemplated by the Duumvirs appears in the diary of Colonel House, October 19, 1916. "It occurred to me yesterday to suggest to the President, in the event of his defeat, to ask both Marshall and Lansing to resign, and then appoint Hughes Secretary of State. He should then resign himself, making Hughes President of the United States. Times are too critical to have an interim of four months between the election and inauguration of the next President...."

"The defect in our government shows itself here, and its

negative quality (as I pointed out in *Philip Dru*) is a source of weakness at such times."

The next day Colonel House unfolds his idea to the President.

DEAR GOVERNOR:

. . . If Hughes is elected—which God forbid—what do you think of asking both Lansing and Marshall to resign, appoint Hughes Secretary of State, and then resign yourself? This would be a patriotic thing to do. . . .

Such a procedure would save the situation from danger and embarrassment. . . .

Affectionately yours,

E. M. HOUSE.

Attorney-General Gregory, with whom House discussed his suggestion, was startled into silence, but, after consideration, gave his unqualified approval. Polk, who heard of it a week later, was deeply impressed. "Lansing," House reports, "was somewhat staggered at first, but recovered himself and finally expressed approval. He said he had worried considerably over the thought of the interim between November 7th and March 4th in the event of the President's defeat, but the way would be immediately cleared if the President would do as I advised."

Two weeks after the election:

H O U S E: Had you made up your mind before election to follow my suggestion about resigning?

W I L S O N: Absolutely. Your suggestion was in line with my lifetime views upon the subject. I took the precaution to write Lansing before the election in order to put myself on record so that I could not be charged with doing something hastily or from pique.

H O U S E: How soon would you have resigned?

W I L S O N: Immediately.

"By immediately," House explains, "was meant just as soon as the result of the election was definitely known. It seems," the Colonel goes on to say, "that during the uncertain hours of Tuesday night, November 7th, both the President and Mrs. Wilson were cheered, as I was, by the thought of the dramatic dénouement we had in mind in the event of defeat."

Would Charles Evans Hughes have accepted the Presidency in such a fashion? I ventured to bring the matter to the attention of Mr. Hughes. Mr. Hughes considered it "most unlikely that the President, on reflection, would have taken any such action." The Chief Justice did not wish to comment upon the hypothetical suggestion or attempt to say what he should have done had the offer been made. This is entirely in accordance with the cautious and judicial attitude of Mr. Hughes—the quality which makes him an excellent Chief Justice, and has cost him the Presidency.

"Do you think Hughes would have had sufficient time to organize a government for the balance of Wilson's term?" I asked House.

"Why not? The Prime Ministers of England, Germany, France and other countries form governments immediately after an election. Mr. Hughes would have considered himself as competent to do this as any foreign Prime Minister. He could have reappointed Lansing, and made every other change at his leisure."

"Was it Wilson's intention to establish a precedent in line with the British theory of government?"

"Wilson's views on parliamentary government were well known. However, I neither made, nor did he accept, my suggestion with the object of tinkering with the American Constitution. The country was in a critical state. Any day might necessitate action. Defeat would have bound Wilson's hands. If Germany had resumed her unrestricted warfare in November as she did in February, what action could Mr. Wilson have taken without embarrassing his successor?

"Frank Polk, Gregory and Lansing all knew of Wilson's intention. Wilson also told me that he put himself on record in a letter to Lansing."

Unfortunately the recollections of Mr. Lansing, published since his death, show no reference to such a letter, and Colonel House has looked in vain in his own papers for some statement from Wilson in reply to his suggestion. Luckily Frank L. Polk, then Counsellor in the State Department, remembers. "I do know," he writes to me, "that Mr. Wilson was planning to resign in 1916 in the event of Mr. Hughes' winning the election. The person I imagine who knows most about this incident except, of course, Colonel House, is the Hon. Thomas W. Gregory who was Attorney-General at the time and who had looked into the constitutional questions involved."

Gregory fully confirms the recollections of Polk and House. This is Gregory's story:

"I went to New York on the day of the National Election in the fall of 1916 and that night I went to the apartment of Colonel House where we received the most discouraging news up to about 10:00 o'clock; it was then apparent that Wilson had lost Illinois by an enormous majority and everything indicated the election of Hughes; the New York *World* and the *Times* had at that hour conceded the election of Hughes and we were both satisfied that the result was as just indicated.

"Colonel House then stated that in case Wilson was defeated he would be discredited at home and abroad and in the then very critical condition of foreign affairs it would be very unfortunate to have the United States represented by a man who had just been discredited and repudiated by his people; I entirely agreed with the views Colonel House expressed; we discussed the method of bringing about Wilson's practically immediate retirement and the succession of Hughes and the plan was this:

"To talk the matter over with Vice-President Marshall and secure his acquiescence; the President to ask for the resignation of Lansing and appoint Judge Hughes Secretary of State in place of the latter; Marshall to resign as Vice-President and Mr. Wilson as President, and Hughes would then automatically succeed to the office and the responsibilities of the hour, backed by the result of the election in his favor.

"I think it was about 10:30 that Colonel House and I went down to the Library of the Lawyers' Club in New York in order that I might carefully examine the provisions of the Constitution and any Acts of Congress bearing on the problem and see if what we had in mind could legally be done; after doing this my conclusion was that the plan was legal and desirable. We parted about 11:00 o'clock that night with the understanding that we would catch an early train to the summer home of President Wilson in New Jersey and go over the entire situation with him.

"I retired about 11:30 that night and when I awakened the next morning I rang Colonel House up to determine on what train we would leave for New Jersey, and Colonel House then told me there was no necessity for going down there, that we had won the election and that the wires which reached him, after we parted the night before and he had returned to his apartment, were to the effect that Wilson had carried California, Vermont and probably Minnesota; the New York daily papers, actually printed that morning, indicated this result and reversed the conclusions printed in their issues of the night before to the effect that Mr. Hughes had won. I stayed in New York several days longer and was in frequent conference with Colonel House until it seemed certain beyond a reasonable doubt that we had won and I then returned to Washington.

"I have no recollection of having had a conversation with President Wilson about this plan, either before or after the incident above set out. I have a recollection that on the night of the conference in New York with Colonel House above described, or thereafter, Colonel House told me that Mr. Wilson would probably pursue, or would have pursued, the course Colonel House and I had discussed, since he was a strong advocate of the practice of the British Government by virtue of which the loss of an election resulted in an immediate change in the governing party."

But where was that letter to Lansing? Had it escaped Wilson's mind? Had he intended to write it and then forgotten? Had he mailed it to Washington while Lansing was in New York and had the letter mysteriously disappeared from Mr. Lansing's files? Further investigation developed the fact that Wilson had kept his promise to House. The letter to Lansing was written. The original of the letter is now in the possession of Mrs. Lansing. The metropolitan newspaper which had printed the editorial denying the authenticity of the story obtained a photostat of the document from Mrs. Lansing's attorney. But neither Mrs. Lansing nor the newspaper in question was able to secure from Mrs. Wilson permission to print the letter.

The incident illuminates the psychology of both Wilson and House. Its verification establishes beyond doubt or cavil the painstaking accuracy of the recollections of him who shared with Wilson the government of the United States. It also establishes the fact that Wilson himself did not cling to the Presidency. He placed the interest of his country above his own tenure of office. He was willing to lay down the Chief Magistracy of the Republic if the people had decided against him in the election of 1916. He again, as we shall presently see, considered resignation before the United States entered the conflict because he doubted his own ability to steer the ship of state in the hurricane of war. Is there any doubt that Woodrow Wilson would have resigned after the stroke that incapacitated him, if he had been himself, and not controlled by others? But after Wichita, Wilson was no longer the master of his fate. Fate assumed the placid but determined features of Edith Bolling Wilson.

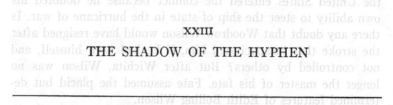

XXIII

THE SHADOW OF THE HYPHEN

Wily Strategy – House Picks a Chairman – A Voice in the Wilderness – How
Presidents Are Made – Wilson's Postmaster General Woos Pro-Germans –
The Hoax That Fooled Roosevelt – The Winning of the West by Woodrow
Wilson

HOUSE had planned the campaign of 1916 too well to make
it necessary for Wilson to resort to a melodramatic exit.
"The strategy of the Democrats," remarks Roosevelt's friend,
Henry L. Stoddard, "was masterful.... The East was abandoned
as 'the enemy's country,' as Bryan had termed it in 1896, but,
more shrewd than Bryan, the 1916 campaigners did not advertise
the fact. Wilson staked his hope of election on his ability to
persuade the West that war sentiment was an Atlantic seaboard
affair and that Hughes was its candidate. He linked Roosevelt
as certain, if Hughes was elected, to plunge us into war, a charge
bound to make an impression, for the two men could not disavow
each other."

At one point of the campaign, before the nomination of
Hughes, Samuel Untermyer told Stoddard that Wilson would
prefer Roosevelt to Hughes as his opponent. Stoddard repeated
the remark to Colonel Roosevelt.

"I refuse to believe that the people out there are pacifists
or that they will endorse Wilson's flabby policy," Roosevelt
snarled.

"But, Colonel," Stoddard persisted, "Wilson's people have
studied the situation carefully and really believe it. They believe
it so much that they would rather have had you nominated. They
feel certain they could defeat you."

"That," Roosevelt retorted sarcastically, "would be the

156

keenest humiliation I could suffer. But Wilson would have a fight on his hands before he licked me."

Being an amateur in politics himself, Wilson at times over-estimated the professional politician. In the beginning of the campaign, the President wanted as Chairman of the National Committee an old-timer, not a high-brow. House, with uncanny political foresight, preferred a newcomer and an amateur. His choice was Vance McCormick.

At the last minute, before the meeting of the Democratic Convention, Wilson implored House to take the job himself. House refused. Wilson admits that House was right. "I was," he explains, "so desperate to get a man I can absolutely trust to judge and act rightly that I for the moment yielded to temptation and asked you."

Once more the Duumvir scores. McCormick is made Chair-man, to the surprise of the politicians. Football, as Seymour points out, had taught McCormick the strategy of the unexpected. He was admirably fitted to carry out the plan of campaign de-signed to catch the progressive vote and to concentrate the main Democratic effort in a few doubtful States.

Wilson reveals a curious apprehension of any foreign sup-port. He does not wish a situation where it appears that Hughes is Germany's candidate and he is the candidate of the Allies. He hopes that the belligerents can be persuaded to let American politics alone. Mr. Wilson troubles himself in vain. He has no friends in either camp. He continues to plead for peace in the hope that his speeches will "soak in" on the other side. In spite of the pro-war sentiment of the metropolitan press, a congenial atmosphere greets the President at a dinner of the New York Press Club. The atmosphere seems to him thoughtfully serious, the sentiment genuine and friendly to him and his policies.

Wilson is not, in the beginning of the campaign, disquieted by doubts of his reëlection. Leaving his personal policies in the hands of his adviser, he concentrates upon Mexico and Europe. He fears that a break with Mexico is "unavoidable" and that all his patience has been in vain. The thought makes him "infinitely sad." He admits that he may have made an error of judgment in not drawing Pershing and his command northward after Villa had slipped through his fingers. He cannot, in looking back, see how he could have acted other than he did. Right or wrong, he feels, the "extreme consequences" seem upon us. But he insists that there shall be no intervention either now or at any other time, if he can prevent it. He desires war neither with Mexico nor with Europe. The Powers at war, he sadly reflects, are in danger of forgetting the rest of the world. He feels that the world at large has a positive right to be heard about peace and reiterates his intention to make an imperative suggestion which neither side can afford to ignore, because the desire of all peoples will be behind it.

He discusses all these problems in a long letter to House, whose friendship alone sustains him. Sadly, wistfully, he concludes: "Good night. God bless you!"

Colonel House divided the country into the smallest possible units. In each unit local workers were to segregate certain Republican and certain Democratic voters. "Roughly speaking," House said, "we must assume that in a unit of 100,000 voters 80% of them will be unchangeable voters, which would leave 20% that can be influenced by argument." It was the suggestion of House to confine the campaign largely to the 20% in question. "We must run the President for Justice of the Peace, not for President; we need not consider the disposition of sixteen or seventeen million voters, but the disposition of the voters in individual precincts."

The Colonel prepared a list of States which Wilson was certain to carry. Events proved that he made no mistake in his calculation. He also made a list of States which the President must carry to be elected. This list included California.

House mapped out the general strategy of the campaign. The detailed organization was in the hands of Daniel C. Roper of Washington. House considered Roper one of the finest political minds in the United States. Mr. Roper worked in close harmony with Vance McCormick and with the Duumvir. Duumvir House remained in the background. His plans included a great campaign rally for Wilson at Madison Square Garden. He walked up to the Garden on the night of the meeting. He was gratified to find that everything had been arranged according to schedule.

Mr. Belasco could have devised his effects with no greater precision. The Garden was packed to the doors. The demonstrations, the cheering, were in accordance with stage directions. He looked in to hear the cheering and then went home. The newspapers reported that it was the biggest demonstration ever given to a President or a candidate for the Presidency in the history of New York.

Mr. Wilson never knew what hand manipulated the "spontaneous" enthusiasm that greeted him. "The President," Colonel House notes in his diary, "thought organization amounted to nothing, and that the people determined such matters themselves. If he had been in politics as long as I have, and knew it from the point of a worker rather than as a candidate, he would understand how easy it is to change the vote of a State in one way or another. To hear him talk, you would think the man in the street understood the theory and philosophy of government as he does and was actuated by the same motives."

Unlike Wilson, House was not worried by the pro-German vote. "The Germans," he told Bernstorff, "are mostly Republican." Nevertheless, strenuous efforts were made to influence the pro-Germans in favor of Wilson. The shadow of the hyphen hung over the campaign of 1916. The National Committee offered to buy one million copies of my magazine, *The Fatherland*, in case it printed an article by James K. McGuire, former Mayor of Syracuse, which asked certain embarrassing questions of Mr. Hughes. A speech by Mr. Hughes, virtually answering McGuire's questions, compelled me to reject the offer. The article was never printed. Postmaster General Burleson told me at Democratic Headquarters in New York City: "I have lived so long among Germans in Texas that I almost feel as if I were a German myself. I experience a sinking in my heart every time I hear of a German defeat." Burleson was regarded as the only pro-German in the Cabinet. When the turn came, this very reputation impelled him to lean far in the other direction.

Count Bernstorff tried, so far as was possible within the limits of diplomatic propriety, to aid the plans of Colonel House. He asked me to stop *The Fatherland's* vitriolic attacks upon Wilson. He based his request ostensibly not upon any desire to influence the election, but upon the fact that the attacks of *The Fatherland* embarrassed his relations with the State Department. Every denunciation of the Administration which I printed was attributed to poor Bernstorff. I was sorry for the Ambassador, but I could not permit my regard for him to interfere with my civic duty. I was a pro-German, true, but I was an American first. Bernstorff, chagrined, told Colonel House: "It is utterly impossible to influence the rabid German-American vote in any way. They are more pro-German than the Germans themselves. To argue with them is futile. They have conceived the idea that the President has branded them as disloyal and they will take their revenge by voting for Hughes."

If only Bernstorff could have told the truth, if he could have revealed the secret negotiations then going on between him and the Duumvirs! But on that point his lips were sealed. In spite of myself, Bernstorff's plea made me pause. I considered the Ambassador the dupe of the Duumvirs. Nevertheless, I might be mistaken. That uncertainty moderated, in some degree, my own attacks on Wilson. The same influence, emanating by the grapevine route, undoubtedly chilled the frantic enthusiasm of many pro-Germans for Hughes. To that extent Woodrow Wilson owes his success at the polls to Bernstorff. His word may have been the grain that tipped the scale against Justice Hughes. In the last analysis, the result depended on fewer than 4,000 votes in California. *The Fatherland* alone had more than 4,000 readers in Hiram Johnson's State. No whisper from Bernstorff would have influenced the anti-British and the pro-German vote if Hughes had not been handicapped by the support of Theodore Roosevelt.

A committee composed of certain pro-German and certain pro-Irish leaders, including Carl E. Schmidt, later president of the Steuben Society, and Jeremiah O'Leary, spokesman of the extreme left wing of the Irish, called upon Hughes and received from him certain assurances which satisfied them that he would hold an even balance between the warring nations. When he promised in Springfield that he would stand "four-square to all nations" and repeated his declaration emphatically at the Academy of Music in Philadelphia, even the skeptical Daniel F.

Cohalan, head of the Clan-na-Gael, joined the Hughes camp with flying colors. When Hughes said at Philadelphia that he did not propose to tolerate any improper interference with American property, with American mails or with legitimate commercial intercourse and that no American who was exercising only American rights should be put on any black list by any foreign nation, he stated an unassailable American doctrine. The pro-Germans who cheered Mr. Hughes did not realize that Mr. Wilson, in his private communications to Colonel House and in his official protests to London, defended American rights with even greater vehemence. They did not know that we were actually on the verge of a breach with Great Britain.

Hughes was entirely ignorant of the dickerings between Republican headquarters and the pro-Germans. "If," Mr. Hughes insists in a statement to me, "history is to be correctly written, it would appear that I had no secret understandings, that I had nothing to do with any intrigues, that I made no promises, but that I stated them to all comers, the committee in question included, but that I made no promise to that committee and did not swerve from my attitude either to please them or their opponents."

Roosevelt played the Mephisto to Hughes' Faust. His truculent war-whoops outshouted the calm judicial pronouncements of the Republican candidate. Mr. Hughes did not dare to pick a quarrel with Roosevelt, for fear of being denounced as pro-German by the Rough Rider. Mr. Hughes did not know that Theodore Roosevelt himself had made an ineffectual bid for the support of the pro-Germans. The episode involved Professor Münsterberg, who, distrusting both Hughes and Wilson, was convinced that Theodore Roosevelt was the one man who could bring to a speedy end the slaughter in Europe. He arranged a meeting between Roosevelt and myself. Mr. Roosevelt had been my friend before the War. Since the War we had crossed swords on several occasions. Roosevelt frankly told me that he considered a German victory a peril to the United States. In that respect the two Colonels, House and Roosevelt, were of one mind.

"The Kaiser," Roosevelt insisted, "is plotting against the United States."

"What proof have you of such a plot?" I asked.

Theodore Roosevelt turned to his desk and shuffled among his papers until he found what he sought.

"Right here," he shouted, "I have the evidence. I told no other German-American why I am against Germany. I shall tell you because you have been my friend. I hold here a copy of the plan of the German General Staff for the invasion of the United States. If Germany wins, America will be the next objective of her aggression."

I pointed out that I could not visualize the German army swimming across the ocean, seeing that they were unable even to cross the channel. But Mr. Roosevelt remained impervious to my argument.

The alleged plan for a German attack on the United States was published after the entrance of the United States into the War. Both Emperor William and General Ludendorff have told me that it was a clumsy forgery. Forgery or not, the spurious plan infuriated Roosevelt and doomed at birth Münsterberg's plan to consolidate German-American sentiment behind the Rough Rider. The only tie between them and Roosevelt was their common hatred of Wilson. When, in the course of the conversation, I mentioned Mr. Wilson and Mr. McAdoo, the Colonel's jaw snapped. "The shepherd and his crook—" he interjected, in the falsetto voice which he assumed on occasion. With the Germans and the Irish aligned against him, Roosevelt was no longer available as a candidate. The battle remained between Wilson and Hughes.

The betting odds throughout the campaign favored the Justice. Gregory has told how, on Election Day, Democratic hopes crumbled. The pivotal States, one by one, went against Wilson. Colonel House, knowing that only morning could bring a final decision, went to bed calmly. The Colonel's ability to withdraw into his shell on occasion accounts for his amazing vitality. Physical frailty taught him how to safeguard his health. A stronger man would have perished under the burdens of the Duumvirate. Seven times he crossed submarine infested seas in the interest of peace. His life preserver beside him, he fell quietly asleep while other passengers walked the deck, watching for periscopes. The calm which served him in the war zone enabled him to rest while the crowds on Broadway celebrated the election of Hughes.

Hughes went to bed that night as President-elect. Wilson went to bed believing that he was defeated, and wondering how the country would take his determination to resign in favor of Hughes. Perhaps he also wondered what would be the fate of the Gentleman's Agreement which he had concluded with Sir Edward Grey. Would Hughes regard himself bound by it? Would the Allies accept from Hughes what they had rejected when it was presented to them on a golden platter by Wilson?

The next morning showed that the West was the pivot of this election. "At daybreak," the Colonel writes in his diary, "the returns began to come in from the Far West favorable to us, and it became evident that the election was to be a close one. I immediately got in touch with Headquarters, where a force had been on duty all night, and advised them to send telegrams to the county chairmen of every doubtful State, urging them to be vigilant and to pay no attention to press reports that Hughes was elected. I called up the *World* and other newspapers, as well as the United Press and urged them to undo, as far as possible, the harm done by the morning press in conceding everything to Hughes. I was afraid if this was not done, everything would go by default, and the States which we carried in the West by close margins would be neglected and we might be robbed of victory."

"Did you," I asked, "think that Hughes would be elected?"

"There was," the Colonel replied, "every chance that he would be. The election hinged on 3,777 votes in California. Normally, this country is Republican. Hughes would have been elected if he had stayed in Washington. But his failure to propitiate Hiram Johnson insured the election of Wilson. I later told his campaign leaders that it would be only fair if we paid for his California trip."

"Did you think on the night of November 7, 1916, that Wilson was beaten?"

"Most of us did. I refused to share in the general gloom. Before the final day, Wilson had firmly believed in his reëlection. I had my doubts. On Election Day, Wilson's hopes sank. My hopes revived when I saw that we had carried Ohio. I believed we had won, even if the margin of victory was slim. The closeness of the election was a shock to Wilson."

"It seems strange that you did not spend that critical night with him."

House smiled.

"Wilson was staying at Shadow Lawn, where he had spent the summer. I was needed more in New York. Much as I detest drudgery, I could not escape it entirely and my place was at the long-distance wire."

"Do you think," I asked, "that Hughes, unlike Wilson, would have kept us out of war if he had been elected?"

"I don't think so. Germany's actions made war almost inevitable. Hughes would have been compelled to draw the sword. It would have been easier for him than for Wilson temperamentally and politically. He would have had a stronger war party behind him than Wilson. In spite of Germany's invasions of our rights, the American people did not want war. Woodrow Wilson went to war against their will—and against his own."

XXIV

BETWEEN THE DEVIL AND THE DEEP, DEEP SEA

Anti-American Tension in London – House Counsels War with the Kaiser –
The Cleavage of the Duumvirs – Wilson's Battle for Peace – Fabian Tactics
– The Note That Made King George Weep – German's Round Robin – Wil-
son's Peace Note – House Sugars a Pill – "Peace Without Victory" – Wilson's
Mistake

WILSON'S reëlection, in November, 1916, aggravated the
tension between England and the United States. Captain
Guy Gaunt reports to House that feeling in Great Britain against
America is "growing apace." It has seized the working people
and it has reached the trenches. Every shell that goes over and
does not explode is called a "Wilson." Gaunt considers the situation so dangerous that he secretly sails for England bearing
confidential letters and messages from Colonel House.

"With their state of feeling," Colonel House says in his
diary, "and with the President's distaste of their methods, I regard the situation as serious.... I had a long conference with
Polk. He agrees with me that we are in deep and troublous
waters. I urged him to have Lansing keep in close touch with
me until the skies are clear. We must do team-work and keep
our wits about us. We not only have foreign countries to deal
with, *but the President must be guided.* He has always been more
interested in domestic problems than in foreign affairs.... This
gives me much concern. His tendency to offend the Allies ... is
likely to lead us into trouble with them. *If we are to have war,
let it be with Germany by all means.* She has forfeited every
right to consideration, and the situation demands, for our own
protection, that we hold with the Allies as long as we can possibly do so with dignity. I will confess that the Allies are irritating almost beyond endurance."

The Colonel's entry in his diary is the gist of his advice to Woodrow Wilson. In spite of the insulting attitude of the Allies, Wilson still attempts to hold an even keel between the two hostile groups. For there are rumblings that Germany may resume unrestricted submarine warfare. Madison felt that he had ample cause to break simultaneously with England and France. Wilson had equal cause to break with both England and Germany. It is futile to speculate what would have happened if the President had sent both Spring-Rice and Bernstorff packing.

The cleavage between the Duumvirs becomes clearly visible. Duumvir Wilson wants to force peace and is willing to go to war (if need be) with Great Britain. Duumvir House also wants peace, but a peace imposed upon Germany by a victorious, if chastened England. He believes that the quickest way to achieve this end will be to join the War on the side of the Allies.

In spite of the cleavage, Wilson still puts his faith in House more than in any one else. On November 25, he entrusts him with a delicate mission. Wilson's instructions to House reveal his passionate desire to remain neutral after the election. His pacifist battle-cry had not been a trap to ensnare the unwary. The President asked House to see Mr. Schiff, of Kuhn, Loeb and Company, formerly the bankers of the German Government, and to suggest to him that in the unsatisfactory and doubtful stage of our relations with Germany it would be most unwise to extend a loan to the Kaiser. He asked House to assure Mr. Schiff of his personal friendship. But in the same breath, he urged House to write a stiff note to Lord Grey.

Wilson wished to convey to the British that the United States would go to any lengths on behalf of a world-wide league for peace. But he told House to stress the fact that the people were growing more and more impatient with the intolerable yoke imposed upon us by neutrality. "Tell them," he said, "that America is as hot under the collar against Great Britain as it was at first against Germany. Leave no doubt in their mind that our temper will wax hotter still, if the deadlock continues indefinitely."

Distracted by the double threat from England and Germany, Wilson determined to act for peace without waiting for an invitation from England. He did not want to drift into a rupture with England, or hostilities with the Germans. Colonel House advised against the dispatch of a peace note. He pointed out to him that the Allies, filled at that time with undue hopes of a speedy victory, would regard any intervention as an unfriendly act.

That night Woodrow Wilson wrestled long with himself. "I was sorry," House records in his diary, "but it could not be helped. I dislike coming to the White House as his guest and upsetting him to the extent I often do." In former days, the visits of Colonel House had no such disturbing effect upon the man who looked upon him as his other self. His love for House battled with his most passionate conviction. His Scotch-Presbyterian soul could not reconcile itself to permit the slaughter. He saw himself driven into a bloody abyss. Innumerable ancestors, ministers of the Gospel, cried out in his heart: "Thou Shalt Not Kill."

In spite of protests from House and Lansing, Wilson drafts his peace note. It was, House admits, "a wonderfully well-written document," but it would make the Allies gnash their teeth, because it did not recognize their special claim to superior virtue. To Wilson the objects of the War were "obscure." House and Lansing almost tore their hair when Wilson grimly read: "The objects, which the statesmen of the belligerents on both sides have in mind in this war, are virtually the same, as stated in general terms to their own people and to the world." It was this phrase that made the King of England burst into tears at luncheon.

House once more counsels delay. Sir Edward Grey had resigned, and Lloyd George was making the welkin ring with songs of hate. House feels that the new Ministry will slam the door in the face of peace. Wilson, undismayed, re-writes his note. He wants House to go to London again. But the Duumvir balks. He even asks Lansing to dissuade Wilson. Wilson changes his mind about sending House to London, and holds back his note once more. Tired of Wilson's vacillations and without a shred of faith in his sincerity, Germany addresses a round robin for peace to the Allies.

"Don't send your note now!" House urges Wilson. "They

will accuse you of pulling Germany's chestnuts out of the fire."
But Wilson refuses to abide by the judgment of his Duumvir.
He sends his own note (December 18, 1916) without asking the
Colonel's advice and without submitting the final draft to him.
This denotes a revolution in the relation between the Duumvirs.
But Wilson excuses himself. He pleads that events had moved
so fast that he could not communicate with House. His mes-
sage was written and sent off within a very few hours, for fear
the Governments of the Entente might in the meantime so com-
mit themselves against peace as to make the situation hopeless.
But House lived with a telephone at his elbow. There was no
interruption in the service between the White House and Park
Avenue and Fifty-third Street!

Like a truant pupil, Wilson lacks the courage to subject his
impulsive act to the keen scrutiny of the Colonel. In spite of
Wilson's brief mutiny, the influence of House remains paramount
in all his decisions. In the end he once more defers to the Colonel's wishes. His peace note expresses pious wishes. But it is
not a clarion call. Only the clarion call of an ultimatum could
save the situation. If Wilson had dispatched a drastic note
threatening intervention to both groups of belligerents, a crisis
would have ensued in every country. That crisis would have
ended the War. If not, Wilson could have replied: "A plague on
both your houses!" America could have "disinterested" herself
in Europe.

It was no secret that Germany was planning a peace offensive. If Wilson had anticipated the German move he would have
disarmed his critics in both camps. But Wilson waited, waited,
waited. His delay eventually forced Germany to play her last
card, to offset, by a submarine blockade of Great Britain, the
paper blockade of Central Europe. Wilson's note, coming on the
heels of Germany's offer, received scant attention. The Allies
could now pretend that Wilson was acting in collusion with
Germany. The arrant hypocrisy of this claim requires no
comment.

On January 22, 1917, Mr. Wilson made in the Senate one
of the finest speeches of his career on "peace without victory."
"Victory would mean peace forced upon the loser, a victor's terms

imposed upon the vanquished." This austere utterance induced Allied hysterics. Like another and greater prophet who wanted to bring peace to the world, Wilson was reviled and rejected. On January 31, Germany announced the withdrawal of her submarine pledge, and a few months later America went to war with Germany instead of Great Britain.

Poor Wilson, like Madison, was forced to make his choice between the Devil and the deep, deep sea. In his chat with House, two months after the War began, Wilson expressed the opinion that President Madison went in on the wrong side. He strove with all his might not to repeat the error of his predecessor. History may decide that Wilson made the same mistake as Madison.

In the calm light of post-war candor it is difficult to escape the conclusion that Wilson's instinct to remain out of the conflict entirely was everlastingly right. No one can tell to-day whether it would have been possible to adhere to this policy. House thought not. In the long duel between the Duumvirs, House prevailed. If it had not been for House, Wilson, like Madison, would have drifted, reluctantly, into war with Great Britain. With the Duumvir beside him, the President drifted, against his will, but less reluctantly, into war with the Kaiser.

XXV

BEHIND THE SCENES OF THE WHITE HOUSE WHEN AMERICA ENTERED THE WAR

Germany and the Duumvirs – The Periscope on the Horizon – The Real Bernstorff – The Ear in the Embassy Wall – If House Had Been the Kaiser – Devious Ways of Duumvirs – Wilson's Suspicions Wane – Torpedo Ahoy! – The Duumvirs Play Pool

THE good faith of the Duumvirs in their relations with Germany has often been challenged. The story of the negotiations between the American Government and the Germans is curiously checkered, criss-crossed with hesitation, vacillation and distrust. The correspondence between House and Wilson reveals the sincerity of both men.

"If Germany really wants peace she can get it, and get it soon, *if she will but confide in me and let me have a chance.*" Addressed by the President to Colonel House two weeks before Bernstorff received his passports, these words exonerate the President from the charge of hypocrisy. He does not speak to be overheard. He is not engaged in framing an alibi for himself before the tribunal of history. When Wilson talks to House, he talks to himself!

Long before January 31, 1917, when Germany officially announced the resumption of unrestricted submarine warfare, the shadow of the periscope, reëmerging from the depths, had fallen over the negotiations between Washington and Berlin. Wilson, still hoping against hope, strained every sinew to avert war.

"Never," says Colonel House, "was Wilson more friendly to Germany and more wroth with the Allies than in the days immediately preceding the rupture of diplomatic relations with the Imperial German Government. 'Find out,' he asked me, 'what

Germany is thinking, or rather, what her rulers think in their hearts.'

"Certain communications from Ambassador Sharp and from Herbert Hoover had convinced him that Germany could have peace for the asking. Perhaps he was mistaken. But he believed it. In the light of his information, he urged me to seek out Bernstorff and try to elicit definite peace terms from him. He suggested that we meet somewhere in secret, where our meeting would not be observed. 'Tell him,' he said, 'that this is the time to accomplish something if they really and truly want peace.'

"Wilson saw that Germany's preparation to resume unrestricted submarine warfare foreshadowed the terrible likelihood of sundering relations completely. 'Feelings, exasperations,' he said, 'are neither here nor there. Do they in fact want me to help? I am entitled to know because I genuinely want to help and have now put myself in a position to help without favor to either side.'"

Vacillating between faith and distrust, between high hopes and gloomy forebodings, he feels "very lonely" sometimes and sometimes "very low in his mind." The President is puzzled by the suave and smiling Bernstorff. Count Bernstorff, he confides to House, is a most extraordinary person. In his letters he is one person, in his interviews, particularly in his confidential interviews with the newspaper men, he is quite another. "I wish," the harassed President sighs, "I knew which, if either, is the genuine Bernstorff." Wilson trusted neither Bernstorff's accuracy nor his sincerity. When he requested the Austrian Government to recall Dr. Dumba he asked House: "If Dumba, why not Bernstorff also? Is there any essential difference?"

The American Secret Service, taking its cue from the Duumvir, glued its ears exclusively to German keyholes. The British Ambassador, Sir Cecil Spring-Rice, ably aided by Guy Gaunt's countryman, John R. Rathom of the Providence *Journal*, poured wild tales of German plots into the horrified ears of Colonel House. There was a time when both House and Wilson, convinced that the country was "honeycombed with German intrigue and infested with German spies," prepared for a possible outbreak in the United States!

Behind every gas plant, behind every dynamo they saw

German agents and disaffected German-Americans. Wilson considers the matter with "the greatest solicitude." He follows every clew, but finds no evidence. He asks House "to focus the danger definitely enough at any one point of the country to suggest a concentration of forces or precautionary vigilance." House is unable to supply definite data because most stories of dangerous German activities in the United States were figments of the imagination and deliberate inventions.

There is no reference in the House-Wilson correspondence to Allied intrigue and Allied spies in the United States. House was exceedingly fond of that irrepressible Australian, Captain Guy Gaunt, naval attaché of the British Embassy, who indulged in activities not unlike those of von Papen and Boy-Ed. Polk, in the State Department, was on intimate terms of personal friendship with Sir William Wiseman, but he did not know that the soft-spoken, bland young Englishman was the head of the British Secret Service and the Propagandist in Chief of Great Britain. House and Wilson knew, but they received him into their confidence. After America entered the War, Wiseman, according to Northcliffe, was the only man who had access at all times to the Colonel and to the White House. He was the bosom friend of the Duumvir. To be always at his elbow, Wiseman rented an apartment in the house where the Colonel lived. David Lawrence referred to the Fifty-third Street house jestingly as the American No. 10 Downing Street.

Notwithstanding their pro-British bias, the correspondence of the Duumvirs was singularly free from intemperate references to the Germans. Even in the hectic days that followed the sinking of the *Lusitania* and the *Arabic*, Wilson wrote without the vehemence which sometimes characterized his utterances about the English. Bernstorff's insistence upon Germany's right to receive cotton for the use of her civilian population placated his Southern heart. Convinced that Germany had at last come to her senses and was playing intelligent politics, he was reconciled to pulling her chestnuts out of the British fire. Wilson was highly pleased with Bernstorff when the Ambassador, exceeding his authority, saved him (Wilson) from drastic action by yielding to the American contention in the *Arabic* dispute.

But unlike House, Wilson never completely trusted Bernstorff. Tapping the telephone of the German Embassy, the Secret
Service had caught, spicing the conversations between young
attachés and their lady friends in New York, now and then in-
discreet references to the President and to Mrs. Wilson. A transcript of these confidences was served the President with his
breakfast. Even if the caustic references to White House personages were not attributed to Bernstorff himself, subconsciously
at least Mr. Wilson's attitude must have been affected by such
reports. It is not inconceivable that they disturbed the tranquillity
of his domestic life.

House deprecates this suggestion. "I doubt," he says, "that
Wilson read the reports, unless they were specifically called to
his attention. The papers submitted to the President of the
United States are so many, the material which he must digest
is so enormous, that even matters of importance escape his
cognizance.

"I grant you that tittle-tattle of this sort may leave in the
mind a focus of disaffection. I, too, received such reports. Bernstorff's cyphers were no secret to us. His cryptic allusions were
not, as a rule, hard to grasp. I know that whenever the Ambassador referred to a 'beam' or a 'window' or anything connected
with a 'house' he was referring to me!

"Talebearers told me that Bernstorff was bragging among
his cronies that he was fooling me. I paid no attention to such
gossip. I believed that Bernstorff was sincere, even if his tongue
ran away with him once in a while. You cannot meet a man day
after day without forming a clear estimate of his real self.
Bernstorff was fundamentally honest. Political exigencies compelled him, at times, to play two parts.

"I never," the Colonel continued, "lost faith in Bernstorff.
If Bernstorff had been Chancellor, the War might have ended
without world wide disaster. Germany should have done one of
two things: she should have chosen a military man, who, em-
ploying every means of force at his disposal, might have forced
peace upon the Allies on his own terms; or she should have
selected a master diplomat who could read the psychology of

foreign nations. If I had been the Kaiser, I would have made either Tirpitz or Bernstorff my Chancellor.

"The War could have been won by diplomacy or by force of arms; it could have been won by a combination of both. But it could not be won by vacillation. The Germans could never quite make up their mind whether to use force or diplomacy with the result that they failed to secure the utmost benefit from either."

I did not quite agree with the Colonel. "Even," I said, "if Germany had been victorious, would not the United States have snatched the victory from her? It is clear from the Gentleman's Agreement that the United States would have intervened if unrestricted submarine warfare brought the Allies to their knees, or if German diplomacy, aided by military victories, had succeeded in imposing upon the Allies a German peace."

House shook his head.

"The Gentleman's Agreement was dead. I do not think that we would have entered the War without Germany's untimely declaration of unrestricted submarine warfare. The country, I repeat, did not want war and Wilson abhorred it. If Germany had not renewed her submarine pledge at the worst possible psychological moment, it is doubtful if Congress would have sanctioned war. It is certain that Wilson would not have sought it.

"In the winter of 1916-1917, Wilson was pressing harder than ever for peace. He would have pressed England to the limit if Germany had not stayed his hands. Bernstorff alone among all the Germans understood his point of view. Wilson could exert pressure upon the Allies by an embargo on money and arms. Against Germany, debarred from American supplies by the Allied Blockade, he had no such weapon. If Germany had played with him, he would have put the screws on her enemies."

"But," I said, "both you and Wilson envisaged only a British peace. The peace terms which you considered 'reasonable' when you made the Gentleman's Agreement included the transfer to France of the ancient German provinces of Alsace and Lorraine."

"The return of Alsace-Lorraine was contemplated in the early negotiations. It was not part of Wilson's program when he proclaimed a 'peace without victory' in January, 1917."

"But you," I persisted, "favored the 'return' of these two provinces."

"I realized long before the end of 1916 that no German Government, unless overwhelmingly defeated, could give up Alsace and Lorraine. I was against their transfer to France even after Germany's defeat. I would have preferred to incorporate Alsace-Lorraine in Switzerland and to create, thereby, an eternal barrier between Germany and France. Neither Germany nor the Entente was in a reasonable mood. The peace terms which Bernstorff submitted to us as his swan song included control of Belgium and annexations of French territory disguised as rectifications of Germany's western frontier.

"But all these differences could have been ironed out, if we had induced the belligerents to meet. 'If,' I said in a letter to Wilson, January 20, 1917, 'we can tie up Germany in conference so that she cannot resume her unbridled submarine warfare it will be a great point gained; and if the conference is once started it can never break up without peace.'"

Almost fourteen years later, Count Bernstorff, in a letter to me, dated January 13, 1931, voiced his agreement with House. The letter reveals the processes of Bernstorff's mind, and the keenness with which he gauged the situation. "I knew nothing about the memorandum of February, 1916 (the Gentleman's Agreement), and could not have accepted it. I only could guess what was going on. My negotiations with Colonel House began much later, when Wilson was sick of the Allies because they did not listen to him.

"I never," Bernstorff goes on to say, "considered Wilson impartial. I knew that he was entirely pro-English. But I knew that he did not *wish* to go into the War, and that was all I wanted. We could not be beaten if the United States remained outside.

"Germany was still very strong and the Russian Revolution was casting its shadow before it. Peace," the Ambassador continues, "would have been possible on the basis of the *status quo*, with compensations, if the United States had not added her weight to that of the Allies. How happy the world would be to-day! All that was possible, if we had accepted Wilson's mediation in 1917. I was never told or offered any terms. I was only asked to name our terms."

The peace conditions did not interest Bernstorff in the preliminary stages of the negotiations. "I was convinced that neither side would re-commence hostilities and that nothing could have induced the United States to be drawn into the conflict if we had once put our feet under the conference table."

House philandered with England as well as with Germany. Bismarck, too, flirted simultaneously with Austria and with Russia. The diplomat, like the juggler, balances many colored balls at the same time. Consistency is not always a virtue. "In politics, as in mathematics, there are," Colonel House remarked, "certain equations that admit of several different solutions. $X =$ action, may stand for minus seven, or plus seventeen, or any other number consistent with the terms of the equation. If I could not solve the problem in my way, I was perfectly willing to try another, provided the final solution was in harmony with certain fundamental conceptions."

This philosophy of statecraft explains the inconsistencies in the Colonel's contradictory actions. He was a friend of Bernstorff. Nevertheless, his suggestion "to let some of the obnoxious underlings of the offending embassies go," persuaded Wilson to send home two of Bernstorff's attachés, von Papen and Boy-Ed. Both were gifted men; neither offended more than their opposite numbers in Allied embassies. Colonel House little dreamed that in 1932 von Papen would be the Chancellor of the German Republic and Dictator of Prussia. House hobnobs with Bethmann-Hollweg and the Kaiser, but demands an ultimatum after the sinking of the *Lusitania*. The *Sussex* incident finds him in a similarly bellicose mood. Again and again he insists upon drastic action. But when Wilson rejects war, House patiently tries the alternate solutions of the equation: peace, mediation.

Bernstorff envisaged the conflicting influences which swayed the Duumvir. He recognized behind apparent duplicities fundamental honesty of purpose. House, in turn, gives credit to Bernstorff. "If," he writes to Gerard, in 1915, "it had not been for his patience, good sense and untiring effort we would now be at

war with Germany." He saved Bernstorff after the sinking of the
Lusitania by placing upon the broad back of Dr. Bernhard Dernburg the alleged excesses of German propaganda. Dernburg, like
von Papen and Boy-Ed, went home; Bernstorff stayed. In the
end Wilson, influenced by House, throttled his distrust of the
German. He carefully read Bernstorff's missives in the fall of
1916 and in January, 1917, and asked him, through House, to
clarify his language. What did he mean by "arbitration," a spe-
cially selected tribunal or an umpire? Where was the exact line
between "arbitration" and "mediation"? Did he want Wilson
to outline tentative peace terms as the basis for discussion? The
President recognizes a "significant change" of attitude on the
part of the German Government. In the month before the break,
Wilson debated the advisability of concluding a Bryan treaty
with Germany. But his suspicions are never asleep. He fears a
trap if Germany should decide to avail herself of intensive submarine warfare during the year of investigation for which the
treaty provides.

His smoldering distrust is fanned once more into flames
by Gerard. "Germany," James Gerard writes in January, 1917,
"wants a peace conference in order to make a separate peace on
good terms to them with France and Russia. Then she hopes to
finish England by submarines. Then later take the scalps of
Japan, Russia and France separately. The Allies ought to remember what Ben Franklin said about hanging together or separately.
I got the above scheme from very good authority."

House, never confident of peace with Germany, nor convinced
of its advisability, attempts to persuade the President to work
out a program of military preparedness. "The State Department" (he writes in his diary), "is worried sick over the President's *laissez faire* policy.... I have promised to go to Washington next week. But I have no stomach for it. It is practically
impossible to get the President to have a general consultation.
I see him and then I see Lansing; and the result is we get
nowhere. What is needed is a consultation between the three of
us and a definite program worked out and followed as consistently as circumstances will permit." He notes (January 2, 1917)

the disturbances in Washington over the President's lack of a "positive" program.

Wilson, undeterred by advices from Page and from Lansing, unmoved even by House, continues to work on his "peace without victory" speech. He does not read it to Lansing before, on January 22, he delivers it in the Senate. Then follows blow after blow. The only answer from the Allies is an angry growl, and Germany, completely shattering Wilson's faith in her, announces on January 1, 1917, her peace terms and the resumption of submarine warfare. Her terms in themselves are not unreasonable. They are certainly more reasonable, in the light of the situation, than the terms discussed in 1916 between Colonel House and Sir Edward Grey. Germany accepts a League of Nations and obligates itself to enter a proposed international conference after the peace conference, on the basis of the President's message.

But the periscope looms over all. "My Government," Bernstorff writes, "would have been glad to postpone the submarine blockade, if they had been able to do so. This, however, was quite impossible, on account of the preparations, which could not be cancelled. My Government believes that the submarine blockade will terminate the War very quickly. In the meantime my Government will do everything possible to safeguard American interests and begs the President to continue his efforts to bring about peace, and my Government will terminate the submarine blockade as soon as it is evident that the efforts of the President will lead to a peace acceptable to Germany...."

Both House and Lansing can see no solution save war. Wilson still resists. In February, 1916, at the Daniels' Cabinet dinner, Woodrow Wilson had told Ida Tarbell: "It is my duty not to see red." Even after the German note announcing the resumption of submarine warfare in 1917, Wilson tries to banish the specter of war. "I shall not allow it to lead to war if war can possibly be avoided. It would be a crime for this Government to involve itself in the War to such an extent as to make it impossible to save Europe afterward. Germany is a madman that should be curbed."

"It is fair," Colonel House retorts, "to make the Allies do the curbing without doing our share."

"Wilson," House records, "noticeably winced at this." The President still clings to his determination not to become involved if it is humanly possible to do otherwise. But he consents to recall Senator Stone from St. Louis. This was to redeem his promise not to dismiss Bernstorff without first notifying the Chairman of the Committee on Foreign Relations, one of the six irreconcilables who had the courage to vote against war.

The President nervously arranges his books and walks up and down the floor. Mrs. Wilson speaks of golf and asks: "Would it look badly, if the President went on the links?" "The American people," House replies, "would feel that he should not do anything so trivial at such a time." "In great governmental crises of this sort," House remarks in his diary, "the public has no conception what is happening on the stage behind the curtain. If the actors and the scenery could be viewed, as a tragedy like this is being prepared, it would be a revelation. When the decision has been made, nothing further can be done until it is time for the curtain to rise. This will be when the President goes before Congress to explain why he is sending the German Ambassador home."

Meanwhile, House and Wilson play pool to kill time!

While the Duumvirs engage in this pastime, Johann von Bernstorff paces restlessly up and down the German Embassy. Already word has gone out to German Consuls everywhere to destroy every document that could be of value to Germany's enemies. The captains of German ships, marooned in American harbors, are instructed to cripple their engines. Whatever hopes may nestle in Wilson's breast, Bernstorff harbors no illusion. Hiding his despair behind a smiling mask, he sees on the wall the handwriting that spells Germany's doom.

XXVI

THE PACIFIST GOES TO WAR

Wilson's Gethsemane – The President's Pacifist Gospel – The Truth About the Sunrise Conference – Frustrated Hopes – House Argues for War – The President Still Hesitates – Zimmermann Sets Off a Bomb – Last Struggles – Woodrow Wilson Salves His Conscience – Wilson and Lenin

WHEN Bernstorff made his farewell call at the State Department, every man, woman and child in the United States, except Wilson, knew that the die was cast. Wilson's pacifist heart still wrestles with the inevitable. The period between Bernstorff's departure and America's declaration of war on April 6, 1917, is Wilson's Gethsemane. "Thou Shalt Not Kill" "He Kept Us Out of War," reëcho through his brain. The Cabinet, vexed by the President's hesitation, is in a mutinous mood. House, having gained his point, retains his composure. He does not share Wilson's horror of staining his messianic mantle with blood.

Peace is the red thread that runs through Wilson's thoughts. The repressed self of his pugnacious Scotch-Presbyterian sires asserts itself. Cornered by circumstance, he has yielded to House on every issue. Must he surrender his last conviction? Wilson's desire for peace is his obsession. Oswald Garrison Villard, editor of *The Nation*, Frank Cobb, of the *World*, and Robert Lansing corroborate Wilson's intractable pacifism. It was not pro-Germanism.

In 1915, Villard, meeting Woodrow Wilson at the Pennsylvania Station in Washington, congratulated him on his *Lusitania* note. Wilson replied: "You need not worry at all. This country will never go into the War while I am President."

A discord is introduced into this pacifist symphony by the

so-called Sunrise Conference. According to William Allen White's *Woodrow Wilson*, the mysterious conference took place in 1915, shortly after the sinking of the *Lusitania*. "The torpedo that sank the *Lusitania*," White says, "seems to have hit Woodrow Wilson's whole foreign policy and all his visions for peace. Few persons knew how terribly he was agitated. What actually happened at that Sunrise Conference is one of the mysteries of the War...."

Here is the story as White received it from Gilson Gardner:

> "As the story was told me, this early morning conference at the White House was attended by Representatives Clark, Flood and Kitchin. It was at this conference that President Wilson announced his intention to put the United States into war and to do so immediately. Clark, Flood and Kitchin were shocked at Wilson's announcement and declared that it was impossible, that the people did not want this country put into war, and that any effort on Wilson's part to force such a result would be met by them with a very bitter fight. Wilson threatened, and said that any man standing in the way would be politically destroyed if he started to carry out his purpose. There were heated words, and the conference broke up with a declaration by these leaders that they would resist the President to the utmost in any such effort."

Shortly afterwards Wilson made his "too proud to fight" speech. White frantically attempts to reconcile this statement with Wilson's effort to wring from reluctant Congressional leaders a declaration of war.

No interpretation, however eloquent, could cover with even the scantiest cloak of respectability such arrant hypocrisy. The story did not ring true psychologically to me. Colonel House considered the incident wholly apocryphal. But the pungency of the smoke pointed to a fire somewhere. There was a Sunrise Conference; there were, in fact, two conferences, but White was mistaken in the chronology.

The two conferences between Wilson and the Democratic leaders did take place, not in 1915, but early in 1916, after Wilson had consented to the negotiations which culminated in the Gentleman's Agreement with England and France. This agreement opened the door to a declaration of war. Although Wilson still eagerly sought a pacific solution, there were moments when he envisaged with relief the possibility of cutting the Gordian knot with the sword.

Every participant in the two conferences is dead. Standing by itself, Claude Kitchin's letter to Gardner, upon which White bases his version of the Sunrise Conference, is not convincing. But two Senators have assured me that, aside from the error in time, the story is substantially correct. Read in connection with Kitchin's letter, their evidence is conclusive.

Senator T. P. Gore of Oklahoma asserts that the Sunrise Conference took place about seven-thirty o'clock on the morning of February 23rd or 24th, 1916. "It could not," he says, "miss that date in either direction more than one day ... it should be borne in mind that there were two conferences instead of one. The Sunrise Conference was the second. In fact it was the sequel of the first conference held at four o'clock on the preceding day.

"The first conference was called by the President and attended by Senator Kern, Majority Leader; Senator Stone, Chairman of the Senate Committee on Foreign Relations; and Representative Flood, Chairman of the House Committee on Foreign Relations. Representative Kitchin, the House Floor Leader, was unable to be present.

"When Flood reported to Kitchin and to Speaker Clark the character of the conference they were much disturbed and arranged a second meeting with the President. This meeting, which took place on the following morning, is known as the Sunrise Conference. The Conference took place very early in the morning to escape the attention of the newspaper men."

Capitol Hill buzzed with rumors after the Conference. Alarmed by the prospect of war, Senator Gore determined to stop the practice of Americans to travel as "guardian angels" upon Allied ships. On February 25, 1916, the fighting Senator from Oklahoma introduced Senate Concurrent Resolution No. 14, which declared it to be the sense of Congress that: "all persons owing allegiance to the United States should forebear to exercise the right to travel upon the armed ships of a belligerent."

In the discussion that followed, the Senator referred, on March 2, 1916, on the floor of the Senate, to the reports about the Sunrise Conference. "I did not," Gore said to me, "make my statement without first consulting many witnesses and gathering testimony in many quarters. I talked to Stone, Kern and Kitchin. Kern related to me in detail what was said at the conference. Stone did not, but admitted that it had excited in him the gravest apprehensions. Stone described the conference in detail to another Senator, who was a confidant of his and a friend of mine. This friend on several occasions repeated to me Senator Stone's account of the conference.

"Stone," Gore insists, "categorically denied the conference, but his denial was, as lawyers say, a 'negative pregnant.' I did not discuss the matter with Speaker Clark or with Flood. I knew, however, that Flood had reported the conference to his Committee, or at least to the majority members in executive session. War was imminent."

Gore's statement is confirmed by his colleague, Senator C. C. Dill of Washington who, when these things took place, was a member of the House. The dauntless Washingtonian received his information from Claude Kitchin, the Democratic Leader, under dramatic circumstances. Here, in substance, is Senator Dill's summary of what happened:

"On the night that war was declared, April 6th, 1917, the Hon. Claude Kitchin, then leader of the Democrats in the House of Representatives, told me of a conference with President Wilson at the White House about a year previous to that date, at which the President stated he believed the time had come when this country should enter the War on the side of the Allies.

"Kitchin mentioned particularly Speaker Champ Clark and Senator William Stone, the Chairman of the Senate Foreign Relations Committee, as being present. I do not recall his mentioning any one else, although he might have done so. He said when the President told them he felt the time had come to enter the War, Senator Stone arose and said to the President: 'I have followed you sometimes when I thought you were right and sometimes when I thought you were wrong in all your policies, but I'll be damned if I follow your leadership if you propose to take us into this hell of a war.'

"According to Mr. Kitchin the President replied: 'When I say the country should go to war, the people and the Congress will follow.' Senator Stone hammered the table and walked up and down the room and shouted 'No.' The President also hammered the table and answered with equal vigor.

"After this had gone on for some few minutes, the President turned to Speaker Clark and asked him what he thought. The Speaker replied: 'This is mighty serious business you are talking about. Senator Stone is angry and you are angry. Neither of you is in a frame of mind to discuss such a serious question. I think we all better go home and sleep over it, and if you still feel the same way about it to-morrow you can call us back here for further discussion.' The President said: 'I think the Speaker is right.'

"Mr. Kitchin said he never heard anything more about it, but he always knew the President had in the back of his mind the idea that sooner or later we must go into this war on the side of the Allies, although Mr. Wilson never told the world of this fact until he delivered his message to Congress on the subject a few days previous to the vote on the declaration of war.

"It was my impression that this meeting occurred in the late afternoon, after adjournment of the House and Senate. But of course I might be mistaken about that. I am certain, though, that it was before the St. Louis Convention that renominated President Wilson.

"I was so shocked by Kitchin's revelation that I could scarcely believe it, and I spoke to Champ Clark about it. The venerable speaker looked at me in amazement and said: 'Who told you that?' I replied: 'Claude Kitchin.' His only comment was: 'The less said about it, the better.' "

With the testimony of the two Senators, the Sunrise Conference emerges from limbo into history. Wilson's psychology is no longer incomprehensible. His pacifism resisted the clamor of Wall Street and the mesmerism of Colonel House until the Gentleman's Agreement forced him to envisage the imminence of war. Harassed, troubled, he tested the temper of Congress in two conferences. The refusal of Stone, while irritating to his pride, coincided with his own deepest impulses. After a temperamental flare-up, he made no further attempt to unleash the hounds of war until events forced his hand. Even House, in Seymour's own phrase, "could only arouse the President's belligerency by appealing to his pacifist instincts." House did not arouse these instincts to martial action until April, 1917.

January 4, 1917, the Duumvir says to the President: "We should not be so totally unprepared in the event of war."

"There will be no war," Wilson retorts. "This country does not intend to become involved in this war. We are the only one of the great white nations that is free from war to-day and it will be a crime against civilization for us to go in."

Innumerable times between 1914 and 1917, President Wilson whispered the word "peace" to the Allies. Innumerable times his overtures were rejected. In May, 1916, Frank Polk reports directly to the President a conversation with M. Jusserand:

> "The French Ambassador called at the Department this afternoon and, in the absence of the Secretary, saw me. After taking up one or two routine matters, he spoke of the rumors in the press of your taking some steps toward bringing about peace. He referred to the construction put on one of your recent speeches and said he sincerely hoped that nothing would be said at present which would indicate an intention on the part of this Government to offer mediation or an intention to take any other steps toward bringing about peace. As he put it, his country wanted peace before the War, but now, after making all the sacrifices that had been made, France could not consider peace until it could be assured that it was a real peace and not a breathing spell for Germany; in other words, the people of France feel that they must continue the War so as to make the result decisive, not a draw, in order to make it a lasting peace.
>
> "The Ambassador spoke with great earnestness and some emotion. His attitude during his talk was most friendly and complimentary toward this Government, but he said, in closing, that any one suggesting peace now would be considered by his people a friend of Germany."

The President was not partial to Germany. His objection was to shedding blood, not specifically to shedding German blood. Lodge taunted Wilson with being "womanish," because he grew white and almost collapsed when American marines lost their lives at Vera Cruz while he was urging peace with Mexico in his peculiar fashion.

Every message to Congress, every private communication to House, corroborates Wilson's aversion to bloodshed. It seems curious that Wilson did not resent the impudence of the French Ambassador who branded his (Wilson's) efforts to bring about peace as an unfriendly act.

"Wilson," House explains, "did not resent the Frenchman's statement because he did not consider it important. To him the War seemed a struggle between two principals, England and Germany. He under-estimated the rôle of France. But he knew as well as I that if England was ready to make peace, France would be compelled to make peace likewise."

"Why did Wilson not resent England's refusal to come to terms?" I asked.

"He did resent it, and he would have enforced an embargo against Great Britain if Germany had not tied his hands with her submarine blunders."

"Is it not a fact that Wilson, while trying to be entirely impartial, was by tradition and inheritance more in sympathy with England than with the Central Powers?"

"Wilson," said House, shaking his head, "strove hard to be neutral and he was often impatient with the English. President Wilson was more critical of the English in the beginning than I. In the end he was more critical than I of the Germans. He lost patience with them completely when they thwarted his hope to keep America out of the conflict. Wilson was intense in his hatred and in his affection. If the Germans had played their game with more political wisdom, if they had known enough to trust Woodrow Wilson, they would have avoided Versailles."

"Why did you ship off von Papen and Boy-Ed without paying the slightest attention to the clumsy activities of the British Secret Service before it was reorganized by Sir William Wiseman?"

"The British," House retorted, "did not commit the lawless actions of which some German agents were guilty. The object of the Germans was to prevent munition shipments from reaching the other side. The British object was to expedite such shipments. Consequently the Germans were necessarily more often in conflict with our laws. We would not have tolerated open defiance of our laws by England, if she had been guilty of the practices of Rintelin and other agents of the German General Staff. On the other hand, I am perfectly willing to admit that we closed one and sometimes both eyes to British offenses. While our people were divided, the Government at times stretched neutrality to the breaking point in favor of Great Britain."

"Did you," I asked sarcastically, "fear a German invasion, like Mr. Roosevelt?"

Colonel House smiled.

"We were bombarded by alarming rumors of concrete foundations supposedly built by the Germans in preparation for an attack. Mr. Wilson asked Wood to look into the matter but I do not think that it weighed very heavily on his mind, except for a few anxious weeks. We were not afraid of a German invasion. But we were afraid of a German victory. A German victory would have turned the United States into a military camp. Such a victory we felt would affect us and might compel vital changes in our form of government."

"But surely," I said, "even if Germany had won, the preponderance of numbers would have been still against her. She could not have imposed upon her enemies a peace treaty like that which she was compelled to sign at Versailles."

Colonel House wrinkled his forehead.

"I am not so sure. Fifty years ago a man could go out and get his rifle, and he was as well armed as any soldier. This is no longer true to-day. A country like Germany, with superior military efficiency, animated by military ambition and commanding large guns, a formidable air fleet and vast arsenals of poison gas, could have held complete domination of Europe if it had won the War, just as the Soviet Government, though constituting only a small minority of the people, completely dominates Russia. Germany could have prevented Italy and France from producing high-powered explosives and airplanes just as they, through the Peace Treaty of Versailles, handicap her."

"Can you point out to me," I asked, "in what way French militarism and British navalism is more commendable than German militarism?"

"I am just as much opposed," Colonel House replied, "to French militarism and British navalism as I am to German militarism. I am opposed to all militarism and all navalism. Once you build up a great military machine, the people behind it cannot resist the temptation to set it going. The British sea lords and the French generals are brothers under the skin to Tirpitz and Ludendorff."

"If I am not mistaken, we are spending to-day more on our army and navy than at any time before the War."

House made a deprecating gesture.

"While the whole world arms, we must continue to keep a jump ahead of them."

"What then have we gained by going in with the Allies?"

"We may not have gained much, but at least we safeguarded the victory of democracy over imperialism in 1918. A German victory would have given a new lease of life to autocracy. The victory of the Allies confirmed democracy everywhere, even in Germany. The German Republic is its progeny."

These are the lines along which the mind of Colonel House moves to-day. It was by reasoning along similar lines that the Duumvir eventually overcame Wilson's scruples against war. Neither foresaw that dictatorship would claim Europe, including Germany. Wilson struggled until the last moment against war. "The President," writes Lansing (in the *Saturday Evening Post*) "though deeply incensed at Germany's insolent notice, said he was not yet sure of the course we must pursue, and must think it over; that he had been more and more impressed with the idea that white civilization and its domination over the world rested largely on our ability to keep this country intact, as we would have to build up the nations ravaged by the War. He said that as this idea had grown upon him he had come to the feeling that *he was willing to go to any lengths rather than to have the nation actually involved in the conflict.*"

Lansing argued with him that if the break did not come now it was bound to do so in a very short time, and that the United States would be in a much stronger position before the world if she lived up to her declared purpose than if she waited for further humiliations. "If we fail to act," the Secretary of State continued, "I do not think that we can hold up our heads as a great nation, and our voice in the future will be treated with contempt by both the Allies and Germany."

Wilson remained unconvinced. "I am not sure of that. If I believed that it was for the good of the world for the United States to keep out of the War in the present circumstances, I would be willing to bear all criticism and abuse which would surely follow our failure to break with Germany. Contempt is nothing unless it impairs future usefulness. Nothing could induce me to break off relations until I was convinced that, viewed from every angle, it was the wisest thing to do."

Lansing continued his efforts to batter down the President's resistance. "The President," he relates further, "showed much irritation over the British disregard for neutral rights and over the British plan to furnish British merchantmen with heavy guns." That was on Wednesday, January 31, 1917. On Thursday, Lansing and Colonel House go over the same ground with Wilson once more. "The Colonel," notes Lansing, "as is customary with him, said very little, but what he did say was in support of my views." Taking a leaf out of the Colonel's book, Lansing insists that peace and civilization depend upon the establishment of democratic institutions throughout the world, and that these would be impossible if Prussian militarism after the War controlled Germany.

"I am not sure of this," Wilson counters. "It might mean disintegration of German power and the destruction of the German nation." On Saturday morning, February 3, Wilson, wornout by the struggle, decides to hand Bernstorff his passports and to recall Gerard. He promises to ask Congress for powers of retaliation in case Germany should carry out her threats. He still refuses to unsheath the sword.

On February 26, Wilson sends House the notorious Zimmermann note. To assure safe delivery, Zimmermann had transmitted his dispatch to Eckhard, the German Minister in Mexico, through four different channels. Every one of these channels was blocked by the English. Every one of his messages was caught and deciphered in London! Although the alliance, involving both Mexico and Japan, which Zimmermann proposed in the note, and the return of the Mexican "lost provinces," was contingent upon America's joining the rank of belligerents against Germany, it betrayed that the German Foreign Office had lost its grasp of realities. There was no doubt that Zimmermann's note would arouse the fury of America. No American could remain Germany's friend if Germany desired to destroy our integrity as a nation. Its publication meant that the country would inevitably be swept into active hostilities.

England knew when she presented that note to Wilson that

she would force his hand. Wilson, House reports, was disturbed and in doubt as to whether the publication of the telegram would bring on a crisis he could not control. House, desiring a positive decision, advised immediate publication. His advice was accepted. The Zimmermann bomb exploded. Pandemonium broke loose.

When the Zimmermann note was published, I declared that no German official could be capable of such stupidity, that the note must be the invention of some imaginative British propagandist or that it must have arisen in the fruitful mind of E. Phillips Oppenheim. I expressed this opinion in a telegram to Mr. Hearst. It was adopted by the Hearst newspapers, and re-echoed by every foe of war in the United States. If Germany had denied the authenticity of the note, pro-Germans throughout the world would have accepted her denial.

Dr. William Bayard Hale, once the friend of President Wilson, and at this time (February, 1917) correspondent for the Hearst papers in Berlin, marched straightforth to the Foreign Office. He did not ask Dr. Zimmermann if the dispatch was authentic. With the subtlety characteristic of him, he asked, lifting his eyebrows: *"Of course,* Your Excellency will deny this story?"

"I cannot deny it," Zimmermann replied. "It is true."

Some years later, talking to Zimmermann about the incident, I tried to find out why he did not foreswear himself like a diplomat and a gentleman. Dr. Zimmermann admitted that, in the jargon of the underworld, the Allies had the goods on him. He knew there was a leak in Washington or in Mexico City. He did not know even then that the message had leaked out in four different places!

Zimmermann's admission ended pro-Germanism in the United States. I declared in *The Fatherland* that I could no longer support a nation which attempted to parcel out American territory. But in spite of Zimmermann, Wilson was not yet ready for war. He resented the efforts of the Roosevelt faction to force his hand and the attempt to impose a coalition Cabinet upon him. "It is Junkerdom," he confides to House, "trying to creep in under cover of the patriotic feeling of the moment. But they shall not get it." He sees no examples of happy or successful coalitions. The nominal coalition in England is a Tory Government in disguise. The American Junkers, the President insists, have the same purpose in mind. I know them too well, he exclaims, and will hit them straight between the eyes if necessary with plain words!

While the country is girding itself for war, Wilson works on his address to Congress. But he delays and delays. Lansing runs despairingly to Colonel House. Wilson is determined that our entrance into the War should be based upon reasoned judgment, not hasty emotion. "We must put excited feeling away." This is the mood in which he composes his message. Dissatisfaction in Washington mounts. Officials grow restless. There is talk of a "strike" in the Cabinet. And still Wilson holds off. The idea of resigning the Presidency flits through his mind.

H O U S E : (March 27, 1917) A crisis has come in your Administration different from anything that you have yet encountered. I am anxious that you should meet it in a creditable way so that your influence will not be lessened when you come to do the great work which will necessarily follow the War. You have met many more difficult situations than this. But this is one for which you are not so well equipped.

W I L S O N : That is true. I do not believe that I am well fitted for the Presidency under such conditions.

H O U S E : You are too refined, too civilized, too intellectual, too cultivated, not to see the incongruity and absurdity of war. It needs a man of coarser fiber, and one less a philosopher, to conduct war brutally, vigorously and successfully. But your position is not as difficult as you imagine. Everything that you must meet in this emergency has been thought out time and time again in other countries. All we have to do is to take experience as our guide and not worry over the manner of doing it. It is not as difficult as it was to take a more or less ignorant, disorganized part in Congress and force it to pass the Federal Reserve Act, the Tariff Act, the Panama Tolls Act and other legislation which you have successfully written into the law of the land. You have taken a gamble that there would be no war and you have lost.

The country will hold it to your discredit unless you prosecute the war successfully.

Wilson still wavers. "I have never," the President tells Frank Cobb on the afternoon of April 1, "been so uncertain about anything in my life as that decision. A declaration of war would mean that Germany would be beaten and so badly beaten that there would be a dictated peace, a victorious peace. It means an attempt to reconstruct a peace-time civilization with war standards, and at the end of the War there will be no bystanders with sufficient power to influence the terms. There won't be any peace standards left to work with. There will be only war standards. It would mean that we should lose our heads along with the rest and stop weighing right and wrong. It would mean that a majority of people on this hemisphere would go war mad, quit thinking and devote their energies to destruction.

"We couldn't," the President insists, "fight Germany and maintain the ideals of government that all thinking men share. I shall try it but it will be too much for us. Once lead this people into war and they'll forget there ever was such a thing as tolerance. To fight, you must be brutal and ruthless, and the spirit of ruthless brutality will enter into the very fiber of our national life, infecting Congress, the courts, the policeman on the beat, the man in the street. Conformity will be the only virtue. And every man who refuses to conform will have to pay the penalty."

"If there is any alternative, for God's sake, let's take it!" Wilson exclaims at the end of a long conversation. Cobb sees no alternative, Wilson wishes to defer the calling of Congress until the 16th of April. Burleson, now a violent protagonist of the War, retorts: "The people wish this country to go into the War actively." The President flares up: *"It does not make so much difference what the people wish as what is right."*

At last the President yields.

On April 2nd Wilson addresses Congress. He does not ask for a declaration of war. He merely asks Congress to recognize that a state of war already exists. That salves his conscience. In his heart of hearts, he still hopes to wage a war of ideas rather than a war of arms. His speech is a clarion call:

"It is a fearful thing to lead this great peaceful people into war, into the most terrible and disastrous of all wars, civilization itself seeming to be in the balance. But the right is more precious than peace, and we shall fight for the things which we have always carried nearest our hearts—for democracy, for the right of those who submit to authority to have a voice in their own governments, for the rights and liberties of small nations, for a universal dominion of right by such a concert of free peoples as shall bring peace and safety to all nations and make the world itself at last free. To such a task we can dedicate our lives and our fortunes, everything that we are and everything that we have, with the pride of those who know that the day has come when America is privileged to spend her blood and her might for the principles that gave her birth and happiness and the peace which she has treasured. God helping her, she can do no other."

In spite of angry protests from the Entente, Wilson does not advocate war against Austria-Hungary until December. Peace may still come by way of Vienna. The United States never declared war against Bulgaria or Turkey. War Wilson cannot tolerate. But this is a war to end war! This ideal sustains him. It raises his stature. Looming over the world, he incarnates for the time being the hopes of mankind.

While Wilson girds himself for war, another intellectual sets out to translate his dreams into action. Another ideologist stretches forth his hand to seize destiny. In a sealed car, with a safe conduct from General Ludendorff, Lenin speeds into Russia. The one thought that inspires Lenin is the dictatorship of the proletariat. Wilson's one thought is peace. Events force Lenin to make concessions to capitalism. Wilson is compelled to wage war for the sake of peace. Both men shook the world. One preached the community of all workers, the other the community of all nations. Both failed and both succeeded beyond their dreams.

WILSON'S PERSONALITY SPLITS

SLOWLY, after April 2nd, Wilson's personality splits. From Wilson the pacifist emerges Wilson the warrior. The pacifist does not permit himself to be subjugated without a struggle. "My message was a message of death to our young men. How strange it seems to applaud that!" Woodrow Wilson said plaintively to Tumulty on his return to the White House after delivering his war message.

The pacifist Wilson never forgave himself the surrender of his dearest convictions. Unwilling to censure either himself or his *alter ego,* Wilson unconsciously transferred the fury of his resentment for himself to "the military masters of Germany." The mind is a magnificent juggler. There is in such transferences no conscious hypocrisy.

House, having steered Wilson's policy into active channels, had no emotional qualms. Calm, imperturbable, he devised ways of winning the War. A shrewd student of men, he sought out moral and psychological weapons to thwart the Big Berthas of Ludendorff. House impressed upon Wilson again and again the advisability of exploiting the cleavage between the German people and the German Government. This thought appealed immensely to Wilson. Henceforth his speeches were emotional outbursts against the Imperial German Government, oblivious of the fact that he could not fight the Government without fighting the people. With House the attack upon the German ruling class was largely a matter of strategy. To Wilson it was a crusade.

Like all schizoids, Wilson was not consistent. Sometimes one personality, sometimes the other, dominated. In the early days, Wilson still envisaged the possibility of a platonic war without actual bloodshed. But when the Allies were at the end of their tether and the Kaiser's helmet cast its shadow over Europe and Asia, Wilson's mood grew more bellicose, until, veering completely around, he demanded "force without stint or limit." Wilson the warrior tortured Wilson the pacifist. Wilson flagellated his own conscience when he signed the Espionage Act. With masochistic enjoyment in self-induced punishment, he saw the fulfillment of his prophecy to Cobb, that war could not be waged without sacrificing free speech at home. War psychosis seized the Government and the people. Wilson, House insists, was not to blame for this metamorphosis of a peaceful people. The Liberty Loan was the battering ram that broke down common sense. Creel, propagandist-in-chief of Uncle Sam, widened the breach in the wall of tolerance to "sell" the War to America. No one fights or pays unless his blood boils!

Lack of enthusiasm became treason, pacifism a crime. Wilson could have moderated this hysteria. He refused to intervene. The reason he gave to himself was the necessity of winning the War against Germany. The real reason was his desire to win the War in his own unconscious against his pacifist self. It was a psychic necessity for Wilson to reverse himself completely. If the handful of pacifists that still remained were right, then he was wrong. Yet, by some strange law of compensation, every conscientious objector, condemned to penal servitude in Leavenworth, was Woodrow Wilson himself.

Wilson's struggle with himself appears in his speeches. In Buffalo, November 12, 1917, Wilson waxes sarcastic at the expense of the pacifists whose suffrage he had asked only a few months before. "What I am opposed to is not the feeling of the pacifists but their stupidity. My heart is with them but my mind has a contempt for them. I want peace, but I know how to get it and they do not. You will notice that I sent a friend of mine, Colonel House, to Europe, who is as great a lover of peace as any man in the world, but I didn't send him on a peace mission yet." The War is justified in Wilson's mind because it is a war to end war, to destroy militarism forever.

"We know now as clearly as we knew before we were ourselves engaged that we are not," Wilson declares in his Flag-Day speech of June 14, 1917, "the enemies of the German people and that they are not our enemies. They did not originate or desire this hideous war or wish that we should be drawn into it; and we are vaguely conscious that we are fighting their cause, as they will some day see it, as well as our own. They are themselves in the grip of the same sinister power that has now at last stretched its ugly talons out and drawn blood from us." The ideas of the speech are the Colonel's, but the eloquence and the emotion are Wilson's.

Fearful of going beyond his mentor, Wilson expressed the hope, in a letter to House, that the Flag-Day speech contains nothing "to which our associates in the War (so I will call them) could object." This is the first time that Wilson speaks of the Allies as our "associates." In this phrase, the repressed pacifist asserts itself. The Sir Galahad of the World War draws a clear distinction between his own idealistic purposes and the selfishness of the Allies. Convinced of the purity of his own heart, and darkly suspicious of others, Wilson shoos back to the Vatican a peace dove of the Pope. He conveys a message to Balfour through Colonel House that he may not even reply to the note of the Holy Father. In his present mood, even to discuss peace with Germany is immoral. "The present German Imperial Government is morally bankrupt. No one will accept or credit its pledges; and the world will be upon quicksand in regard to all international covenants which include Germany until it can believe that it is dealing with a responsible government."

House is less passionate. "Personally," he adds in the note to His Britannic Majesty's Secretary for Foreign Affairs, "I feel that the door should not be shut abruptly. It will give the Prussian militarists the advantage of again consolidating sentiment in Germany." He replies in the same vein to Wilson. "Answer the Pope's proposal in such a way as to throw the onus on Prussia."

Wilson takes the hint. In a formal reply to the Pope he stresses the point that it is impossible to accept the word of the existing rulers of Germany and intimates that he welcomes reconciliation with a "liberalized Germany." Like all important documents, the letter to the Pope is submitted to Duumvir House. Wilson, suffering from the psychic conflict within himself, attributes his weariness to overwork. "I am doing daily about twice as much as I can do, and the pace is telling." Wilson the warrior banishes into the remotest recess of the unconscious the nascent resentment of Wilson the pacifist against House, the War Maker. "I think of you every day with the greatest affection." The tender phrase hides an internal struggle.

Even in ordinary life, every action is the resultant of many factors, conscious and unconscious. Wilson's attitude toward the Vatican's peace plans is influenced not merely by his own psychic disturbance. He knows that the Allies want no peace, now that America has joined their ranks with its might. There are also vague hints of a Catholic conspiracy. This rumor, crystallized in a letter from Page, must have reached Wilson and House from other sources. "Rome," Page whispers, "wishes to preserve Austrian loyalty to the Vatican. Devout Roman Catholics of all nationalities are influenced by the Church's wishes. Even English and French Catholics thus find their loyalty divided between their countries and their church, and the resolution of many good men is weakened unconsciously."

House, swayed both by his fear of an inconclusive peace and the attitude of his friends in London and Paris, redoubled his efforts to make America's war aid effective. When England's financial backbone was nearly snapping, she turned for help to the Duumvir. House talked to Wilson. Wilson talked to McAdoo. Thus was struck the rock from which gold poured like water. Great Britain played her cards with masterly skill. Sir William Wiseman, England's super-Ambassador, was always at the elbow of the super-Secretary of State. He had access to the two White Houses—the modest retreat of the Colonel at 53rd Street and

Park Avenue, New York, and the stately mansion on Pennsylvania Avenue in Washington, D. C.

Together with House, Wiseman works out a shrewd memorandum on American coöperation for his Government. Before sending it home, he submits it to President Wilson. The President pronounces it "an exact summary." It contains a sop for Downing Street and a sop for Wilson.

"It is important to realize that the American people do not consider themselves in any danger from the Central Powers. It is true that many of their statesmen foresee the danger of a German triumph, but the majority of the people are still very remote from the War. They believe they are fighting for the cause of Democracy and not to save themselves.

"There still remains a mistrust of Great Britain, inherited from the days of the War of Independence, and kept alive by the ridiculous history books still used in the national schools. On the other hand, there is the historical sympathy for France, and trouble could far more easily be created between the British and the Americans than with any of our Allies. German propaganda naturally follows this line, and has been almost entirely directed against England. . . .

"Any pronouncement the Allied Governments can make which will help the President to satisfy the American people that their efforts and sacrifices will reap the disinterested reward they hope for will be gratifying to him, and in its ultimate result serve to commit America yet more wholeheartedly to the task in hand.

"The Americans need a slogan. The President realizes this when he gave them the watchword that America was fighting 'to Make the World Safe for Democracy.'

"Our diplomatic task is to get enormous quantities of supplies from the United States while we have no means of bringing pressure to bear upon them to this end. We have to obtain vast loans, tonnage, supplies and munitions, food, oil, and other raw materials. And the quantities which we demand, while not remarkable in relation to the output of other belligerents, are far beyond the figures understood by the American public to-day.

"The Administration is ready to assist us to the limit of the resources of their country; but it is necessary for them to educate Congress and the nation to appreciate the actual meaning of these gigantic figures. It is not enough for us to assure them that without these supplies the War will be lost. For the public ear we must translate dollars and tonnage into the efforts and achievements of the fleets and the armies. We must impress upon them the fighting value of their money."

Until this moment Great Britain had minimized the submarine peril. Now for the first time Great Britain permits the American Government to learn that Germany was by no means reckless when she staked her all on the submarine. In the first three months of the unrestricted submarine campaign Germany had sunk one thousand vessels. One out of every four ships leaving England never returned to port. England was groggy. France staggered. Italy was knocked out. Russia was no longer a help but a menace. "Unless a change for the better comes," writes Colonel House, "the Allies cannot win and Germany may. For six months or more the ground has been steadily slipping away from the Allies."

Adversity stiffened Wilson's determination. He could not afford defeat. To lose the War was to lose the peace! This was the moment when Wilson could have imposed his own conditions upon the Allies. Balfour told President Wilson of the existence of the Secret Treaties for dividing the prospective loot among the Allies. They were no secret to House. He had told the President of the Treaty of London with which the Allies bought the support of Italy. Now was the time to throw these agreements into the discard. But House, fearing dissension among the Allies, hopes that Wilson will not make the Secret Treaties an issue. "If," he says to Wilson, "the Allies begin to discuss terms among themselves, they will soon hate one another worse than they do Germany, and a situation will arise similar to that in the Balkan States after the Turkish War. It seems to me the only thing to be considered at present is how to beat Germany in the quickest way." Wilson acquiesced. That was unfortunate for Wilson. The emergency of the Allies was his opportunity.

The position of House was rational. But the general who consults reason too much may lose his campaign. Only audacity wins. House, ordinarily audacious, was timid now. Perhaps, knowing Wilson's heart, he feared a relapse into pacifism if the hideous truth of the Secret Treaties flashed across his consciousness, like the handwriting Belshazzar saw on the wall. House justified his attitude by persuading himself that England and the United States would be able to dictate broad and generous terms at the end of the War.

Balfour entrusted to Colonel House a map with the Secret Treaty lines traced on it. Unfortunately this map has disappeared. It cannot be found among the House papers. Alsace-Lorraine, Danzig, an outlet for Poland to the sea, the ambitions of Italy, constitute the topics of lengthy discussions between House and Balfour. This conference was followed by a joint conference between Balfour and both Duumvirs. In this conference, according to the diary of Colonel House, the same ground was covered as on previous occasions. The discussion lasted for two hours, at the end of which Balfour promised to send copies of the Secret Treaties to Wilson. Neither Balfour nor House deceived Wilson. But neither impressed upon the President the importance of the Secret Treaties.

Wilson himself once said that he had a "one-track mind." The Secret Treaties were shoved off to a side-track in the unconscious. But every now and then a whistle blew or a wheel rattled. Even if he repressed the unwelcome knowledge, he was not unmindful of it when, some months later, he drafted the Fourteen Points. Spurred by House, Balfour now wrote a letter to Wilson in which he apologetically confirmed the Secret Treaties once more. He admitted that England and France were bound by them in letter and spirit, but added that Italy, the principal beneficiary, was not in a position to prolong the War to attain her objectives. Wilson, certain that America's economic power would be the final dictator of the peace, once more dismissed the Secret Treaties from his mind.

Some two years later, on August 19, 1919, President Wilson testified before the Senate Foreign Relations Committee that he had no knowledge of the Secret Treaties as a whole before he reached Paris. The whole series of understandings, including the Treaty of London, he said, were disclosed to him for the first time then. Both Balfour and House contradict Wilson's testimony. But the Colonel immediately rallies to Wilson's defense:

> "There was no man living at that time who had more varied information and misinformation brought to him than President Wilson. How could he on the spur of the moment know when he first heard of this or that?
>
> "There are those who believe the President laid too little stress

upon the treaties and that he should have had some understanding with the Allies regarding them before he committed the United States to war. This was not practicable. We had our own quarrel with Germany, and if we had waited until he could have gotten a satisfactory understanding regarding the Secret Treaties the War would have been over before we entered the lists. England and France might have come to a quick decision, but, of necessity, they would have had first to reach an agreement with Japan, Italy, and Russia. Could any satisfactory agreement have been reached with them? I doubt it. Meanwhile, Germany would have sunk our ships and we should have been standing idly by, waiting for a termination of negotiations regarding the secret treaties."

Wilson did not deliberately misstate the facts. Like Roosevelt, he had the gift to forget what he did not wish to remember. Disagreeable facts disappear in the unconscious, unless they bulk so enormously that we cannot submerge them. Wilson's advisers represented the Secret Treaties to him as matters of minor importance. Subsequently, his mind repressed his knowledge of them, together with other disagreeable facts that did not fit into his ideology. Other troubles, more immediate, engaged his attention. The shipping tangle, the manufacture of munitions, and the problem of long-distance war. Roosevelt occupied his mind more than did the Secret Treaties.

Wilson was determined not to send Roosevelt to Europe. Perhaps he was afraid that Roosevelt would steal the War from him. Perhaps he resented Roosevelt's diatribes in *The Outlook*. But he undoubtedly summoned from the depths of his mind some satisfactory moral and intellectual reasons to justify his decision. Reason is always the servant of our wishes. Moreover, the General Staff upheld Wilson. A pacifist, keenly conscious of his shortcomings as a strategist, Wilson hesitated to overrule his military advisers, especially in a case where their counsel coincided with his inclinations.

The General Staff, Colonel House explained to me, decided against any volunteer army. "Many of my friends wanted to lead brigades and legions, including the late Mayor Mitchel. I advised them to wait until Wilson had decided the Roosevelt problem. The General Staff thought it better to stick to the regulars, and not to re-create the conditions brought about by political appointments in the Civil War. I was in favor of using Roosevelt, Hughes and Taft on some special commission meeting once a month in Washington to discuss ways and means of winning the War. I would have appointed to such a commission three Democrats of the Olney type. In that way the country would have had the benefit of their experience and the Administration would have had more friends. Certainly I would have sent Roosevelt rather than Root to Russia. That would have been good politics. Roosevelt, instead of eating out his heart, would have felt that he was serving his country."

Perhaps to propitiate those who looked upon Theodore Roosevelt as the embodiment of the nation embattled, the Duumvirs planned to give Roosevelt's friend, General Wood, an important command. But Pershing, who detested Wood, protested.

"What," I asked Colonel House, "was Wilson's attitude toward Pershing?"

"Wilson," House replied, "realized that the World War had produced no military genius of the first order. There was no reason for believing that we would be more favored in that respect than the rest of the world. He was not especially favorable to Pershing. But he knew no one better. Secretary Baker chose him, and we confirmed his choice. It is not impossible that General Wood would have received the appointment if he had played his cards more skillfully, for he was an able man. I asked Wilson to hold Wood. In fact, it was probably the first advice I gave him. I knew that Wood had studied Mexico and would be very useful in case of complications in that region. But Wilson did not treat Wood as he was accustomed to being treated by Roosevelt and Taft. He did not send for him or ask his advice. When he had anything to communicate to him he did so through the Secretary of War."

Shortly after we entered the War, we sent twelve major-generals to Europe to study conditions and to prepare the way for our troops. Wood was one of the twelve. Every one of the other eleven went silently. No one knew that they were in Europe. No one knew when they came back. But Wood, like Roosevelt, had a flair for publicity. He was on the front page of the newspapers continually. After he returned from his tour of inspection, he was cited to appear before a committee of the Senate. All this irritated General Pershing. Wilson did not care very much. His attention was concentrated on larger problems. Pershing probably felt that Wood's temperament would not permit him to play second fiddle. As a result, Wood was recalled abruptly on the point of departing for Europe, and sent back to Kansas.

Wood's biographer, Herman Hagedorn, relates that Wood called on House in New York after he received the orders in question and asked the Colonel's advice. House arranged an interview for Wood with Wilson and Baker. Neither Wilson nor Baker gave Pershing away. They did not tell Wood that it was Pershing's message that ended his hope of active participation at the front. The friends of Wood and Roosevelt stormed and fumed. Wilson could have disarmed all criticism by publishing Pershing's unequivocal demand. But without wincing he took the blame upon himself.

Although House admired Wood, he made no attempt to change Wilson's decision. "Pershing," House says, with conscious or unconscious irony, "possessed what we most needed: the spirit of Prussian discipline. We Americans are a lawless people. Pershing was the one man who could teach us the lesson without which we could not win the War. He was a better drill-master than Leonard Wood. It may be that Wood was as able as Pershing. But he was not, like Pershing, the supreme embodiment of military discipline. A look at Pershing's picture, always erect, never relaxing, suffices. His disciplinary qualities made him at times unpopular in the army. That was inevitable. It was to his credit rather than to his discredit. It was a part of the price we paid for victory."

It was not the only price. Free discussion became impossible. When Colonel House suggested a debate between the *Berliner Tageblatt* and the New York *World* on the peace terms of the two groups of belligerents, to strengthen "liberal" sentiment in Germany, Wilson, though much interested, refused to sanction the bold experiment. His primary reason was the fear that such a discussion would prove a double-edged sword. It would arouse

dissension in Germany. But it would probably be equally dangerous to the peace of mind of the Allied Governments.

For similar reasons he thwarted the movement for a Labor
Congress in Stockholm, where German Socialists were to discuss
peace with representatives of labor groups from England, France,
Belgium and the United States. He asked House to tell Samuel
Gompers that the people of this country are intolerant of politics
and impatient of special missions. "Outrageous" and "fraught
with mischief," he exclaims. William II assumes in his mind the
shape of the Evil One. To "knock the Kaiser off his perch" becomes his preoccupation.

But, realizing that the Allies, greedy for loot, must be disci-
plined, Wilson urges House to gather data for the Peace Conference and to initiate a propaganda campaign to disseminate
the peace aims of the American Government. He assures House
that Lansing, far from objecting, considers the choice (of House)
most appropriate. If Lansing had objected his tenure of office
would not have outlasted the proverbial snowball in hell. Wilson
ventures to suggest Professor Frankfurter of Harvard, President
Mezes of City College and Walter Lippmann as assistants. The
emphasis placed by Wilson on the unselfish war aims of the
United States calmed pacifists everywhere. Where such methods
failed, Wilson resorted to drastic measures to assure that
unanimity without which victory did not seem possible. Eventually American propaganda culminated in the Fourteen Points.

While guarding American liberals and labor leaders carefully from any infection even remotely resembling German
measles, American agencies succeeded in establishing contacts
with revolutionary forces in Germany. House especially fostered
these efforts. "Our advices," he writes to Lord Bryce, "are that
the liberal movement in Germany is strong and is constantly
receiving new recruits of influence. They complain, however,
of the little help they receive from the outside." Some day, it
may be possible to determine from archives yet unpublished who
"they" were and to whom "they" complained.

House uses the information to moderate statements emanating from London and Paris.

"Every reactionary utterance made by those in authority in England and in France is quoted in Germany and used to prove the Government's contention that the Allies' purpose is to crush Germany both politically and economically.... The President is trying to get the truth into Germany in order to wage war against the Prussian autocracy from within as well as from without. I hope you also will lend your great influence in the same direction."

Partly to exert pressure in this direction, partly to unify America's war efforts with those of the Allies, Duumvir House proceeds to England at the head of the American War Mission. His conversations with British officials constitute what is practically a personal meeting of governments. The London *Times* says of Colonel House that he is himself for this purpose virtually the Government of the United States.

The Allies were agitated at this time by the demand for a unified command. House told the British Government that President Wilson favored the Supreme War Council contemplated in this connection. But Tumulty, though physically closer to the President than the Duumvir, evidently misinterpreted his master's voice. A wireless denial, based upon some statement by Tumulty, delighted the by no means inconsiderable opposition in England to any plan subjecting British troops to a French command. The incident, which has never been fully explained, shocked House to such an extent that he missed the important meeting of the British War Cabinet with the American Mission. Bainbridge Colby and the various technical heads of the American Mission took his place while the Colonel tried to undo the mischief. An original cable from President Wilson endorsing his spokesman enabled Bonar Law to assure the House of Commons that the British Government had the "official guarantee of American approval." But House realized forcibly that he was not President.

It is possible that this incident was a straw in the wind, revealing a struggle for independence in the White House. Whatever may have been its origin, Wilson's new freedom did not last long. Colonel House continued to dominate and direct the foreign policies of the United States.

The Allies, on the brink of disaster, established a Supreme

War Council. The choice of the Commander-in-Chief was between Petain and Foch. Clemenceau favored Foch. "Petain," House remarked to me, "had more gifts, Foch more faith. Clemenceau chose Foch because Foch believed in an Allied victory. Petain, right from the purely military point of view, misjudged the imponderables."

"Events," I interjected, "justified Foch, not Petain. Would you say that Foch was a genius?"

House smiled.

"I would say that Foch was an optimist. But sometimes optimism is genius."

Other problems emerge. The Russian collapse, the breakdown of Italy, the extent of American participation in the War, led sometimes to acrimonious debates. The minutes of important conversations held by Colonel House with the Allied leaders were omitted from the post-war publications issued by the State Department, in deference to objections from Great Britain, France and Italy.

"Both France and England," Colonel House explained to me, "pressed us to secure our consent to a Russian expedition. I insisted that any invasion of Russian territory would only strengthen the Bolshevists. I had in mind what would happen in our own country in a similar case. A nation invariably rises to the defense of its own government against a foreign invader. Moreover, any effective intervention would have required an enormous number of troops. The Japanese Ambassador told me that it would take the entire Japanese Army to guard the Trans-Siberian Railroad. Japan agreed with me. France was strongly for intervention. England sided with her. After the Armistice, these two powers wanted to hurl a huge army of a million and a half into Russia."

"Where," I interrupted the Colonel, "would you have recruited this army?"

"Foch thought they might be gathered in Czecho-Slovakia, Poland, Rumania, Greece and Jugo-Slavia. I then asked: 'Where will you get the money?' The French replied: 'From you' (meaning America). I told them as politely as possible to dismiss the thought. But the Allies continued to work upon the

President after the Armistice. England and France sent numerous intermediaries to the United States to win over Wilson. One ambassador of intervention was the great philosopher, Bergson. That was a very clever move. Wilson would be more in sympathy with a philosopher than with a politician. Finally, Wilson was persuaded and gave his consent to our participation in an ill-starred Russian expedition. I would have preferred to send Hoover with food."

"How many men did we send to Russia?"

"I believe," House replied, "ten thousand, under General Graves—a useless and expensive experiment. The English sent an army, which likewise accomplished nothing. A part of the French troops sent to Crimea caught the infection of Bolshevism."

"Some legal authorities," I interjected, "considered the shipment of our troops to Russia after the Armistice a violation of the Constitution."

"Whether," House remarked deprecatingly, "it was a violation of the Constitution or not, it was certainly a futile and unfortunate gesture."

"Are you telling me these facts from memory or have you had the opportunity to go over your suppressed notes of 1917?"

"I have," House replied. "With the exception of the proposed invasion of Russia, most questions which were so vital then are now academic. The British were holding a comparatively short line against the Germans, whereas the French line was very long. Clemenceau insisted that the English line be lengthened. The British maintained that the greatest aggregation of German troops was massed against the short English line. I agreed with Clemenceau and the English were compelled to take upon themselves a larger responsibility by increasing their lines."

"What convinced you that Clemenceau was right?"

"I talked with him for half an hour before the conference. We reached an agreement to which we both adhered."

"Did Clemenceau usually keep his engagements?"

"He always did. Once he made an engagement, he stood by it." The friendship between House and Clemenceau, formed in those days, was to bear fateful fruit in the Peace Conference.

In the case of Russia House disagreed with the Tiger. Clemenceau demanded forcible intervention. The Duumvir recommended a moral offensive to weaken Germany and uphold Russia. The Russian dilemma gave birth to the Fourteen Points.

XXVIII

WILSON AND HOUSE RE-MAKE THE WORLD IN TWO HOURS

The Genesis of the Fourteen Points – The Regrets of Colonel House – The Four Objectives of the Duumvirs – How Poland Got the Corridor – The Puzzle of Austria-Hungary – Alsace Lorraine Falls under the Table – House Incorporates the Freedom of the Seas – Everybody's Business – Lloyd George Steals Wilson's Thunder – The Fourteen Points and the Secret Treaties – Wilson's Tongue Sharper than Pershing's Sword

JEHOVAH needed seven days to make the world. It took the Duumvirs only two hours to re-make it. It is not the first time that the world was thus divided. Pope Alexander VI once apportioned the globe between Portugal and Spain with a stroke of his goose quill. Wilson's task was more complex.

On January 5, Colonel House made the most astounding entry ever set down in a political diary.

> "Saturday was a remarkable day. I went over to the State Department just after breakfast to see Polk and the others, and returned to the White House at a quarter past ten in order to get to work with the President. He was waiting for me. We actually got down to work at half past ten and finished re-making the map of the world, as we would have it, at half past twelve o'clock."

On January 5th, House and Wilson agreed on the Fourteen Points. It was Clemenceau who noted that Woodrow Wilson promulgated fourteen commandments while God himself was satisfied with ten! Clemenceau was responsible for the situation which compelled Wilson to state his war aims. House had vainly pleaded with the Allies to re-state their objectives in terms of the new ideals championed by Woodrow Wilson. The Allies, especially Clemenceau, could not be budged. The Secret Treaties hung around their necks like millstones. Wilson was not so hampered. House scented the necessity of setting the world's imagination on fire. On December 1, 1917, he cabled to Wilson: "I hope you will not think it necessary to make any statement concerning foreign affairs until I can see you. This seems to me very important."

"I find it useless," he notes in his diary, "to try to get either the French or British to designate terms. Great Britain cannot meet the new Russian terms of 'no indemnities and no aggression,' and neither can France. Great Britain at once would come in sharp conflict with her colonies and they might cease fighting, and France would have to relinquish her dream of Alsace and Lorraine. . . ."

The very first subject which the Duumvirs took up when House returned was the re-statement of war aims. Eventually this manifesto assumed the shape of the Fourteen Points. The most effective piece of propaganda ever designed by any human brain in the history of mankind, the Fourteen Points owe their effectiveness to Wilson's sincerity. Wilson and House literally believed in the gospel they promulgated. There were liberal men in other belligerent countries who saw a new star, like that of Bethlehem, rise over Washington. But the men in control in London and Paris had no faith in that star.

The Duumvirs, on January 5th, did not depend entirely upon the spirit of the moment or their own inspirations. They had often debated the various points, drawing for their information now upon the Inquiry, now upon the private correspondence of Colonel House. Wilson expresses his chagrin that he could not reduce the number of points to thirteen, his lucky number. He confessed to House that he had made the attempt but had failed. Psychologically, it is not without interest to note the very human foibles of the man who took upon himself the task of re-modeling creation. Historically, it is important that the map of the world as it exists to-day, coincides largely with the one which Colonel House made with Woodrow Wilson between 10.30 and 12.30 on Saturday, January 5, 1918.

Wilson made no notes of his momentous conference. The world owes its knowledge of the scenes behind the curtains of the White House to the Colonel's diary. Many have questioned the wisdom of the division made by Wilson and House. Dr. Isaiah Bowman, executive officer of the Inquiry, in a discussion of their joint labors, bestows praise upon both Duumvirs:

> "No one can doubt that H[ouse] ... was the wisest counselor that ever a President had. This because of the temper of H no less than the temper of W[ilson]. H's mind is like a sleeve valve: no friction! His thoughts come clearly to one, through simple words directly spoken. This is not craft but art and genius. Yet W[ilson] too had an altogether extraordinary character: he was a genius, a very great man."

It would lead us too far to discuss every one of the Fourteen Points in detail. Students of history will find the material in the *Intimate Papers*. The Duumvirs took up their work systematically. First they outlined general terms such as open diplomacy, the freedom of the seas, the removal of economic barriers, the establishment of equality of trade conditions, guarantees for arms reductions, adjustments of colonial claims, and an association of nations to preserve peace.

The Fourteen Points deftly embodied the doctrine proclaimed alike by the German Socialists and by Kerensky in Russia: "Peace without annexations or indemnities on the basis of the rights of nations to decide their own destiny." These basic demands coincided with Mr. Wilson's message to Congress of December 4, 1917, made in response to an appeal from the Russian Ambassador:

> "The wrongs, the very deep wrongs, committed in this war will have to be righted. That, of course. But they cannot and must not be righted by the commission of similar wrongs against Germany and her allies. ... Statesmen must by this time have learned that the opinion of the world is everywhere wide awake and fully comprehends the issues involved. ... The congress that concludes this war will feel the full strength of the tides that run now in the hearts and consciences of free men everywhere. Its conclusions will run with those tides."

House was insistent upon the Freedom of the Seas. The original paragraph framed by House demanded "absolute freedom of navigation on the seas outside territorial waters alike in peace and in war." As an afterthought, the Duumvirs added that the seas might be closed by international action in order to enforce international covenants. House, misled by the assurances of his liberal British friends, expressed the opinion that England would accept this doctrine. He believed that it assured harmonious coöperation between English-speaking nations, which was, in his opinion, the most solid foundation of permanent peace. Wilson hoped more for peace from the League of Nations.

The Duumvirs had no difficulty in agreeing upon the restoration of Belgium. They differed on Alsace-Lorraine. House advised Wilson not to mention the two provinces specifically. He also suggested that the message on this point should read "If Alsace and Lorraine were restored to France Germany should be given an equal economic opportunity." The matter worried Wilson for several days. He modified his language, but retained the specific reference. The President wrote that the "wrongs" done to France by Prussia in 1871 *must* be righted. House suggested *should* instead of *must*. Here House prevailed. Both the President and his Duumvir agreed that certain clauses in the Treaty of London, giving Italy sovereignty over foreign nationalities, were plainly in conflict with the principles espoused by the United States. A marginal remark written by Wilson on a report of the Inquiry on this question became Point Nine. The two men agreed that Turkish rule in Europe must end.

Point Six, a fine summary of Wilson's idealistic position, insists that the treatment of Russia by her sister nations would be the acid test of their good will. Point Thirteen guaranteed an independent Polish State. This was in accordance with the avowed principles of the Colonel and with his promises to his friend Paderewski. It was a German friend of both men who introduced Paderewski to House! Poland owes the Corridor to this visit. Point Eleven, dealing with Balkan complexities, complicated still further by the uncertain future of the Dual Monarchy, was vague and general. Wilson still envisaged the preservation of Austria-Hungary as a federal state. The head of the Serbian Mission to this country, Mr. Vesnitch, assured House that no solution of the Balkan problem was possible without Austria-Hungary's destruction. This news depressed the President. But, on the advice of

House, he did not change his original statement. He could not advocate the partitioning of the Hapsburg dominion without strengthening the bonds between Berlin and Vienna.

In the turmoil of the Peace Conference, Wilson forgot that if Austria-Hungary did not exist it would have been necessary to invent it. It was the only formula capable of sustaining the economic balance in that part of Europe. But, as one of her own statesmen said, Austria-Hungary's clock had run down. It is possible that nothing could have saved Austria-Hungary. But it was unnecessary to make the map of Central Europe a crazy quilt.

The Allied leaders were annoyed because Wilson took up some of the delicate problems which they preferred to discuss privately among themselves. They intimated to him that the details of the settlement were none of his business. Wilson's jaw assumed its most determined angle. "A just peace," he said, "is everybody's business." That was one of his finest statements. It emphasizes more than any other phrase the spirit of the Fourteen Points.

Three days before Wilson delivered his speech on the Fourteen Points, Lloyd George tried to steal his thunder. But Lloyd George's statement lacked Wilson's fiery sincerity. He supported the League of Nations, but did not make it a fundamental condition of the new peace.

The question has often been raised: who first conceived the Fourteen Points? "The suggestion of a statement of Allied war aims," Colonel House replied to my inquiry, "first appeared in my cable to Wilson from Paris, in which I asked him not to commit himself until I returned. Subsequently, I spent a week with him in Washington. Jointly we labored upon a document which afterwards became known as the Fourteen Points."

I: Did Wilson consult any one except you about the Fourteen Points?

HOUSE: I do not think so. When he had finished writing them, he thought they should be printed before he delivered his speech. He sent for the printer and told him that he would hold him personally responsible for any leakage. The Fourteen Points were our secret until Mr. Wilson appeared before the joint meeting of the two houses of Congress.

I: What inspired you to call your program the Fourteen Points?

HOUSE (*smiles*): We did not christen the child. The name grew afterwards. I presume the Decalogue was not labeled the Ten Commandments when it was first promulgated by Moses.

I: No statement of Wilson's could brush aside the secret agreements of the Allies.

HOUSE: Even if the Allies gave only lip service to the Fourteen Points, they formally adopted them. It seemed to us that the Fourteen Points, being of later date, superseded all secret covenants of the past. That was the reason I fought so hard to make the Fourteen Points and Mr. Wilson's subsequent speeches, interpreting their spirit, the basis of the Armistice Agreement.

I: Was that also the opinion of President Wilson?

HOUSE: It was.

I: You are quite certain that Wilson knew about the Secret Treaties?

HOUSE: He did.

I: But he denied this knowledge before the Senate Committee?

HOUSE: Mr. Wilson's denial was based on a misunderstanding or some confusion of memory.

I: Why did Mr. Wilson in Paris consent to secret negotiations, in spite of his insistence upon open covenants openly arrived at?

HOUSE: The United States asked for open discussions in Paris from the very beginning, but did not make that point a condition of its participation in the Peace Conference. Open covenants openly arrived at does not necessarily mean that every preliminary discussion must be a public debate. It merely means that the larger lines of policy shall be made known and maintained without secret reservations.

I: Why did you permit the transference of Alsace-Lorraine to France without a plebiscite?

HOUSE: Point Eight, though somewhat equivocal, committed us to the return to France of these provinces. I originally objected to the inclusion of the phrase about Alsace-Lorraine. I had it out with Wilson one night. Before dinner Wilson agreed to drop it. After dinner he put it back.

I: What solution did you have in mind with regard to this problem?

H O U S E: I wanted to make Alsace-Lorraine an autonomous province of Switzerland, creating a neutral barrier between Germany and France, and giving both nations free access to its resources. The people of Alsace-Lorraine are much more akin to the Swiss than to the French or to the Germans. They were not happy under German rule and they do not seem to be happy now.

I: Why did Wilson drop the Freedom of the Seas at Paris?

H O U S E: He had come to the conclusion that a war contrary to the judgment of the League would automatically bar the offending nations from the seas. I did not agree with this view. I fought for the Freedom of the Seas at all times. I have rarely longed for the power and the responsibility of office. The Freedom of the Seas was the only question which made me regret that my power was vicarious. If I had been President of the United States, I would have put the Freedom of the Seas first on my program. I would not have dropped it overboard under any conditions. The United States could have used sufficient pressure to wrest this concession from England, if we had made the effort seriously enough. We should have secured the Freedom of the Seas at Versailles. Failing there, American diplomats had a second opportunity to win the recognition of the doctrine of the Freedom of the Seas from Premier MacDonald.

I: To what extent did you receive inspiration for the Fourteen Points from British sources?

H O U S E: We owe nothing to England. The Fourteen Points were evolved entirely between Wilson and myself. But naturally others were thinking along similar lines. Lloyd George decorated his pudding with plums from the same tree. I had just left the President in his study and got downstairs when Irving Hoover, the White House usher, handed me an afternoon paper with Lloyd George's speech. I immediately rushed back with the news to Mr. Wilson. I remember his consternation when he discovered some passages paralleling his own in the Lloyd George speech. "I am afraid," he said, "that kills our effort." "By no means," I replied. "Just hold back for two or three days and then issue your message. No one now living can contend with your magic.

You are to-day the most powerful man in the world. These thoughts, uttered by others, are leaden. Your eloquence gives them wings."

The purpose of the Fourteen Points was fourfold:

1. To secure the adhesion of the new Russian Government, which was distrustful of the purposes of the Allies.
2. To weaken the German Government by strengthening the revolutionary forces in Germany.
3. To align liberal opinion everywhere on the side of the Allies.
4. To compel the Allies to reconsider their war aims and to revise their secret agreements.

Wilson failed in his first objective completely. He succeeded completely in the second and third. The last objective remained undetermined. Lenin and Trotsky suspected the skeleton of secret treaties under the cloak of Wilson's rhetoric. But the promise of the Fourteen Points enthralled the Germans. Austria, coquetting with a separate peace, listened sympathetically to the siren voice of the American President. To liberal opinion in America, in the Allied countries, in fact everywhere, the Fourteen Points were a Holy Grail. The Allies accepted Wilson's war aims with their tongue in their cheek. To them the Fourteen Points were a stratagem of war, not a new political gospel. Both Wilson and House saw the fighting value of their program. That in no way detracts from their honesty.

Wilson's moral offensive, which reaches its culmination in the Fourteen Points, was more decisive than the millions in men and materials which America poured into Europe. God, as Napoleon surmised, may be on the side of the strongest battalions. But in this case victory was on the side of the most eloquent pen. Wilson's pen, mightier than the sword of Pershing or Foch, won the War for the Allies.

XXIX

THE NEW SANCTION IS BORN

The League is Born – Multiple Fathers – Snatched from the Womb of Time – Long-Distance Debates – Austria's Secret Peace Offer – Allied Statesmen Shake in Their Boots –"Force without Stint or Limit"– A League Symposium – House Writes a Covenant – History Stalks Through Magnolia

I T'S a wise child that knows its own father, especially where the paternity is divided. Multiple paternity is by no means infrequent in the realm of ideas. The League of Nations has many fathers. Foremost among them are the two men whose friendship is strangely interwoven with the fate of the world between 1912 and 1919. A League of Nations of some sort was present embryonically in the mind of the Duumvirate when Colonel House first set forth upon his great adventure in 1913.

During the World War able minds in many lands created patterns upon which such a League could be formed. England, the nation most interested in holding on to her slice of the globe, was fertile soil for the idea. Lord Parmoor, Lord Cecil and many others exchanged thoughts on the subject with Colonel House. It was a frequent topic of conversation between the Colonel and Sir Edward Grey, and frequent references to an association of nations guaranteeing the peace of the world appear in the correspondence between the Duumvirs. Elihu Root, William H. Taft and others associated with the League to Enforce Peace revolved similar ideas in their minds. It was Colonel House who, encouraged by Wilson, worked out the plan most completely. The conception that sprang from his head, fully armed and accoutered like Pallas Athena, was more or less the scheme that was finally adopted. House, as usual, gave the notion, Wilson the passion and the rhetoric. It was a perfect example of their intellectual symbiosis.

Wilson's interest in the League idea, growing gradually, spread like a tree until it overshadowed all else. The peculiar intellectual infatuation which bound him to House and his own pacifist obsession combined to make this consummation inevitable. If a League of Nations could be reared upon the ruins of the World War, then no price in blood was too high to pay. A League of Nations, a covenant between the peoples of the earth, was the only achievement that justified Wilson the warrior before his own Scotch-Presbyterian conscience. Without a covenant of peace, the blood of all those fallen in battle cried out against him—for all his rhetoric.

Colonel House faced the problem practically for the first time when he negotiated a Pan-American covenant to guarantee peace and territorial integrity with the A. B. C. Powers. The proposed Pan-American pact died still-born, but the idea of an association of nations was too vital to be pigeon-holed or smothered by red tape. It bobs up again in May, 1916. In the meantime, Duumvir House had discussed his peace plan applied on a large scale to all nations with the British Foreign Secretary. Wilson was so impressed with the idea that he proposed to promulgate the new doctrine in a speech before the League to Enforce Peace. He asked House to embody in concrete suggestions the essence of his discussions with Grey. The speech engaged the President's mind intensely. It seemed to him "the most important I shall ever be called upon to make." After that the idea of a League of Nations always persists in Wilson's mind. In December, 1916, he asks the belligerents to state their peace conditions, and holds out a "consort of nations" as "immediately practicable." A covenant of coöperative peace is the main thesis of his speech of January 22, 1917. The climax of the Fourteen Points is Wilson's insistence upon a General Association of Nations formed under specific covenants for the purpose of affording mutual guarantees of political independence and territorial integrity to great and small States alike.

Wilson's official biographer, Ray Stannard Baker, admits that not a single idea in the covenant of the League was original with the President. But, irrespective of authorship, Wilson became its most eloquent mouthpiece. Originality is not the prime requisite of great statesmanship. The philosopher originates ideas. The poet cloaks ideas in colorful language. The statesman translates them into reality. House was the philosopher. Wilson combined the functions of the poet and of the statesman. He voiced the idea and he forced it, perhaps prematurely, from the womb of time.

France and England, too much preoccupied with their own troubles to consider the League seriously as a part of the Peace Treaty, nevertheless appointed commissions to investigate the problem. House suggests an unofficial commission to study the League idea to Wilson. Wilson refuses. He wants no discussion, no "wool-gatherers." He entrusts the nurture of the embryo entirely to his Duumvir. From that moment House sends out feelers in every direction, anxious to collect all varieties of opinion. Sir William Wiseman assists the Colonel. It is interesting to see House in action through the eyes of Sir William:

> "He (House) sought the views of conservatives such as Root, of distinguished soldiers and sailors, labor leaders, pronounced pacifists, and extreme Socialists. He did not by any means confine his inquiries to American opinion, but tried to get the views of thoughtful men in every country. Busily occupied with many other urgent matters, he asked me and one or two other trusted friends to gather opinions regarding the League. In this way, House was able to give Wilson a very fair summary of world opinion about the Covenant so far as it was developed at that time."

Receiving the essence of all his information from House, Wilson prepared a message to Congress on the League in the first week of February, 1918. House found much to criticize in the draft. "I have never," House notes in his diary, "advised a quarter as many eliminations in any previous address as in this one." For several days the discussion waged. Wilson made a number of minor changes, and adopted two or three suggestions made by Lansing. The day before the speech was scheduled, February 10, House was still ill at ease. Wilson had laid too much stress upon peace, too little upon the war in which the nation was engaged. House advised the President to focus the world's attention on the military party in Germany. "I thought he should say that the entire world was now in substantial agreement as to a just peace with the exception of this small group who seemed determined to drive millions of men to their death in order to have their will.

"The President," House relates, "took a pad and pencil and began to frame a new paragraph. This paragraph begins: 'A general peace erected upon such foundations can be discussed,' and ends with the sentence, 'The tragic circumstance is that this one party in Germany is apparently willing and able to send millions of men to their deaths to prevent what all the world now sees to be just.' ..." Intended solely as an instrument of peace, the speech, by the intervention of House, became an instrument of war.

When Wilson delivered his speech before the joint session of Congress, he connected it directly with his Fourteen Points and their echo in all Central Europe. He curtly rejected certain suggestions made by Count Hertling, because the program of Bethmann-Hollweg's successor was based on the principle of barter and concession. "The method the German Chancellor proposes is the method of the Congress of Vienna. We cannot and will not return to that. What is at stake now is the peace of the world. What we are striving for is a new international order based upon broad and universal principles of right and justice—no mere peace of shreds and patches." In conclusion, Wilson stressed four fundamental principles upon which peace must be based:

> "First, that each part of the final settlement must be based upon the essential justice of that particular case and upon such adjustments as are most likely to bring a peace that will be permanent;
> "Second, that peoples and provinces are not to be bartered about from sovereignty to sovereignty as if they were mere chattels and pawns in a game, even the great game, now forever discredited, of the balance of power; but that
> "Third, every territorial settlement involved in this war must be made in the interest and for the benefit of the populations concerned, and not as a part of any mere adjustment or compromise of claims amongst rival states; and
> "Fourth, that all well-defined national aspirations shall be accorded the utmost satisfaction that can be accorded them without introducing new or perpetuating old elements of discord and antagonism that would be likely in time to break the peace of Europe and consequently of the world."

Within a week the British Intelligence Service picked up a secret peace offer from the young Austrian Emperor, Karl. Even before this, an Austrian Liberal leader, Dr. Lammasch, had flirted with Wilson's unofficial spokesman, Dr. George Herron, in Switzerland. Six days after the Emperor's message had been decoded in London, the Spanish Ambassador gravely presented it at the White House. Wilson had difficulty in composing his face and in trying to look surprised. If he had followed his first impulse, Wilson would have grasped the hand thus extended. But, swayed by House and the Allies, he made a noncommittal reply and ostensibly sought more information.

Wilson missed a great opportunity to put a halt to the futile slaughter. But the Allies were not ready for peace. The Treaty of Brest-Litovsk, denoting the complete collapse of Russia as an ally, and German victories on the Western Front weighed heavily on the minds of Allied statesmen. Why should they talk peace, while the fortunes of war were against them, when American blood and American money were pouring freely forth to tilt the scales in their favor? House feared that Germany would yield to Wilson's propaganda while still retaining her military strength. This did not coincide with his plans. He persuaded Wilson to shift the emphasis of his speech from salvation to victory. The Allied statesmen were shaking in their boots. Wilson's speech, stressing the necessity of meeting force with force, allayed their panic. Together, the Duumvirs prepared the speech. Wilson the warrior completely dominated Wilson the pacifist. But even here he pleads for a righteous and triumphant force which shall make right the law of the world. Beyond the bloody battlefield he sees a glimpse of the Covenant.

Wilson's speech, inaugurating the campaign for the Third Liberty Loan, rallied, as House had foreseen, the drooping spirits of the Allies:

> "For myself, I am ready, ready still, ready even now, to discuss a fair and just and honest peace at any time that it is sincerely proposed—a peace in which the strong and the weak shall fare alike. But the answer, when I proposed such a peace, came from the German commanders in Russia, and I cannot mistake the meaning of the answer.

"I accept the challenge.... Germany has once more said that force, and force alone, shall decide whether Justice and Peace shall reign in the affairs of men, whether Right as America conceives it, or Dominion as she conceives it shall determine the destinies of mankind. There is, therefore, but one response possible from us: Force, force to the utmost, Force without stint or limit, the righteous and triumphant Force which shall make Right the law of the world, and cast every selfish dominion down in the dust."

Wilson, while determined to fight to the limit, was equally determined to fight not for the selfish ambition of the Allies, but for world peace. He encouraged House to throw out his net, a fisher of men and ideas. House confers at a luncheon with Root, Taft, Lowell, with Mezes and with the Archbishop of York. He delivers to them a message from Wilson on the League:

"My own conviction, as you know, is that the administrative constitution of the League must grow and not be made; that we must begin with solemn covenants, covering mutual guarantees of political independence and territorial integrity (if the final territorial agreements of the peace conference are fair and satisfactory and ought to be perpetuated), but that the method of carrying those mutual pledges out should be left to develop of itself, case by case. Any attempt to begin by putting executive authority in the hands of any particular group of powers would be to sow a harvest of jealousy and distrust which would spring up at once and choke the whole thing. To take up one thing and only one, but quite sufficient in itself: The United States Senate would never ratify any treaty which put the force of the United States at the disposal of any such group or body. Why begin at the impossible end, when it is feasible to plant a system which will slowly but surely ripen into fruition?"

Most of the Colonel's guests thought that Wilson did not go far enough. Root volunteered to draw up a memorandum embracing concrete proposals for a machinery establishing a court or bureau of arbitration. House gathered mead from many chalices. While he conveyed to Wilson the essence of his negotiations with peace lovers in the United States, the Phillimore Committee in London drafted a constitution for the League. House now urges upon the President that the time has come to make at least a tentative draft of the American plan: "The trouble that I see ahead is that the English, French, or the groups here may hit upon some scheme that will appeal to people generally and

around it public opinion will crystallize to such an extent that
it will be difficult to change the form at the Peace Conference.
It is one of the things with which your name should be linked
during the ages. The whole world looks upon you as the champion
of the idea, but there is a feeling not only in this country but in
England and France as well that you are reluctant to take the
initiative."

Wilson, sweating blood over the Russian problem, did not
even read the Phillimore report. He turned it over to the Duumvir and asked him to supply data for an answer. The relations
of the two men once more reach their zenith, but there are gaps
in their communications. The President hails all letters from the
Duumvir with "deep satisfaction." "Unspoken thanks" go out to
him, even when there is no message from the White House. The
President is "very tired." There never were so many problems
per diem, it seems to him, as there are now. "But," he adds, "I
am well." Then, as an afterthought, "We are well." Evidently the
President had not replied to the Colonel's letters for two weeks.
Was a mutiny shaping itself in his mind against the overpowering
influence of the Colonel? Was it "I," his ego alone, that rebelled,
or did "we," Edith Bolling Wilson, incite the reaction?

Meanwhile, House, instead of merely collecting data for a
reply to the Phillimore report, wrote a covenant of his own,
christened it by that name, and returned it to Woodrow Wilson.
He was assisted on legal and technical points by David Hunter
Miller.

"In spite of the skepticism of the financial world," he writes
to Wilson, "panics have been made impossible and impending
disaster has been lifted. Now if war can be made impossible,
what a glorious culmination of your other accomplishments!"

This argument carried conviction. House's plan, with minor
variations, was laid before the Peace Conference by Woodrow
Wilson. He forced it, at Versailles, upon conqueror and vanquished alike. But he was unable to secure its adoption at home.

The Covenant submitted to Wilson by House proclaims a
new code of international morals and affirms the right of any
nation to "butt in" for the purpose of preserving peace. Although
Wilson made several important changes, the essence of the in-

strument remained untouched. He incorporated two or three preliminary clauses into the Preamble, eliminated the World Court
provided by House, and added military to economic sanctions.
In order to read his version of the covenant to Colonel House,
Wilson left Washington and arrived at Magnolia on the North
Shore of Massachusetts, where House was summering, on August
15, 1918. The Presidential train waited on a siding at Magnolia
Station. Mrs. T. Jefferson Coolidge, a member of the branch of
the Coolidge family descended from Thomas Jefferson, put her
beautiful country house, a few minutes' walk from the residence
of Colonel House, at Wilson's disposal.

I visited the historical spot on the North Shore where Wilson, in a secret conclave with his Duumvir, put the finishing
touches upon the Covenant. I retraced with Colonel House the
path which the two men had trodden and the ideas which they
had exchanged. "This," Wilson said to House, "is what I have
done to your constitution of the League of Nations." The immediate exigencies of the War were forgotten. Wilson the pacifist,
released from the tyranny of Wilson the warrior, embraced his
friend. Their souls met in a common ideal. Sir William Wiseman,
who was always at the elbow of Colonel House, vividly recalls
the meeting of the Duumvirs. "Withdrawn for a brief space from
the atmosphere of Washington, Wilson was able to discuss with
House, and give his mind to, the broader questions of war aims
and the League. I remember one afternoon in particular the President and Colonel House sat on the lawn in front of House's
cottage with maps of Europe spread out before them discussing
ways and means of organizing Liberal opinion to break down the
German military machine, and how the nations which had suffered from oppression might be safeguarded in the future. The
Allied embassies in Washington," Sir William adds, "were keenly
interested and somewhat disturbed about the conferences at
Magnolia. Rumors of peace overtures were flying around, and,
with one excuse or another, various embassies tried to reach that
part of the North Shore, where they felt the destinies of Europe
were being decided."

Thus the New Sanction was born. History stalked through
Magnolia.

XXX

HOUSE SAVES THE FOURTEEN POINTS AT THE ARMISTICE CONFERENCE

Germany's Imperial Scapegoat – The German Government Tricks the Kaiser – Uncle Sam's Trojan Horse – Five New Commandments – Pershing's March to Berlin – The Colonel's Tiff with Lloyd George and the Tiger – House Threatens a Separate Peace – German Collapse Weakens Wilson's Hand

WHEN Germany crumbled under Wilson's bombardment, the German Government promptly offered the Kaiser as a visible scapegoat on the altar of the New Sanction. In spite of the hunger blockade, Germany, victoriously holding her own against twenty-two nations, could have held out many more months. But what was the object of continuing to fight when the Moses in the White House was showing the way for all mankind to a new promised land across the Red Sea of war? The diplomats of Wilhelmstrasse forgot in their calculations that the Emperor was the keystone of the German arch. Without him the whole structure tumbled. The High Command, equally blind, failed to thwart the conspiracy of Berlin. The Imperial Chancellor, Prince Max of Baden, told the Kaiser: "Blood is flowing on the streets of Berlin." It was a lie. Hindenburg, his most trusted military admirer, assured the Emperor that the army would refuse to fight or march under his command. Men close to William II assert that the Field Marshal's statement was not based upon a careful survey of the army. It was the opinion of a few political generals, influenced by the Cabinet in Berlin.

The Germans, like Wilson, took the Fourteen Points seriously—too seriously. Hindenburg told the Kaiser: "Stay, and we shall have war abroad and revolution at home. Go, and we shall have peace at home and an honorable peace based on the Fourteen Points with the Allies." The harassed Emperor had no choice. Ill-advised and misinformed, William II laid down his imperial crown. But he refused to abdicate as King of Prussia. His cousin, the Chancellor, Prince Max of Baden, took the unwarranted liberty of proclaiming William's abdication as Emperor and King. Without consulting the Crown Prince, he simultaneously announced that the Emperor's heir had relinquished the right of succession. Father and son were sacrificed on the altar of the Fourteen Points. To his people, the Emperor's abdication and exile seemed like desertion. Everywhere in Germany thrones toppled. Few realized that the revolution received its impetus from above. It was the Government itself which cynically thrust the reins into the hands of the Socialists. German Socialism was not prepared for the task.

Apologists for the German Revolution claim that Ludendorff's demand for an immediate armistice made the débâcle inevitable. Ludendorff attempted to explain his act to me and to others. It still remains incomprehensible. He suggests that his demand was a bluff to force the vacillating Chancellor into action. He expected to rally the German people for a last desperate fight, once the peace terms of the Allies were known. If so, the Fourteen Points upset his game. Others claim that Ludendorff lost his nerve when he realized that upon his shoulders lay the entire burden of responsibility. Some insist that he acted under a momentary spell of hysteria. We shall never know the full truth. History is ever a patchwork of facts and fancies. But there is no doubt that Ludendorff never contemplated surrender. He saw no possibility of victory. But he was far from acknowledging defeat. The German army, he claimed, was undefeated in the field. Woodrow Wilson's Fourteen Points were the Trojan horse that carried defeat into Germany. House was the Ulysses, Wilson the Agamemnon of this siege. But their intentions, unlike those of their Greek predecessors, were honest. They thought that their Trojan horse carried in its belly liberty enlightening the world. They did not foresee the conflagration that followed.

Germany, though hamstrung by the revolution, did not lay down her arms unconditionally. Her peace offer was based upon the Fourteen Points and the subsequent speeches of President Wilson. The Allies themselves, nearly collapsing, were willing to make peace on this basis, until it became apparent that Germany was a rudderless ship. When the truth dawned upon the Allies they deemed it convenient to forget the new solemn gospel enunciated in their behalf by the President of the United States. It was here that Duumvir House leaped into the breach. He saved the Fourteen Points.

Wilson had not handicapped his Duumvir with instructions. "I have not given you instructions," he said, "because I feel you will know what to do."

"I have been thinking of this before," House notes in his diary, "and wondered at the strange situation our relations had brought about. I am going on one of the most important missions any one ever undertook, and yet there is no word of direction, advice or discussion between us. He knows that our minds are generally parallel and he also knows that where they diverge I would follow his bend rather than my own."

Wilson designated House officially to represent the United States in the Supreme War Council. Nevertheless, his power flowed less from this designation than from Wilson's friendship. In a letter dated October 14, 1918, To Whom It May Concern, Woodrow Wilson writes:

> "Mr. Edward M. House, the bearer of this letter, is my personal representative, and I have asked him to take part as such in the conferences of the Supreme War Council and in any other conference in which it may be serviceable for him to represent me. I commend him to the confidence of all representatives of the Governments with which the Government of the United States is associated in the War."

Similar notes went out to the Premiers of all nations and to the ambassadors of the United States at London, Paris and Rome. The spectacle of a private citizen armed with the affectionate confidence of the President, sailing back from the New World to redress the balance of the Old was, as E. P. Gooch remarks, indeed unique.

It was necessary to rescue not merely the Fourteen Points, but the pledges solemnly made in two subsequent speeches by President Wilson. Wilson's speech of September 27, at the Metro-

politan Opera House, reiterated the necessity of a League of
Nations as the most essential part of the peace settlement. He
made certain other stipulations:

> "First, the impartial justice meted out must involve no
> discrimination between those to whom we wish to be just
> and those to whom we do not wish to be just. It must be a
> justice that plays no favorites and knows no standard but the
> equal rights of the several peoples concerned.
>
> "Second, no special or separate interest of any single
> nation or any group of nations can be made the basis of any
> part of the settlement which is not consistent with the com-
> mon interest of all.
>
> "Third, there can be no leagues or alliances or special
> covenants and understandings within the general and com-
> mon family of the League of Nations.
>
> "Fourth, and more specifically, there can be no special,
> selfish economic combinations within the League and no
> employment of any form of economic boycott or exclusion
> except as the power of economic penalty by exclusion from
> the markets of the world may be vested in the League of
> Nations itself as a means of discipline and control.
>
> "Fifth, all international agreements and treaties of every
> kind must be made known in their entirety to the rest of
> the world."

The President's eloquence reverberated throughout the
world. It aroused responsive chords in Central Europe. Before
transmitting the German demand for an armistice and peace to
the Allies, President Wilson exacted from the Germans a clear-cut
acceptance of the Fourteen Points and their progeny, assurances
that the Chancellor spoke in the name of the German people and
not of its "military masters," and the evacuation of the invaded
territories.

At first, the military aspect of the Armistice engaged the
attention of Duumvir House. House asked Foch: "Will you tell
us, M. le Marechal, solely from the military point of view, apart
from any other consideration, whether you would prefer the Germans to reject or to sign the armistice as outlined here?" Foch

replied: "Fighting means struggling for certain results. If the Germans now sign ... those results are in our possession. This being achieved, no man has the right to cause another drop of blood to be shed."

The Allied generals, aware of the crack in their armor, regarded the German offer of an armistice as a godsend. Pershing had visions of marching at the head of his troops into Berlin. Colonel House laid Pershing's memorandum before Clemenceau and Lloyd George without recommendation. The Allied leaders brushed it aside contemptuously. The word is Seymour's, not mine.

Haig, the British commander, wanted to impose generous conditions. Foch, while desiring peace, insisted on harsher terms. The terms finally agreed upon were more severe than necessary. The Allies still could not believe their good luck. No one realized the extent of Germany's demoralization. No one seriously expected her to bend her neck under the yoke. The German armies were still holding Belgium and vast stretches of France. The Allies had advanced, but they lacked the equipment to follow up their success. Foch expected the Germans to hold certain strategic lines behind the front until the spring. He told me so himself. The roads were destroyed. Allied resources were failing. Their peoples were tired of war. The Allies could not disentangle their transportation snarl, and advance. American troops were only beginning to get into action. Without America, the Allies were more thoroughly defeated than Germany. With America they could hold their own. The Duumvirs held in their hands the scales of history.

House, Clemenceau and Lloyd George were the Big Three who made the Armistice. The Italian, Orlando, played a subordinate part. House opposed the Tiger's sometimes unreasonable demands, but he would have opposed them even more resolutely if it had not been for the fascination which Clemenceau exercised over him. But, underneath his velvet, House now and then displayed steel. He made many concessions, perhaps too many, but he was adamant when Clemenceau, Sonnino and Lloyd George, each for a different reason, wanted to discard the Fourteen Points. He was prepared to defend the new map of the world which he had drawn up with Wilson on that historic Saturday between 10.30 and 12.30.

"Have you ever been asked by President Wilson," Clemenceau remarked to Lloyd George, eyebrows uplifted, "whether you accept the Fourteen Points?"

"I have never been asked."

"I have not been asked either," retorted the French Prime Minister.

"What"—he turned to Colonel House—"is your view? Do you think if we agree to an armistice we accept the President's peace terms?"

"That is my view," replied the Duumvir.

"I cannot consider the Freedom of the Seas," Lloyd George insisted, "unless the League of Nations is established first. If the League of Nations is a reality I am willing to discuss the matter."

"The Freedom of the Seas," House explained, "does not necessarily mean the abolition of the blockade. It merely signifies a new code, guaranteeing immunity to private property at sea during war. In case of another war, British interference with American trade would throw the United States into the arms of Great Britain's enemy, whoever that enemy might be.

"Great Britain," he continued, "might find itself at war with some other Power, possibly France; in the past war the sympathy of the United States had been with the Allies, because of Germany's abominable naval practices; in a future war if France did not resort to any of these practices and was the weaker naval power, the sympathy of the United States might be with France."

Lloyd George held that the doctrine of absolute freedom of navigation upon the seas would wrest sea power from the hands of Great Britain.

"I do not believe," Colonel House expounded, "that the United States and other countries will submit to Great Britain's domination of the seas any more than to Germany's domination on land. The sooner the English recognize this fact, the better it will be for them. Challenged, our people will build a navy and army greater than yours."

When the Allies balked, House threatened. "I shall advise the President to go before Congress and say: 'We have attained

our war aims. Shall we make peace upon the terms which we
ourselves have proposed, or shall we pursue the War until all the
separate war aims of Great Britain, Italy and France are
achieved?' "

The threat of Colonel House to telegraph to the President
excited both Lloyd George and Clemenceau.

"That," Clemenceau shouted, "would amount to a separate
peace between the United States and the Central Powers."

"It might," the Duumvir replied firmly, but cautiously.

"If the United States made a separate peace," argued Lloyd
George, "we would be sorry, but we could not give up the
blockade, the power which enables us to live; as far as the British
public is concerned, we will fight on."

"Yes," interposed Clemenceau, throwing his weight on the
side of his British colleague, "I cannot understand the meaning
of the doctrine. War would not be war if there was Freedom of
the Seas."

The Colonel's diary records the vehemence of the discussions
between himself and the English. "Great Britain," Lloyd George
insisted, "would spend her last guinea to keep her navy superior
to that of the United States or that of any other power. No
Cabinet could officially continue in the Government in England
that took a different position."

"It is not," replied House calmly, "our purpose to go into
a naval-building rivalry with Great Britain. But it is our purpose
to have our rights at sea adequately safeguarded, and we do not
intend to have our commerce regulated by Great Britain whenever she is at war."

When George sent Reading to argue the matter, House told
him bluntly: "You are wasting your breath. Under no circumstances will we yield the point about the Freedom of the Seas."

The policy of House throughout the war had been to guarantee coöperation between the English-speaking nations. The sole
menace to that coöperation was the naval policy of Great Britain,
which was responsible for the War of 1812 and very nearly en-
gulfed us in the War of 1914 on the side of England's enemies.
If that danger was not removed, then his policy had failed disas-
trously.

Wilson seconded the Duumvir. "I feel it my solemn duty to authorize you to say that I cannot consent to take part in the negotiations of a peace which does not include the Freedom of the Seas, because we are pledged to fight not only Prussian militarism but militarism everywhere.

"Neither could I participate in a settlement which does not include a League of Nations because such a peace would result within a period of years in there being no guarantee except universal armaments, which would be disastrous. I hope I shall not be obliged to make this decision public."

Faced with this ultimatum, the Allies at last relented. Wilson was more powerful in Washington than in Paris. House could appeal to the absent Cæsar. If Cæsar had been present, Cæsar himself might have weakened.

"Would Wilson have backed you up?" I asked.

"He always did," House replied. "Wilson never disavowed any act of mine."

But House was unable to prevent Lloyd George and Clemenceau from making certain significant reservations. The French inserted a clause reserving the "future claims" of the Allies. Apparently innocuous in itself, this sentence became the focus of an infection from which Europe may never recover. The reservation made by Great Britain may prove an apple of discord between the United States and England in the next World War.

The Freedom of the Seas was not "rejected." Its discussion was merely postponed for the consideration of the Peace Conference.

Sonnino, speaking for Italy, made certain complaints concerning Point Nine which touched upon the Italian frontiers, but his argument was ignored on the ground that this was a matter which concerned Austria, not Germany. The Austrians were in such a hurry for an armistice that the Fourteen Points were not formally included in the agreement between them and the Allies. Unlike Sonnino, House considered that the benefit of the Fourteen Points extended to Austria as well as to Germany. He advised Wilson to accept the reservations of Lloyd George and Clemenceau.

Wilson replied: "I am proud of the way you are handling the situation," and did as he was advised.

The postponement of the issue of the Freedom of the Seas was a costly, perhaps a fatal, blunder. Duumvir House fought bravely to secure the acceptance of that fundamental American doctrine. If he failed, the blame rests partly upon his shoulders. When Wilson was willing to respond to Austrian and German peace feelers, the Duumvir urged delay. If Wilson had acted more swiftly, the complete collapse of Germany would have been averted. A week or a fortnight gained would have saved the Government of the Kaiser. After the War the German people could have asked for an accounting from its leaders. But the Revolution, on the verge of peace, bred chaos and ruin. Germany's weakness militated against the unreserved acceptance of Wilson's program. It weakened Wilson's position because America was no longer indispensable to the Allies. To that extent Colonel House must share the responsibility for the miscarriage of his own high hopes with the Kaiser's Chancellor, Prince Max of Baden.

But House has no such reflection. On November 11, 1918, Armistice Day, Duumvir House, for once emotional, cables to Duumvir Wilson: "Autocracy is dead. Long live democracy and its immortal leader. In this great hour my heart goes out to you in pride, admiration and love."

XXXI

MOHAMMED COMES TO THE MOUNTAIN

Wilson Decides to Make Peace in Person – House Upsets the President –
Roosevelt Thunders in the Index – Wilson's Puppets in Paris – The Duumvir
Moves – Allied Plot to Poison President – Wilson's Infelicitous Joke – Wood-
row Wilson's Obsession – The Duumvir and the Tiger – Clouds with a Purple
Hue

MESSIAHS should travel alone. Woodrow Wilson set forth
to save Europe with Edith Bolling Wilson. Caparisoned
from head to foot in purple, a purple dress, a purple hat and a
purple plume, she cast a purple shadow athwart the friendship of
the Duumvirs.

Long before we entered the World War, House had suggested to Wilson the convocation of a meeting of world powers
for the purpose of forming a League to prevent future wars. It
seemed to him that no such League could be founded without
the propulsion of Wilson's powerful personality. When the time
for the Peace Conference came, the seed planted by Colonel House
in Wilson's mind began to sprout. But now conditions were different. The Colonel no longer favored the personal participation
of Wilson under the changed conditions. But in Wilson the idea
of presiding over the Peace Conference had taken root so firmly
that it could not be plucked out, even by Colonel House.

Forgetting his temperamental and physical limitations, Wilson decided to make the peace in person. Whether there was in
this decision a touch of megalomania, or whether he suspected,
rightly or wrongly, that he could rely on no one save himself, it
is difficult to determine. Possibly something of both elements entered into the decision. Other factors exercised a powerful in-

fluence. *Cherchez la femme* plays an important part in politics as well as in detective fiction. Wilson's second term was drawing near its end. The War had played havoc with the social ambitions of the Mistress of the White House. The European trip enabled Edith Bolling Wilson to play First Lady of the World.

The opposition which arose almost at once only strengthened Wilson's determination. George W. Wickersham, former Attorney General, and ex-Senator George F. Edmunds issued opinions that Wilson would cease legally to be the head of the Government if he left the soil of the United States. An effort was made to secure a court order to declare the office of President vacant. Newspapers and orators proclaimed that ninety-five per cent of the American people viewed Wilson's contemplated trip to Europe with "misgiving and dislike."

The Colonel's position was difficult. "It is always dangerous," he explained, "for Mohammed to come to the mountain. While Wilson was in Washington he could control the situation. If we went too far in our concessions, he could disavow them. We could always gain time by asking for instructions from him. At the proper moment he could hurl a thunderbolt from the heights in which he dwelled securely like Jove. But the moment he came down to earth, he lost his divine status. He became a mortal among mortals.

"It was Wilson's original idea that he would be asked to preside over the Peace Conference. I pointed out to him that such a procedure violated tradition. Diplomatic usage reserves that distinction for the head of the State where a conference takes place. Wilson occupied a position like a monarch. Lloyd George spoke to him as if he were a king with whom one does not argue or debate. He was not only a king, but he was the greatest king in the world.

"The moment he stepped among the delegates and became a delegate, they could wrangle freely with him as with one another. He was merely one of the Big Four. In fact he put himself slightly under Clemenceau who was the chairman. Moreover, Wilson did not confine himself to conferences with the Big Four. He attended regular conferences which were more like town-hall meetings.

"He dominated some of these meetings by virtue of his personality. But nevertheless he was no longer king, no longer Jupiter thundering on Olympus. The minute he entered the door of the council chamber he lost his crown. He was also somewhat handicapped by not being familiar with men and localities. When Wilson returned to America, I immediately got Clemenceau to restore the meetings of the Big Four which had functioned so well at the time of the Armistice. When Wilson returned to Paris he accepted the change."

The situation at home, as well as abroad, made Wilson's trip inadvisable. Wilson had told House, before the Duumvir sailed for Europe, of his contemplated appeal for a Democratic Congress. House made no reply to that suggestion. His silence indicated his disapproval. Wilson's only error was verbal. He should have asked not for a Democratic Congress but for a Congress which, irrespective of party, supported America's war aim. Under the circumstances it was unwise to irritate the opposition. In spite of these complications, the Colonel could not strongly urge the President to stay at home. If he had done so, his motives would have been maligned.

Indirectly, he voiced his dissent. If Wilson did not understand, his obtuseness was intentional. The Duumvir wired that Americans in Paris were "practically unanimous" in the belief that it would be "unwise" for him to sit in the Peace Conference. Clemenceau, he added, thought that no head of a state should sit there. The same feeling prevailed in England. Cobb, Reading and Wiseman held similar views. But recognizing that Mr. Wilson's mind was made up and that Mrs. Wilson was packing her trunks, the Colonel suggested a compromise. Why not limit his participation to the preliminary conference to determine the larger outlines of the settlement? "In announcing your departure I think it important," the Duumvir cautiously insinuated, "that you should not state that you will sit at the Peace Conference. That can be determined after you get there."

Wilson's reply, preserved in the archives of Yale, shows that he was annoyed by the Duumvir's cable. It upset every plan "we" had made. "We" presumably refers to himself and Edith Bolling Wilson. The change of program throws him into "complete confusion." He considers the suggestion that he should not participate as a delegate a way of "pocketing" him. He infers that the French and British leaders desire to exclude him from the Conference because they fear he might lead the weaker nations against them. Reverting to his favorite theory, he points out this: the President plays the same part in our Government as the Prime Ministers play in theirs. The fact that he is head of the State seems of no practical importance to him. He objects very strongly to a dignity that prevents the attainment of the results upon which he and House have set their hearts.

Wilson's isolation from the currents of public opinion in the United States had already begun. For, with complete disregard of all opposition, he insists that America "universally expects and generally desires" his attendance at the Conference. No one, he adds acidly, would wish me "to sit by and try to steer from the outside." He hopes House will be "very shy of the advice of others," and give him his own independent judgment "after reconsideration." House reassures the President that the forces of reaction are not conspiring against him. "As far as I can see all the powers are trying to work with us rather than with one another." Wilson's decision to come to Paris remains adamant, but he issues the non-committal statement suggested by House on his status in the Peace Conference.

The Congressional election of 1918 had gone against the Duumvirs, not merely because of Wilson's unguarded statement. The pro-Germans and the pro-Irish wanted to punish the pacifist President for having gotten us into the War. The pro-Allies wanted to punish him for not having gotten us into the War sooner. There was, moreover, a lively reaction against the restraints imposed by war legislation, especially the infamous Espionage Act, and the drastic manner in which the Post Office Department under Burleson had throttled public opinion. Wilson's obstinate refusal to consult the opposition leaders embittered the men who had hoped to invade the citadel of governmental power through the breach of patriotism. House would have used the occasion to ingratiate himself with the opposition, since, under the changed circumstances, Wilson could no longer count upon Congress.

Roosevelt, writing from his sick-bed in the hospital, assailed the Fourteen Points. "Our Allies and our enemies," he exclaimed, "and Mr. Wilson himself, should all understand that Mr. Wilson has no authority whatever to speak for the American people at this time. Mr. Wilson and his Fourteen Points, and his four supplementary points, and his five complementary points, are all assurances for which we have ceased to have any shadow of right to be accepted as expressive of the will of the American people. Let them (the Allies) impose their common will on the nations responsible for the hideous disaster which has almost wrecked mankind." Mr. Roosevelt added that the only supporters of the Fourteen Points were "Mr. Wilson, Mr. Hearst and Mr. Viereck."

To Roosevelt, in the throes of war psychosis, Mr. Hearst and I seemed the embodiment of all villainy. But Roosevelt was not the Republican Party. House suggests the appointment of Taft and Root as peace commissioners. With their support, Wilson would have been invincible both at home and in Paris. But Wilson balks. He desires for once to hold the reins entirely in his hands. He even refuses to name his own son-in-law, McAdoo, and appoints a colorless commission which he and his alter ego dominated completely. In his new mood, Wilson wants only tools, men who will do his bidding without question. He selects General Bliss, accustomed to obey orders, Secretary Lansing, the shadow Secretary of State, and Henry White, a colorless Republican without party backing. Lansing, choking his smoldering resentment, was a puppet in Wilson's hands. Bliss and White were not consulted in important decisions. Their position was unfortunate. House was the only man on the committee whose opinions received consideration from Wilson. The symbiotic ties between them, though weakened, were not yet broken. Perhaps Wilson thought of himself as the sun and of House as his moon. But the moon did not disappear when the sun emerged. The simultaneous appearance of both luminaries wrought confusion in Paris.

Wilson sailed for Europe with high hopes. In a talk on shipboard he told members of the Peace Commission that America was the only disinterested nation at the Peace Conference. The men with whom she was compelled to deal did not represent their own people. The Paris meeting was the first peace conference in which decisions depended upon the opinion of mankind, not upon previous determinations and diplomatic schemes. If the conference was not dominated by this principle, he predicted another break-up of the world. "Such a break-up, when it comes," he said, "will not be a war but a cataclysm." The League of Nations would vouchsafe the political independence and territorial integrity of all nations. Terms and boundaries could be altered, if it could be shown that injustice had been done, or that conditions had changed. It would be easier to bring about such alterations after the passions of war had subsided. To quote further from the notes of Dr. Isaiah Bowman:

> "Anticipating the difficulties of the Conference in view of the suggestion he had made respecting the desire of the people of the world for a new order, he remarked, 'If it won't work, it must be made to work,' because the world was faced by a task of terrible proportions and only the adoption of a cleansing process would recreate or regenerate the world. The poison of Bolshevism was accepted readily by the world because 'it is a protest against the way in which the world has worked.' It was to be our business at the Peace Conference to fight for a new order, 'agreeably if we can, disagreeably if necessary.' "

Mrs. Wilson's arrival gave rise to various problems of etiquette which were solved without difficulty. Sudden illness prevented House from welcoming the President and Mrs. Wilson at Brest. Wilson had planned to reach Paris on his lucky day, Friday the 13th. But once more, as in the case of the Fourteen Points, Fate decided otherwise. The President did not arrive until the 14th. His arrival was a holiday for Paris. Europe looked upon its Saviour. The masses everywhere clamored for Wilson. House, the prime mover of Wilson's politics, was unheeded by the people. But he continued to be heard by the Cabinets. When the President arrives in the French capital, House moves over from his headquarters at 78 Rue de l'Université to the Crillon, henceforth the official home of the American Peace Commission. He is reconciled to play a subordinate part. In his diary he notes: "The President is in European waters now and can be easily reached by wireless. Therefore, I shall make no further decisions myself."

The masses jubilated, but the governments were alarmed by

Wilson's determination to take part in the Peace Conference. Major Herbert O. Yardley charges an Allied plot to administer slow poison to President Wilson by giving him the influenza in ice. This message came through in an intricate code which Yardley deciphered. "I have no way," he remarks in *The Black Chamber*, "of knowing whether this plot had any truth in fact and if it had, whether they succeeded. But there are these intangible facts. President Wilson's first sign of illness occurred while he was in Paris and he was soon to die a lingering death." House pooh-poohs this suggestion. The fact remains that both he and Wilson were victims of the "flu" in Paris.

The dread of Wilson in England and France was real enough. It was so real that House, with Sir William Wiseman, mapped out an interview for Wilson outlining his views, to allay the alarm in French and British hearts. The interview in the *Times*, unfortunately, showed that Wilson was weakening on the most important of the Fourteen Points. Wilson admitted that Great Britain's historical tradition entitled her to an exceptional position in the discussion of naval problems. He practically drowned the Freedom of the Seas on his trip from New York to Brest.

More logical than psychological, Wilson maintained that the League of Nations made a special agreement of this type superfluous. "The Freedom of the Seas," he blithely remarked in Paris. "I must tell you about that. It's a great joke on me. I left America thinking the Freedom of the Seas the most important issue of the Peace Conference. When I got here I found there was no such issue. You see, the Freedom of the Seas concerns neutrals in time of war. But when we have the League of Nations there will be no neutrals in time of war. So, of course, there will be no question of the Freedom of the Seas. I hadn't thought the thing out clearly." But the League, in Wilson's mind, was a League with teeth.

Wilson still thought that he could enforce his ideas in Paris. House knew that, with the complete breakdown of Germany, Wilson's power to impose a peace treaty on his own terms was gone. He also gauged correctly the influence of the political opposition to Wilson at home. Unfortunately the severe attack of influenza to which I have already referred crippled House in the formative period of the Peace Conference. As soon as he could stand on his feet he resumed his burdens.

André Tardieu had prepared a tentative peace treaty based on the Fourteen Points. But the Duumvirs permitted this document to be thrown into the discard. It was not even discussed. Subsequently Wilson, Clemenceau, Lloyd George and Orlando whittled away the Fourteen Points one by one. No one warned Wilson. No one, except House. When both Duumvirs attended a conference, little slips of paper constantly passed from the one to the other. He still was, as William Allen White calls him, the generalissimo of his army of trained genii. "Facts came to his hand when he rubbed his wishing ring, and truth, separated from the facts like gold from ore, always was at his hand ready for his chief."

But there was one who was more constantly at Wilson's side. That was Edith Bolling Wilson in her dark purple suit with her purple plume and her purple hat. She rode beside the President on every occasion. House arranged for a private telephone wire, guarded against tapping, between himself and Wilson. They could reach each other without intermediary. But the second Mrs. Wilson was closer still. She instinctively resented Wilson's dependence on House. His visits left Wilson often irritated, in doubt of himself. What wife would not be annoyed by such a friend?

"At one time," House says, "I had persuaded him not to participate in the conferences. Clemenceau had raised the point that if Wilson attended, President Poincaré might also wish to attend the conferences. It was pointed out in that case that King George, the King of Italy, and King Albert of Belgium could not be prevented from participating in the meetings if they desired to do so. 'If that is true,' Wilson said, 'I am willing to relinquish the idea.'

"But Clemenceau, after some reflection, changed his mind and induced Lloyd George to do likewise. They may have realized that by going into the conferences Wilson sacrificed his most effective thunderbolt."

Wilson concentrated his efforts upon the League of Nations. The Covenant became to Wilson the symbol of his achievement. The Covenant alone justified the War as a war to end war. He insisted upon the Covenant before the Treaty. It must be an integral part of the Treaty. Wilson's own version of this instrument follows closely the draft of Colonel House. It was House who reconciled the differences between the American and the British conception.

The work on the Covenant was finished on the thirteenth of February. The number of articles was twice thirteen. Both facts were pleasing to Wilson. On February 14, 1919, Wilson addressed the Peace Conference on the League Covenant. That was the climax of his first visit to Paris. It was, as William Allen White describes it, "a typical Wilsonian performance, a great thing done insignificantly."

"All the notables crowded about him stiffly, shaking mannikin hands with him, apparently congratulating him. But Mrs. Wilson, who had exchanged smiles with him as he spoke, smiled proudly when he finished, and her smiles were the only human thing of the occasion; the only indication in the hour that this man had done a big thing, who, by sheer force of will, from unwilling governments had wrested a radical covenant of democracy. From the whole tone which he set for the day, a stranger, not understanding his words, might have thought he was bidding on a list of livestock at a country fair."

It was now necessary to gain the consent of Congress to the Covenant. Wilson, more than ever convinced of his power, did not envisage the difficulties involved. House advised the President to confer with the Committee on Foreign Relations of the Senate immediately on his return. Wilson grudgingly made the arrangement through Tumulty. But meetings of this type went against his grain.

Before his departure, Wilson explains: "In technical matters most of the brains I used were borrowed. The possessors of the brains are in Paris." He leaves with an easy mind, convinced that his principles have won. Nevertheless, when House suggests the possibility that everything could be "buttoned up" in the next four weeks, Wilson is startled and even alarmed. He wants no final conclusion before his return. House agrees. "Please," he asks, "bear in mind that it is sometimes necessary to compromise." "I did not," he writes in his notebook, "wish him to leave expecting the impossible in all things."

In January, House has a conference with Hoover. In the

light of present events, the report of the conversation which he sets down in his diary assumes prophetic significance:

"Hoover and I had a long talk upon the food situation and upon the situation in general. He takes, as usual, a gloomy outlook and I must confess that things do not seem cheerful. There is every evidence that the Allies have a growing intention not to repay us the money we have loaned them. One hears the argument, both in France and England, that we ought to pay our full share of the Allies' war debt; that we ought to have come in sooner; and that their fight was our fight. I for one have never admitted this. I have always felt that the United States was amply able to take care of herself; that we were never afraid of the Germans, and would not have been afraid of them even if France and England had gone under. We would have had a serious time, I admit, and there would have been a war in all human probability; but that we ever feared that they could defeat us or dominate us, has never seemed to me probable."

Events make House again and again the ally of Clemenceau. The wily Frenchman accepted Wilson's Covenant under the spell of House. But in return he exacted the sacrifice of the remaining thirteen points. The affection between House and Clemenceau was real. "I think of you as a brother," said Clemenceau, embracing the Duumvir in the demonstrative fashion of his race. "I want you to tell me everything that is in your mind and we will work together just as if we were parts of the same government." It is dangerous to fraternize with a tiger!

On February 15, 1919, Wilson goes home, the Covenant in his pocket. No other problem is settled. Every one in Paris breathes a sigh of relief when the inconvenient idealist departs. The members of the American Peace Commission are no exception. House uses all his mesmerism to compose ruffled feelings. The Duumvir organizes at this time the Council of the Big Four. A gesture on his part creates the new Poland. A word from him changes a boundary line. He has many friends. But there are also foes. Having emerged from his self-imposed obscurity, he becomes the target of envy and intrigue. A cabal shapes itself against him in the immediate environment of the President. Every day the forces against the Duumvir gather momentum. Suspicion crowds suspicion. Shadows fall; clouds gather. And every cloud has a purple hue.

WOODROW WILSON DROPS THE PILOT

WHEN Woodrow Wilson first went to Europe he was a god. When he came the second time he was a politician who had lost his constituency. His loss of prestige at home became more apparent with every fresh outburst from the office of *The Outlook* and from Capitol Hill. Wilson's first visit was a triumphal procession. He was the saviour of the world, the prophet of a new dispensation. It was the high tide of idealism. When he returned again, the dreams for which he had fought were carried away by the backwash of national greeds.

France attempted to make the League an anti-German Alliance. Clemenceau, unlike Wilson, had his people and his parliament behind him. He wanted a realistic peace, a peace of conquest, and he got what he wanted. False rumors reached Wilson that House had consented to separate the Treaty from the Covenant and that he was making innumerable concessions obnoxious to Wilson. At first, the opposition criticized both House and Wilson; then they hit upon the strategy of attacking Wilson and praising House. This finally got under Wilson's skin. The star of the Duumvir begins to pale, the star of Edith Bolling Wilson rises on Wilson's horizon. Innumerable busybodies, basking in the sun of the Presidential favor, put not one but a host of fleas into the President's ear. Wilson impatiently brushed their tales away, but they left, nevertheless, an indelible trace. He was con-

vinced that his hand alone could pilot the ship of the world into
the harbor of permanent peace. He rushed to Paris once more,
but, being a poor negotiator, sacrificed more than House. On
March 3, 1919, House writes in his diary:

> "It is now evident that the peace will not be such a peace as I
> had hoped. . . . If the President should exert his influence among the
> liberals and laboring classes, he might possibly overthrow the govern-
> ments in Great Britain, France, and Italy; but if he did, he would
> still have to reckon with our own people and he might bring the
> whole world into chaos. The overthrow of governments might not
> end there, and it would be a grave responsibility for any man to take
> at this time. . . . I dislike to sit and have forced upon us such a peace
> as we are facing. We will get something out of it in the way of a
> League of Nations, but even that is an imperfect instrument. . . ."

In all his utterances before reaching Paris, Wilson championed
the idealism of the New World against the diplomacy of the Old.
But when he was on the spot himself, he was unable to hold his
own against the intrigues that seethed around him. On March
4th, the day before the President set forth on his second trip,
thirty-seven Republican Senators, headed by Senator Lodge, sent
a round robin protesting against the inclusion of the League of
Nations in the Peace Treaty. Hedged in with invisible walls by
the coterie around him, the cheers of Europe reverberating in his
ears, Wilson believed in his own omnipotence and ignored the
warning. When House suggested a plan to start the League of
Nations functioning at once, the President was disturbed. He did
not want anything to be settled in his absence, except strictly
military and naval terms. House, on the other hand, felt that it
was necessary to speed up the Treaty unless the whole world was
to drop into the abyss of Bolshevism. He dickered now with the
French, now with the English, now with Japan, now with Italy,
giving and taking in turn.

The chance of imposing the Fourteen Points without reservations had passed. The best that could be done was to save the
wreckage. The Duumvir used every ounce of energy in his frail
body to rescue the dream which he had dreamed with Wilson.
He was powerful, resourceful, indefatigable, but he was not an
Atlas who could carry upon his shoulders the weight of the world.

Wilson, too, in spite of his indomitable idealism, lacked the strength for such a task. Together the Duumvirs could function. Together they might have negotiated a different peace. But when they did not work in conjunction, their plans went awry. The very perfection of their intellectual symbiosis made even a partial divorce a hazardous risk.

"Many people," House remarked, "came to see me. People began to say that I was setting up a little White House."

Colonel House interviewed on the average forty callers a day. Every great figure in Paris sat opposite him, on a little chair in the Crillon, at one time or another. It was presented to the Colonel by the Hotel Crillon. I have sat in the chair, while a babble of ghostly voices seemed to reverberate in my ear. King Albert of Belgium, Prince Feisal, now King of Irak, Clemenceau, Foch, Wilson, every Premier, every Ambassador, visitors from many lands, called daily upon the Duumvir.

House continued to do in Paris what he had done in America, to save Wilson the effort of personal contacts which would have crushed him. But the great part which he necessarily played aroused jealousies in the entourage of President Wilson. There is a story that on one day when the President called Clemenceau was announced. The Duumvir excused himself for a few minutes to receive the head of the French Government. It is said that this angered Wilson. "This story," Colonel House says, "is not true. I immediately took Clemenceau to see Wilson. While we were still talking, Cecil Spring-Rice called on a similar mission, but I asked him to wait. Wilson did not resent my intimacy with the Allied statesmen. He himself had authorized these activities to ease his own burdens. But it is quite likely that much was made of the incident by others to bedevil the relations between us."

The trifling occurrence would not have annoyed Wilson if his mind had not been goaded and irritated by intrigue without, while his health was shattered by insidious attacks of disease within. Since his first attack of the influenza, Wilson was never again the same.

"If," Colonel House said, "Wilson had been well, mischief-makers could not have made trouble between us."

There were other psychic conflicts which troubled him, like

the grim shapes which invade the Monarch's high dominion in Poe's *Haunted Palace*. Of these I shall speak anon.

According to some reports, not only Clemenceau, but Lloyd George and Orlando collided with Wilson on the same day in the Colonel's study. Each time, the story goes, House excused himself and left Wilson to fret alone. The Colonel's diary does not bear out this hypothesis. I have vainly scoured his visitors' book for a conjunction of these constellations. But there is a grain of truth in the story, nevertheless.

"People," House explained, "got into the habit of looking to me as Wilson's spokesman. I had been his intermediary for many years. Wilson, being inaccessible to them even in Paris, they still came to me." This fact, distorted by tale-bearers, may have affected Wilson.

The Allied Premiers knew House. They had tested and tried him. Wilson orated, or shut down like a clam. He did not speak nor understand their language. Wilson resented the reliance of his colleagues upon Duumvir House. There was, as yet, no evidence of an open break. But the two minds no longer harmonized completely. Of what avail was it if House labored to secure information which Wilson too often disregarded? Sometimes the extraordinary partnership functioned as of old. At other times Wilson, seated alone at the wheel, formed fateful decisions without consulting with his Duumvir. Confusion ensued. In that confusion lickspittlers and scandal-mongers prospered.

Now, according to Lawrence, Stoddard, White and other correspondents, Edith Bolling Wilson takes a hand. A London newspaper had said that Colonel House was the "brains" of the Peace Commission. Mrs. Wilson showed the clipping to Colonel House. He paid no attention to the matter, which seemed of very minor importance at a time when the fate of the world itself was at stake. Mrs. Wilson did not forget, and she did not permit the President to forget. Can we blame a wife if she resents statements such as this, printed with malice aforethought: "What Colonel House thinks to-day, Wilson says to-morrow." Some smart Aleck called Wilson "the Jack that House built." Surely some faithful retainer must have brought this epigram to the attention of Wilson's consort.

We see the tragic, almost biological, conflict between the friend and the wife. The first Mrs. Wilson, from all the data I have been able to gather, accepted House as the complement of her husband. Knowing Wilson's strength, she also knew his weakness. The second Mrs. Wilson desired to make Wilson independent of others. Jealous of the camaraderie between Wilson and House, she prejudiced Wilson's mind against the Duumvir. She was aided and abetted by the men whom House himself had placed near the throne.

Some of Mr. Wilson's friends began to discover that there was "nothing hard, clear and definite" in the Colonel's intellectual processes. The seed of distrust was sedulously sown. There was some buzz about friends and relatives of House who played a part in the peace commission. Hostile newspaper men called it "the Austin Delegation." House went his way without being disconcerted by such tittle-tattle. He wrestled with the Allied Premiers. He knew that Clemenceau, Lloyd George and Orlando could not sanction some of the compromises which their reason dictated, because they were caught in the trap of their own propaganda. The expectations of their nations were so exaggerated that they would not accept half a loaf. House saw civilization itself going to pieces.

"Better," he exclaimed, "an unsatisfactory settlement in April than the same sort of settlement in June!" The Duumvir recognized the insanity of the French demands for reparation. He fought the French desire to build up a buffer State between Germany and herself, and her rapacious demand for the Saar Valley. But, being accustomed to dealing with realities and having no messianic complex, he compromised to achieve his end. It would have been wiser, perhaps, if both Wilson and House had packed their trunks and gone home!

But the men about Wilson, who flattered him day and night, did not admit the possibility of failure. To them it seemed, rightly or wrongly, that House was a liability in Paris. "The Colonel would make peace," writes Ray Stannard Baker, "quickly by giving the greedy ones all they want." That was not the Colonel's program. He wanted to give Wilson all he could. But Wilson's weakened position at home also weakened his hand in the peace game. Wilson was irritated by his failure to placate the Senate. Almost the first thing he said to House was: "*Your* dinner to the Senate Foreign Relations Committee was a failure as far as getting together was concerned." Wilson referred to the get-together dinner with the Senate Foreign Relations Committee which House had suggested. Wilson's temperament unfitted him congenitally for such a task. The dinner had widened the breach between him and the Senate. Wilson was particularly angry with Senators Knox and Lodge, who seemed to have behaved like the stony guest in the opera. His hatred of Lodge was implacable. House could have found a formula to unite them. Without House it was war and—defeat.

Every day now brings new troubles and disagreements to Wilson's harassed nerves. "How did you get along with Lloyd George and the President?" the Duumvir asked the French Premier. The Tiger growls: "Splendidly. We disagreed about everything." On March 22, House writes in his diary: "We are not moving as rapidly now. From the look of things the crisis will soon be here. Rumblings of discontent every day. The people want peace. Bolshevism is gaining ground everywhere. Hungary has just succumbed. We are sitting upon an open powder magazine and some day a spark may ignite it."

House urges the President to insist upon an immediate settlement. "Tell them that the Covenant for the League of Nations would either be written into the Treaty of Peace or we would have none of it; that the only excuse we could give for meddling in European or world affairs was a league of nations through which we hope to prevent wars. If that was not to be, then we would not care to mix again in their difficulties."

Every one who argued for moderation was branded as a "pro-German." Wilson had the right instinct when he desired to hold the Peace Conference in Switzerland. But the Allies, with the consent of House, overruled Wilson. Wilson saw even the Covenant slip from his hand. In a panic, his nerves worn threadbare, he agreed to buy French support of the Covenant as an integral part of the peace settlement by a guarantee of French security. House protested at first. Such a treaty, he argued, would be looked upon as a direct blow at the League of Nations. "If it is necessary for the nations to make such treaties then why a League of Nations?" But Wilson had committed himself to Clemenceau, and did not wish to withdraw his promise. Considering the guarantee the lesser of several evils, House yielded, and himself drafted the memorandum which Wilson accepted and the Senate rejected.

But the Tiger was insatiable. "Gentlemen," Wilson said, after a stormy conference with Clemenceau, to Dr. Isaiah Bowman and other members of the American Peace Delegation, "I am in trouble. And I have sent for you to help me out. The matter is this: the French want the whole left bank of the Rhine. I told M. Clemenceau that I could not consent to such a solution of the problem. He became very much excited and then demanded ownership of the Saar Basin. I told him I could not agree to that either because it would mean giving 300,000 Germans to France. ...I do not know whether he will return to the meeting this afternoon. In fact, I do not know whether the Peace Conference will continue. M. Clemenceau called me a pro-German and abruptly left the room."

Clemenceau insisted that no French Prime Minister could sign a treaty that did not satisfy France's claim to the Saar Valley. "Then," Wilson asked sharply, "if France does not get what she wishes, she will refuse to act with us? In that event, do you wish me to return home?"

"I do not wish you to go home," said Clemenceau, "but I intend to do so myself."

Eventually Wilson agreed wryly to a compromise. Physically worn out and racked by influenza, he once more asks Colonel House to take his place temporarily in the council of the Big Four. He no longer sees eye to eye with the Duumvir. But there is no one else who has his trust. Battered almost beyond endurance, Wilson finally consented to name no definite sum for reparations in the Peace Treaty. Most of the economic troubles from which the world suffered after the War result from this indefinite clause:

> "I [writes House] went in and out of the President's room at various intervals so as to keep him informed as to the progress we were making.... I suggested that in the event there was no agree-

ment by the end of next week (April 12) he draw up a statement of what the United States is willing to sign in the way of a peace treaty, and give the Allies notice that unless they can come near our way of thinking we would go home immediately and let them make whatever peace seems to them best. My suggestion was to do this gently and in the mildest possible tone, but firmly."

Wilson threatens to end the meetings of the Big Four and to insist upon Plenary Sessions where all the delegates of the smaller Powers would be present. Discouraged, he sends a message through Admiral Benson to the Navy Department to inquire how soon the *George Washington* can be sent to France?

This cable became known almost immediately. It was undoubtedly translated by the Intelligence Departments of the Allies even before it reached Washington. But the bluff did not work. Lloyd George continued to support the French demand for the Saar, and it is Wilson who made concessions. He refused the "alienation" of the territory from Germany, but consented to a lengthy occupation and French control of the mines.

Guided only by the star of the Covenant, rejecting the knowledge of House, Wilson steered now to the left, now to the right, now forward, now backward. Dropping the pilot, House, he sailed alone in the treacherous waters of Paris.

XXXIII
THE WRECK OF THE FOURTEEN POINTS

Fourteen Points Overboard – House on Reparations – Wilson's Change of Mind – The Blunder of the Brenner Pass – The Secret Treaties Come Home to Roost – The Abstemiousness of Woodrow Wilson – The Last Talk of the Duumvirs

SKIPPER WILSON threw overboard almost every one of the Fourteen Points to save his League of Nations. The Germans learned that they had built their hopes on fourteen scraps of paper. The Peace Treaties of Versailles and St. Germain Balkanized Europe and upset the financial structure on which the globe revolved.

House alone, or united with Wilson, could have exacted more rational terms. Both House and Wilson made blunders. But they blundered most when they failed to harmonize. House, thinking more realistically than Wilson, saw the folly of yielding on reparations and bartering promises to secure adhesion to the League. Wilson thought in ideas, not in figures. House thought in both, balancing the one with the other. His plan for reparations was essentially sane.

"I advised the Allies to limit their reparation demands to fifteen or twenty billions. But by that time Lloyd George had gone off electioneering with the battle cry of: 'Hang the Kaiser and make the Germans pay the cost of the War,' and Wilson had lost his trumps. Lord Cunlif, Governor of the Bank of England, welcomed my suggestion. 'Germany,' he said, 'can pay that over the counter.' The money would have been available commercially. It would have saved the franc as well as the mark.

"In those days," House explains, "the mark was still nearly

252

at par. Later the mark went to the devil and all Europe went with it. It would have been better for France if she had consented to some such arrangement. She did not know it then. Today no intelligent Frenchman denies that the question was solved in the most unsatisfactory manner. If the United States had been a member of the League, it would have been possible to remedy matters. Voting with England and Italy, we could have prevented France and Belgium from deadlocking the question.

"Both Wilson and I hoped that the League, with the United States as a member, would undo some of the blunders to which he was compelled to consent. Wilson never dreamed that the United States Senate would reject the League."

"Is it not true that Wilson was abysmally ignorant of European history and geography?"

House denies this impeachment.

"Naturally," he says, "like most Americans and Englishmen, he was not as fully conversant with European affairs as men who were born and trained on the continent. But he was aided by our commission of experts. These experts compared by no means unfavorably with those of European countries. In many cases where there was a controversy, the judgment of our experts was eventually confirmed."

"It seems to me," I said, "that some of these experts were biased grotesquely against Germany."

"It was impossible," House admitted, "even for historians, even for men ordinarily accustomed to think along objective lines, to escape entirely from the bane of war psychosis. Moreover, the voices reaching our experts from home were stridently insistent upon a peace that made Germany pay. Wilson objected to the impossible burdens which the Allies, encouraged by enthusiastic plaudits from the Republican Senate and the contributing editor of *The Outlook*, Theodore Roosevelt, imposed upon the tricked and vanquished foe.

"I advised the President to throw the responsibility for all measures upon the Republican Party, to place the Peace Treaty before Congress without recommendations. In any logical system of government, the Republicans should have had the executive as well as the legislative department of the government in their hands. Since such a thing is not possible under our Constitution, I suggested the next best thing, that is to say, for the Executive to yield to Congress in all matters requiring its consent. But Wilson, trusting in his own strength, hoped to force the Peace Treaty through Congress by an appeal to the people."

"Did you never," I asked Colonel House, "when the Fourteen Points were up for discussion, insist upon safeguarding them from being slaughtered?"

"The Fourteen Points," Colonel House answered gloomily, "were not slaughtered in a day. It was a matter of negotiations stretching for many months. Wilson made a concession here and a concession there, dropping his own premises without realizing the extent of the sacrifice."

"How could Wilson consent to the flat denial of his Fourteen and subsequent points?"

"Wilson, I repeat, believed that the remedy for the injustices of the Peace Treaty was in the League. Nor can it be denied that he had not yet regained the detachment of the philosopher who had once viewed the World War as no concern of ours. He could not forgive the Germans for having forced him into the War."

"James Kerney," I interjected, "editor of the Trenton *Times,* reports that Wilson said to him in the year of his death: 'I should like to see Germany clean up France, and I should like to meet Jusserand and tell him that to his face.' "

"Wilson," House replied, "was a man of quick changes. After it was too late he stiffened against England and France."

"Did Wilson," I asked, "insist that Italy was bound morally, if not legally, to abide by the Fourteen Points in her dealings with Austria-Hungary?"

"Unfortunately," House said, "Austria was already dismembered. She had fallen apart. Wilson, beset by other problems, failed to disembowel the Secret Treaties and their sinister brood."

"Why did Wilson yield the Brenner Pass to Italy?"

"That," House admitted, "was the most serious slip he made."

"Are you sure it was only a slip?"

"I feel sure," House replied, "that he did it inadvertently. But it undoubtedly was one of the worst things in the Peace

Treaty. My colleague, Henry White, seems to feel that I was pro-Italian and that I helped Italy to obtain Dalmatia. In that he was mistaken.

"My sympathies were with the Jugo-Slavs rather than with the Italians. What I was trying to do was to bring about a settlement that was measurably fair to both sides.

"It would have been possible to give Italy Dalmatia immediately, if the same pressure that was put on Italy had been applied also to Czecho-Slovakia and Jugo-Slavia. The President permitted me to bring all the pressure I thought advisable on Orlando and Sonnino. But he would not allow me to exert any pressure on Trumbitch and other Jugo-Slavs. The result was a failure to agree, and the Italians after the Conference adjourned got much more than I was willing to give when I was carrying on the negotiations. I have thought that the President's reasons for letting me put pressure on the Italians and not on the Jugo-Slavs was because he had inadvertently agreed to allow Orlando the Brenner Pass line, and he resented the fact that he had done so.

"The President was fully informed of my negotiations with both parties at interest, and approved of what I was doing. White's thought that this incident was the beginning of the breach between Woodrow Wilson and myself is wide of the mark.

"I might have given Italy Dalmatia. In Dalmatia the races were inextricably intermingled. I would never have given her that bit of purely German territory, the Brenner Pass, delivering one hundred and fifty thousand pure Germans to an alien flag. Both Clemenceau and Lloyd George were against this decision."

"Why did they not prevent it?"

"Their chickens came home to roost. Both were bound by Secret Treaties. Wilson was not. They hoped Wilson would object. But for some strange reason, Wilson's mind, usually so agile, failed to grasp the situation. He said: 'I give you the Brenner Pass. I cannot give you Dalmatia.' So Orlando took the one and D'Annunzio took the other.

"Having yielded too much in one direction, Wilson occasionally was too stubborn in other directions. It took a hard struggle to persuade him to accept Japan's promise that she would return Shantung to China, but he finally agreed with me.

The Japanese just gave Wilson and me privately their word of honor that Japan would return Shantung, but she wanted to do it of her own accord, without pressure from others. I never doubted for a minute that Japan would live up to her word. And she did."

"Did not some of the experts protest against the violation of the Armistice and Woodrow Wilson's pledge?"

"Some of the experts threatened to resign in protest against some provisions of the Peace Treaty. But it was too late to unravel what had been done. Delay would have been worse."

"Then you admit that the Fourteen Points were slaughtered in Paris?"

"The Treaty did not conform with the Fourteen Points. I was sure of that. Wilson tried to persuade himself that it did. I am afraid," the Colonel sighed, "the wish was father to the thought."

"Then you are dissatisfied with the peace?"

"I do not wish to criticize Wilson," House looked earnestly at the picture of Woodrow Wilson above the couch in his study where he was seated, "but I would have made a different peace. I would have tried to resuscitate the Fourteen Points in the Peace Conference as I did in the Armistice Conference. Germany's only claim to a revision of the Peace Treaty rests in the fact that the Fourteen Points and the President's subsequent speeches were the premise upon which she laid down her arms."

"Why did not Wilson try harder to modify the Allied peace terms?"

"He tried very hard. If it had not been for Wilson the peace would have been infinitely worse. In fact, it would have been so bad that the Germans would have gone home the moment they read it."

"Perhaps," I countered, "that would have been better. It would have forced a revision before the wrongs and the blunders of the Allied statesmen crystallized into States and boundary lines. Your moderating influence," I insisted, "did not prevent the Allies from imposing upon the Germans the most humiliating treaty ever forced upon a great nation since the destruction of Carthage."

"We did all we could. A clause put into the pre-Treaty agreements by our insistence obligated the armies of occupation to do nothing that could embarrass or impair the work of the Peace Conference. This clause nipped in the bud the attempt of the French militarists to set up an independent Rhineland."

"We should never have entered the War without first compelling the Allies to accept whatever conditions Mr. Wilson laid down."

"Such things," House replied, "are only possible theoretically. Once the rupture was inevitable we could not drift. We would have been paralyzed by inaction."

"Why was not Germany admitted to the League of Nations at once?" I asked.

"Neither the Allies nor Germany wanted that. It was a mistake on both sides. It would have been better for the Allies if Germany had been in the League and it would have been better for Germany."

"What was Woodrow Wilson's attitude toward Clemenceau?"

"He liked him better at the end than in the beginning. I told him he would. It was just the opposite with Lloyd George, whom he liked better in the beginning."

"What did Wilson think of Foch?"

"He saw little of him. He did not like the idea of Foch of setting up a separate State in the Rhineland."

"It has been claimed that the Allies diverted Wilson's mind from the Peace Treaty by entertaining him with gay frolics and pretty actresses. His subsequent physical breakdown has been ascribed to alleged debauches in Paris."

"There is no truth whatever in this scandalous imputation. If one can vouch for any man, I can vouch for Wilson in this respect. Diversions of this type were utterly alien to his temperament. He disliked all frivolities. He even attempted to escape legitimate social obligations. The only dinner I can recall that he attended in Paris was one given by the President of the French Republic before his departure. Wilson accepted finally after I urged him to a point that almost exhausted his patience, but he harbored resentment against me for my insistence."

Before Wilson leaves Paris he has two more interviews with House. On June 11 the Colonel writes:

> "My interview with the President was in the nature of a farewell. The main thing we talked about was the appointment of an international lawyer of great standing to sit in London during the summer in the formation of the International Court as required by Article 14 of the Covenant. After we had talked the matter over, he too thought Root would be the best selection, because of the prominent part he has taken in urging an international court. Then too, the fact that he is a Republican will add something to the strength of his appointment.
>
> "We discussed the Adriatic question, Germany's entrance into the League of Nations, reparations, and a number of other matters. He asked me to suggest names for the different commissions on which the United States would have representatives in the event the Treaty was signed.
>
> "I was disappointed to hear him say that he had agreed to have a plebiscite in Silesia. I am afraid it cannot be honestly carried out."

Evidently the discussion was purely along formal lines. There is no touch of emotion, not a flicker of the old flame. On June 29, House records his last talk with Woodrow Wilson. This last conversation, he himself reports, was not reassuring. House urged Wilson to meet the Senate in a conciliatory spirit.

"Treat them with the same consideration which you have used with your foreign colleagues in Paris, and all will be well."

Wilson stiffened.

"House," he said combatively, "I found one can never get anything in this life that is worth while without fighting for it."

"Anglo-Saxon civilization," the Duumvir retorted, "is built upon compromise."

These two sentences illustrate clearly the different mental attitude of the two friends. House never saw Wilson again in life. He was not even permitted to see him in death. But there were still innumerable ties that could not be immediately severed. There was still (a favorite phrase of House) much to be "buttoned up."

House still acts as Wilson's spokesman in the farewell week. He suggests a pronunciamento, after the signing of the Peace Treaty by the Germans, to Wilson. Wilson authorizes him to make this statement in his name:

"By the terms of the Treaty of Peace, the greatest possible measure of compensation has been provided for those people whose homes and lives were wrecked by the storm of war, and security has been given them that this storm shall never rise again. In so far as we came together to ensure these things, the work of the Conference is finished.

"But in a larger sense, its work begins to-day. In answer to an unmistakable appeal, a League of Nations has been constituted and a Covenant has been drawn which shows the way to international understanding and to peace. We stand at the crossroads, however, and the way is only pointed out. Those who saw through the travail of war the vision of a world made secure for mankind must consecrate their lives to its realization."

Personally, House feels less cheerful.

"When the Germans had signed and the great Allied Powers had done so, the cannons began to boom. I had a feeling of sympathy for the Germans who sat there quite stoically. It was not unlike what was done in olden times, when the conqueror dragged the conquered at his chariot wheels. To my mind, it is out of keeping with the new era which we profess an ardent desire to promote. I wish it could have been more simple and that there might have been an element of chivalry, which was wholly lacking. The affair was elaborately staged and made as humiliating to the enemy as it well could be."

Dissatisfied and disgruntled, Wilson returns to the United States after signing the Peace Treaty. House leaves Paris on the 29th with mixed emotions to aid in the distribution of mandates in London.

"There is little left for me to do in Paris," he writes in his notes. "The answer to the Germans is practically ready, and it is not intended that I should remain in Paris with Lansing, White, and Bliss to button up the matters that will be left over after Germany signs. I have been away from home for eight strenuous months, and while I do not feel at all tired, yet I would like to shift the scene. In a way I realize that in breaking up here it means the end of an epoch in my life, for after the Peace Conference is wound up I feel that I shall do other things than those I have been doing for so many years."

"How splendid it would have been," he writes in his *Intimate Papers*, "had we blazed a new and better trail! However, it is to be doubted whether this could have been done, even if those in authority had so decreed, for the peoples back of them had to be reckoned with. It may be that Wilson might have had the power and influence if he had remained in Washington and kept clear of the Conference. When he stepped from his lofty pedestal and wrangled with representatives of other states upon equal terms, he became as common clay. . . ."

> "To those who are saying that the Treaty is bad and should never have been made and that it will involve Europe in infinite difficulties in its enforcement, I feel like admitting it. But I would also say in reply that empires cannot be shattered and new states raised upon their ruins without disturbance. To create new boundaries is always to create new troubles. The one follows the other. While I should have preferred a different peace, I doubt whether it could have been made, for the ingredients for such a peace as I would have had were lacking at Paris. And even if those of us like Smuts, Botha, and Cecil could have had our will, as much trouble might have followed a peace of our making as seems certain to follow this. . . .
>
> "And yet I wish we had taken the other road, even if it were less smooth, both now and afterward, than the one we took. We would at least have gone in the right direction, and if those who follow us had made it impossible to go the full length of the journey planned, the responsibility would have rested with them and not with us."

One can almost hear the sigh of the Duumvir as he lays down his pen. "What is happening in the world to-day," Colonel House added in a marginal remark at the end of this chapter, which I submitted to him, "is largely the result of the kind of peace we made in Paris."

XXXIV

THE END OF A FRIENDSHIP

Estrangement – Many Hypotheses – The Friendships of Woodrow Wilson – What Wilson Said to Sir William Wiseman – Seibold's Theory – More Conjectures

T HERE had been rumors of a rift in the relations between Wilson and House ever since the beginning of their fateful friendship. Wilson and House had laughed at these stories.

But they had laughed once too often.

The estrangement of the Duumvirs was the gossip of Paris.

Many theories for the break between Wilson and House have been advanced. David Lawrence refers to Mrs. Wilson's tiff with Colonel House over the London dispatch. "Undoubtedly," he adds (in *The True Story of Woodrow Wilson*) "the President absorbed Mrs. Wilson's viewpoint which, together with the attacks that had been made on Colonel House for his alleged compromises, served to end the warmth of the relationship between these two statesmen."

But the attacks upon the Duumvir came from many sides. A prominent New York editor, whom Mr. Wilson held in high esteem, wrote that Colonel House was too conciliatory in his negotiations. "Thus," Lawrence says, "the campaign against Colonel House began almost immediately after the Armistice. It succeeded in the early spring of the following year. The man who for so many years had worked tirelessly and without compensation of any sort for the United States Government was cast adrift by President Wilson."

As a rule Wilson expressed his appreciation of the Duumvir's services in effusive terms. But his thanks for the work at the Armistice Conference was confined to one short sentence. The Armistice marks the beginning of the end. That end, though perhaps inevitable, was still on the knees of the gods.

"It was natural," Lawrence insists, "that the Colonel who had been given so much power should be the victim of his own efforts to please Woodrow Wilson and at the same time make a practical peace."

Another distinguished student of politics, the late Henry L. Stoddard, avows himself puzzled. "Who," he asks, "knows the facts of that sundering of the most intimate ties that ever existed between the executive of a great nation and a man in civil life? The relation began in silence, it continued in silence, it ended in silence. Was it a myth—that unity of purpose and of mind? Or was it real? Mystery of mysteries! Politics never saw its like. There can be only one opinion," he says, "about the relations of the two men up to March, 1919; there is room for more than one opinion from that time."

Stoddard suggests that the Allied statesmen did not realize that the House proxy from Wilson ceased when the giver of the proxy was present. He relates a variant of the Clemenceau story. "One afternoon after an unsatisfactory talk with Wilson, Lloyd George had hurried to the Crillon to talk it out with House. While the two men were talking Wilson entered. The President excused himself and said he would call again when House was at leisure." House remembers no such incident!

"In Paris, Wilson did not want tea-party talks," said one of Wilson's Paris intimates to Stoddard. "He needed practical suggestions. House was good at tea parties where he agreed to everything and undertook to carry it through with Wilson. The President needed a man who would take orders from him and not make compromises with others. House simply couldn't fill that bill. They had captured him as they had captured Page, and Wilson turned from both." Stoddard tried to get the indictment against House bit by bit from different individuals and put the pieces together. In the end, he gave up in despair. "President Wilson never uttered a word to House to indicate a separation from him. He just forgot, more and more each day, that such a man existed. No charges, no dissensions, no explanations. House saw him off for home, exchanged cables with him after he reached the White House, but there was another tone to their relations, and shortly it died away entirely."

H. A. Kohlsaat (in his book, *From McKinley to Harding*), tries to answer the question: What caused the break between President Wilson and Colonel House? and recalls the remark of one of Wilson's admirers: "I believe Mr. Wilson is constitutionally incapable of sustaining a lasting friendship." This theory, too, is contradicted by some of Wilson's friendships which lasted a lifetime! Frederic L. Paxson, in a review of the *Intimate Papers*, ventures another guess. "Even if the Treaty negotiations had been a success," he says, "it might have been hard to share the glory on terms consistent with friendship and devotion. But with the Treaty headed for rejection, it is not strange that one of them might have come to think that had his advice been taken the result were otherwise; or that the other might have remembered the moments when he felt impelled to depart from advice that was ever asked and often given."

Professor Seymour does not accept the explanations given. He admits that the relations of Wilson and House had undergone a certain change during the course of the Peace Conference. He denies that House betrayed Wilson's policies or that Wilson withheld his trust. He points out the demonstrable fact that when the President fell ill in Paris, he chose House to take his place in the Council of Four, and endorsed all the steps taken by the Duumvir. He used House during delicate negotiations in April, 1919, and authorized as his own the Colonel's final statement on the work of the Peace Conference. He selected House as his representative in the discussions with Lord Robert Cecil that led to the establishment of the League of Nations, and sent him to London to work out a system of mandates. This, he points out, would hardly have been possible if Wilson had lost confidence in his *alter ego*.

Seymour makes light of the Clemenceau incident. "There is," he concludes, "no scrap of evidence in all of House's papers indicating any specific reason for a rift in their relations during the course of the Peace Conference. Then, as always, they agreed absolutely upon principles. When, as in days past, they disagreed as to methods or details, there was no hint of friction. The cables exchanged between House and Wilson after the two parted company in Paris, on June 28th, never to meet again, were friendly. The President writes: 'I am glad your letters have begun to come. ... I am very well satisfied with the mandates you sent me ... etc. We unite in the warmest messages.' "

At the end of August, 1919, a story that Wilson and House had broken bursts into print. House writes to the President: "Our annual falling out seems to have occurred." The President replies, three days later: "Am deeply distressed by malicious story about break between us and thank you for the whole message about it. The best way to treat it is with silent contempt."

About the same time Sir William Wiseman, propagandist-in-chief of Great Britain in the United States, the head of its secret service and the special Ambassador of His Britannic Majesty to the small apartment in Fifty-third Street near Park Avenue where Colonel House held his court, has an informal conversation with Mr. Wilson.

> "The President," he reports, "was obviously a sick man. His face was drawn and of a gray color and frequently twitching in a pitiful effort to control nerves which had broken down under the burden of the world's distress. ...
>
> "In my notes of the conversation, I find this remark of Wilson's: 'I ask nothing better than to lay my case before the American people.' We naturally talked a lot about Colonel House, and the President spoke of him•most affectionately, and I find this recorded: 'Colonel House,' I remarked, 'is trusted by all the statesmen in Europe.' 'And rightly,' said the President, 'for he is trustworthy.'
>
> "The President retired directly after lunch, and bade me good-by most kindly. I never saw him again. The doctors were urging him to abandon his speaking tour, and had warned him of the danger, the almost certainty of a breakdown, but he was convinced that it was his duty to lay his case before the American people, and nothing would deter him."

Seymour points out in *The Intimate Papers of Colonel House*, that four days after sending his last cable to House, President Wilson left on the Western tour which ended in his collapse. During October, both Duumvirs were ill. "But," Seymour goes on to say, "the question arises, why, after House regained his health, was he not called down to the sick man in Washington?

House's papers show that he expected such a call. They also show that he realized how ill the President was and felt that in view of his condition he could not go down without a special summons. But there is nothing to show why the call never came. ...What is certain is that there was never anything approaching a quarrel between the two. On three occasions after the defeat of the Treaty, Colonel House received notes from President Wilson, in answer to those in which the Colonel sent him good wishes and hopes for restoration of his health."

Wilson's response was cordial. But his epistles were signed "faithfully yours" or "sincerely yours" and not "affectionately."

"Thus," Seymour observes, "the friendship lapsed. It was not broken."

Seymour makes no attempt to explain the mystery of the "lapse." House himself claims to be unable to pierce the veil. In the attempt to peer behind it, I sought out Louis Seibold, the brilliant interpreter of political news. Seibold was on excellent terms with Woodrow Wilson. He is conversant with the attitude of those who now claim to speak for him.

An article by Louis Seibold in the *World* of December 8, 1919, "Diplomats and Politicians Believe Colonel House Has Lost Favor With President Wilson—Why?", was the first sensational disclosure of the break between the Duumvirs from a source close to the White House. In a conversation with Colonel House, I summarized my impressions of a talk with Seibold based on his extraordinary analysis.

I: Seibold insists that you led Wilson to believe that the Peace Conference was held in Paris by the unanimous choice of the Allies. Afterwards he discovered that this was not the case. The President concluded that you had permitted yourself to be unduly influenced by the French.

H O U S E: That is nonsense. Wilson and I agreed that Switzerland was the best place for the Conference. But after reaching Paris, I found that all Switzerland was threatened with Bolshevism, and it was decided that it was inadvisable to hold the Conference there. There was no disagreement between Wilson and me in the matter. It was merely a question of Brussels or Paris, with everything favoring Paris.

I: Seibold claims that you eliminated the Freedom of the Seas from the Armistice Agreement, and that, under the gentle guidance of Sir William Wiseman and Lord Cecil you agreed to leave the issue to the League of Nations instead of discussing it at the Peace Conference.

HOUSE: The Freedom of the Seas was my particular child. I brought up the subject during my visits to Germany and England, without any suggestion from Wilson or any one else. Wilson approved it, and when I returned to America he made it one of his Fourteen Points. I fought for it at the Armistice Conference and tried to get the consent of Lloyd George to discuss it at the Peace Conference. However, at Paris Wilson did not insist upon a clear understanding, arguing, if I remember rightly, that the League of Nations would make it unimportant since there would be no neutrals.

I: It is claimed that you surrendered on Fiume and told Orlando that Wilson did not know his own mind, and that you could make him agree to anything you considered right.

HOUSE: I did not surrender Fiume and I did not criticize Wilson to Orlando, nor did I say that I could make him agree to anything I considered right.

I: It is further stated against you that you came to this country instead of sticking to your job, which Wilson had assigned to you in Europe. Your coming back was kept from him because it would have irritated him unduly.

HOUSE: I did come back to the United States without Wilson's approval. He was in no condition to pass on the question. I was sick myself. My work in Europe was finished. My place at such a critical moment, when death seemed imminent, was at Wilson's side.

I: Seibold says that the substance of the charges of the Wilsonians against you appeared in his article. He says that, on December 8, you passed through Washington and remained there for several hours. If you had stopped at the White House, even if you had not seen Wilson at all, he would not have dared to publish his startling revelations.

H O U S E : Seibold is correct when he says that his article in the New York *World* was the first sensational discussion of our "separation." If I remember rightly it covered two full pages. He is wrong about my having passed through Washington and remaining four hours without calling at the White House. The only time I was in Washington after my return from Europe and before Wilson died was when he was living on S Street. I called on him but he was out driving. My friend, James J. Lyons, was with me, and I was stopping with Justice James McReynolds.

I: I am told that Wilson, enraged by your actions, instructed Tumulty to refer all your letters hereafter to the State Department, not to him personally.

H O U S E : I do not believe that this story is true. Why not ask Tumulty?

In accordance with the Colonel's suggestion, I asked Wilson's secretary, Joseph P. Tumulty, whether he received instructions from Mr. Wilson to refer all communications from the Colonel to the State Department. "Frankly," Mr. Tumulty writes, "I do not recall ever having received the instructions you mention. . . . Personally, I do not know anything about the so-called 'break' between the Colonel and the President. No information was volunteered and I made no attempt to find out what it 'was all about.' I can say to you, however, that by no act of Woodrow Wilson, during my association with him, did he ever show a lack of faith or confidence in Colonel House."

One important dignitary, even closer to Woodrow Wilson than Tumulty, told me that the President resented a book entitled *The Real Colonel House* by Howden Smith. "House," he told me, "was staying in the White House at the time when the articles were syndicated. After Wilson read these effusions, he absolutely refused to see House. Thereupon," my informant added with a significant smile, "Colonel House fell sick. . . . Some one said to Wilson: You cannot have the man die on your hands in the White House. Then Wilson relented and peace was patched up."

This story is good. But it is not true. A letter from Wilson to House, written May 6, 1918, clearly reveals Wilson's attitude. Wilson knew that House was annoyed by the articles. This did not surprise Wilson. He consoles House with the thought that they were written in an "excellent spirit." While, he says, I have known in reading certain passages that you would "squirm," on the whole I think the writer has tried to treat you "fairly" and he certainly has treated you in "the most friendly spirit." We just, he philosophically adds, have to "grin and bear it" when these things happen.

I discovered in the House archives a letter from Mrs. Wilson commiserating with Colonel House on account of the undesired publicity he received when the article appeared in the New York *Evening Post*. The tone of her letter is exceedingly friendly.

XXXV

WHY WOODROW WILSON BROKE WITH
EDWARD MANDELL HOUSE

Colonel House Takes the Stand – Why Colonel House Did Not Ask for a
Showdown – Five Minutes That Might Have Restored the World's Equi-
librium – What Wilson Did Not Know – Colonel House Calls at S Street –
The Silence of Colonel House – The Human Reasons for the Break – The
Wall Around Wilson – A Deathbed Message from Doctor Mezes – What
Did Edith Tell?

WHAT ended the friendship between the Duumvirs? Colonel
House invokes Isis and other mythical deities to express
his own mystification. "Theories I have and theories they must
remain. These you know," he writes to Seymour in 1928. His
attitude to-day is unchanged. "I cannot," House insists, "solve
the riddle."

Every writer who has studied the relationship between House
and Wilson attributes the dissolution of the ties between them
to a different cause. According to Ray Stannard Baker, the break
began because House consented to separate the Covenant and
the Treaty. There is no truth, Colonel House avers, in the assertion that he ever consented to such a separation. It is possible,
however, that Wilson may have thought so. If so, he was mistaken.

Baker attempts to build up his own hero by belittling House.
A study of Wilson's letters to House shows that Wilson would
not be smaller if the whole truth as exposed in these pages were
known. They show two fine minds, each acting on the other.
Baker's method of attack is very subtle. He attacks not the Colonel's character, but his judgment. If he accused him of being
a rascal it would be easy for House to defend himself. It is diffi-

cult for any man to prove that he is not a fool. Naturally the
Colonel's advice and his decisions were modified by currents and
cross-currents invisible and imperceptible to those who were not
in the midst of events. Baker's interpretations of many documents reveal his ignorance. If Baker impeaches the Colonel's
judgment, he impeaches Wilson's as well, since Wilson's own
letters to House conclusively prove that for seven years he was
guided almost invariably by the Colonel's advice in all matters
pertaining to foreign as well as to domestic affairs.

It is sometimes asserted that House made concessions in
connection with Danzig, the Polish Corridor and the Saar Valley
contrary to Wilson's wishes. House maintains that he made no
concessions that were not in accordance with Wilson's ideas. It
is possible, of course, that some one subsequently planted in the
President's mind the idea that he did such a thing. Wilson himself never revealed any indication of disapproval.

Some writers insist that Wilson and House split over
Shantung. As a matter of fact, House was the only one of the
American Peace Commissioners who agreed with the President.
It is evidence of Wilson's continued confidence in House that he
asked him to stay in Europe to assure an equitable distribution
of colonial mandates. Presumably he wanted House to be ac-
cessible for consultation on the minor peace treaties which were
still pending.

After his return to the United States, House wrote to Lodge
that he was willing to appear before the Senate Committee to
defend the Treaty. House had communicated with Lodge before,
on various occasions, at Wilson's own request. It was one of his
primary functions to keep in touch even with Wilson's enemies.
House had known Lodge for thirty years. However, his letter to
Lodge was used against him to create the impression that he was
conspiring with the enemy. It was this incident which prompted
the statement that House broke Wilson's heart by his disloyalty.

"I was loyal to Wilson," House says, "and I was loyal to
our common ideal."

Unlike Wilson, House did not think the Peace Treaty perfect. It contained, in his opinion, much of inestimable value, but
it was not sacrosanct.

The report of any friendliness between House and Lodge, distorted by malice and gossip, must have enraged the sick President in his mattress tomb. The enmity between Wilson and Lodge was implacable. Although Lodge was one of the first men to encourage Wilson's literary ambitions, their old friendship grew into a violent animosity when Lodge, in the campaign of 1916, cast aspersions on Wilson's veracity. House himself frequently comments upon the intensity of Wilson's feelings and his inability to forgive easily.

When Wilson drifted away from House, the Duumvir was hurt deeply. But he was not surprised. Wilson needed House more than House needed Wilson. Their friendship was, after all, only of seven years' standing. It was not rooted in their youth. House would have been far more deeply hurt if some old friends like Governor Hogg, Attorney General Gregory or Senator Culberson had treated him as Wilson did. Moreover, as the Colonel repeats again and again, there was only a drifting apart, no break. Colonel House does not believe this drifting apart would have happened if Wilson had remained himself. It was Wilson's illness that wrought many changes in him. House deeply regrets that his collaboration ceased at the moment when he could have been most useful to him.

The query suggests itself: Why did Colonel House fail to insist upon a frank talk with Wilson before the President left Paris? The pressure of affairs was too great. Wilson was tired and worried. History was being made. House did not wish to interfere selfishly with his private affairs. But he made up his mind to have it out with Wilson in Washington. In the light of subsequent events, it would have been better if House had insisted upon a showdown in Paris. If he and Wilson had worked together as heretofore, House would have succeeded in persuading him to accept the Treaty reservations of the United States Senate, and Uncle Sam would be, for better or for worse, a member of the League of Nations.

Unfortunately, House could not foresee the future. He was so busy with great affairs that he was hardly conscious of the apparent change in Wilson's attitude. He had ignored the slight alteration in Wilson's salutations to him. He attributed no importance to it, because their intimacy itself remained what it was. He still thinks that in his heart Wilson never changed.

Irrespective of Wilson's strange silence, one of Wilson's selves never ceased to think of House with affection. There was a Wilson House loved and understood. There was another Wilson whom he did not understand and love so well, whose existence he denies even now. That other Wilson rarely came to the surface in the seven years of their intimacy. Certain psychic conflicts within Wilson's own soul made it difficult to predict his actions. In his heart of hearts, House must have always felt that it was necessary to be on guard against sudden reversions. This uncertainty, which creeps out now and then in his diary, at least between the lines, must have prepared him for the dénouement, although he himself denies this supposition.

Forewarned by such premonitions, House was able to brace himself for the shock. But he feels that any passing misunderstanding could have been swept aside if Wilson had not broken down physically. "I have not the slightest doubt," he once said to me, "that Wilson and I would have come to a complete understanding if we had been vouchsafed the opportunity of talking to each other after he left Paris."

One brief talk, eye to eye, between the Duumvirs, would have restored the equilibrium, but when House came back to the United States, Wilson was convalescing. There was nothing House wanted, nothing that Wilson could give him, except his friendship. While he was wrestling for life, Wilson did not know that House was back in America. House fears that Wilson died without ever knowing that he had come home to see him. Wilson certainly never knew how eager House was to be with him during the distressing days that followed the stroke. It may be that Wilson's heart hardened against House because he did not hear from him. He may not have even seen the letters House wrote to him. Perhaps he wondered why the Colonel did not come to the White House. Perhaps he thought his Duumvir had deserted him because he was at the end of his tenure and of his political strength. It may be that Wilson died in this belief.

Why didn't the Colonel take the bull by the horns and call at the White House? That would have been at variance with his temperament. The supposed break had been exploited sensationally in the press. Under the circumstances, the Duumvir could not go to the White House without an invitation. If he had gone and had been refused permission to see the patient, the situation would have been most distressing. He tried to bridge the gulf by writing Wilson about the Treaty. To make sure that the letter was not intercepted House sent it through Attorney General Gregory, who personally placed it in Mrs. Wilson's hands. He said in this letter that the President's reputation was in the balance. He suggested to Wilson to tell the Senate that he did not feel at liberty to change the terms of the Treaty which he had made with the Allies, but that the Senate had the constitutional right to make such amendments as it deemed proper, and that he would be prepared to accept any changes made by the Senate, provided these changes were agreeable to the Allies.

This stratagem would have placed the burden of a failure of the Peace Treaty upon the Allies and upon the Senate. Wilson was unpopular at that time. The Allies were popular. The step House suggested would have assured the adherence of the United States to the Peace Treaty. House feels that the economic débâcle that followed the War would have been avoided or mitigated, if the United States had been a member of the reparations commission.

Wilson did not reply to this letter, nor to another in a similar vein. It seems strange that House did not attempt to straighten out the tangle after Wilson retired from the Presidency. He himself tells of his attempt to reëstablish the old contact. Upon his first visit to Washington, after Wilson's illness, while stopping with Justice McReynolds, House went around to S Street and left his card. Wilson was "not in." The occasion of the Colonel's visit to Washington was a luncheon with President Harding, Vice-President Coolidge and members of the Cabinet on Cyrus Curtis's yacht.

The call on Wilson was a gracious gesture. House did not seriously think that the friendship could be resurrected. After Wilson's long illness it was too late for explanations. There was too much to be said. Too many deep things stirred in the depths. A meeting then might have been a fatal shock to the invalid.

House is consoled by the knowledge that never, by spoken or written word, did Wilson criticize him. Once Wilson rebuked a member of the Cabinet for a slighting remark about the Colonel. There are those who saw Wilson shortly before his death who tell that he spoke kindly of the man who shared the powers of the Presidency with him for almost seven years.

Friendship, like love, blossoms, bears fruit, and dies. The causes of its decay are always many. Some are external and some are internal. Some are impersonal and some are human. Pushing aside the veil of the mystery behind the House-Wilson break, one finds behind it, enthroned in purple, the figure of Mrs. Wilson. Like every woman, she resented every friendship in her husband's life which preceded her own entrance.

House chivalrously refrains from even hinting at such a possibility. He resolutely refuses to discuss the widow of Woodrow Wilson. There are some rumors that Mrs. Wilson was annoyed by the fact that, after the death of Ellen Axson Wilson, Mrs. House, traveling in Europe, was royally received by the great ones of the earth, while Mrs. Wilson remained at home. But House pooh-poohs this suggestion. The Colonel's relations with Wilson's daughter are friendly. His relations with Mrs. Wilson are mutually polite.

But I have vainly scanned the newspapers for any account of a ceremony in honor of Wilson in which both Mrs. Wilson and Colonel House participated. Colonel House is the godfather of the New Poland. His statue, like Wilson's, graces the city of Warsaw. When Poland desired to honor Wilson, Mrs. Wilson sailed over the seas. But Colonel House was not of the party.

Colonel House maintains a cryptic silence when such topics come up for discussion. He has never pointed out that Mrs. Wilson could have brought about a meeting between him and Wilson had she so desired. But the documents in the House archives and the facts speak for themselves. Mrs. Wilson's attitude in Paris elicited comments from many observers. The only one who did not comment upon it was Colonel House himself. Mrs. Wilson kept the news of the Colonel's return from her sick husband. It was she who answered the letters of Colonel House. Having shared her husband with the Colonel and with the world, feminine instincts, natural enough in themselves, prompted her to isolate the President, to keep him exclusively to herself.

She was ably assisted by Dr. Grayson's desire to shield his patient. Grayson was the Colonel's friend, as well as Wilson's. He could have said the redeeming word, but he never did. They were the only people who had access to Woodrow Wilson in the interregnum that followed Wilson's breakdown. There was one other, who later became one of Wilson's spokesmen, but he never lifted a finger to bring House and Wilson together. He knew the great work that House had done. In looking over some photographs in the House collection, I saw one with a fervid inscription from the person in question. But he evidently preferred to sun himself in the favor of the dying man without inconvenient rivals.

Mrs. Wilson, with Grayson's aid, immured Wilson completely. She is the main human reason for the break between the Duumvirs. I do not attribute to either the slightest ignoble motive. Like every wife, Mrs. Wilson desired to protect her husband. She undoubtedly resented the stories spread by their enemies, in order to cause dissension, stories reflecting unkindly and unjustly upon their unique intellectual coöperation.

The enemies who thus widened the breach were inspired by personal malice and selfish ambition.

Colonel House refuses to accept the statement that Mrs. Wilson was the real cause for the lapse in his friendship with Wilson. Fortunately I was able to substantiate my theory from another source. Accident or good luck blew across my way a letter from the late Dr. Sidney E. Mezes to a friend in Boston. Dr. Mezes, it will be remembered, was the head of The Inquiry. He was the brother-in-law of Duumvir House, and if Arthur Howden Smith is right, stood toward House in precisely the same relation which Colonel House occupied with President Wilson. Mezes, Smith insists, worked along the same lines and saw things in the same perspective. The attacks upon Colonel House by the professed friends of Wilson outraged his sense of justice.

"You are right," Mezes exclaims. "In spite of strong and wanton provocation, House stayed true ten years after Wilson's death. If Wilson had been endowed with similar loyalty, the history of the last ten years would have been different, more cheering, I believe. Far from yes-yessing, House was constantly urging Wilson on and as an agent constantly taking the longest chances."

"I don't know how much of this he will stand," House once confided to Mezes, "I may go into the scrap heap in a day." That remark illuminates dark corners like a powerful flashlight. "During those years," Mezes goes on to say, "I picture his political life as hanging by a hair. But he knew his Woodrow better even than he realized. . . ."

When Mezes penned these words in Tucson, Arizona, he was a dying man. "I have worked out the technique of staying in bed and am quite comfortable," he writes. "But," he adds pathetically, "pencil writing is hard on my friends."

The moment I saw this notable letter, I communicated with Dr. Mezes. On January 10, 1931, his answer came. Consideration for House had sealed his lips these many years. But on the brink of Nirvana, Mezes cast aside conventional restraints. His letter, which strangely moved me, has the ring of death-bed sincerity. "While we have not met, you are so well known as a son of the college that I feel as if I almost knew you. *You speak of the three* [human] *reasons for the fading out of Wilson's friendship for House. From what I know of that most unfortunate happening, I am sure you are right. . . .*"

Mezes, like House, tends to exonerate Wilson. "Wilson's record shows him not to have been a staunch friend, but I am inclined to hold him nearly, it may be quite, blameless in the matter of the waning of his friendship for House. Up to the time of his leaving Paris, in fact up to the time of his stroke, in the face of much tension, and what was probably strong and constant pressure, he remained true to House. And after he was stricken he heard about the latter only what his *entourage* wanted him to hear."

Mezes had not lost, even in the shadow of death, his analytic faculty. Piecing together the evidence from many sources, he says: "It is highly probable that no letter of any moment from House ever reached him (Wilson). He thus felt that House, for reasons he was too ill to work out, had failed him in his need, and that there was nothing he could do about it. But we have one highly illuminating indication of his feeling. In the spring of '20, Edward Bok called on him to tell him of the lectures being given in Philadelphia on the Peace Conference, and spoke of what House was doing in his, Wilson's, interest. Turning, the latter said, 'I told you, Edith, House was all right.'

"What had Edith told him?"

XXXVI

THE FOUR SELVES OF WOODROW WILSON

The Verdict of the Jury – The Ambivalence of the Duumvirs – The Schizoid President – Two Portraits – The Revenge of an Artist – The Lady or the Blarney Stone? – Woodrow Wilson and Mrs. Hulbert Peck – Ten Shares of Steel – Wilson the Covenanter, House the Pagan – Woodrow Wilson's Heart of Hearts –"Tremendous Storms"– The Return of Colonel House – Wilson Immures Himself – The End of the Duumvirate – The Judgment of Woodrow Wilson

COLONEL HOUSE could function without Woodrow Wilson in his own fashion. Woodrow Wilson could not function adequately in the sphere of politics without Colonel House. Nevertheless, their friendship was broken.

It would not be difficult to find an indictment against Mrs. Wilson and Dr. Grayson for the murder of the friendship between Woodrow Wilson and Edward Mandell House. But the jury would recommend both to the mercy of the court. There are many extenuating circumstances. Although I have cited the situation before, I may be permitted, in justice to both, to rehearse it once more. Mrs. Wilson turned against House because, in certain circles, his fame was beginning to overshadow her husband's. She may have been conscious that the psychic struggle which kept Woodrow Wilson awake night after night was intensified by every contact with House. There is no question that she resented the dominance of the Colonel in her husband's life nor that she, aided by Grayson, built a wall around Wilson which House was unable to penetrate. Dr. Cary T. Grayson fulfilled his professional duty when he isolated his patient from any disquieting influence. When the story is told in full it will involve others, especially one whose overmastering ambition plays an important but obscure part in the tragedy of Woodrow Wilson and Colonel House.

Intrigue, whispering behind closed doors, and Mrs. Wilson's antagonism were powerful factors in the severance of the Duumvirs. Wilson was sensitive to the gossip which constantly beats against the ears of all rulers. But no one could have separated this David from this Jonathan except for the strange schism in Wilson's soul.

Psycho-analysis reveals what the poets always knew, that every affection has both a plus and a minus sign. Hate and love dwell together in the same bosom. We love and we hate at the same time. Love has a cruel as well as a kindly face. The most tender friendship, the most ardent love, hides a death-wish in the unconscious. The most fervent admiration is reared upon dormant antagonism. This explains why both admiration and love so easily change, almost overnight, into their opposites. Perhaps ambivalence is necessary to save the soul from vassalage, to protect the integrity of the ego.

Wilson needed House. He was exceedingly fond of him. But, at the same time, he hated him for his dependence upon him. House was devoted to Wilson. He made him President. He wove a halo around his head. Yet underneath his devotion there must have been, concealing itself under various masks, an unconscious envy.

A physical element enters in every human relation. Friendship, as well as love, has a physiological basis. The law governing both may be formulated some day in terms of biochemistry or in terms of the mysterious oscillations which are the basis of life itself. But in friendship the purely physical element is rarely accentuated. It was barely perceptible, if not entirely unconscious, in the friendship between Woodrow Wilson and Colonel House.

Where the sex element enters, physical attraction stabilizes affection. Love intoxicates the brain centers. It makes us blind to the faults of the beloved object. Friendship is clear-eyed. Neither Wilson nor House was blind to the faults of the other. The only intoxicant stimulating the brain centers of the Duumvirs was their love of power. Love of power stabilized their friendship.

Their complete interdependence made it almost unassailable from without.

The astonishing psychic messmateship between these two exceptional men was strong enough to withstand the shock and strain of a World War. It would have outweathered disease and disillusionment, irritation and intrigue, except for the division in Wilson's own nature. A powerful component of Wilson's personality allied itself with the diverse forces from without, which, for reasons of their own, desired to terminate his alliance with House.

The curious fluctuations in the rhythm of Wilson's personality have been noted by many observers. In Wilson, as in all of us, the instincts of a thousand ancestors stirred. But in most of us one personality completely subjugates the others. Wilson's soul was a tetrarchy in which four dominant personalities strove for mastery. There was an intellectual self, an emotional self, a practical self and a moral self, each dominating at times. The effort to maintain his psychic balance led to amazing inconsistencies of behavior and judgment.

Self Number One, the intellectual self, detached, philosophical, academic, spoke with a British accent. Self Number Two, the emotional self, stubborn, passionate at times, vindictive, flowery in language, had an Irish brogue. Self Number Three, the practical self, had acquired in some strange fashion, certain characteristics which Europe attributes to the Yankee. It was shrewd, humorous, inclined to be sharp in its dealings. It is the self of the "weasel words." It is the self that inspired Roosevelt's description of Wilson as a Byzantine logothete. There was in this self an almost Levantine touch. Self Number Four, recognizable by its burr, was Scotch. It drew strength from all the ancestors of Woodrow Wilson who preached the word of a Scotch-Presbyterian God. Intractable, unflinching in its hard idealism, it was the strongest of all his selves.

The perplexities of the psychologists are increased by the fact that in every human being both sexes meet. Our mothers as well as our fathers impart their heritage to us. Each of Wilson's selves had a masculine and a feminine phase. The masculine dominated. The feminine and masculine aspects of Woodrow

Wilson's personality are startlingly revealed by the portraits of Sir William Orpen and John S. Sargent. Sargent, who hated Wilson, deliberately brought out all that was soft and feminine in his nature. Orpen, who painted him in Paris, brought out all that was masculine and robust.

An Irish nobleman had bought a blank canvas by Sargent in an Allied charity drive. On his death, he willed all his possessions, including his option for a portrait by Sargent, to the City of Dublin. The City decided to commission Sargent to paint Woodrow Wilson. Sargent had no choice in the matter. Unwillingly he accepted the commission. His portrait of Wilson is his revenge. Detesting Wilson's pacifism, he refused to respond to Wilson's approaches. President Wilson put himself out to win over the furious painter, but his magic failed to work. Sargent remained icily polite. He wanted to portray a pusillanimous Wilson, but being a great artist, he could not help giving some nobility to the soft countenance.

Sargent painted Wilson in his most pacific mood. When Orpen painted him in Paris, his mood was belligerent. He was determined to fight not only the Germans, but the Allies as well, to establish his Covenant. Colonel House himself in his diary contrasts the two portraits. "Went to see Sir William Orpen's portrait of the President. . . . I like the portrait, although it shows up some of the President's prominent features . . . it is an entirely different looking gentleman from Sargent's æsthetic scholar and has more of the 'rough and tumble' look. I have seen him look as Sargent sees him one time in twenty, but I have seen him nineteen times out of twenty look as Orpen sees him. I think I never knew a man whose general appearance changed so much from hour to hour. . . ."

It is not the President's face alone that changes kaleidoscopically. "He (Wilson) is one of the most difficult and complex characters I have ever known. He is so contradictory that it is hard to pass judgment upon him. . . . When," Colonel House goes on to say, "one gets access to him, there is no more charming man in all the world than Woodrow Wilson. I have never seen any one who did not leave his presence impressed. He could use this charm to enormous personal and public advantage if he would...."

William Allen White paints in words still another portrait. "Care," he says, describing the last phase of Woodrow Wilson, "had chiseled down the face of the Princeton professor of the nineties, and the years in the White House had changed even the proud, happy features of the Governor of New Jersey to a certain sphinx-like reserve. Grief and worry had not brightened his face. The forehead, the eyes, the sensitive nose, still held their nobility. But the hammer and chisel of time and care had cut away the soft lines from his jaw. It revealed a certain carnal coarseness that shocked a stranger." Yet, White adds, that coarseness was only a pretense. "An honest study of his life, shrinking at nothing, has revealed no justification for the implication of that heavy jaw."

An old Confederate veteran, standing near President Wilson when he delivered an address at the Arlington Amphitheatre, was asked: "What is your impression of the President?"

"I saw something in the President's face," he replied, "I don't think I ever noticed before in a human countenance. I found that the upper and lower half of his face belonged to two different men."

While the four selves of Woodrow Wilson, with their masculine and feminine aspects, do not exhaust the gamut of his personality, they explain his contradictory character. Now battling for ascendancy, now allied with each other, they puzzled even Wilson's other self—Colonel House. House could play best upon Wilson's intellectual self. He harnessed the practical and the emotional self, but he could dominate Wilson only while the moral self, the self of the Covenanter, stepped in tune with the others. Occasionally Wilson's emotional self, now and then obstreperous, upsets the calculations of his other selves. Its momentary ascendancy accounts for some impulsive actions. It was the emotional self, the self with the Irish accent, that engaged in numerous intellectual flirtations. Wilson liked to be adored by pretty women, but it is obvious that he kissed more often the Blarney Stone than their lips. His Libido sought refuge in words.

Woodrow Wilson's friendship with Mrs. Hulbert Peck was a mildly platonic affection such as blossoms pallidly in the shadow of American universities. The friendship with Mrs. Peck, like the friendship with House, lasted for seven years. He took it from Princeton to the Governor's Mansion in Trenton, from Trenton to Washington. It was wrecked in the end by gossip.

The so-called Peck scandal furnished the zest for the whispering campaigns of two Presidential elections. Circumstantial stories of Wilson's susceptibility to feminine charm and of his relations with Mrs. Peck made the rounds. Wilson had written hundreds of letters to the charming divorcee. There were rumors that these letters had been bought for fabulous sums by friends of the President. John Devoy, in the *Gaelic American*, playfully referred to Woodrow Wilson as "Peck's Bad Boy." *The Fatherland*, slightly more sedate, alluded to the President's "peckadillos."

"I know," Colonel House remarked to me, when we were discussing the subject, "that innumerable stories were invented to discredit Wilson. On one occasion a person very close to Wilson came to me and told me that Mrs. Peck was going to bring suit the following week before such and such a judge. I replied: 'Go and stay on the job and let the suit come off on schedule, without the slightest attempt to hush up anything whatsoever.' Needless to say, the case never came up. There was no such case. No one ever paid one cent for the Peck letters. Mrs. Peck never demanded and Woodrow Wilson never paid hush money or blackmail. I never met Mrs. Hulbert Peck but once. I was not surprised to find her a woman of culture, beauty and charm. Wilson never paid a cent of blackmail to any one. His friendship with Mrs. Peck was purely intellectual. I have seen many of his letters to her and her letters to him. He corresponded with two or three other women. All these relations were singularly free from passion."

It is not likely that, in relations of this type, Wilson strayed from the conventional path of marital rectitude. His emotional self was controlled too strongly by the moral and the intellectual self. Wilson's exuberant letters were the revenge of the repressed romantic young Irishman who slumbered somewhere in the soul of the stern college professor.

It seems that the Peck letters were finally acquired by the Wilson estate. At any rate, Mr. Baker, in his *Woodrow Wilson: His Life and Letters,* quotes freely from them to destroy the last lingering suspicions of scandal. The excerpts which have been published reveal Wilson in a gentle mood. They are bids for sympathy of a soft feminine soul, contrasting strangely with the truculent Covenanter. Something of the same soft note creeps now and then into his letters to Colonel House.

It was Wilson's intellectual and his moral self, aided by his emotional self, that wrote the Fourteen Points. It was his practical self that suffered the Allies to exploit his gospel as a *ruse de guerre.* His moral and intellectual self agreed with the English on the Panama Tolls, but his practical self exacted a price for his conversion. The practical self planned the trick that forced Congress to reverse itself. Wilson's intellectual and moral self refused to surrender the principle of the Freedom of the Seas. But his practical self slyly consented when the British silenced American protests by purchasing our cotton. It winked at the Secret Treaties. It proclaimed that the Peace Treaty of Versailles was in consonance with his pledges. His practical self persuaded him to accept Bryan, by convincing him that in politics the end justifies the means. It is the practical self which is responsible for the charges of ingratitude made against him by those who aided him in his political career. But so strong was the intellectual and the moral note in him that he rarely took action of this type without first persuading himself that his motive was highly moral. Wilson's moral self never gave up without a struggle. In the end it invariably prevailed.

The moral self asserted itself at times to the point of absurdity. Colonel House discovered among Woodrow Wilson's investments ten shares of United States Steel. Feeling that the Administration might be compelled to attack the Steel Trust, House advised the President to sell them. Wilson refused. For, at that time, he had determined to take action against the company, which was likely to depress the market value of its securities. "I have no right," he said, "to avail myself of my prior knowledge at the expense of the other stockholders." It so happened that the contemplated action never eventuated. The gesture, nevertheless, was fine.

House sympathized with the first three of Wilson's selves, but philosophically he was at the opposite pole of Wilson's moral self. House, like Wilson, was a humanitarian. His heart, as his friend Bob Washburn says in the Boston *Transcript*, was set on the amelioration of humanity and a broader and higher purpose than that of himself or "America first."

But the Colonel never imposed upon his soul the straitjacket of a creed. Wilson was a Presbyterian, House a Pagan and a Pantheist. Where Wilson turned to the rugged gospel of his forefathers, House delicately fingered the elegant pages of Plato and Marcus Aurelius. When Wilson takes counsel with the God of the Covenanters, House turns to Confucius and Buddha.

Both McAdoo and Josephus Daniels dwell on the almost primitive religious feeling of Woodrow Wilson. Once McAdoo told a harmless joke remotely involving the Deity. Wilson objected to it on the ground that it was "irreverent." Wilson, like Emperor William, felt that one man and God make a majority. "You cannot fight God!" he exclaimed. When Lodge "cut out the heart of the Covenant," House would have compromised. Wilson refused. When the American people, by an overwhelming vote, rejected the League of Nations and all its works he said to McAdoo: "I am not so sure that the delay is not for the best. The people should be unmistakably back of the Government's action. After all, Providence knows more about these things than any of us. Any one is a fool who questions its ways."

"I am sometimes very much interested," he said on some other occasion, "when I see gentlemen supposing that popularity is the way to success in America. The way to success in this great country, with its fair judgments, is to show that"—the statement is curiously reminiscent of Bismarck—"you are not afraid of anybody except God and His final verdict. If I did not believe that the moral judgment would be the last judgment, the final judgment, in the minds of men as well as at the tribunal of God, I could not believe in popular government."

In a little book, *When a Man Comes to Himself*, Woodrow

Wilson unfolds his creed. "The ethical code He (Christ) taught may no doubt be matched, here a piece, there a piece, out of other religions, other teachings or philosophies. Every thoughtful man born with a conscience must know the code of right and of pity to which he ought to conform, but without the motive of Christianity, without love, he may be the purest altruist and yet be as sad and unsatisfied as Marcus Aurelius."

Wilson's moral self was his pacifist self. He resisted the suggestion of war even when his three other selves were united against his moral self. He finally yielded only when he was convinced that a war to end war was moral. When war became a moral duty, all his selves were united, and the intense energy of the combined selves of Woodrow Wilson almost terrified those who knew him. Something in himself still could not forgive bloodshed. But he deflected this resentment, as we have seen, from himself to the Germans. The German Government became to him, for the time being, the very principle of evil. Some remnant of this resentment rankled in his heart against House and against himself. When events in Paris and at home made him realize that he had deceived himself, he suffered the agonies of the damned. Nothing could justify the slaughter which he had caused, the blood he had shed, except the Covenant. If he brought peace to the world he could wash the bloodstains from his hands.

When House advised moderation and compromise, he spoke a language which the Scotch-Presbyterian self could not understand. The fury of the President's disappointment, the resentment against himself and against war, became the ally of the Duumvir's foes. No whisper, no intrigue, no reproach, justified or not, could touch House until the Scotch-Presbyterian supplanted the intellectual self. When the insinuations of others coincided with the voice of his own conscience, the break became inevitable. But the separation was not absolute. It is impossible to sever all the cords which, in an intimacy so profound, bind soul to soul. Deep in Wilson's heart there still remained an attachment for House. His emotional, his intellectual, his practical self, still admired the Duumvir. Fearing a return of the old dominance, he could not see him, he could not even, except in the most conventional tone, reply to his letters. The communications between the Duumvirs after the Peace Conference are still cordial. On August 15, 1919, Wilson hopes that certain difficulties raised by the French Government will be overcome by "patience and argument." He is delighted to hear that Viscount Grey will be the new Ambassador of Great Britain. The President refers to a tremendous "storm of all sorts of difficulties" through which he is going. He adds the assurance that the ship is "steady" and the officers "undismayed." But there is no reference to the pilot nor to the need of his guidance.

Somewhat later, Colonel House suggests in a cable to Wilson the desirability of his return. Wilson rejects this suggestion and asks the Duumvir to remain in London. In response to Wilson's request, House postpones his return trip until he hears of Wilson's collapse. Then, though sick himself, he hurries back. His condition was so serious that he was unable to leave the boat without assistance. While the Colonel was slowly recovering at his home on Fifty-third Street, Wilson lay stricken in the White House.

The House archives at Yale reveal an exchange of mutual condolences and courtesies between Mrs. Wilson and Mrs. House. Mrs. Wilson, writing on October 17th, feels that the President is gaining a little every day, but does not expect the miracle of a quick restoration, since every nerve in the sick man's body had been crying out for weeks before he gave up the struggle. The writer admits that she did not inform the President of the Colonel's return or of his illness because she wishes to keep everything from him on which his advice is not needed or which would annoy or distress him. House, it seems, had returned from London to Paris. "I have not yet told him of the Colonel's illness or that he has left Paris, for I knew how anxious he was that he remain there for the time." The letter ends with conventional greetings and the hope that the cloud of illness will soon lift.

On November 18th, another note from Mrs. Wilson, acknowledging a letter from Colonel House to the President, flutters from the sick man to Fifty-third Street. The President, she assures the Duumvir, is sorry to hear of the Colonel's illness. But there is no suggestion of any meeting.

Meanwhile, the Peace Treaty faces a decisive defeat in the

Senate. To save the Treaty and the League, House overcomes his pride and writes a powerful letter to Woodrow Wilson on November 24th. This is the letter which he entrusted to Gregory and which was delivered personally to Mrs. Wilson. There is no evidence that Wilson saw the letter, which is preserved for posterity in *The Intimate Papers of Colonel House*.

"DEAR GOVERNOR:

"I hesitate to intrude my views upon you at such a time, but I feel that I would be doing less than my duty if I did not do so, since so much depends upon your decision in regard to the Treaty. Its failure would be a disaster not less to civilization than to you.

"My suggestion is this: Do not mention the Treaty in your message to Congress, but return it to the Senate as soon as it convenes. In the meantime, send for Senator Hitchcock and tell him that you feel that you have done your duty and have fulfilled your every obligation to your colleagues in Paris by rejecting all offers to alter the document which was formulated there, and you now turn the Treaty over to the Senate for such action as it may deem wise to take.

"I would advise him to ask the Democratic Senators to vote for the Treaty with such reservations as the majority may formulate, and let the matter then rest with the other signatories of the Treaty. I would say to Senator Hitchcock that if the Allied and Associated Powers are willing to accept the reservations which the Senate see fit to make, you will abide by the result, being conscious of having done your full duty.

"The Allies may not take the Treaty with the Lodge Reservations as they now stand, and this will be your vindication. But even if they should take them with slight modifications, your conscience will be clear. After agreement is reached, it can easily be shown that the Covenant in its practical workings in the future will not be seriously hampered and that time will give us a workable machine.

"A great many people, Democrats, Progressives, and Republicans, have talked with me about ratification of the Treaty, and they are all pretty much of one mind regarding the necessity for its passage with or without reservations. To the ordinary man, the distance between the Treaty and the reservations is slight.

"Of course, the arguments are all with the position you have taken and against that of the Senate, but, unfortunately, no amount of logic can alter the situation; therefore my advice would be to make no further argument, but return the Treaty to the Senate without comment and let Senator Hitchcock know that you expect it to be ratified in some form, and then let the other signatories decide for themselves whether they will accept it.

"The supreme place which history will give you will be largely
because you personify in yourself the great idealistic conception of a
league of nations. If this conception fails, it will be your failure.
To-day there are millions of helpless people throughout the world
who look to you and you only to make this conception a realization.

                            "Affectionately yours,
                                "E. M. HOUSE."

No reply came. But there must have been rumblings from
Washington that Wilson was determined to fight to the bitter
end, giving no quarter to himself or his enemies. Three days
later Colonel House writes once more.

"DEAR GOVERNOR:
    "I am wondering if I made myself clear to you in my letter of
the other day.
    "I wish to emphasize the fact that I do not counsel surrender.
The action advised will in my opinion make your position consistent
and impregnable. Any other way out that now seems possible of
success would be something of a surrender.
    "Practically every one who is in close touch with the situation
admits that the Treaty cannot be ratified without substantial reservations. You must not be a party to those reservations. You stood for
the Treaty as it was made in Paris, but if the Senate refuses to ratify
without reservations, under the circumstances, I would let the Allies
determine whether or not they will accept them.
    "This does not mean that no effort will be made by those
Senators and others who favor the Treaty as it is to make the
reservations as innocuous as possible. Neither does it mean that the
Allies will accept the Treaty as the Senate majority have desired it.
    "If you take the stand indicated, it will aid rather than hinder
those working for mild reservations. It will absolutely ensure the
passage of the Treaty and probably in a form acceptable to both
you and the Allies.
    "I did not make the suggestion until I had checked it up with
some of your friends in whom I felt you had confidence, for the
matter is of such incalculable importance that I did not dare rely
solely upon my own judgment.
    "In conclusion, let me suggest that Senator Hitchcock be warned
not to make any public statement regarding your views. When the
Treaty is ratified, then I hope you will make a statement letting your
position become known.
    "I feel as certain as I ever did of anything that your attitude
would receive universal approval. On the one hand your loyalty to
our Allies will be commended, and, on the other, your willingness to

accept reservations rather than have the Treaty killed will be regarded as the act of a great man.

"Affectionately yours,
"E. M. House."

Again there is no answer whatever. Wilson, having yielded so often, refused to compromise when compromise alone could save his dream. His conscience, overruling his reason, permits no concession. It does not even allow him to reply to House, to listen to any argument that could possibly weaken his determination. The fourth self of Wilson is in complete control. The eternal struggle of the last few months has consumed his strength. He can bear no more. A meeting with House would lead to a psychic catastrophe. Such a meeting would have stirred the depths of him. It would have killed him. Edith Bolling Wilson and Dr. Cary T. Grayson are wise in shielding the patient. His own protective instinct rallies to their aid. The walls about him rise, until he is completely immured.

There is no message from Woodrow Wilson to House from November 18, 1919, to March 11, 1920. House makes every effort consistent with self-respect to reëstablish his contact with Wilson. In the letter of March 11, signed by Wilson himself, the President thanks him for the return of a check for one thousand dollars, the unexpended balance of a small fund which Wilson had put to the Duumvir's credit to defray the expense of himself and his secretary in the fall of 1918. He adds that he is regaining his strength slowly and assures House that he is having the very best care. He hopes that the Colonel and Mrs. House are well. The letter is signed, "Always, Faithfully yours, Woodrow Wilson." But there is no hint that the President desires to meet his *alter ego*.

It is evident that Wilson dreads such a meeting. On June 7, 1920, before sailing for Europe, House once more reaches out his hand to Wilson:

"DEAR GOVERNOR:

"We are sailing Saturday for a short trip abroad and I am sending a word of good-by. God grant when I return in September you will have fully recovered.

"These last few difficult months have been a source of deep

regret to me and I am sure you know that I am as concerned as ever in the noble policies you have sought to effectuate. You lifted statesmanship to a higher plane and in doing so our country assumed a place in world affairs without parallel. The great captains of the past sought to dominate mankind by force and failed; you essayed to influence the world by justice and succeeded.

"One would have thought that every American heart would have been filled with satisfaction because it was a day when every American head could be held high. But envy and malice corroded the finer impulses of many of our fellow citizens and no art has been left unemployed to drag down the American colossus. Future generations will read with amazement and shame the story of the warfare waged upon you. It has been an unholy effort and will merit the condemnation of posterity.

"Affectionately yours,
"E. M. HOUSE."

"P. S. In view of my past activities and in order not to mislead any one, I shall state before leaving and again upon reaching the other side, that my visit has no official status whatever and is made for purely personal reasons."

The postscript of the letter is most important because it definitely severs the formal relationship between the two men. It is the notification to Wilson that the Duumvirate is at an end. Wilson, in his reply, makes no reference to the termination of their long coöperation. There is no word of either thanks or reproach. The President intimates that councils are as "confused" on the other side of the water as they are on this. He stresses the fact that his health is improving. It is "uphill work" and the hill is "very steep," but it can be breasted with perseverance and patience. Wilson expresses perfect confidence that the "confusions of the time" will clear. But he does not grasp the outstretched hand.

House crosses the ocean, no longer the astral body of Woodrow Wilson. For the first time in seven years, he belongs entirely to himself. Once more, one week before the election of 1920 that carried Harding to victory and the League to the discard, House writes to Wilson:

"DEAR GOVERNOR:

"During these last anxious days of the election, I should like you to know how often I think of you and wish for the triumph of the great cause which you have sponsored and have advocated with such eloquence and force. I have an abiding faith in the aggregate wisdom of the people and I feel that it will not now be long before America will join her sister nations in the League.

"Faithfully yours,
"E. M. House."

Wilson replies two days later. He appreciates the Colonel's thoughtfulness and his hopeful expectations of the ultimate results of the contests through which the world is now darkly struggling.

The rest is silence.

But in shutting out House, Wilson condemned himself to spiritual starvation. No one else could complement his complex personality. No combination of men and minds could possibly fulfill the complicated symbiotic function upon which the achievements of Woodrow Wilson rest. Wilson was neither young enough nor strong enough to seek a new intellectual alliance.

Wilson himself killed the thing he loved. He sacrificed his friendship with House on the altar of his Scotch-Presbyterian conscience. Perhaps it was a gesture of atonement for having violated the injunction: "Thou Shalt Not Kill!" With House he could not live. Without him, he was condemned to death and frustration.

Woodrow Wilson was his own judge and his own executioner.

XXXVII

THE GREAT COLLAPSE

Wilson's Psychic Shocks – Dr. Grayson Makes a Blood Test – The Truth About Wilson's Blind Eye – Messengers of Death – The Great Crusade – Bullitt's Bullet – Lansing's Excuse – The Chink in the Armor – Wilson Weeps in Pueblo – Mrs. Wilson Takes Command – The Verdict of the Specialists – Lansing Invokes the Constitution – Tumulty and Grayson Defy the Secretary of State – Who Ruled America?

FOR six and one-half months, from September 26, 1919, to April 13, 1920, a woman was virtually President of the United States.

For six and one-half months Edith Bolling Wilson fulfilled the dream of Susan B. Anthony. For six and one-half months she was, so to speak, not only Acting President, but Secretary to the President, and Secretary of State.

From mid-April to the end of Wilson's term on March 4, 1921, Edith Bolling Wilson shared with Woodrow Wilson the responsibilities and duties of the Chief Magistracy of the Republic.

To understand this, perhaps the most extraordinary, chapter in American history we must briefly sketch Woodrow Wilson's crusade on behalf of the Covenant and the League of Nations, which ended with his physical and nervous collapse. This collapse seems all the more astounding since Woodrow Wilson was never more fit physically than he was before the catastrophe. I have this assurance from Colonel House. It is corroborated by Admiral Grayson. "I am in better health than I have been in forty years," Wilson himself said to his doctor, prior to America's entrance into the War. Dr. Grayson's régime enabled the President to bear his war burdens with undiminished vitality. He had laid aside coal-tar tablets and found golf a substitute for the stomach pump. Even strenuous speaking campaigns did not tax his strength unduly. Woodrow Wilson, if Henry Morgenthau is right, actually drew energy from his audiences. Their applause recharged the batteries of his nervous system.

Clinton Gilbert, who met Wilson in Paris at the apex of his career, describes him as marvelously fresh and young, his color warm and youthful, his eye alive to pleasure. "His League Covenant had just been agreed to. The world had accepted him. Fate had led him far from those paths of defeat and obscurity into which his sensitiveness and shyness had turned him as a youth. He was elated and confident."

Dr. Grayson insists that Paris upset Wilson's constitution. It limited his exercise and French hospitality made it impossible to carry out the rigid diet to which Wilson had accustomed himself. The circumstances cited by Dr. Grayson were no doubt important. But Wilson's mysterious physical breakdown was probably due largely to psychic causes. Wilson's physical deterioration was the inevitable consequence of his estrangement from House.

All his life Wilson shrank from contact with other men. Every one who knew Wilson closely testifies that such contacts, except under conditions chosen by himself, were a torture to him. The analytical Clinton Gilbert ascribes this tendency to a neurotic sense of inferiority. "When all his personal history becomes known, when his papers and letters have all been published and read, when the memoirs of others have told all that there is to be told, there will stand clear something inadequate, a lack of robustness, mental or nervous, an excessive sensitiveness, over self-consciousness, shrinking from life, a neurotic something that in the end brought on defeat and the final overthrow. He was never quite a normal man with the average man's capacity to endure and enjoy, but a strange, impeded, self-absorbed personality."

This coincides with the facts with which we are familiar. But Wilson had found an escape from his difficulty by his alliance with House. The Duumvir permitted the outside world to filter through his mind to Wilson, but he protected his sensitive partner from the harsh winds that blew. When Wilson himself flung open all the windows, he exposed himself to perils he had never successfully braved. For seven years House had functioned as his defensive against the slings and arrows of outrageous fortune. The collapse of his symbiotic alliance with House compelled him to bear unendurable frictions and combats. Wilson's conferences with Clemenceau, Lloyd George and Orlando undermined his strength and destroyed the psychic and nervous balance he had so laboriously acquired. In addition to these assaults from without, he was assailed by inimical forces battling for mastery within himself. That battle was waged at the expense of his nervous surplus. Some people ascribed his rapid physical collapse to a specific ailment which sometimes, even after it is ostensibly cured, revenges itself upon the organism. In order to spike this rumor, Dr. Grayson took several blood tests. The reports of eminent physicians and bacteriologists to whom the specimens were submitted agree that Wilson's blood was free from taint. The trouble was not with his blood but with his soul!

Wilson's organic inferiority combined in a vicious circle with psychic complications. Eyestrain, in all likelihood, aggravated both conditions. We can understand Wilson's mentality better if we realize that he was constrained to make one eye do the work of two. Years before the Peace Conference a retinal hemorrhage had deprived him of the sight of his right eye. The strain on his optical nerve, and that messenger of death, hardening of the arteries, explain the violent headaches which began to plague him again in Paris. People noticed that one side of his face twitched ominously.

His encounter with the Senate Foreign Relations Committee had compelled Wilson to face the unpleasant reality that he would have to wage battle for the Covenant unless he accepted certain senatorial reservations. But he was in no mood for compromise. Standing sternly by the letter of the law, Wilson, in his fundamentalist mood, preferred to fight. He compelled his followers to vote against all reservations. The Covenant was defeated not by its enemies but by its friends!

Undismayed by the tokens of Wilson's illness, pro-League

Senators impressed upon the President that he could not secure the acceptance of the Peace Treaty and the Covenant unless he personally undertook a great moral crusade. Remembering his recent European apotheosis, Wilson determined to take his case to the people. Tumulty and Grayson both urged him to delay the contemplated swing around the circle. But the stern moral Scotch-Presbyterian self overruled every other consideration.

Wilson met Grayson's objections with a grim smile. "I know why you are here. You want to persuade me not to go. I know all your arguments and I admit their truthfulness. But the boys who went overseas did not refuse to go because it was dangerous. Many of them sacrificed their lives in an attempt to bring about a permanent peace. The thought of their sacrifice makes me more determined to put forth my utmost endeavor to have the League ratified, for I believe it will prevent another such world-wide catastrophe. No, despite your advice, I must go."

With the same grand gesture Wilson waved away Tumulty's advice to take a needed rest.

"Disastrous consequences may follow if you insist upon this trip," Tumulty objected.

"I know," Wilson replied wearily, "that I am at the end of my tether, but my friends on the Hill say that the trip is necessary to save the Treaty, and I am willing to make whatever personal sacrifice is required, for if the Treaty should be defeated, God only knows what would happen to the world as a result of it. In the presence of the great tragedy which now faces the world, no decent man can count his own personal fortunes in the reckoning. Even though, in my condition, it might mean the giving up of my life, I will gladly make the sacrifice to save the Treaty."

Darkly, in Wilson's Scotch-Presbyterian soul, another thought seems to shape itself. He must chastise his body to atone for the blood shed in the War. Deliberately he chooses the dolorous road of salvation by self-crucifixion. Possibly his intellect offered the counter-suggestion of a triumph over his foes without the ultimate sacrifice. Keenly aware of the dramatic element of his crusade, he saw himself an embattled knight in shining armor and expected the country to be carried away by that vision. And a voice in his heart urged him to venture the trip if only to prove to himself, to the world and to his *alter ego,* Edward Mandell House, his ability to snatch victory from defeat with his own hands. All these elements combined to make his decision irrevocable, but his wrecked and racked body could not bear the weight of his cross.

Tumulty made a mental comparison between the Woodrow Wilson who now stood before him and the man he had met many years before in New Jersey. "In those days he was a vigorous, agile, slender man, active and alert, his hair but slightly streaked with gray. Now, as he stood before me discussing the necessity for the Western trip, he was an old man, grown grayer and grayer, but grimmer and grimmer in his determination, like an old warrior, to fight to the end."

On September 3rd the battered, broken, one-eyed Covenanter sets forth upon his crusade. He makes a notable speech in Columbus, Ohio. Others follow, in quick succession. His reception by the crowds is not over-friendly. Wherever the Presidential train arrives, the fiery Judge Daniel Cohalan and his indefatigable Irish cohorts, who were fighting the League, had preceded him with advertisements asking embarrassing questions which Wilson was unable to answer. Tossing logic aside, he draws upon the mighty arsenal of his rhetoric. His phrasing and his delivery are exquisite. He pits the batteries of his eloquence against the stone wall of destiny. Day after day his emotional ecstasy grows. Then comes a shock, an attack that can neither be ignored nor laughed off.

On September 12, he receives a news dispatch that unnerves him. William C. Bullitt testifies before the Committee on Foreign Relations that Secretary Lansing had criticized the League of Nations severely. To Wilson and his friends this seems like a stab in the back. Lansing's lame explanation in a dispatch fails to improve Wilson's temper.

"Were I in Washington," he says to Tumulty, "I would at once demand his resignation. That kind of disloyalty must not be permitted to go unchallenged for a single minute."

His memory travels back to Paris.

"The testimony of Bullitt," he said, "is a confirmation of

the suspicions I have had with reference to this individual. I found the same attitude of mind on the part of Lansing on the other side. I could find his trail everywhere I went, but they were only suspicions and it would not be fair for me to act upon them. But here in his own statement is a verification at last of everything I have suspected. Think of it! This from a man whom I raised from the level of a subordinate to the great office of Secretary of State of the United States. My God! I did not think it possible for Lansing to act in this way. When we were in Paris I found that Lansing and others were constantly giving out statements that did not agree with my viewpoint."

It is significant that Wilson does not include House in his indictment of those who disagreed with him in Paris.

"When," the President continued his confidences, "I had arranged a settlement, there would appear from some source I could not locate unofficial statements telling the correspondents not to take things too seriously; that a compromise would be made, and this news, or rather news of this kind, was harmful to the settlement I had already obtained and quite naturally gave the Conference the impression that Lansing and his kind were speaking for me, and then the French would say that I was bluffing."

Tumulty is convinced that only Wilson's illness a few days later prevented his immediate dismissal of Lansing. Identifying himself with his cause, Wilson, like a true crusader, persuaded himself that any one who disagreed with him was an enemy of the Lord. The archfiend in his universe was no longer the Kaiser but Lodge, who led the fight against the Peace Treaty. Lansing, by admitting in a confidential conversation that the Peace Treaty was not perfect, aligned himself with the powers of evil.

Living in a dream world of his own, Wilson planned, upon the completion of the Western trip, to make a sally into Senator Lodge's own territory in Massachusetts. But every day shattered more completely the confidence of the American people in Wilson's handiwork at Versailles. At last a ray of the truth must have pierced a chink of the fantastic armor in which Wilson accoutered himself, like the poor Emperor in the story who suddenly realizes that his robe of State is a nightshirt. Perhaps it was Bullitt's statement or Lansing's long-winded excuses. Perhaps newspaper comment—one of Judge Cohalan's full-page broadsides—perhaps the fiery oratory of Johnson or Moses, perhaps the stinging invective of Jim Reed; Colonel House was the only man who could have softened the blow to Wilson's pride without concealing from him the realities of the situation. But Colonel House was in Paris!

In Pueblo, on September 25, no longer master of his emotions, Woodrow Wilson bursts into tears when he addresses the crowd. His headaches rob him of sleep. When he sleeps, saliva drops from the corners of his mouth. Fever assails his body. Catastrophe is at hand.

At four o'clock in the morning, on September 26, Grayson knocks at Tumulty's compartment. "The President is seriously ill. I greatly fear that the trip may end fatally if he attempts to go on."

When Tumulty arrives at the President's drawing-room, he finds him fully dressed and seated in his chair. Speech no longer flows freely. His tongue stumbles. His lips refuse to articulate. His face is ghostly pale, one side of it seems to have fallen, like a ruined house. Tears stream down the President's cheek.

"My dear boy," he mumbles, painfully, "this has never happened to me before. I felt it coming on yesterday. I do not know what to do."

Tumulty agrees with Grayson. The trip must be cancelled. The sick man pleads with his doctor and his secretary. "Don't you see that if you cancel this trip, Senator Lodge and his friends will say that I am a quitter and that the Western trip was a failure, and the Treaty will be lost."

Reaching over to him, Tumulty takes both of his hands: "What difference, my dear Governor, does it make what they say? Nobody in the world believes you are a quitter, but it is your life that we must now consider. We must cancel the trip, and I am sure that when the people learn of your condition there will be no misunderstanding."

Wilson is unable to persuade Tumulty. His left arm and leg no longer function. His whole left side is paralyzed. But the indomitable Scotch-Presbyterian soul continues to argue. "I want to show them that I can still fight and that I am not afraid. Just postpone the trip for twenty-four hours and I will be all right."

No one can read unmoved Tumulty's account of Wilson's collapse in his *Woodrow Wilson As I Know Him*, which enables us to trace Wilson's way to Golgotha.

The train slides into a siding near Wichita, Kansas. Mrs. Wilson, now thoroughly alarmed, takes command of the situation. The Wichita engagement is cancelled. A sign from her ends the sad crusade. With the assistance of Grayson she takes hold of the reins, never to relinquish them while Wilson lives. Riding around the town, the train turns homeward. Blinds drawn, it swiftly heads to Washington.

Skeptics among the newspaper men believed that the President was shamming illness. The majority were not surprised. They had seen unmistakable signs of the approaching collapse. When the train arrives in Washington on a Sunday morning, Wilson, controlling the agony that racks his limbs, walks briskly through Union Station.

A few days later, October 4, at four o'clock in the morning, Mrs. Wilson, hearing the President calling from the bathroom, finds him prostrate on the floor, his left leg crumpled under him. Grayson is summoned in haste. When the President regains consciousness he asks his wife and his doctor to keep his condition a secret. Such, at least, is the statement vouchsafed by Josephus Daniels. No one talked to the invalid immediately after his stroke except Grayson and Mrs. Wilson.

Dr. Grayson summons a Philadelphia specialist, Dr. Francis X. Dercum, Rear Admiral E. R. Stitt of the Naval Medical Corps, and Mrs. Wilson's family physician, Dr. Sterling Ruffin of Washington. The doctors agree that Wilson has suffered from a cerebral thrombosis, a blood clot in the right side of his brain, which paralyzed the left side of his body. Dr. Dercum is grave. "Mr. Wilson," he says, "may live five minutes, five months, or five years."

The last part of his prediction came nearest the truth. Shut off completely from the world of reality, Wilson survives from October 4, 1919, to February 3, 1924. But was he the same Woodrow Wilson after the stroke? To Lawrence he was never the same. "Every criticism, every coolness which old friends experienced, every expression on the part of Woodrow Wilson with reference to the few problems that he was permitted to consider or discuss cannot be appraised in retrospect without being mindful of the tired brain that once swayed the world and then feebly sought to retain its hold on the Presidency and public opinion."

No hint of the President's true condition was permitted to percolate through from the White House. Mrs. Wilson and Dr. Grayson threw around the sickbed the screen of professional secrecy and wifely devotion. Meanwhile rumor was rife. Bars which Roosevelt had put up, to protect the White House windows from his children playing ball on the lawn, suddenly assumed a sinister significance. It was whispered in the Senate cloakroom that the President was insane. Behind the bars the Senators pictured a raving maniac. No member of the Cabinet, not even the Secretary of State, was permitted to approach the sick man's bedside. Even Tumulty was compelled to wait in the anteroom. The Vice-President of the United States was left in the dark, like the rest of the country. Conscious of his duty to keep the machinery of the government moving, Lansing, in a private talk with Tumulty, suggests the advisability of calling upon the Vice-President to act for the President. He opens Jefferson's manual and reads to Tumulty a clause of the Constitution:

> "In case of the removal of the President from office, or of his death, resignation or inability to discharge the powers and duties of the said office, the same shall devolve on the Vice-President, and the Congress may by law provide for the case of removal, death, resignation or inability, both of the President and Vice-President, declaring what officer shall then act as President, and such officer shall act accordingly until the disability be removed or a President shall be elected."

Tumulty, already wroth with Lansing, is enraged. "Mr. Lansing," he sharply retorts, "the Constitution is not a dead letter with the White House. I have read the Constitution and do not find myself in need of any tutoring at your hands of the provisions you have just read. And who," he asks, shaking with indignation, "should certify to the disability of the President?"

"That," Lansing diplomatically intimates, "would be a job for either Dr. Grayson or for you."

"You may rest assured," Tumulty thunders, summoning all the fighting instincts of his race, "that while Woodrow Wilson is lying in the White House on the broad of his back, I will not be a party to oust him. He has been too kind, too loyal and too wonderful to me to receive such treatment at my hands."

At that moment, wafted hither by some magic foreknowledge, Dr. Grayson enters the Cabinet room. Who guided Dr. Grayson's steps in that epic moment?

"I am sure," Tumulty says, every tone an impeachment of Lansing, "that Dr. Grayson will never certify to his disability. Will you, Grayson?"

Dr. Grayson emphatically concurs with Tumulty. Tumulty, then, in no uncertain terms, notifies Lansing: "If any one outside the White House circle attempts to certify to the President's disability, Grayson and I will stand together and repudiate his statement."

"No further attempt," Tumulty says in his recital of the incident, "was made by Mr. Lansing to institute ouster proceedings against his chief."

Loyalty won at the expense of the Constitution!

"If," Tumulty adds, as Lansing turns to the door, "the President were in a position to know of this episode, he would take decisive measures."

October, November, December and January passed. For more than one quarter of a year, until February 13, 1920, Lansing remains Secretary of State. But Wilson takes no steps to end Lansing's régime in the State Department. The President is unable to discharge, for over one-fourth of a year, the functions of his office, even with the aid of Mrs. Wilson and Dr. Grayson.

From March 4, 1913, to Wilson's débâcle in Paris, June, 1919, the United States was governed by a Duumvirate consisting of Wilson and House.

Wilson ruled alone after his return, until September 26th, when his Western trip ended.

Between September 26 and October 4, when Wilson was paralyzed by a blood clot on the brain, Mrs. Wilson held the reins of government. She continued in command from that day until April 13, 1920, when Wilson resumed meetings with his Cabinet. But she remained his co-regent until the end, March 4, 1921.

If Mrs. Wilson did not virtually rule the United States throughout that period, who did?

Not Woodrow Wilson!

XXXVIII

THE INACCESSIBLE PRESIDENT

Guardians of the Sick-room – Misleading Information – The Isolation of
Woodrow Wilson – The Ignorance of the Cabinet – The Resentment of Vice-
President Marshall – Senator Moses Explodes a Bombshell – Dr. Grayson
Makes a Statement – The Chinese Wall Grows Higher – The President's
Callers – The Senate's Smelling Committee – Wilson Forces Out Lansing –
Colby steps into Lansing's Shoes – Grayson Tiptoes – The Woman in Purple

LIKE the two angels standing with fiery swords before the
gates of Paradise, Edith Bolling Wilson and Rear-Admiral
Dr. Cary T. Grayson guard the sick-room of the President. They
protect the paralytic from the intrusion of the world without.
They protect, with equal zeal, the truth about Woodrow Wilson
from seeping through the doors of his chamber.

From the very beginning, misleading accounts of the President's condition appear in the press. The deception begins with
Wilson's collapse on the train. Grayson (see the New York *Times*
of September 27, 1919) calls the President's trouble "nervous
exhaustion" and adds that it is "not alarming." Tumulty declares
that the President's exertions brought on a "nervous reaction in
his digestive organs."

The following day, September 28, Edith Bolling Wilson and
Admiral Grayson are in control on the President's train. "Under
instructions from Admiral Grayson, all dispatches concerning the
Treaty situation and other public questions were withheld from
the President." "The President has not been permitted to see
any one to-day but Mrs. Wilson, Admiral Grayson and Secretary
Tumulty."

No one, not even Senator Hitchcock, Wilson's personal
spokesman in the Senate, sees Wilson after his arrival in Wash-

ington, September 29. On October 3, the visit of the specialists summoned to the President's bedside is noted in the press. The President's son-in-law, William G. McAdoo, arrives in Washington. He leaves, according to the dispatches, without being permitted to see his father-in-law.

Official statements are lacking in candor. While Wilson lies unconscious and paralyzed, the newspapers indicate that the President is "chafing under restraint." Grayson is "constantly with him." On October 6, the public hears that Mrs. Wilson and Grayson still "guard" the President, who is so anxious to get to work that he calls for a stenographer, but is persuaded to give up the idea.

In the absence of authentic news from the White House, rumors spring up overnight like mushrooms. Press and public founder in a sea of uncertainty. On October 7, Wall Street hears that McAdoo has been called in to take supervisory charge of the executive branch. It is announced that Colonel House is hurrying to Washington. Both reports are false.

"All sorts of rumors," remarks the *Times*, "have been running the gamut of gossip in the capital regarding the exact nature of the President's illness. . . . One of the most insistent reports has had it that the President's real trouble has been a slight abscess of the brain. . . . When this rumor was brought to Dr. Grayson's attention to-night he stated informally that there was no foundation for it. Another persistent report has had it that the President has suffered from a slight cerebral leakage and hemorrhage, but this was also discounted to-night when brought to the attention of Dr. Grayson."

Still completely in the dark, leading press organs print dispatches such as these: "The President fully realizes his condition. . . . His spirits have been variable, however, and recurrently he indicates a desire to be out of his bed." No visitor is admitted. "There are numerous visitors to the White House daily . . . but no person outside of the members of the immediate White House family and the physicians are permitted to see the President."

The *Times* reports a special meeting of the Cabinet "to consider phases of the situation created by the illness of the

President." We know that such was indeed in Lansing's mind. Tumulty loyally insists that the rumor is without foundation.

We learn that "Admiral Grayson and those in charge of the case have prescribed an 'absolute rest cure' for the President.... For this reason no business whatever is being brought to the attention of the President." On October 8, the *Times* writes: "The President was again impatient to-day over his confinement as a bed-ridden patient and wanted to transact business, but Rear-Admiral Grayson insisted that it would be very unwise." Dr. Dercum, consulting physician, is quoted in a Philadelphia paper as saying: "The President's mind is clear and alert." "I agree with him entirely," says Grayson.

More news of the same type follows. The New York *Times*, of October 9, carries a Washington dispatch representing the President as "very urgent that he be permitted to leave bed," but Grayson continues to "deal with him as a bed patient." Apparently it is hard to keep Wilson inactive. "It has been a good day for the President, but not the best day for me," says Grayson. The headline reads: "Wilson Stronger, but Kept in Bed."

The New York *Herald* likewise reports that Wilson is "restive." "Mr. Wilson is particularly anxious to see several Democratic Senators.... After considerable difficulty, he succeeded in inducing Mrs. Wilson to telephone to Joseph P. Tumulty ... and have him locate them. Up to a late hour to-night, however, Mr. Tumulty had been unable to find any of the Senators. Dr. Grayson made some inquiries, too, but had the same experience. When the reports reached the President he commented adversely on the fact that nobody seemed able to get in touch with anybody he wanted to see...."

The darkness in which the President's condition is still shrouded on October 14 appears in the following excerpt from the New York *Times:*

DETAILS OF ILLNESS KEPT FROM CABINET

Members Get Reports on Wilson Only Through Press, Says Palmer.

Philadelphia, Oct. 13.... A. Mitchell Palmer, Attorney General of the United States, to-night declared that no member of President Wilson's Cabinet knows any more about Mr. Wilson's condition than appears in the newspapers.

Mr. Palmer was questioned on this point before he spoke at the Columbus Day celebration at the Academy of Music.

"What is the President's condition?" was the first question.

"You read the newspapers, don't you?" was the reply.

"Don't you know any more than that?" Mr. Palmer was asked.

"I do not," the Attorney General replied.

"Does any Cabinet member know any more about it than what he reads in the newspapers?" Mr. Palmer was asked.

"No," was the answer.

D. F. Houston confirms Mr. Palmer's statement. We learn from his book, *Eight Years with Wilson's Cabinet,* that the Vice-President of the United States, like the Cabinet, was ignored by the guardians of the bed-chamber. Mr. Houston happened to meet the Vice-President and Mrs. Marshall at the Shoreham. Marshall was "much perturbed" and expressed "regret" that he was kept in the dark about Wilson's condition. The Vice-President asked Mr. Houston to give him the real facts, which Houston said he was unable to do. "I could not," Mr. Houston comments, "even repeat what had been told to me, because it had been said in confidence. The Vice-President expressed the view that he ought immediately to be informed; that it would be a tragedy for him to assume the duties of President, at best; and that it would be equally a tragedy for the people; that he knew many men who knew more about the affairs of the Government than he did; and that it would be especially trying for him if he had to assume the duties without warning. He showed resentment that the doctors were keeping the situation a mystery so far as he especially was concerned, and asserted that they ought to be frank with the public."

On October 10, 1919, Washington dispatches once more picture a President improved to the point of being apparently about to over-rule his physicians and wife and get back to work. But this picture is greatly changed by the Washington dispatches of October 12th. The Associated Press story, carried by both the New York *Times* and the New York *Tribune,* begins: "Hope that President Wilson might soon regain his normal health and resume fully the duties of his office was swept away to-day by his physicians." The bulletin of the previous day was then quoted: "The President," reads a bulletin signed by Grayson,

Ruffin, Stitt and Dercum, "shows signs of continued improvement, but his condition is such as to necessitate his remaining in bed for an extended period."

The Associated Press dispatch goes on to say that in view of this decision that Mr. Wilson must be bedridden for "an extended period" there is "renewed discussion as to what expedient might be adopted should the press of executive business reach a point demanding more attention than he could give it. The disposition on all sides (the dispatch continues) seems to be to refrain from raising the question of the President's disability to act under the Constitution, but officials are known to have considered it as one of the possibilities of the situation." The dispatch further indicates that there is much discussion in Washington of the question as to how disability should be determined, and by whom.

On this same date a bombshell explodes—the first guarded challenge to those who, keeping the physical person of the President virtually prisoner, insist on retaining control of the executive business of the country in his hands, or ostensibly in his hands. The charge of T.N.T. is the publication of a letter written by Senator George Higgins Moses of New Hampshire to a friend in Manchester, in his home State.

The sensational nature of Senator Moses' allegations (which the next day are "ridiculed," not very convincingly, by Dr. Dercum) lose nothing in the elaboration in the Providence *Journal* of October 13th.

"President Wilson is suffering from a very dangerous cerebral hemorrhage. . . . There is partial physical paralysis and the brain lesion is of such a character that Mr. Wilson has suffered several periods of aphasia. . . . From a high government official . . . it is learned that even if the President should show signs of improvement by the gradual absorption of the hemorrhage, any mental strain . . . would mean . . . a more dangerous condition. It is also declared there is no possibility that Mr. Wilson would be able to perform the functions of his office either in the immediate or the remote future."

But if the information of Senator Moses was correct; if Woodrow Wilson was partly paralyzed and subject to loss of memory, who was President? The Providence *Journal* assumed that McAdoo and Colonel House had control of the Government. We now know that this assumption was wrong.

By October 14, Washington dispatches began to speak of "the demand to know what is really the matter with the President." The New York *Tribune* reports "private advices" that Mr. Wilson had a "blood clot on the brain," and recalls that it was the breaking of such a clot that caused the death of Theodore Roosevelt. Dr. Grayson states that "if any public matters really needed Mr. Wilson's attention they might be attended to." The situation in the Senate becomes agitated. Senator John Sharp Williams asks the Committee on Foreign Relations to postpone certain questions it wants to submit to the President, on the ground that it "would not be in good taste, in view of his condition." Senator Fall quickly responds: "If you think the President's condition is such that he could not answer this, of course you are right that it should not be referred to him, but I think you ought to move on the floor of the Senate that further consideration of the Peace Treaty be postponed until the President's recovery."

Secretary Lansing denies the report of another Cabinet meeting. According to the *Tribune,* it is asserted very flatly in some quarters that the "Democratic leaders are seriously discussing the possibility of Vice-President Marshall assuming the duties of the Presidency." An equally significant item in the same issue records that Secretary Tumulty, "though noticeably irritated by the rumors of the President's condition, declined to make official denial of any of the stories. Mr. Tumulty indicated that the President was in the hands of Dr. Grayson and other physicians."

A bulletin issued by Grayson, Ruffin and Stitt on October 14, discloses that the President has passed a restless night and day owing to a swelling of the prostate gland. The *Tribune* of October 15, reporting this, indicates a crescendo in Washington in the discussion of whether steps should be taken to transfer the executive functions of the Federal Government to some other person or group of persons during the President's illness. Under the headline: "Cabinet Decides to Act," the *Tribune* says: "It became apparent to-day that Mr. Wilson's Cabinet ... is about to become a power in government, and is expected to take up many of the problems which the President laid down when he took to his bed several weeks ago. The prospects of an illness long continued on the part of Mr. Wilson seems to have convinced the Cabinet members that they cannot afford longer to ignore some of the more pressing situations of domestic policy which confront the nation. If the President is kept to his bed for months to come it is highly improbable that the Government will continue to go along without an actual head. ... It is not questioned that eventually something will be done to appoint a successor."

Responsible Government officials began to feel that the President's case should be considered as one of "disability," requiring congressional action. If the little coterie that immediately surrounded the sick President wished to retain the executive power, they could not have exploited the situation with greater dexterity. On October 15, the New York *World*, Administration organ, flaunts a letter from Dr. Grayson to an anonymous friend, saying he did not know "any disease that had not been included in the rumors about the President"; and that he, *Grayson, would be glad to be as sick as Mr. Wilson if he could also be as alert mentally!*

The American people, noted by Northcliffe to be docile, begin to grumble. Faced with this situation, the physicians give out longer, apparently franker, but really no more revealing bulletins. The New York *Herald*, of October 16, prints an "unofficial explanation" to the effect that "the President is being kept in very general touch with affairs, but he is not permitted to know any details of the Treaty fight (etc.) ... Dr. Grayson and Mrs. Wilson inform the President in a general way what is happening."

An Associated Press dispatch from Washington lets the cat out of the bag: "With the exception of the news furnished him by Mrs. Wilson, the President has learned very little of national and international developments." A writer in the *Tribune* uses stronger language on Sunday, October 19: "The ingenuity of his (the President's) retinue was taxed with appearing to carry out

his wishes, while secretly thwarting them." The writer goes on
to say: "While the 'politics' of the situation has been talked...
little has been played.... The outstanding criticism has not been
so much that any one has tried to take advantage of an unusual
situation, as that Mr. Wilson's attending physicians, by their
mysterious secrecy, have created fears that have been, perhaps,
unwarranted."

On October 21, the President for the first time performs an
executive function (according to a headline in the *Tribune*) by
appointing Owen D. Young of Schenectady to a vacant place in
the Industrial Conference then going on in Washington. The
Times account of the same incident has this significant passage:
"It was learned at the White House that during the day the President had occasion to send for some papers of an official character
which he went over with Mrs. Wilson. Mrs. Wilson does most of
the President's reading for him, as the physicians do not wish
to have him do his own reading at this time."

On this day also the newspapers carried the story that four
bills had become laws without the President's signature and in
default of any action by him, because these bills had not been laid
before him, and he had not been permitted to know about them.
"It is explained that... these bills... were not presented to him
under the policy of keeping as much business as possible from
him." (New York *Times*, October 21.) Evidently it lay in Mrs.
Wilson's hands to submit to or withhold from the President legislation passed by the Congress.

The hierarchical rank of those surrounding the President at
this time may be gleaned from a report in the New York *Tribune*
of October 22, 1919. Telling how the day before the President
had been well enough to dictate and sign (in pencil) a letter to
Secretary Lane, it says: "The letter was written after Bernard
Baruch and Thomas L. Chadbourne... visited the White House
and conferred with Secretary to the President Tumulty. Tumulty
in turn conveyed their message to Dr. Grayson, who told the
President.... The rule still applies against visitors to the President's sick room, only Mrs. Wilson and the nurse, and an occasional visit from the President's daughters, being permitted. Only
rarely does Secretary Tumulty go to the bedside." The next day's

papers (October 23) report that the President was able to sign bills which had been "handed to Dr. Grayson by Secretary Tumulty."

On November 18, a curious dramatic situation occurs. The President is permitted, for the second time since he is stricken, to sun himself on the south lawn of the White House. "From the windows of the Cabinet Room the members of the Cabinet, while in session, could see the President in his wheel chair." They could see him but not reach or communicate with him. Senator Gilbert M. Hitchcock is equally unlucky. He leads the fight for the Treaty that is most dear to Wilson's heart, but the sick-room is locked against him. The efforts of Hitchcock to keep in touch with Wilson constitute material for gossip and speculation.

On November 30, the *Times* reports that the President's physicians, after consultation, will not allow him to hold a conference scheduled with Senator Hitchcock at that time. This is a month and one-half after Dr. Grayson gleefully declared he would be "glad to be as sick as Wilson if he could be as alert mentally," seven weeks after Dr. Dercum announced in Philadelphia that the President's mind was "clear and alert." But Secretary Tumulty denied the "alarmist reports" of a setback in the President's health.

On December 3, more than two months after the breakdown in Wichita, the New York *Times* records that Hitchcock is still barred from the President. Those close to President Wilson are quoted as stating that the condition of his health is improving steadily. "Some uneasiness is being shown in the Senate and House over the President's prolonged lack of participation in public activities. A considerable number of Congressmen believe that the President is in much worse condition than his physicians have indicated, while others assert that whatever the state of his health it is time that Congress and the country should know the facts. Another reason advanced for the widespread belief that the President is in a serious state of health is his failure to keep his engagement with Senator Hitchcock."

This fermentation of adverse comment leads to the decision headlined in the New York *Times* of December 5, 1919, "Grayson to Let Wilson Transact More Business." The dispatch categorically states: "The President's only callers during his illness have been Secretary Tumulty, Senator Hitchcock, who has seen him three times, Attorney General Palmer, who saw him once, Secretary Baker, who saw him just before starting for Panama, William G. McAdoo, Dr. Axson, a relative by marriage, King Albert of Belgium, the Prince of Wales, and the consulting physicians." Hitchcock must have seen the President three times between December 3 and December 5.

A crisis in the relations between the United States and the Carranza Government in Mexico brings the situation to a dramatic head. Senator Albert Bacon Fall, who was destined to be the scapegoat of the Teapot Dome Scandal, had offered a resolution to withdraw American recognition of Carranza. Fall, a severe critic of the Wilson Administration in other matters, and a leader in the fight against the Covenant, is appointed, with Senator Gilbert M. Hitchcock, a Special Committee of the Senate Committee on Foreign Relations, to "seek a personal interview with President Wilson on the Mexican situation." The real purpose of this Special Committee is not to discuss the Mexican situation, but, according to the New York *Times* of December 6, "the ill-concealed purpose on the part of the members of the Foreign Relations Committee to ascertain the truth or falsity of the many rumors that he was in no physical or mental condition to attend to important public business."

The request for this interview, "had been made to Joseph P. Tumulty ... who had referred it to Rear-Admiral Grayson. The request was granted after Admiral Grayson had consulted Mrs. Wilson." Mrs. Wilson was present during the interview, which lasted about forty minutes. The two Senators "came away from the White House convinced that his (the President's) mind is vigorous and active." Senator Fall was specific in reporting this finding.

The President, according to other reports in the New York *Times*, seemed to be familiar with the Mexican situation. This was all the more surprising since Secretary Lansing had assured the Committee that he had not talked with the Chief Executive about Mexico for two months!

The President received the two Senators propped up in bed, his whole body covered except his right arm and shoulder. Mr. Wilson made no movement with his legs during the interview. Neither Senator was able to deny the report that he was paralyzed from the waist down. The Senators noticed no impediment of his speech. Dr. Grayson took the Senators to the door but did not remain. No one was in the room when the conference took place except Mrs. Wilson. Wilson jocularly referred to the letter by Senator Moses, which stated that he had suffered a brain lesion that affected his mind. "I hope," he said, with biting sarcasm, "the Senator will now be reassured. But he may be disappointed."

During the conversation, Secretary Lansing called the White House on the telephone and announced that Jenkins, an American Consular Agent, had been released from the penitentiary at Pueblo, Mexico.

"That helps some," said the President.

Some time after the meeting, the President told D. F. Houston that he never wanted to hit a man in his life as badly as he did Senator Fall when he called at the White House as a "member of a smelling committee" to discover whether he was "all there" or not. "I was lying flat on my back. After the Committee had discussed certain matters with me and had discovered, I think, that I was very much all here, the committee turned to leave. Senator Fall paused a moment and said: 'Mr. President, I want you to know that I am praying for you.' If I could have got out of bed I would have hit the man. Why did he want to put me in bad with the Almighty? He must have known that God would take the opposite view from him on any subject."

Wilson's ability to chat or to be epigrammatic does not establish his ability to discharge his constitutional duties. On December 7, it was announced that the President would not read his annual address to the Senate and to the House, but that it would be transmitted by messenger and read to both bodies in separate session. The December message was the joint work of various members of the Cabinet. But here and there a Wilsonian touch appears. "Congress," according to David Lawrence, "took the message with an outward show of scorn, indifference and captious doubt as to the true authorship of the document." The message did not mention the Peace Treaty. The President did not comment upon the Treaty until January 8, 1920, when he wrote a letter on the occasion of the Jackson Day banquet.

During January and February, 1920, the President continues to be a sick man under tutelage of his wife, and in close seclusion. From time to time he takes a sun bath on the portico. Five months after his stroke, he is said to walk unaided on the second floor of the White House.

On February 10, the Baltimore *Sun* prints a copyrighted dispatch from a staff correspondent in Washington, recording an interview with Dr. Hugh H. Young of Johns Hopkins, one of the consulting physicians. Dr. Young insists that the clot in the blood vessel affected only the President's left arm and leg. "At no time," he declares, "was his brain power or the extreme vigor and lucidity of his mental processes in the slightest degree abated." Dr. Young goes on to describe the manner in which the President is resuming daily a greater share of his executive duties.

If the President's mental vigor was at all times unabated, why was he kept from all participation in public affairs? If he was mentally vigorous, what was the reason for guarding him so closely from his friends and from the members of his official family?

On February 13, 1920, the newspapers report that Mr. Wilson will preside at the next Cabinet meeting. But, in spite of his alleged mental alertness and vigor, the meeting is postponed for another month. Wilson did not meet with his Cabinet until the second week in April. However, Wilson (or those who act for him) decided that Lansing must go. Tumulty, realizing the state of public opinion, argues with the President that the dismissal of Lansing is the right thing at the wrong time. The President sits up in his invalid's chair.

"Tumulty, it is never the wrong time to spike disloyalty. When Lansing sought to oust me I was on my back. I am on my feet now, and I will not have disloyalty about me."

On February 14, Lansing receives a letter signed: Woodrow Wilson.

"MY DEAR MR. SECRETARY:

"Is it true, as I have been told, that during my illness you have frequently called the heads of the executive departments into conference? If it is, I feel it my duty to call your attention to considerations which I do not care to dwell upon until I learn from you yourself that this is the fact.

"Under our constitutional law and practice no one but the President has the right to summon the heads of the executive departments into conference, and no one but the President and the Congress has the right to ask their views or the views of any one of them on any public question...."

The Cabinet had been meeting week after week. Lansing claims that Tumulty and Grayson originally endorsed his plan of calling Cabinet meetings. The fact that more than twenty-five meetings were held, had kept the Government running. Mr. Lansing communicated with the President on two important matters which were taken up by the Cabinet, and Mr. Wilson (or those acting for him) acknowledged these communications by adopting Lansing's advice. Had Mr. Wilson (or those acting for him) forgotten? Did Wilson not learn of these meetings until February 14?

Lansing, in his reply, stresses the fact that Wilson was kept incommunicado from his own Cabinet:

"Shortly after you were taken ill in October, certain members of the Cabinet, of which I was one, felt that, in view of the fact that we were denied communication with you, it was wise for us to confer informally together on interdepartmental matters and on matters as to which action could not be postponed until your medical advisers permitted you to pass upon them. Accordingly, I, as the ranking member, requested the members of the Cabinet to assemble for such informal conferences and in view of the mutual benefit derived the practice was continued.

"I can assure you that it never for a moment entered my mind that I was acting unconstitutionally or contrary to your wishes and there certainly was no intention on my part to assume powers and exercise functions which under the Constitution are exclusively confided to the President...."

Wilson's rejoinder reminds the Secretary that no action could be taken without him by the Cabinet and therefore there "could have been no disadvantages in awaiting action with regard to matters concerning which action could not have been

taken without executive approval." Wilson's language seems confused and repetitious. His meaning, nevertheless, is clear. Lansing
resigns.

The Republicans in the Senate and in the House pointed to
the President's letter as proving that he was not yet quite fit
either mentally or physically. The country at large sided with
Mr. Lansing. Franklin K. Lane said: "We all thought the meetings were a good thing." He felt that his responsibility in attending the meetings was on a full level with that of Secretary
Lansing. The New York *Times* learns that practically all the
members of the Cabinet were in accord with Lansing's views.

The popular indignation evoked by Lansing's dismissal left
Wilson undisturbed. "Well, Tumulty," he asked smilingly, "have
I any friends left?"

"Very few, Governor," the faithful Tumulty answered.

Wilson replied that it would be another two days' wonder.
The truth was not very palatable to him. It was even less
palatable to those in his entourage. They could not permit the
intrusion of the outside world, even through Tumulty's kindly
lips. There was now no window through which the light came
to Wilson!

Meanwhile public business is delayed. Ambassadors vainly
wait for the opportunity to present their credentials. Bills lan-
guish. A successor for Lansing must be found. Now is the opportunity for Bernard Baruch to realize his dream. He could become
the American Disraeli by stepping into Lansing's shoes. Perhaps
the bedside Cabinet did not share the enlightened mental attitude of England, which made a Jew Queen Victoria's Premier.
Perhaps Wilson's own prejudice against Wall Street men re-
asserted itself. Perhaps Baruch preferred the shoes left vacant
by House!

There is some talk of Baker as Lansing's successor. But
Baker is unacceptable because of his independence in refusing
a request by those in charge of the sick President. The country
is astounded when Wilson offers Lansing's post to Bainbridge
Colby. Colby owes his nomination not to his indisputable intellectual qualifications but to the fact that Wilson is convinced of
his absolute personal loyalty to himself.

Wilson, or those who rule the country in Wilson's name, cannot brook independence. For that reason House is kept from Wilson and even Tumulty, for all his faithfulness, loses favor. McAdoo's advice is not asked. But Bernard Baruch gives interviews in the New York *Times* as President Wilson's adviser. Wilson remains inaccessible, except to the chosen few. Dr. Grayson silently tiptoes around the capital, and behind the scene rules, undisputed, a woman in purple.

WHEN A WOMAN WAS PRESIDENT OF THE UNITED STATES

UPHELD by the warm, firm hand of a woman—the woman who was President—Woodrow Wilson, palsied, paralyzed, clung desperately to power. Edith Bolling Wilson had no political ambitions. But events conspired with her vanity to perpetuate her reign. Woodrow Wilson's intellectual self lay dormant, his practical self was asleep, his emotional self, wide awake, was the vassal of his moral self. Completely dominating the wrecked body and the wrecked mind of Woodrow Wilson, his emotions and his conscience convinced him that he could, even from his sick-bed, entice America to accept his cherished Covenant.

Edith Bolling Wilson nurtured this illusion.

"Never," Colonel House remarked to me, "was there a more devoted wife." Mrs. Wilson's predominant desire was to shield Wilson from pain. But, surely, under the threshold of consciousness other motives came into play. It was delightful to toy with omnipotence, to hurl the thunderbolts of Jove! The purple which Mrs. Wilson affected in Paris became the color of a queen regnant. While Wilson was on his back, she exercised the functions of the President. When he was able to participate, she became his Duumvir, sharing with him the government of the United States. No Senator, no member of the Cabinet, not the President's own secretary, could gain a glimpse of Wilson without her permission. Her whim decided whether a king or an ambassador was to be received, whether a bill awaiting the President's signature would become law or not. Wilson, judging by echoes from his sick-bed conversation, sometimes longed for other friends, but he did not have the strength or the courage to summon them. No act of Woodrow Wilson, from this period until the end of his life, was undertaken without the knowledge and consent of Edith Bolling Wilson.

With shaky hand Wilson signed the few letters and documents placed before him by his wife. Everything likely to disturb his peace of mind was withheld. Nevertheless, there were days when he wept and cried like a child. His oldest daughter, Margaret, assisted his wife. Their devotion kept the flickering flame burning. Mrs. Wilson, remarks the astute David Lawrence, stood between her husband and the Government, indeed between him and the outside world. "It was she who acted as personal secretary, taking notes and writing memoranda and messages to the various Cabinet officers and officials of the Government generally. Even the Private Secretary, Mr. Tumulty, refrained from entering the bed-chamber except when sent for. He placed his memoranda on vital questions before Mrs. Wilson, leaving it to her to discover the proper moment to ask the President for his opinion or decision. She was, so to speak, the reigning monarch."

Even before he came under the sway of Edith Galt, Wilson was strongly susceptible to wifely influence. He was, William Allen White remarks in his penetrating study, tremendously "uxorious." Marriage, like friendship, was a crutch upon which he leaned heavily. Wilson's instinctive timidity made him falter before every audience and made every speech an ordeal. He gave up his law career, and became a teacher in a lady's seminary, because he could not face the odds against him in a trial court, although the subtlety of his mind and the flow of his eloquence would have made him a pillar of the bar. He could have not overcome his temperamental weakness without his first wife, Ellen Axson. Without Ellen Axson, he would have remained a teacher in a girl's school. Princeton, Trenton, Washington, would have remained day dreams. Ellen Axson, McAdoo says, was the only human being who fully understood Wilson. Wilson himself speaks of her as the most radiant creature he had ever known.

In spite of her strong, artistic personality, Ellen Axson possessed the supreme gift of self-effacement. Without this self-effacement she would have resented the predominating influence of Colonel House. She not only encouraged this friendship, she countenanced her husband's platonic flirtations with Mrs. Hulbert Peck. Wilson needed feminine sympathy. When Ellen Axson died, Wilson wrote at once to Mary Hulbert "I want you to be the first to know." When he was betrothed to Mrs. Galt, Mrs. Hulbert was his first confidante. After his second marriage the correspondence with Mary Hulbert lapsed, and his friendship with House lost its glow.

Feminine devotion usually includes a strong sense of possessiveness. This sense of possessiveness was evidently more marked in the second than in the first Mrs. Wilson. Tumulty, who has no reason to love Edith Bolling Galt, pays a touching tribute to the heroic quality of her devotion. Edith Bolling Wilson accompanied the President on his tour of the country in 1916. Chicago and other centers, William E. Dodd, one of Wilson's biographers tells us, received the sprightly woman with enthusiasm. She was his companion on his two trips to Paris. She shared with him the harrowing experience of his Last Crusade. Concealing her anxieties, she turned a smiling face to the crowds in San Diego. Mrs. Wilson consistently disavowed any intention to participate actively in public affairs. Yet, Tumulty remarks, in many a crisis she, out of her strong intelligence and sagacity, was able to offer timely wise suggestions. In his illness she became not only Wilson's nurse but, assuming Tumulty's place, his secretary, and Lansing's, his Secretary of State. She, Tumulty admits, was the chief agent in keeping him informed of public business.

"Her high intelligence and her extraordinary memory enabled her to report to him daily, in lucid detail, weighty matters of state brought to her by officials for transmission to him. At the proper time, when he was least in pain and least exhausted, she would present a clear, oral résumé of each case and lay the documents before him in orderly arrangement.

"As woman and wife, the first thought of her mind and the first care of her heart must be for his health. Once at an acute period of his illness certain officials insisted that they must see him because they carried information which it was 'absolutely necessary that the President of the United States should have,' and she quietly replied: 'I am not interested in the President of the United States. I am interested in my husband and his health.' "

But in spite of her devotion to her husband, Edith Bolling Wilson did not relish the thought of permitting Wilson to exchange the White House for a sanitorium. She had tasted the sweet draught of power. She had basked in the sunshine of high station. If she had been asked to sacrifice both to save Wilson's life, she would not have hesitated an instant. But the human mind is so constituted that problems do not present themselves in this undisguised fashion. Her own ambition assumed the shape of his. She persuaded herself that she must keep the pretext that Wilson was still actively President of the United States for his sake, not hers.

A distinguished physician, Dr. Arthur Dean Bevan, had stated in the Chicago *Tribune* that Wilson's trouble was permanent and not a temporary condition, and that Wilson should, under no circumstances, be permitted to resume the work of such a strenuous position as that of President of the United States. The strain and responsibility would bring with them the danger of a recurrence of such attacks and might hasten a fatal termination. Surely this point of view must have come to Mrs. Wilson's attention. But evidently she evaded the advice of physicians who disagreed with her desire (and Wilson's own) not to relinquish the reins of government.

White House propaganda occasionally represents the Presidency as a Herculean task that no ordinary mortal can endure without paying for it with his life blood. Propaganda exaggerates. Roosevelt, Taft, Wilson, and Coolidge worked hard. But they had also ample time to play. Harding was the most hard working of Presidents. This was due not to his multitudinous duties but to his own incapacity for quick thinking. Nevertheless, being President of the United States is a man-sized job. Wilson, even when he was in the possession of all his powers, delegated some of his major duties to House. Now, broken in health and spirit, he was utterly incapable of discharging his constitutional obligations.

Even after his partial recovery in the fall, Wilson's public appearances were rare. A few friends were admitted at the White House. These, William Allen White remarks, knew that he was not able to discuss large matters seriously. According to Kohlsaat (*From McKinley to Harding*) Wilson was unconscious for nearly a week, and semiconscious for over a month. His recovery, as Mrs. Wilson herself admits, was a "slow process." For three months no one entered his bedroom except his wife, his daughter, his doctors and his nurses.

In December, 1919, two or three months after the breakdown, Franklin K. Lane, Secretary of the Interior, wrote to a friend: "The President is getting better slowly, but we communicate with him almost entirely through his doctor (Grayson)." In another letter (the same month) Lane enlarges upon the same topic. "Things," he assures his correspondent, "are going well notwithstanding the President's illness. No one is satisfied that we know the truth, and every dinner table is filled with speculation. Some say paralysis, and some say insanity. Grayson tells me it is nervous breakdown, whatever that means. He is, however, getting better, and meantime the Cabinet is running things."

Lane wished to resign in order to accept an offer of a lucrative position. For months he was stopped from this action by the inaccessibility of the President. At last, on January 5, he puts his dilemma before Rear-Admiral Grayson. He asks him to "be perfectly frank" in advising him what to do, as he did not wish to "do anything to hurt our Chief." This is a rather remarkable situation. Three months or more after the attack that laid Wilson low, a Cabinet officer cannot approach his superior except through this young doctor-admiral. It is difficult to reconcile this situation with the statement that Wilson carried on the duties imposed upon him by the Chief Magistracy of the Republic. There are witnesses galore to the contrary.

No member of the Cabinet was more devoted to Wilson than Houston. Wilson himself, in a letter to House, wishes that there were more than one Houston. Both Mrs. Wilson and Wilson reposed their trust in the Secretary of Agriculture, as we shall presently demonstrate. Yet Houston did not have access to Wilson. And it was Mrs. Wilson who offered him the Treasury. Houston himself tells how, one morning, January 25, 1920, when he awoke with the grippe, he received a summons to the White House from the Woman Who Was President, to call at 4.30 in the afternoon. Houston thought that Wilson might ask his advice on the Treaty situation, on the Treasury Department, or on the vacancy created in the Department of the Interior by Lane's resignation. He telephoned Mrs. Wilson that he had a severe cold and expressed the fear that he might carry with him the danger of infection. Mrs. Wilson insisted, however, upon his visit.

When Mr. Houston arrived, the mistress of the White House received him graciously in the sitting-room. The conversation leaped from one topic to another until the servants had cleared away the tea table. Then Mrs .Wilson said: "You are wondering why I wanted to see you and why I sent for you this afternoon. Of course, you know that I did not ask you to take the trouble to come merely to drink tea. The President asked me to tell you that he is very anxious for you to accept the Secretaryship of the Treasury. He is reluctant to have you give up Agriculture, but still thinks he now needs you more in the Treasury. He thought of putting you there twice before—first, when McAdoo thought of resigning, and second, when he did resign—but could not make up his mind to have you leave the Department of Agriculture."

When Mrs. Wilson had finished, Houston said: "Please give my greetings to the President and tell him that I am very grateful to him for this further evidence of his confidence. I am in the harness until March 4, 1921, if he wishes it, and as long as I am with him I will dig stumps, or act as Secretary of the Treasury, or assume any other task he assigns to me."

"That is very interesting. That is just what the President said you would say."

"Mrs. Wilson [Houston continues] said that the President would like to know whether I had anybody in mind to suggest for Secretary of Agriculture. I asked if he was thinking about anybody. She answered: 'Yes, Meredith.' I replied that Meredith came from the right section, that he was in touch with agricultural problems through his newspaper, and that it seemed to me that he ought to fill the position acceptably. I told her that I had at one time sounded him out as to whether he would take the Assistant Secretaryship, that

I had suggested him for membership on the War Agricultural Council, and that I had mentioned his name for membership on the Industrial Conference, but that I knew very little about his intellectual ability and whether he was Cabinet size or not. I added: 'If I had to select a Secretary of Agriculture, I would draft President W. O. Thompson of the University of Ohio. He is a man of very independent judgment. He is an independent in politics, but I understand that he voted for Mr. Wilson both in 1912 and in 1916. He is a man of unusual ability, of great wisdom, and of sound views. He has been the Dean of the Presidents of the Land-Grant colleges. I know of no one who stands higher in the agricultural field among leaders and sensible thinkers.'

"She then asked whether I had anybody in mind whom I could suggest for the position of Secretary of the Interior. She added: 'The President is somewhat embarrassed. Secretary Lane has resigned —in the press. The President has not yet been officially informed of his going. He would like your judgment.' "

It is difficult to escape the conclusion that in this period, the fifth month of Wilson's disability, Mrs. Wilson was his regent. Grayson, too, enters into the picture the following month. Houston reports how, on February 14, he discussed with Dr. Grayson the desirability of the President's filling vacancies on the tariff commission, and sending certain messages to Wilson through Dr. Grayson. When Grayson told him that the President had asked for Lansing's resignation, Houston was not surprised.

"Do you know," he asked, "who will succeed the Secretary of State?"

Grayson did not know.

"The President is very much worried. In fact, he is worrying himself sick over the matter."

"Why?"

"Because the President is no longer in the position to write his notes and papers as he formerly was and he wants somebody who has great facility in this direction."

Houston suggests Frank Polk. However, the following morning the appointment of Bainbridge Colby is announced in the papers. To what extent was Wilson consulted? Was his mind able to grasp the facts presented to him by Mrs. Wilson?

Houston's own description of the first Cabinet meeting in the President's study, in the seventh month of Wilson's physical incapacity [April 13th—note the date—1920] throws some doubt on the matter. It was the first meeting of the President with his Cabinet since August, 1919. When Mr. Houston arrived several minutes late, Mr. Wilson was already seated behind a desk at the far end of the room. As Houston entered, he was ushered into the President's presence by the White House aide who announced his name to the President. Was Wilson unable to recognize the members of his own Cabinet? What was at fault? His mind, his memory, or his vision?

The incident struck Mr. Houston as "singular" and he "wondered" why it was done. "The President," he goes on to say, "looked old, worn, and haggard. It was enough to make one weep to look at him. One of his arms was useless. In repose, his face looked very much as usual, but, when he tried to speak, there were marked evidences of his trouble. His jaw tended to drop on one side, or seemed to do so. His voice was very weak and strained. I shook hands with him and sat down. He greeted me as of old. He put up a brave front and spent several minutes cracking jokes. Then," to quote further, "there was brief silence. It appeared that he would not take the initiative. Some one brought up the railroad situation for discussion. The President seemed at first to have some difficulty in fixing his mind on what we were discussing. Dr. Grayson looked in at the door several times as if to warn us not to prolong the discussion unduly for fear of wearying the President. The discussion dragged on for more than an hour. Finally, Mrs. Wilson came in, looking rather disturbed, and suggested that we had better go."

This picture, drawn by a trusted friend, demolishes the contention that Wilson was mentally himself. In spite of the occasional resurgence of his old brilliance, in spite of what Mr. Houston himself calls his attempt to maintain a "brave front" by cracking jokes, he was disabled, in the sense of the Constitution. Who took his place in the six and one half months that had elapsed since his collapse in Kansas?

There was apparently some improvement in the President's condition two weeks later. Houston reports on April 27 that the President seemed "rather better" and took a more lively part in the discussion. He does not state if Mrs. Wilson hovered in the background. However, Daniels relates that when Cabinet meetings were resumed Mr. Wilson was "never far away." Evidently Wilson's condition fluctuated. He had his good days and his bad days. But there is no indication that even on his good days he was able to give more than an hour or two to his work. Who was President the remaining twenty-two hours?

There were, admits the well-informed Lawrence, days when Woodrow Wilson seemed to be mentally as keen as ever. "Shutting one's eyes to the drooping figure and listening only to his fiery logic, the illusion of an unchanged personality would not have been difficult to maintain." Little by little, Lawrence continues, as gradual improvement in his condition was evident, more executive work was undertaken but always at his side stood the devoted wife and the physician, Admiral Cary T. Grayson.

> "Together they carried the secrets of the sick-room while Private Secretary Tumulty played the rôle of everything-as-usual in the Executive Offices, a mark of loyalty to his Chief which alone should have earned him something better than the brusque treatment he later received.
>
> "But those were topsy-turvy days and many an old friend who had served Mr. Wilson in the past was turned away. The tragic events that followed Mr. Wilson's breakdown cannot be explained by any theory of logic. Those who had it in their power to persuade President Wilson to permit advisers to reach him failed to realize the immensity of their responsibility in shutting him off so completely from the outside world."

How did Woodrow Wilson communicate from his sick-bed with members of the Cabinet?

"I know no reason," writes Newton D. Baker, Wilson's Secretary of War, "why I should not give you all the knowledge I have about the questions you ask. I do not know how the President communicated with the State Department after his breakdown. I can only answer as to myself. I wrote the President many memoranda and received replies, usually noted on the memorandum itself, indicating his concurrence or dissent. After his recovery began to be more promising I saw him frequently for verbal discussions of important things. As he continued an ill man to the end of his Administration I brought to his attention for decision only the most necessary matters."

Although Mrs. Wilson acted only in the name of the President, some communications from the White House bore her signature. "Please bear in mind," says Frank L. Polk, the legal adviser of the State Department, "that I was in Paris as Head of the American Peace Delegation from the middle of July, 1919, to the middle of December, so I have no personal knowledge as to what took place immediately after Mr. Wilson was taken ill. On my return from Paris, communications from the White House were signed by the President and in some instances by Mrs. Wilson, but the letters I wrote the President in regard to foreign affairs would have notes in pencil on the margin in his handwriting, approving or disapproving the suggestions therein contained. I understand he communicated with the Cabinet through Mrs. Wilson, Mr. Tumulty, and by notes signed by himself."

Wilson may have scribbled consent or disagreement on the margin of the notes submitted by the State Department. But after his stroke, as White remarks, the world was practically shut off from Woodrow Wilson. "All his life he had been afflicted with a mild Narcissus complex, desiring to see himself in everything, his views, his faith, the facts as he knew them. This complex did not hold him completely, but it stood in the wings of his consciousness always too ready to act. And when the public was shut away from him, he knew nothing of the truth about public sentiment in the country. It was as though the curtain had fallen upon him with the roar of applause which greeted his speech at Pueblo always reverberating in his heart."

When, William Allen White points out, Wilson decided to reject any reservations to the Treaty, his ears were full of that applause. He thought it represented public sentiment. His devoted wife, who was surrounding him with every physical comfort and every spiritual easement, was not trained in public affairs. She was almost as isolated as he:

> "Admiral Grayson had no access to the truth about public opinion, no means of interpreting the facts, no great interest in the clamor outside the sick-room. Tumulty saw his chief rarely, with Mrs. Wilson standing at the head of the bed to shake her head when Tumulty broached a subject that might irritate the President. It was easier for those about him to hold to his face the mirror of his own

conception of public opinion than to irritate him with the story of a gradual, inevitable change in the American attitude to the League of Nations. It was a statesman's job to convince Woodrow Wilson that the jingoism which follows war had alienated the people from the generous pacifist President of Princeton. And the only statesman who could have told him, he had put away when he banished House. The autumn of 1919 deepened into winter, and his friends outside saw with fear and consternation that the President was determined stubbornly to face the incoming Congress with an immovable determination that the Treaty should stand or fall as it was. But he called no counsel about him and saw few visitors."

Baruch acted at times as Wilson's spokesman in public. But unlike Grayson, he did not have ready access to the sick-room. Baruch first appeared in 1912 as a substantial contributor to the Wilson campaign fund. Wilson was so deeply prejudiced against the man who manipulated Wall Street that he did not wish to see him, in spite of McComb's recommendation. Finally Wilson relented, but expressed the wish that House should be present at his first interview with Baruch.

After a while, Baruch took over important functions in the conduct of the War and the Peace Conference. He became head of the War Industries Board in Washington and became one of the economic experts of the American Peace Delegation. After the break with House, he figured in the public prints repeatedly as the President's "adviser." He remained Mrs. Wilson's adviser after the death of the President.

On the day before Wilson's funeral, Colonel House had occasion to speak to Baruch about some matter. He mentioned that he had not been invited. Baruch called him back in the afternoon, but did not mention the funeral. Under the circumstances House decided that he was not wanted in Washington. Bernard Baruch never occupied the niche vacated by House in Wilson's regard. If the financier's advice reached Wilson in the White House, it came to him chiefly through Grayson and Mrs. Wilson.

Grayson's influence did not rest entirely upon his professional ability. The relationship between the two men began the evening of the inauguration. Mrs. Howe, the President's sister, having injured herself, a Philadelphia friend advised him to send for Dr. Grayson, who was on duty in Washington as a naval surgeon. From that moment to his death, Josephus Daniels avers, Wilson and Grayson were closely associated. The association ripened into regard until it burgeoned into complete understanding and tender friendship. Wilson, Daniels says, loved youth, particularly young men of clear thinking and clean living.

> "He had no son. Perhaps that was a regret he never uttered. His paternal regard embraced the younger physician. They rode and walked and played and talked together. Dr. Grayson knew his constitution, knew how he must take care of himself and conserve his strength. But he knew his responsibilities and how he would meet them, sick or well. He was the skilled physician who studied to keep the President fit. He was the skilled physician who in Paris brought him through a serious illness. He was the skilled physician who was with him almost daily for more than eleven years. But he was much more than that: he was the true and trusted friend, the agreeable companion who brought him good stories and kept him advised about what went on in the world about him, who shielded him and was toward him all that a son might have been, if God had given the world a second Woodrow Wilson."

There is no reason to assume that Grayson abused Wilson's confidence, nor to question his genuine affection for his stricken chief. But no one who carefully studies the testimony adduced can deny that Grayson exercised more influence than any Secretary of State, nor that he leagued himself with Mrs. Wilson to surround the sick President with a Chinese Wall. It was natural that both physician and wife should guard Wilson from injurious contacts. But it is unfortunate that their judgment was less reliable than their devotion. Nor is it difficult to trace, in the selection of those who were banished from the Presence in the White House, a feminine bias. Consciously or unconsciously, the Woman Who Was President, or shared the Presidency with Woodrow Wilson, rationalized her own prejudices. One of the victims of the feminine animus was Colonel House.

We have seen the callous manner in which House was kept at a distance. And we have discussed the very human motives— by no means unintelligible—which inspired Mrs. Wilson's distrust of the ex-Duumvir. But apparently Mrs. Wilson's distrust extended to all who were her husband's friends before her marriage. It included even that warm-hearted Irishman, Joseph P.

Tumulty. Tumulty, in spite of his knowledge of Wilson's real condition, was kept at a distance. His final reward for his loyal services was a black eye in public.

Wilson, or those responsible for his actions, went out of his way to repudiate his secretary in 1922—after his retirement—by seizing upon what was at worst a trifling misunderstanding. Tumulty had conveyed a perfectly harmless message expressing pious wishes for Democratic success to a dinner at which Governor Cox was present. This message, based on a casual conversation, was repudiated formally by Woodrow Wilson, in spite of the convincing and touching explanation made by his secretary. Tumulty's letters to Woodrow Wilson were answered not by the ex-President but by Edith Bolling Wilson. In his reply to Mrs. Wilson, Mr. Tumulty aptly expresses his own feelings by a quotation from *Liliom*:

> LOUISE: Is it possible for some one to hit you hard like that—real loud and hard—and not hurt you at all?
>
> JULIE: It is possible, dear, that some one whom you love may beat you and beat you and beat you—and not hurt you at all.

"That," he writes, "is the way I feel toward the Governor."

In a conversation with William Allen White, Tumulty unburdens his heart. Here, more than in his own book, we catch a glimpse of the shadow moving behind the drawn blinds of Wilson's sick-room. "Then," he says, "the President got sick and no one saw him. Oh," he adds, correcting himself, "I came in once in a while and saw him when he was in the White House, but not much." Tumulty was one of the three people who was supposed to have constant access to the sick President. This remark eliminates him.

Mrs. Wilson, no doubt, had reasons of her own which justified her snubbing of Tumulty. But it is difficult to escape the conclusion that she was influenced, at least unconsciously, by the fact that the first Mrs. Wilson had called Tumulty one of her own boys.

Nor was this all. When Tumulty heard of Wilson's intention to marry, he warned him, for political reasons, to postpone the announcement as well as the marriage until after the election of

1916. These facts hardly endeared him to Edith Bolling Wilson.

"Well then," Tumulty continues his confidences to White, "he married Mrs. Galt. Now remember that his first wife was my dearest friend, and she said she loved me like one of her own boys, and I felt pretty bad, and I talked a good deal with Wilson about how I felt. And one day, about a week after the wedding, I picked up the Philadelphia *Public Ledger* with a story of how Cary T. Grayson had made the match. After that some more things began to happen. When we would all go away on official trips, my name would not be on the list. . . ."

When Wilson's letter of rebuke to Tumulty appeared in the press, the latter vainly attempted to see his erstwhile chief. When subsequently he called at the house on S Street he was unable to see any one except Grayson.

"It seems to me," he implored the all-powerful doctor, "that ten years' faithful service have earned me the right to go in and look once into his eyes, or maybe just pat his forehead before he goes."

"And Grayson (I am quoting Tumulty's own account) said: 'Yes, Joe, you're right, and he will be glad to see you, but he's asleep now.'

"And he promised and promised over and over to call me if there was any real danger before the end. But the end came too quickly and when it came poor Joe was on the sidewalk with the rest.

"And at the funeral—not a word. Finally, McAdoo comes to town, and on the last day, about noon, calls me on the phone and says: 'I'm going to see that you're invited.'

"And pretty soon Mrs. Grayson calls up and says of course Mrs. Tumulty and I are expected to the house for the funeral. And we go, and they let us in, and we come out afterward, and they call out the names for the carriages and I listen, and all the other names of friends and statesmen are called out there before the reporters, and then, after the names of two doormen from Keith's Theatre, at the very end of the list, comes poor Tumulty! And I got in and followed the hearse."

The vindictive attitude of Edith Bolling Wilson toward

Tumulty was not mitigated by the death of her husband. Some years ago a friend of Wilson, Judge James Kerney of the Trenton *Times*, wrote an article on Woodrow Wilson for the *Saturday Evening Post* in which he quoted a letter from Woodrow Wilson, dated October 30, 1923, suggesting that, in canvassing the field of candidates for the United States Senate he should not ignore Tumulty. His political training, Mr. Wilson insisted, was more varied than that of any other man he knew. He also pointed out Tumulty's formidable equipment as a debater, which he proved when he was a member of the New Jersey Assembly. With waxing enthusiasm, Mr. Wilson concluded that Tumulty would make some of the reactionary Senators "sit up and take notice" of the advent of modern times and circumstances. The *Saturday Evening Post* had printed a full-page advertisement in all the larger newspapers of the country announcing the fact that they were about to publish the article, and a very large part of the edition had been actually printed, when Mrs. Wilson, standing on her copyright, sent a lawyer both to them and to James Kerney, the author, forbidding the publication of any letter from Woodrow Wilson.

Legally, Wilson's letters to Kerney, like his letters to House, are the property of his estate. In stopping the letter Mrs. Wilson did not carry out the wishes of Woodrow Wilson. In fact she thwarted her husband's intention. The letter was written to further the ambitions of Tumulty. Wilson's feelings for Tumulty were friendly, in spite of the influences that poisoned his mind. But he lacked the physical or the moral strength to make a breach in the wall that shut him in.

It would have been natural if Wilson had turned in his distress to his son-in-law, McAdoo. At one time McAdoo occupied more positions under the American Government than any other human being in history, and creditably acquitted himself of his multiple job. But, unless all reports are misleading, McAdoo, too, was kept away from Wilson by the unfriendly atmosphere created by those who guarded the President. McAdoo was the son-in-law of the President. He was the husband of the first Mrs. Wilson's stepdaughter!

I do not find any record that Prof. Francis B. Sayre, who

married Wilson's second daughter, was called to his father-in-law's sick-bed. Woodrow Wilson's will left his fortune entirely to his wife, except for a small pension to Margaret, his eldest daughter. Under the terms of the will, marriage would deprive Margaret Wilson even of this little stipend. Wilson's will seemed all the more incredible to his friends since Edith Bolling Wilson is reputed to possess a fortune in her own right, and since there was no question of the mutual devotion which existed between Woodrow Wilson and his three daughters. Wilson, detained by war from entertainment, had saved a large part of his salary. He was a rich man when he died.

Wilson's estrangement from members of his family accentuated his loneliness; it did not affect his destiny. But the political result of the isolation of Woodrow Wilson from his friend and adviser Colonel House, brought about the frustration of all his hopes. Wilson's fight for the League of Nations miscarried completely. His intractable attitude doomed his own child beyond hope of resurrection. He made every possible error in his dealings with his friends and with his opponents. Colonel House, with one twist of his little finger, could have straightened out the tangle. It did not even take the political genius of a House to accomplish Wilson's end. Only the blundering of Wilson's advisers after the pilot was cast out explains the débâcle. The Woman Who Was President could not help the invalid in the White House to translate his dreams into political action.

Wilson's major blunder in the treaty fight was his letter of January 8, on the occasion of the Jackson Day dinner, in which he categorically declared that he could not accept the action of the Senate in rejecting the Treaty without reservations as the decision of the nation.

"We cannot re-write this Treaty. We must take it without changes which alter its meaning, or leave it and then, after the rest of the world have signed it, we must face the unthinkable task of making another and separate kind of treaty with Germany. But no mere assertions with regard to the wish and opinion of the country are credited. If,"—and here we come to the crux of the letter—"there is any doubt as to what the people of the country think on this vital matter, the clear and single way out

is to submit it for determination at the next election to the
voters of the nation, to give the next election the form of a great
and solemn referendum, a referendum as to the part the United
States is to play in completing the settlements of the War and
in the prevention in the future of such outrages as Germany
attempted to perpetrate."

The references to the November election was Wilson's bid
for another mandate from the American people. What evil angel
induced Woodrow Wilson to thrust his hat into the ring for a
third term? In 1920, McAdoo was an active candidate for the
Presidency. One word from Woodrow Wilson would have given
the nomination to McAdoo. No one could give the nomination to
Wilson. Day after day McAdoo led in the vote before the convention. His friends, reports White, besieged the White House
with long-distance telephone calls and telegrams across the continent asking for some word from Wilson, not in public but in
private, that would swing the New York delegation to his son-
in-law. "No word came. The White House was sealed. As it had
been picketed against Colonel House, so it was closed to the
appeal of McAdoo's friends. No one knew why." We know why
to-day. A statement by Lawrence that Wilson had previously
expressed his willingness to disavow any ambition for a third
term displeased Wilson, and prompted Mrs. Wilson to ask
Tumulty if the Washington newspapermen had access to Mr.
Wilson's cables from Paris. The question, an insult in itself,
clearly shows the direction in which the wind was blowing.

Wilson was able to confer, now and then, with members of
the Cabinet; his health had improved. But he was unequal to
the strain of resuming his duties in full. A renomination would
have been a sentence of death. Was the woman beside him as
blind as her ailing husband? Forgetful of his paralyzed left side
and his useless eye, oblivious to the deeply ingrained prejudice
of the people against a third Presidential term, ignorant of the
suspicion aroused even in the ranks of his own party by his
mysterious seclusion, uninformed òf the gathering storm against
his Administration, he seriously harbored the mad delusion that
his party would make him its standard bearer by acclamation.

To accomplish this end, he sent two members of his Cabinet

to San Francisco to whisper the word that he was receptive into the ears of the delegates. Clutching for the chimera of a third term, he saw himself not only as standard bearer of his party but as the saviour of the world. Nothing reveals more clearly the ruin of his mind and his complete dependence upon inexperienced advisers. The reëlection of Woodrow Wilson would have meant another term in the White House, a full draught of the intoxicating ichor of power, for the woman in purple.

Other Presidents' wives may have influenced their husbands, but surely no spouse ever held in her hand the Government of the United States like Edith Bolling Wilson! The human mind is so constituted that Mrs. Wilson no doubt persuaded herself that she was seeking solely the benefit of her country and of her man. That was the reason that never a word, never a hint, from the White House favored the Presidential ambitions of the husband of Mrs. Wilson's stepdaughter. One whisper would have swayed the New York delegation and made McAdoo the nominee.

The Democratic Convention in San Francisco ignored Wilson's candidacy. When his emissaries failed to accomplish their mission, Woodrow Wilson was so angry that he did not speak to them for weeks. The Republicans took up Wilson's phrase that the election was a solemn referendum to decide the fate of the League. The Democratic candidate, Cox, was snowed under. But Cox did not matter in the campaign. The real candidate was Woodrow Wilson, carrying upon his shoulders the Covenant of the League of Nations, and the woman who wore the purple.

Woodrow Wilson's last bolt was shot. There was no Colonel House to smooth his path with wise counsel, no generalissimo to direct his political fortunes. Even Colonel House would not have undertaken to secure the renomination of Woodrow Wilson. Wilson, on his sick-bed, was a Don Quixote, willing to challenge windmills and dragons for the honor of his Dulcinea, the League of Nations. House was too much of a realist to attempt the impossible.

If House had directed his affairs, he would have made Woodrow Wilson's exit more dignified and less tragic. Stricken in body if not in spirit, Wilson rides beside President-elect Harding to Capitol Hill on March 4th. From Election Day to his funeral in a church not of his own faith, Woodrow Wilson is a dying man. Disease stamps itself upon his wasted features. A ghostly caricature of the man, they still retain a heroic mold. Something in Wilson remains undefeated. Something in his Scotch-Presbyterian soul fights to the end. Thus Wilson's shattered self becomes the symbol of the shattered world he has failed to save. The vanquished idealist, the slain god, he embodies humanity's struggle for the ideal. Soon, from the wreck and ruin of his body and of his life, will rise, like Osiris and Baldur, glorified and exalted, the Wilson myth.

THE WILSON MYTH

THE Wilson of the Wilson myth is the Baldur of Democracy, the Osiris of Freedom. His figure over-shadows the World War, as the Statue of Liberty dominates New York harbor. He is impeccable; he is perfect. He is the hero, foully betrayed by the powers of darkness, rising like spring itself from the grave—Titan, superman, god.

Before he became a myth, Wilson identified himself with what Francis Delaisi calls "the Democratic myth." The new doctrine which he taught gave the humblest soldier in the trenches and the most untutored workman in the factories a new purpose. "Over and above the national ideal which served the allied peoples, he superposed the democratic ideal which bound them together—just as once upon a time the Lorraine shepherdess had reënforced the royal myth which momentarily had become impaired, by calling in the religious myth at the coronation of Rheims. Merely by tapping his typewriter, the American statesman had given a meaning and a purpose to the War—which now became a crusade for universal democracy."

If to the Frenchman the Pacifist Wilson seems a male Joan of Arc, to his own devoted disciples he is the Messiah of a new political era. Wilson fostered in himself this messianic illusion. Sensing this, Clemenceau uttered the famous *bon mot* that it was hard to make peace, seated between one man who imagined he

was Napoleon and another who thought he was Jesus Christ. That
was the wicked Frenchman's characterization of Lloyd George
and Wilson. He admitted, with twinkling eyes, the authenticity
of the epigram to me when I saw him in his little Paris apartment shortly before his death.

The same idealists who stood at Armageddon and battled
for the Lord Roosevelt now battled for the prophet of the Fourteen Points. Some deserted him when he, too, failed to establish
a Kingdom of Heaven on earth, and the Fourteen Points disappeared in the sewers of Versailles. Those who remained were
only fortified in their faith by the tribulations of their Scotch-
Presbyterian Redeemer. The last crusade in which he risked and
lost his health increased the frenzy of their admiration. His solitary fight from the sick-bed, behind the veil of secrecy thrown
around him by Grayson and Edith Bolling Wilson, the lonely
years in the house on S Street, made him a legend.

Bit by bit the legend grew. Here and there a touch was added.
Unconsciously those who were near him and loved him obliterated
his weaknesses and his errors. Inch by inch, they increased his
stature until he assumes colossal proportions. The mark of the
nails in his hands and feet, the wounded side and the wounded
head, cease to be human. They become symbols of his godhead.
Some of his disciples deny his physical deterioration. Or they
claim that his spirit burned more brightly than ever in the ruined
lamp of his body.

The World War revealed the legend-building capacity of the
human mind. The men who saw the angels at Mons did not foreswear themselves. To them the heavenly vision was real. The
men and women who beheld German soldiers cutting off the
breasts of Belgian women and the hands of French babies were
not deliberate prevaricators. Hysteria, patriotism, the fact that
the brain is the bondsman of the emotions, explains all such phe-
nomena to the complete satisfaction of any student of human
psychology.

We have seen D. F. Houston's description of the pitiful
spectacle when Wilson, attempting to preside once more over a
Cabinet meeting, was unable to recognize or to see the members
of his own official family. His speech rambled and a pathetic col-

lapse was prevented only by the intercession of Admiral Grayson and Mrs. Wilson. Technically, Mrs. Wilson was only her husband's spokesman. Actually she had assumed the duties which should have been delegated to the Vice-President of the United States, to Tumulty, the President's Secretary, and to the Secretary of State. Yet, only a few years after his own book, Houston looks upon the events which he himself describes in a different light.

"I know," he writes to me, "of no occasion when Mrs. Wilson was practically President of the United States. I am not aware that she ever decided or attempted to decide anything. It is true that when Mr. Wilson's condition, for a time, was especially unsatisfactory, communications were transmitted in writing. Of course, we bothered the President with as few things as possible. The matters which I submitted to him bore his own notations. On at least one occasion, he communicated his wishes to me through Mrs. Wilson, but in no sense was her intervention more than that of an intermediary. I did not on any occasion transmit anything to him through either Admiral Grayson or Mr. Baruch. I am not aware that at any time Mr. Baruch had anything to do with Presidential matters.

"You refer to my account of a meeting where I spoke of the seeming difficulty the President had with his vision. You speak of the meeting having been broken up by Mrs. Wilson. What actually happened was that after we had been in session some time Mrs. Wilson, with a wife's apparent solicitude that her husband should not overstrain himself, appeared in the hall. I do not recall that she made any communication. It was not difficult for us, however, to sense her solicitude. Soon thereafter the President adjourned the meeting, especially as we had nothing further to discuss."

Mr. Houston himself describes in his book the dissatisfaction aroused by the secrecy with which those who controlled the body of Woodrow Wilson shrouded his illness. He himself relates how he entrusted messages for Wilson to Dr. Grayson. He forgets that his associates in the Cabinet discussed among themselves the rumor of Wilson's insanity. The diplomatic corps gossiped with the rest when Wilson was unable to receive Sir Edward Grey and other accredited emissaries. We have seen that important bills passed by Congress could not secure the President's signature. We know that the very men designated by Wilson to lead the fight for his Treaty vainly clamored at the door of his sick-chamber. All this has vanished from Mr. Houston's memory.

"At the time the President was quite sick, I know of nothing which demanded action on which action was not secured in reasonable course. The situation, in my judgment, was not such as to call for the assumption of the duties of President by Mr. Marshall, especially as no authority had determined that the President was incapable.

"When Mr. Wilson was in Paris we had, at his request, been holding regular meetings. We held one meeting after his return from the West and, therefore, after his illness. At that meeting we asked Dr. Grayson if he would come in and tell us how the President was getting on. He came in smiling and said the President wanted to know what we were doing, meeting while he was in the city and without his authority. This does not seem to indicate that he was not aware of what was going on. Neither does his remark to me, which I quoted in the book about Senator Fall, indicate that he was not aware of what was going on."

The years lend a rosy glow to events. The invalid in the shuttered room with the iron bars assumes for Mr. Houston an air of omniscience.

"I do not agree with you," Mr. Houston goes on to say, "that the fight in the Senate was lost because Mr. Wilson was inaccessible to Colonel House and other friends. During a good part of that fight we were holding Cabinet meetings; and it was during one of these Cabinet meetings that Mr. Wilson was called up by a Senator and told that Senator Lodge had agreed to certain reservations. Mr. Wilson, after consulting us, told him to go ahead. Later the Senator called him up again, while we were in session, and told him that Senator Lodge had backed down.

"My judgment is that the fight for the League was lost because of the unalterable opposition of Senator Lodge and his followers to anything that was at all reasonable, and to their determination to kill the Treaty after they found they could do so. The partisanship is best evidenced by the round robin which they sent to Paris and which met Mr. Wilson there, warning Europe that Mr. Wilson no longer represented America.

"Personally, I am convinced that the Treaty would have been lost if Mr. Wilson had not had his illness. Public opinion had been terribly misled and inflamed. You recall that he made his trip West, during which he was stricken, because he felt that the public had to be aroused, if there was to be any chance of securing the assent of the Senate, to the ratification of the Treaty. As a matter of fact, I think the fight was lost before he started on the trip."

If Houston is right, Wilson lost the Treaty fight not because he failed to take, and probably did not even hear, the advice of his ex-Duumvir. He lost it because Senator Lodge, the Lucifer of the Senate, the personal Devil of the Wilsonian myth, led his legions against heavenly hosts!

Mr. Houston's is a beautiful letter. It is a fine tribute to his loyalty. But it clearly shows how his brain rationalizes what his heart wants to believe. This is no impeachment of his mental capacity. It merely shows that Mr. Houston is subject to the same psychological influences which dominate all mankind. If Mr. Houston should write another letter ten years from now to another writer, holding up, however tremblingly, a little lantern to seek the truth, Wilson will have grown several cubits more in his estimation. The image of the idol will continue to grow in stature. Folklore, conspiring with his historians, will divest the new saviour of all frailties of the flesh.

Bainbridge Colby, Wilson's only real Secretary of State, does his share to magnify Wilson's dimensions. Colby wrote some notes which the world attributes to Woodrow Wilson, although the invalid merely changed a comma or interjected an adjective. But when the Wilson myth is challenged, Colby rushes instinctively, loyally, to its defense.

To admit that Mrs. Wilson played the part of President is to cast a doubt upon Wilson's perfection. Any one who judges Wilson by his third-term ambition and by the inconceivable political blunders made in his name, cannot escape the conclusion that, while at times his mind still functioned with the old vigor, such moments were the exceptions. The pathological picture of his disease coincides with this conception. Slowly, the patient loses his clearness of mind, his sense of proportion. His brain, no longer the arbiter of its actions, is constantly bombarded and besieged by the inimical process that assails his arteries. Mrs. Wilson may not have recognized the gradual deterioration of his brilliant mind. Love has the happy faculty of closing its eyes to unhappy conclusions. But Colby must have known, except for the myth-building propensity of the human mind which weaves about its heroes a cloak more colored than Joseph's!

"I note," Colby writes, "that you have in contemplation writing on 'the last phase of the Wilson Administration,' and, as you say, 'when the President was on the sick-bed and Mrs. Wilson was practically at the helm of affairs.'

"I recall no time during the final year of his Administration, which was the period of my membership in the Cabinet, when Mrs. Wilson was practically, or in any other way, at the helm of affairs, and at no period during that year was the President on any sick-bed. He was very much on the job and there was no person with whom I came in contact during that period who gave prompter or more effective attention to public business than did the President."

Colby did not see Wilson in the six months that followed his collapse in Wichita. When, by a sudden whim of the sick man, or by a strange vagary of his bed-side cabinet, Colby became Lansing's successor, Wilson had recovered to a large extent his power of speech, although there were periods when, as in the famous Cabinet meeting which Houston describes, his faculties seemed to desert him. Evidently Mr. Colby does not remember that Cabinet meeting!

Mr. Colby courteously replies to three inquiries: "You ask three questions—first, did President Wilson preside over any meetings of his Cabinet after his break-down?

"He presided at every Cabinet meeting that I attended, and these meetings were held during the year of my residence in Washington regularly every week, with perhaps an adjournment now and then when there was no occasion for a Cabinet meeting, although any such interruptions in the regular course of affairs I do not now specifically recall.

"Second—you ask, did he communicate with the Cabinet through Mrs. Wilson, and if not, through whom?

"I received no communications from Mrs. Wilson on official or public matters. My communications with reference to the affairs of my office were to and from the President directly. His communications with me were by letters which were frequent; by telephone (I had a private telephone which connected between my office and his study at the White House), and by personal interviews with me at the White House. These interviews were had whenever occasion arose, with no ceremony, and they were most satisfactory. In fact, it was always a pleasure to discuss official business with the President. His mind was alert. He had the ability, which is widely known, of coming directly to the essential of any subject and disposing of it with facility and brevity.

"Third—you say, was the question of Vice-President Marshall's assumption of the duties of the Presidency considered by the Cabinet, and if not, why not.

"It was never mentioned during my membership in the Cabinet, and as to your further question, 'if not, why not,' there was neither reason nor occasion for considering it."

If Colby received no communications from Mrs. Wilson on public business his experience was different from that of his associate, Polk, and from that of most Cabinet members. It seems to me that Colby's memory unconsciously represses or glosses over many difficulties of communication between himself and his chief. He looks at Wilson through the golden haze of the Wilson myth.

"What you say in your closing paragraph," Colby concludes, "gives me much pleasure. No one can be conversant with the character of Mr. Wilson without feeling as you express yourself, that is to say, without realizing his 'fundamental idealism, his sincerity and his desire to keep the country out of war.'"

Attracted and repelled by his very inconsistencies, the Wilson myth grows. The contradictory elements in Wilson's character enable the historian to portray him as a hero or as a villain, as a god or a fool. I should say that, like most heroes, he was also something of the villain, and that like most gods, he was not incapable of folly. To the Germans, with the exception of Count Bernstorff, Wilson seems the embodiment of Anglo-Saxon hypocrisy. To his worshipers he is, and remains the inspired prophet, the faultless lamb of God.

Wilson was puzzled by the inability of the world to understand his contradictory character. "I have never," he exclaims, "read an article about myself in which I recognize myself, and I have come to have the impression that I must be some kind of a fraud because I think a great many of these articles are written in absolute good faith. I tremble to think of the variety and falseness of the impressions I make—"

Some students of Wilson's psychology regarded him as a thinking machine, detached from his body. But, conscious of the turmoil within himself, even if he could not discover its causes, Wilson saw himself as a boiling caldron. "I am not aware of having any detachable apparatus inside of me. On the contrary, if I were to interpret myself, I would say that my constant embarrassment is to restrain the emotions that are inside of me. You may not believe it, but I sometimes feel like a fire from a far from extinct volcano, and if the lava does not seem to spill over it is because you are not high enough to see into the basin and see the caldron boil."

Wilson's *alter ego*, Colonel House, confesses himself baffled by Wilson's enigmatic ego. McAdoo, after an intimate association with Wilson every day for six years, says: "There were wide and fertile ranges of his spirit that were closed to me; and, I think, to every one else except the first Mrs. Wilson. As far as I am aware, she was the only human being who knew him perfectly."

From whatever angle we approach Wilson, we find ourselves entangled in contradiction. Some who met Wilson describe his manner as curt and unresponsive. Others who knew him intimately paint him as a picture of austere politeness. His courtesy, said Colonel House, is instinctive. Aloof and democratic at once, his mind was at war with his taste. "I am a Democrat like Jefferson with aristocratic tastes," he once said to House. "My reason leads me where my taste rebels." The deeper we probe, the more are we mystified by this orator who suffered from stage fright, this humanitarian who disliked human beings, this shy and embarrassed person whose audacity shook the world!

Wilson's perplexing personality will furnish material to playwrights and poets for centuries to come. Emil Ludwig in his play, *Versailles*, makes Wilson the protagonist of the new spirit against the old. Wells Wells, author of *Wilson the Unknown*, portrays Wilson as a superman who plotted America's entrance into the War to save America and humanity and who, for the same reason, stretched out his hand for a third term. According to Wells, Wilson deliberately wrecked the Peace Treaty to create an issue for his campaign. He envisaged America dominating the League and saw himself as President of the World, until the cerebral thrombosis thwarted the success of his plan. Here we have a diabolic interpretation of Wilson.

To Josephus Daniels, on the other hand, Wilson assumes the radiance of a saint. Three weeks before his death Wilson gave a reception, his last. One of the guests, a member of the Democratic National Committee, drew for Daniels a pathetic picture of Wilson's condition. "He plainly showed the effects of his long illness. He has aged perceptibly; his hair has grown whiter, and his face was stamped with marks of pain. His left arm, limp at his side, rested against the cushions of the chair. His right hand was raised with an effort to clasp the hands of his callers. It was with difficulty the women kept back their tears."

But when death comes, behold a miracle! "One of the most striking things concerning his passing from human life," says Daniels, quoting one of Wilson's oldest and most intimate friends, "was his extraordinary appearance after death. Near the window in his bedroom in which the sunlight fell softly and freely upon a couch lay Woodrow Wilson, in appearance thirty-five or forty years of age. His hair was prematurely gray for his features. The lines of care, of anxiety, and of weakness had disappeared. The outlines of the face were smooth and beautiful. It was as if a distant sunrise had touched the features."

Wilson lived up to his legend. Hardly able to move, he summoned all his powers to deliver a last message to his countrymen on Armistice Day, November 11, 1923. There was, in spite of his bitterness and his contempt for his enemies, a fine spirit in the speech in which the ghostly voice of a dying man once more avowed his abiding faith in the righteousness of his cause, recalling "the high levels of vision and achievement upon which the great war for democracy and right was fought and won." He sees "these stimulating memories" marred "by the sullen and selfish isolation which is deeply ignoble because manifestly cowardly and dishonorable."

> "That we should thus have done a great wrong to civilization, and at one of the most critical turning points in the history of mankind, is the more to be deplored because every anxious year that has followed has made the exceeding need for such services as we might have rendered more and more manifest and more pressing.
>
> "As demoralizing circumstances which we might have controlled have gone from bad to worse, until now—as if to furnish a sort of sinister climax—France and Italy between them have made waste paper of the Treaty of Versailles, and the whole field of international relationships is in perilous confusion.
>
> "The affairs of the world can be set straight only by the firmest and most determined exhibition of the will to lead and to make the right prevail."

On the same day, from the front steps of his house, Wilson makes a brief, impromptu talk to World War veterans. His voice is hardly audible:

> "I am not one of those that have the least anxiety about the triumph of the principles I have stood for. I have seen fools resist Providence before and I have seen their destruction, as will come upon these again—utter destruction and contempt. That we shall prevail is as sure as that God reigns."

This was Wilson's last public utterance.

Not long before the end, Wilson discusses the League of Nations in private.

"I am not sorry I broke down."

Wilson's friends look at him with amazement. They point out what a triumph it would have been if he himself had led the cause to universal acceptance.

Wilson replies: "As it is coming now, the American people are thinking their way through, and reaching their own decision, and that is a better way for it to come."

The echo of his bitter speech over the radio has hardly died, but Wilson undergoes a srange metamorphosis. His features soften. The meekness of the martyr supplants his intellectual pride. To hate is human, to forgive divine!

Thus, drawing its sustenance from fact and fancy, the Wilson myth expands. Ray Stannard Baker, in his *Woodrow Wilson: Life and Letters,* admits Wilson's minor weaknesses, but only to magnify his strength. His faults are like flyspecks on the granite face of the Sphinx. The colossal statue of Wilson carved out of his life and letters by Baker throws a gigantic shadow.

House, the man whom Wilson called his Other Self, capers through Baker's volumes like a garrulous, elderly errand boy, for whom Wilson harbors an affection that is almost inexplicable. To Baker, House is merely a "political reporter and adjuster," carrying messages which he does not understand, dabbling with problems beyond his ken. He sees in House's letters and in his "eagerly written diary the assumption, naïve at times, of the magic of his influence with his great and good friend." To acknowledge the symbiotic relationship between House and Wilson would be to detract from the Wilson myth. Hence the claims advanced on behalf of Colonel House are deftly touched with the brush of ridicule.

No one who delves into Wilson's history can deny his genius. His name is written against the sky as lasting as the stars. Controversy will wage over his dust for centuries to come. The Wilson myth may overshadow Lincoln and Washington. But, like David and Jonathan, Castor and Pollux, like Salmacis and the son of Hermes and Aphrodite, the enigma of House will be entangled eternally with the enigma of Wilson.

To recognize the amazing spiritual coöperation between these men in no way diminishes the greatness of Woodrow Wilson. Potentially Wilson's energy was sufficient to move a world. Some biological accident, some psychic shock, cleft his soul asunder. Paralyzed by the war between the various personalities of his composite self, handicapped by innumerable inhibitions, he could not function fully without drawing upon the strength of others. Destiny or chance made House the most important of those upon whom this giant leaned. Wilson's time was out of joint. With House he could set it right. Without House he was impotent.

Thus Woodrow Wilson was, in a sense, only half a man. In another sense, he was a superman. Half a Wilson weighs more heavily in the balance of history than half a dozen Presidents of mediocre capacity. Even the torso of Hercules, even a Headless Victory, is more divine than any figure fashioned by the hands of a tyro.

For all his might, Wilson could not stand alone. In every fruitful enterprise he borrowed the Colonel's brain. I shall not impute feet of clay to the idol. I concede they are living flesh. But they are not his own. Woodrow Wilson stalks through history on the feet of Edward Mandell House.

APPENDIX

APPENDIX

CODE BETWEEN THE PRESIDENT AND E. M. H.

Allies	Wilmot	Gerard	Youth
Germany	Zadok	Kaiser	Dante
England	Zenobia	Sharp	Keen
France	Warren	Thomas N. Page	Yew
Russia	Winter	Penfield	Zebra
Greece	Wendell	Mayre	Zenith
Rumania	Whitney	Whitlock	Zenda
Italy	West	Van Dyke	Zion
Austria	Zeus	Willard	Zeal
Bernstorff	Walter	Hindenburg	Bonder
Spring-Rice	Winkle	Crown Prince	Yammer
Jusserand	Young	Stovall	Pelham
Russian Ambassador	Wizen	E. M. House	Beverly
Sir Edward Grey	White	Dumba	Wisdom
Zimmermann	Wolf	Italy	Irritancy
Asquith	York	Rumania	Principal
von Bethman-Holweg	Alto	Bulgaria	Conform
von Jagow	Othello	Servia	Recliners
Walter Page	Yucca	Greece	Grogshops

CABINET NICKNAMES ARRANGED BETWEEN PRESIDENT WILSON AND E. M. H.

Bryan	Priam.	Daniels	Neptune
McAdoo	Pythias	Lane	Alley
Garrison	Mars	Houston	Mansion
McReynolds	Coke	Redfield	Bluefields
Burleson	Demosthenes	Wilson	Vulcan

CODE

(PARTIAL; MADE UP BY H. M. R. FROM PAPERS IN HOUSE COLLECTION)

Balfour	Altona
Drummond	Adonis
House	Tabriz
Lansing	Charlie

McAdoo ....Manisa
Northcliffe ....Manisa
Northcliffe ....Mainz
Polk ....Memel
Reading ....Sundgan
Spring-Rive ....*Drogden*

Alsace-Lorraine ....Banks
British Foreign Office ....Conchiform Gambol
Constantinople ....Detriment
Germany ....Maine
Great Britain ....Texas
Luxembourg ....Legitimize
Russian Minister of Finance ....Propounder of Frigidi

Armaments ....bluebird
belligerents ....claver
disarmaments ....ensnarles
peace ....nodal
terms ....silvering
final terms ....frighted
territorial integrity ....slothful inscient
war ....yriable

Manufacture of munitions of war and the building of battle-
    ships ....limkins of medallion and the confluent of tricking.
Relative strength of the armies and navies.......Pinkroot Sayer (D.C.)
    of the Blurred and Messenger.

HOUSE CODE—1915

THIS SHEET MADE UP BY H. M. R. FROM PAPERS IN HOUSE COLLECTION

Aaron ....Wilson
Abacus ....Bryan
Abstraction ....Spring-Rice
Adder ....von Tirpitz
Affection ....Grey
Aftermath ....Balfour
Alimony ....Crewe
Alluvial ....Bryce
Aloe ....Page
Aloft ....Grasty
Alpha ....Lansing
Altruist ....U. S. Congress
Aptitude ....Great Britain (British Govt.)
Assignation ....American Embassy, London
Aura ....U. S.

Aurelia ....Germany
Autograph ....War Dept., Washington
Automaton ....British Press

Balearic ....the matter is of extreme urgency
Calumny ....armed intervention certain
dado ....suspend action until you receive my letter
ebony ....public opinion
fibre ....freedom of the seas
fiction ....command of the seas
fief ....munitions
figaro ....manufacture
fairy ....cotton
organise ....Plunkett

WILSON'S 4 U'S

Justice ....Italy ....West
Temple ....Austria ....Zeus
Zenith ....Allies ....Wilmot
Zion ....Germany ....Zadok
Zero ....England ....Zenobia
Zodiak ....France ....Warren
Yam ....Russia ....Winter
Smilax ....Bernstorff ....Walter
Whig ....Spring-Rice ....Winkle
Wisdom ....Jusserand ....Young
Trojan ....Bakhmeteff ....Wizen
Mogus ....Sir E. Grey ....White
Gypsy ....Zimmermann ....Wolf
Force ....Asquith ....Hork
Simon ....Chancellor ....Alto
Leander ....Von Jagow ....Othello
Marcus ....Walter Page ....Yucca
Oliver ....Gerard ....Youth
Noah ....Kaiser ....Dante
Owen ....Sharp ....Keen
Michael ....Tom Page ....Yew
Thomas ....Penfield ....Zebra
Valentine ....Francis ....Zenith
Thaddeus ....Whitlock ....Zenda
Timothy ....VanDyke ....Zion
Robert ....Willard ....Zeal
Peter ....Stoval ....Pelham
Olympia ....Crown Prince ....Yammer
Roland ....E. M. H. ....Beverly

Lansing ....Justus
McAdoo ....Pythias
Burleson ....Mark
Lane ....Street
Baker ....David
Gregory ....Lex
Daniels ....Dan
McCormick ....Yale
Morgenthau ....Jacob
Tumulty ....Mike
F.L.P. ....Paul
E.M.H. ....Roland

CODE MADE BY BRITISH GOVERNMENT FOR THEIR CONFIDENTIAL COMMUNICATIONS WITH E. M. H.

Remus ....U. S. Gov.   Slavius ....Lloyd George
Minos ....British Gov.   Damon ....Balfour
Plato ....Spring-Rice   Cæsar ....E. M. H.
Syntax ....Northcliffe   Ajax ....President
Brown ....McAdoo

CODE NAMES IN USE WITH SIR WILLIAM WISEMAN, BT.

April 5, 1918

President Wilson ....Angus   Austrian Emperor ....Nunn
Colonel House ....Bush   Court Czernin ....Osler
Mr. Balfour ....Craig.   Lammasch ....Pond
Lord Reading ....Dent   German Government .....Prowse
The Prime Minister ......Esmond   German Emperor ....Raven
Sir Eric Drummond ....Fergus   von Kuehlmann ....Stone
Lord Robert Cecil ....Grice   von Hertling ....Tree
Mr. Lansing ....Hurd.   Spanish Government ....Vesey
Mr. McAdoo ....Inman   Spanish Ambassador ....Wilde
Mr. Newton D. Baker .....Jessop   F. M. Sir Douglas Haig ....Ashby
Lord Northcliffe ....Kidd   Gen. Foch ....Bagot
Mr. Polk ....Lock   Gen. Pershing ....Clegg
Gen. MacLachlan ....Monck.   Gen. Bliss ....Dowie
Mr. Arthur Henderson ......Nash   Mr. Frazier ....Ely
Mr. Samuel Gompers ....Okey   Allies ....Filson
Mr. Gordon Auchinchloss ...Pryor   United States ....Grogan
Gen. Bridges ....Quirk   Morgans ....Haslam
Sir Richard Crawford ....Rye   W. R. Hearst ....Inglis
Sir Hardman Lever ....Sloan   I. N. S. ....Kemp's
M. Andre Tardieu ....Todd

H. M. Government	Upton	Trotzky	Keble
U. S. Government	Venn.	Soviets	Lucas
U. S. Treasury	Wright	Siberia	Veldt
State Department	Yates	Austrian Government	Marsh
U. S. Ambassador	Avery	British	Blue
M. Clemenceau	Blunt	French	Red
French Government	Cutler	American	White
French Ambassador	Dobbin	Italian	Orange
Italian Government	Edge	Japanese	Green
Italian Ambassador	Flint	Russian	Brown
Japanese Government	Giles	Polish	Buff
Japanese Ambassador	Book	Spanish	Olive
Russian Government	Imrie	German	Black
Russian Ambassador	Joyce	Austrian	Yellow
Bolsheviki	Judd	Bolsheviki	Canary

WILSON-HOUSE CODE

B 6	C 7	D 2	F 3	G 8	H 3	K 1	L 6	M 5	N 4	P 1	R 7	S 8	T 4	V 2	Z 5	
ab 07	ac 41	ad 69	af 12	ag 82	ah 25	ak 78	al 02	am 43	an 31
ap 83	ar 56	as 33	at 90	av 24	aw 01	ax 15	az 68	eb 53	ec 89
ed 32	ef 91	eg 08	ek 64	el 40	em 81	en 11	ep 52	er 63	es 10
et 79	ev 44	ex 19	ez 23	ib 14	ic 77	id 42	if 30	ig 49	ik 67
il 70	im 18	in 57	ip 29	ir 00	is 39	it 73	iv 51	ix 06	iz 48
ob 13	oc 28	od 76	of 58	og 22	oh 46	ok 35	ol 16	om 88	on 21
op 92	or 71	os 45	ot 27	ov 38	ow 26	ox 62	oz 05	ub 17	uc 66
ud 97	uf 59	ug 80	uk 04	ul 84	um 34	un 65	up 47	ur 54	us 36
ut 85	uv 37	ux 60	uz 93	yb 72	yc 61	yd 99	yf 94	yg 74	yk 87
yl 03	ym 95	yn 98	yp 75	yr 50	ys 86	yt 55	yv 96	yx 09	yz 20

WILSON-HOUSE CODE

	1 k/p	2 d/v	3 F/H	4 N/T	5 M/Z	6 B/L	7 C/R	8 G/S	
00 ir	01 aw	02 al	03 yl	04 uk	05 oz	06 ix	07 ab	08 eg	09 yx
10 es	11 en	12 af	13 ob	14 ib	15 ax	16 ol	17 ub	18 im	19 ex
20 yz	21 on	22 og	23 ez	24 av	25 ah	26 ow	27 ot	28 oc	29 ip
30 if	31 an	32 ed	33 as	34 um	35 ok	36 us	37 uv	38 ov	39 is
40 el	41 ac	42 id	43 am	44 ev	45 ox	46 oh	47 up	48 iz	49 ig
50 yr	51 iv	52 ep	53 eb	54 ur	55 yt	56 ar	57 in	58 of	59 uf
60 ux	61 yc	62 ox	63 er	64 ek	65 un	66 uc	67 ik	68 az	69 ec
70 il	71 or	72 yb	73 it	74 yg	75 yp	76 od	77 ic	78 ak	79 yd
80 ug	81 em	82 ag	83 ap	84 ul	85 ut	86 ys	87 yk	88 om	89 ad
90 at	91 ef	92 op	93 uz	94 yf	95 am	96 yv	97 ud	98 yn	99 et

I arrived today
42330   16789

to code
NEZIL PIKEC

decode
42330

Edward   is   favorable
34150   45232   36931

code   FACYR—GEPED—HADAN
decode   34150—45232—36931

COLONEL HOUSE ABROAD — ITINERARY

1914-1918

(AS INDICATED BY HIS DIARY)

1914

May 16 "We sailed to-day on the *Imperator* at ten o'clock...."

May 23 "We had a featureless voyage.... At Cherbourg I had a cable-gram.... At Cuxhaven we found Lanier Winslow.... We went to Hamburg...."

Date? (No date here; next date after May 23 is May 27) "...We reached Berlin at 9.30...."

June 1 "...Gerard and I set forth for Potsdam at half past nine o'clock...."

Date? "We left Berlin at eleven o'clock for Paris and arrived on the afternoon of June 2nd."

June 12 London. "We came from Paris on the 9th...."

July 21 "We left London on the steamer train at twelve o'clock for Liverpool.... We sailed on the Cunard *S.S. Franconia* at five o'clock...."

July 29 Boston. "The voyage was entirely uneventful... we arrived on time...."

1915

Jan. 30 On board *S.S. Lusitania*. "We sailed this morning at ten o'clock...."

Feb. 6 London. "We docked at Liverpool early this morning. Our train left for London at eleven o'clock...."

Mar. 11 Paris. "We left Victoria Station at 8.30 for Paris...."

Mar. 17 "...We left Paris this morning at eight o'clock for Berlin via Bale.... We arrived at Bale at 8.30 in the evening...."

Mar. 18 "We arrived in Berlin at nine o'clock this morning...."

Mar. 28 Bale. "We left Berlin this morning...."

Mar. 29 "...We went over to Lausanne on the six o'clock train...."

Mar. 30 "We spent the morning in Lausanne and took the boat to Geneva where we are to spend the night...."

Mar. 31 "We left Geneva at five o'clock for Nice...."

Apr. 1 Nice, France. "We arrived here to-day just after noon...."

Apr. 5 Pau, France. "...We left for Pau and Biarritz an hour later [than noon]...."

Apr. 6 Biarritz. "We left Pau at one o'clock and reached here around five...."

Apr. 9 Bordeaux. "...We left Bordeaux this afternoon, reaching here in time for dinner...."

Apr. 10 Paris. "We reached Paris to-night at eight...."

Apr. 27 "I have seen many people ... preparatory to leaving for England in the morning. ..."

Apr. 28 London. "We went ... to take the train for London. ..."

May 23 "This morning we came out to Coombe Warren to spend the week end with Lady Paget. ..."

May 24 "X (Carver) telephoned this morning. ... I returned to London at once. ..."

May 28 } "The Ambassador and Mrs. Page, Mr. and Mrs. Wallace and
29 } ourselves motored down to Bath and over to Dunster in Somer-
30 } set. ..."

May 30 "... I left the crowd at Bath and took the train for London. ..."

June 4 "... We left on the six o'clock train for Liverpool. ..."

June 5 On board *S.S. St. Paul.* "We sailed around five o'clock this afternoon. ..."

Dec. 28 On board *S.S. Rotterdam.* "... There were a number of friends to see us off. ..."

1916

Jan. 5 Falmouth, England. "We arrived at Falmouth ... this afternoon at three o'clock. ..."

Jan. 6 London. "We arrived in London this morning around seven o'clock. ..."

Jan. 20 "We left this morning for Paris via Folkestone-Boulogne. ..."

Jan. 21 Paris. "We left Boulogne this morning at eleven o'clock by train. ... We reached Paris around seven o'clock. ..."

Jan. 23 "... We are leaving to-night for Geneva."

Jan. 24 Geneva. "... Stovall went a part of the way with us to Bale which we reached in time for dinner."

Jan. 25 Bale. "... Our trip across the frontier was without incident. ..."

Jan. 26 Berlin. "We arrived in Berlin in the early morning. ..."

Jan. 29 "... We went to the train at nine o'clock. ..." (P.M.)

Jan. 30 Geneva. "We arrived at Bale at one o'clock ... we were enabled to catch a two o'clock train for Geneva, where we arrived at half past seven o'clock. ..."

Jan. 31 "... We leave to-night for Paris."

Feb. 1 Paris. "Frazier ... was at the station to meet us. ..."

Feb. 8 "We left Paris to-day at 8.45. ... We arrived at Boulogne about two o'clock. ... I ... went directly to the King's motor which was waiting to take me ... to La Panne. ... We reached Calais in twenty-five minutes. ... We made the trip ... to La Panne in about an hour and a half. ... We reached Boulogne in time for a late dinner. ..."

Feb. 9 London. "We crossed on a troopship leaving Boulogne at 12.15. ..."

Feb. 23   "...We leave here at 9.30 P.M. for Falmouth."

Feb. 24   Falmouth, Eng. "We arrived at Falmouth this morning. The *Rotterdam* does not arrive here until to-morrow morning."

Feb. 24   "...The Admiralty sent us out to the *S.S. Rotterdam* this morning...."

Mar. 4   At sea. "Our voyage has about come to an end...."

Mar. 5   New York. "We arrived in the lower harbor this morning around noon...."

1917

Oct. 29   "Our private car was ready...at the Pennsylvania Station last night.... We were picked up at four o'clock in the morning by the special train from Washington which is to take our party to Halifax."

Oct. 30   "We reached Halifax this morning at about half past nine.... Our party took a launch to the Cruiser *Huntington*...."

Nov. 8   "We docked last night at 6.30 o'clock...." At Plymouth. "There was a special train waiting to take us to London...at twelve o'clock arrived at Paddington Station...."

Nov. 22   Paris. "We left this morning at 11.40 from Charing Cross...."

Dec. 6   "...After dinner we left...for the special train which is to carry us to Brest...."

Dec. 8   On board *S.S. Mount Vernon.* "We arrived at Brest at 12.45 P.M...."

Dec. 15   "We are to land this afternoon...."

1918

Oct. 22   Mid-Atlantic. On board *U.S.S. Northern Pacific.* "...We drove to the Battery and took the Dock Commissioner's boat at nine P.M. on Thursday the 17th.... We did not get under way before four o'clock Friday morning...."

Oct. 24   "...We expect to arrive to-morrow in the forenoon."

Oct. 25.   At sea.

Oct. 26   Paris. "The weather was so thick before we landed at Brest that it was necessary to run up and down the coast for several hours.... We left [Brest] on a special train for Paris, reaching here at eleven o'clock...."

(Remained in Paris during the rest of 1918)

INDEX

INDEX

West Point, 29
Wheeler, H. A., 47
When a Man Comes to Himself,
Woodrow Wilson, 285
White, Henry, 238, 255, 259
White House, The, 6, 11, 12, 14, 19,
23, 25, 34, 37, 47, 48, 106, 110, 133,
148, 168, 172, 205, 209, 211, 221,
225, 235, 263, 266, 267, 272, 282,
287, 302, 305, 311-315, 322, 324,
328-336, 344
White, William Allen, xii, 24, 181, 182,
241, 242, 247, 255, 282, 320, 323,
328, 331, 332
Whitlock, Brand, 48, 118
Why We Fought, C. Hartley Grattan,
108
Wichita, Kansas, 155, 300, 312, 343
Wickersham, George W., 235
Wiggin, A. H., 36
Wilhelmstrasse, 82, 83, 90, 104, 105,
123, 225
Willard, Joseph E., 48, 101
William I, Emperor, 23
William II, Emperor, xi, xii, 7, 40; interview with Col. House, 55, 58,
62-68, 72, 85, 94, 95, 97, 103, 104,
118, 120, 137, 146, 161-162, 169,
174, 176, 195, 204, 225, 226, 232,
252, 285
Williams, Senator John Sharp, 309
Wilson, Mrs. Edith Bolling, as co-
regent, xiii; refuses husband's letters, 6, 149, 154, 155, 173, 179, 223;
ambitions of, 234-243; in the ascendant, 244, 247, 248; tiffs with
Col. House, 267; commiserates
with Col. House, 268; and the final
break with Col. House, 273-277;
builds wall around Wilson, 279;
letter to Mrs. House, 287; House's
letter delivered to, 288; shields
patient, 290; shares duties as Chief
Magistrate, 293; holds reins of
government, 300-303; guards the
President, 304-306, 310-318; as regent, 319-336; and the veil of
secrecy, 339-344
Wilson, Mrs. Ellen Axson, 10, 11; illness of, 12; death of, 13, 25, 73,
149, 248, 274, 320, 321, 331, 333, 345
Wilson, Margaret, 320, 334

Wilson the Unknown, Wells Wells, 346
Wilson, W. B., 39
Wilson, Woodrow, *passim* (see Duum-
virs, The, and Friendship of Wood-
row Wilson and Colonel Edward
Mandell House)
Wilson, Woodrow, William Allen
White, xii, 181
Windsor, 18
Wiseman, Sir William, xii, 172, 186,
197, 219, 224, 236, 240, 264, 266
Wood, General Leonard, 187, 202, 203
Woodrow Wilson and His Work, Wil-
liam E. Dodd, xii
Woodrow Wilson As I Know Him,
Joseph P. Tumulty, xii, 300
Woodrow Wilson: Life and Letters,
Ray Stannard Baker, xii, 284, 348
World Court, The, 224
World War, The, 13, 55, 62; as an
abysmal blunder, 65; Kaiser Wil-
liam on, 67; House's policy on, 77;
those who profit by, 105; contraband in, 125; causes House to lose
his temper, 135; and Theodore
Roosevelt, 161; Wilson's aims in,
196-200; and General Pershing,
202, 203; and the League of Nations, 217; and English naval policy,
231; Wilson on, 254; and the economic debâcle, 273; and its legends,
339
World War Veterans, The, Wilson's
speech to, 347
World's Work, 18, 39

Y

Yale University, archives of, 7, 10, 11,
91, 236, 268, 287
Yardley, Herbert O., 83, 122, 240
York, Archbishop of, 222
Young, Dr. Hugh H., 315
Young, Owen D., 311

Z

Zadak (Germany), 100, 101
Zenobia (England), 100, 101
Zeppelins, 136
Zimmermann, Dr., 61, 82, 83 (Wolf),
101, 102, 105, 189, 190